MW00529856

KENT
STATE

ALSO BY BRIAN VANDEMARK

Road to Disaster

American Sheikhs

Pandora's Keepers

In Retrospect
(with Robert S. McNamara)

Into the Quagmire

KENT
STATE

An American
Tragedy

B RIAN V AN D E M ARK

W. W. NORTON & COMPANY
Independent Publishers Since 1923

For information about permission to reproduce selections from this book, write to
Permissions, W. W. Norton & Company, Inc., 500 Fifth Avenue, New York, NY 10110

For information about special discounts for bulk purchases, please contact
W. W. Norton Special Sales at specialsales@wwnorton.com or 800-233-4830

Manufacturing by Lake Book Manufacturing
Book design by Chris Welch
Production manager: Lauren Abbate

ISBN: 978-1-324-06625-5

W. W. Norton & Company, Inc.
500 Fifth Avenue, New York, N.Y. 10110
www.wwnorton.com

W. W. Norton & Company Ltd.
15 Carlisle Street, London W1D 3BS

1 2 3 4 5 6 7 8 9 0

To all those touched by the Kent State tragedy

Contents

Prologue

People don't withhold the whole truth unless the whole truth is too much to bear. For years, he didn't tell people the whole truth—not even his wife. He knew, of course, that he should tell the whole truth, but he always hesitated. His decision initially reflected the danger of legal jeopardy, then the burden of personal responsibility. Telling the whole truth would lead only to harsh criticism and endless speculation about his motives, and he had no desire to deal with either. And he failed to see how it would benefit the victims. Critics couldn't punish him any worse than he had punished himself.

He had spent years in pain, reliving memories of the shooting. Vivid and disturbing, they resurfaced unpredictably, flickering like fish in murky waters. They haunted him, but he could not switch them off. They magnified what he withheld, but it was its very smallness that made it so terrible. Whenever he thought about the victims, it was about what went through their minds in their last seconds, all the things they would never do, their devastated families. Reporters, investigators, and historians did question him—at first every day, then every few weeks, then every year or so around the anniversary of the shooting—but he never told anyone exactly what happened. He convinced himself that this had been the right decision, and he did not see how reversing the decision would serve any useful purpose.

He was an introspective man who spent a lot of time alone pondering what happened; it had worn a deep groove in his mind. But no matter how controlled a person is, keeping a secret gets heavy and tiring and lonely. He could only hold out for so long. He sought relief from the heavy burden that had dogged him for decades. He wasn't happy about going over all of it again, but he had reached a certain age. The past few years had not been good ones for him. He had undergone two serious heart operations and felt he needed to get something off his chest that he had been holding back, make peace with things, and correct the historical record before it was too late. He wanted a clear conscience and an end to the tension. He hoped he would feel better, but he could just as easily end up feeling worse.

"Enough time has passed," he told me. A long silence followed. "I'm willing now to talk with you about it. I'm going to tell you only the truth. I'm not afraid of what's down the pike." It was the only story about the Kent State shooting that nobody but him would ever be able to tell.

Matt McManus was a twenty-five-year-old platoon sergeant in Company A, First Battalion, 145th Infantry Regiment of the Ohio Army National Guard on May 4, 1970. The eleventh of twelve children, he was orphaned when five years old and never adopted. He joined the guard at eighteen and became a leader among the enlisted guardsmen. He was intelligent and confident, he liked his men and they liked him, and he was firm but kind. But for more than fifty years, he withheld exactly what happened at Kent State University shortly after noon on that sunny, breezy spring day—the events that led to the death of four students and the wounding of nine others during a protest against the Vietnam War. He came to think of May 4 as a separate, private world that he guarded against all kinds of inconvenient questions. His elusiveness wasn't readily apparent because it had been cultivated to such a degree that it became almost invisible. There were some things he would discuss only in the abstract. He avoided others so subtly one hardly noticed him doing it.

When I wrote him to request an interview, his wife opened the letter and told him, "If you read this, you know there will be sleepless nights." But he read my letter and responded with an eight-page letter of his own. He agreed to talk with me, but he wanted "a face-to-face discussion" because "it's best to look into one's eyes and feel the pain he or she may be experiencing." "It's because of what I saw that I hate to go back to that day," he told me in a phone call a few days later. "My mind goes back to an incident that I'd prefer not to remember, but that I can't forget." A long pause. "We need to remember the students who died and were wounded that day," he then said.

Three weeks later, I traveled to his home in Wooster, Ohio. A part of me feared that he would change his mind at the last minute. My hopes lifted as I drove up and saw him standing in the street waiting for me. The autumn sky above him was heavy with cold clouds. He had a sad face and looked exhausted—not the kind of exhaustion that can be healed by a good night's sleep. His burden showed in the lines of his face as he led me into the living room of his modest ground-floor apartment and took an easy chair opposite me, his hands on the chair arms. His wife sat on a sofa between us. There was something enormous moving through the air of that room. As I placed my tape recorder on the coffee table, he gave me a brief, measuring look. He unfolded and refolded his hands, not wary of me but being careful. I sensed how rigid with tension his body was. I could feel him thinking, and I didn't want to interrupt. He was gearing up toward something big. He took his time before he finally started to talk.

As the interview got under way, he slowly loosened up. His initial reserve and bodily tension gradually fell away. For the next two and a half hours, he unburdened himself completely about Kent State for the first time, narrating his way to the very soul of his regret. Much of the time he looked at me, but his haunted eyes never quite met mine. His mouth quivered often and grief stirred under his voice. Occasionally he cast his eyes at the floor or stared out the window, concentrating on something only he could see, shut away in a private world of thought. Waves of sadness crossed his face. He never dreamed that his action might not do what it was intended to do; that his fellow guardsmen might not react the way he anticipated; that with good intentions he could set in motion a terrible tragedy. But there was no undoing what happened, no fixing it or explaining it away. I wondered how many times he had rerun that day in his head. The pain in his voice went so deep that I had to force myself not to look away. It was a long-postponed catharsis, painful but purgative. Deep down, a part of him felt relieved at last. But I couldn't tell which one was strongest: the relief or the shame. It wasn't over and done with; it was never going to be over and done with for him.

Much of what Matt McManus told me was unexpected. Yet it fit the known facts and was crucial to understanding how and why the shooting happened. Things that had baffled people for years suddenly made perfect sense. It also laid to rest many myths surrounding the events at Kent State. It was as if things suddenly rearranged themselves and clicked neatly into place, making visible what had been obscured for so long.

I thought of the victims and their families. They needed to know, to understand; cause and effect isn't a luxury. When we can't see a reason, we make assumptions and force facts into preconceived patterns until a reason takes shape because we want to find sense in the senseless. It is a reminder that reality is tumultuous, disordered, and unpredictable and that learning the truth can be devastating.

———

On May 4, 1970, on the campus of Kent State University in northeastern Ohio, the cultural and political crosscurrents that had been building in the United States for years reached critical mass. One group of young Americans, student protestors wearing bell-bottom pants and many with long hair, hurled epithets and rocks at another group of young Americans, National Guardsmen wearing helmets and gas masks and armed with rifles. About half past noon, a spasm of violence unfolded with chaotic speed as the National Guardsmen opened fire on the protestors.

This was the day the Vietnam War came home and the sixties came to an end. American soldiers shot American students on American soil. The Kent State shooting was a shocking event that dramatized the tension of social conflict, the theater of confrontation, the poignancy of life and death, and the horror of pure chance, revealing the choices individuals make, those that are made for them by others, and their lifelong ramifications.

The Kent State shooting gave rise to two competing narratives that over-simplified the motives and characters of the people involved, lacked nuance, and ignored ambiguity, complexity, unpredictability, confusion, chaos, and cruel pathos. One narrative depicted the shooting as lethal violence in the name of the state directed against those who sought to defy its writ. The other narrative depicted the shooting as law enforcement giving trouble-makers the comeuppance they deserved. For more than fifty years, little to no middle ground has existed between these competing narratives. Opinions remain as sharply drawn as ever. Most Americans, when they look at Kent State, have not allowed themselves to understand the opposing viewpoint or to accept shared responsibility.

Because of these competing narratives and because of incomplete and sometimes contradictory evidence, the full story of the Kent State shooting has remained elusive. But now the time has come to move beyond the partisanship of competing narratives. This means telling the story of the fatal encounter between Vietnam War protestors and the National Guard at Kent State through multiple perspectives, critically and with understanding, but without taking sides. It means searching out and piecing together the story in all its intimate, vivid, and painful detail from previously published accounts, untapped archival documents, and original interviews with participants. Only then can one grasp the full dimensions of this great American tragedy and, perhaps, help to heal the wounds it inflicted.

KENT
STATE

Chapter 1

THE DIVIDED AMERICA OF 1970

Unraveling the full story of Kent State requires understanding what the shooting grew out of—what emotions and antagonisms brought it forth. Young Americans in 1970 came of age during a tumultuous era. They entered their teens when John F. Kennedy fell victim to an assassin amidst a bloody civil rights struggle in the South, which was followed by a succession of shocks: escalation of the Vietnam War, urban riots, and the assassinations of Martin Luther King, Jr., and Robert F. Kennedy.

World War II had been a talismanic paradigm for them as youngsters growing up during the 1950s. Television shows and movies made the war appear heroic and romantic. There were "good guys" and "bad guys," and the Americans were always the good guys. The business of killing and being killed seemed sanitized and safe—just like in movies and on television. The U.S. military always did right, it always overcame adversity, and it always prevailed in the end. The Cold War was widely seen as a Manichean struggle between American virtue and Communist evil.

These idealized notions collided during the 1960s with the messy realities of Vietnam. A war had been under way there since 1946, initially between the Vietnamese and their French colonial occupiers, then between communists in the North supported by the Soviet Union and China and anticommunists in the South supported by the United States. In 1961, President Kennedy began sending increasing numbers of American military advisors to South Vietnam to shore up the declining fortunes of its autocratic leader, Ngo Dinh Diem. The 1963 coup that resulted in Diem's death worsened circumstances in the fragile, troubled country. This led JFK's successor, Lyndon Baines Johnson, to vastly expand U.S. involvement to avert South Vietnam's collapse. In 1965, LBJ initiated the bombing of North Vietnam and committed American combat troops to South Vietnam—the first steps in what would become a massive and futile U.S. military effort.

Vietnam was America's first—and last—uncensored war. Television brought its violent realities into living rooms, making the ugly, obscene truth of war—death and destruction—concrete and emotionally immediate. Young Americans saw U.S. soldiers dying in jungles and rice paddies and the American military unleashing a torrent of devastation on the people and countryside of Southeast Asia. The bloodshed shocked and angered those whose childhood had been sanitized and idyllic. Many of the ideals and illusions that baby boomers had been raised with began to fall away with astonishing speed.

There was another reason for young Americans' discontent. Up until 1965, U.S. involvement in Vietnam had been limited, as had conscription quotas. Now, draft calls increased dramatically because LBJ elected to fight the war with draftees rather than reservists. College students received draft deferments—"the 2-S sanctuary"—as long as they did not fail their courses or drop out. The potential loss of deferment status made students feel vulnerable, and witnessing the poor, the working-class kids, and the farm boys going to Vietnam in their place uneased them. These anxieties fed resistance to the draft. During 1964, not a single protest against the draft occurred. During 1965 and 1966, draft calls rose to forty thousand a month. During 1967 and 1968, antidraft demonstrations took place at nearly half of all universities. Some of those involved in these demonstrations would develop a hatred for the military and everything associated with it.

The first protests against the Vietnam War were polite affairs involving a few hundred marchers carrying signs back and forth in front of the White House. Most of the young men wore ties, and most of the young women wore skirts. As 1965 went on, the number of protestors grew—fifteen thousand in Washington in April, twenty thousand in New York in October—and the rhetoric heated up. On college campuses, "teach-ins" exposed the growing rift between the Left and the Right. At Rutgers in New Jersey, a history professor declared, "I do not fear or regret the impending Vietcong [South Vietnamese communist guerrillas] victory in Vietnam. I welcome it." This prompted a sharp letter of reply to the *New York Times*. "The victory for the Viet Cong which Professor Genovese 'welcomes' would mean, ultimately, the destruction of freedom of speech for all men for all time, not only in Asia but in the United States as well. . . . Any individual employed by the state should not be allowed to use his position for the purpose of giving aid and comfort to the enemies of the state." The writer was future Republican president Richard Nixon.

During 1966, the antiwar movement grew larger and louder as casualties mounted. Students protested the presence of Reserve Officers' Training Corps (ROTC) units on college campuses. Some refused to register for the draft, to accept deferment or exemption, or to be inducted, which meant the possibility of jail or exile. Others urged draftees not to report and soldiers not to reenlist—even to desert. Still others organized mass registrations of conscientious objectors in order to jam the system. The Selective Service System retaliated by ordering local boards to reclassify draft resisters 1-A (most eligible for conscription).

In October 1967, nearly seventy thousand college and high school students gathered near the Lincoln Memorial in Washington for a massive antiwar demonstration. The difference in atmosphere from the 1963 civil rights march on Washington when Martin Luther King, Jr., delivered his stirring "I Have A Dream" speech in the same spot reflected the dramatic change in national mood provoked by Vietnam in just four years. Protestors carried a forest of placards, some reading "Get the Hell Out of Vietnam!" and "Where Is Oswald When We Need Him?" One participant lauded the "responsible people who thought enough to come down here in a show of protest"—then nervously added, "I just hope to God the whole day stays this way." Following several speeches, including one by a speaker who declared that "violence will not come from us," a smaller group of about twenty thousand protestors streamed over Memorial Bridge toward the Pentagon, the heart of America's "war machine."

As the late afternoon sun cast a lengthening shadow, about three thousand of the most radical demonstrators, chanting "Hell no, we won't go!" and denouncing "white honky cops," surged toward the steps of the Pentagon's Mall Terrace entrance in an attempt to storm the "belly of the beast." In front of the steps, a line of three hundred white-helmeted U.S. Marshals with nightsticks and military police armed with rifles and tear-gas grenades confronted the loud and jeering demonstrators, some of whom were carrying Vietcong and North Vietnamese flags, brandishing sticks, and shoving against the line. Amidst an exchange of fists and clubs, two dozen demonstrators crashed through the line and sprinted toward an auxiliary entrance, where soldiers inside forced them out with rifle butts. U.S. Marshals intercepted and beat the demonstrators as they came out, spattering the Pentagon steps with blood. Back at the line, demonstrators shouted obscenities, spit in soldiers' faces, taunted them—"Hit them—they won't hit back," yelled one protestor—threw bottles and rocks, and urinated on the side of the building. "It is difficult to report publicly the ugly and vulgar provocation of many of the militants," wrote James Reston in the *New York Times*. Other demonstrators placed flowers in soldiers' rifle barrels in what became an iconic image of the antiwar movement.

The day ended on a tragic note. Most of the demonstrators left by nightfall, but a few thousand decided to camp overnight on the plaza in front of the Mall Terrace entrance where they built bonfires out of wooden barricades they had broken through, lit draft cards that burned like fireflies in the night, and continued to taunt and curse soldiers and military police with self-righteous invective, while some female protestors unbuttoned their blouses and pawed at soldiers' zippers under the glare of floodlights the military had wheeled up to illuminate the plaza. Around midnight—after most reporters had left and network television cameras had been turned off, meaning the country wasn't watching—U.S. Marshals backed by troops of the U.S. Army's 82nd Airborne Division moved in a wedge toward the remaining demonstrators and began clearing the plaza. At this point, some U.S. Marshals who had been rapping their nightsticks against their hands and soldiers who had been glaring at protestors began brutally clubbing demonstrators, including young women, whose faces were soon covered with raw skin and blood.

The midnight beatings and the arrests that followed enraged the protestors who endured and witnessed them. "Something happened to many of us there that is hard to describe, harder to explain," a demonstrator observed. "We went down to protest and returned ready to resist. . . . Many who were not anti-government now are; many who were committed to using legal channels to change governmental policy now have what they consider the governmental attitude—cynicism, violence, covertness—which they may use for the same end. . . . Reason is starting to slip, and like the inmates of concentration camps who gradually took on the values of their oppressors, I fear many are beginning to see violence as the only alternative to futile discussion." The antiwar movement's fury at the government and military intensified dramatically, feeding its growing sense of apocalypse in national life, with consequences that would become apparent in the years to come as antiwar protestors became more radical and prone to violence. Yet the March on the Pentagon had the opposite effect of that intended by its organizers: a Harris survey the following month revealed that 70 percent of Americans felt the march had hurt the antiwar cause, and a nearly equal number viewed it as an act of disloyalty to American servicemen in Vietnam. Nevertheless, nearly 60 percent of the public still supported demonstrations against the war as long as they remained peaceful.

In late January 1968, Vietnamese communists launched the massive Tet Offensive. Casualties on both sides of the conflict skyrocketed. Demonstrations erupted at universities across the United States. The most notorious one began on a cool, gray April day at Columbia University in New York City. Using bullhorns to harangue the crowd, protest leaders wearing jeans and berets raised their fists and demanded Columbia sever ties with the Institute for Defense Analyses, a university consortium for military research, and cease construction of a gymnasium in Morningside Park that would be closed to African American residents of Harlem, chanting, "Gym Crow must go!" Students took hostage a college dean and ransacked the president's office in Low Memorial Library, breaking into his files and urinating in his wastebasket. Low and four other buildings became "liberated zones." During the occupation, polls showed a large majority of the campus to be against the protestors. University faculty asked the protestors whether they would abide by a university referendum on whether to end the strike. The protestors responded, "We believe in democracy; we will abide by the results of a vote . . . uh, as long as the people of Vietnam and Harlem can vote, too, since it is their lives that are most affected by these decisions."

News media headquartered in Manhattan reported the events at Columbia around the country and the world. The takeover ended seven days later when the university ordered in police to evict its own students, further radicalizing protestors. About seven hundred were arrested and more than one hundred fifty injured. Excesses occurred on both sides. A student protestor wearing a red armband confronted a law professor who was walking with his wife near the campus gates and punched him in the stomach. Police wielded batons against faculty and reporters as well as protestors. Columbia closed for the remainder of the semester.

In late August, antiwar protestors disrupted the Democratic National Convention in Chicago. The day before the convention began, hundreds of protestors assembled in Lincoln Park a mile north of the Loop began heckling and taunting the police, chanting "Fuck the pigs!" "Ho-Ho-Ho Chi Minh, NLF* is gonna win!," and "Two-four-six-eight, organize and smash the state!," some of the protestors waving Vietcong flags. Many of them wore red headbands and carried small backpacks stuffed with Vaseline, gloves, and goggles to protect them from tear gas; a first-aid kit; a hammer to smash windows; marbles to scatter before approaching police; and a homemade blackjack fashioned from a piece of garden hose that had a weight jammed into one end and was wrapped outside with electrical tape. Helmeted police armed with billy clubs, truncheons, and tear gas charged into the crowd and brutally drove protestors out of the park, sparking a running street battle that lasted well into the night. Skirmishes continued for the next several days, the police wielding batons and the protestors throwing rocks and bottles, shouting "Sieg, heil!" and "Kill the pigs!"

* National Liberation Front, the political arm of the Vietcong.

The climax (or low point) came on August 28, when protestors chanting "Fuck you LBJ!" started out from Grant Park toward the International Amphitheater on the night of presidential balloting. At the intersection of Michigan and Balboa Avenues, across the street from the Hilton Hotel housing convention delegates, a triple line of angry policemen awaited them. Television crews covering the convention recorded the melee that followed. Nightsticks and rocks flew through the air as police tear-gassed demonstrators, reporters, and bystanders and dragged protestors kicking and screaming, blood running down their faces, to waiting paddy wagons while the wounded and terrified shouted, "The whole world is watching!" The images of helpless demonstrators beaten senseless swept live across a stunned and disbelieving nation. As civil order collapsed in the streets, unity in the convention hall fractured as well. Liberal U.S. senator Abraham Ribicoff of Connecticut condemned "Gestapo tactics in the streets of Chicago," sparking Mayor Richard Daley on the convention floor to shake his fists at Ribicoff and shout back obscenities. "How hard it is to accept the truth," retorted Ribicoff from the podium. "How hard it is."[*] Vietnam had become a war within the Democratic Party and America itself.

Events galvanized not just radicals but conservatives as well. During the 1968 presidential campaign, Richard Nixon tapped into growing resentment among traditional Republicans and blue-collar Americans that decency and social order were under assault. Nixon defeated Democrat Hubert Humphrey by less than five hundred thousand votes out of more than sixty-three million cast. But independent right-wing candidate George Wallace received nearly ten million votes (13.5 percent), most of which would have gone to Nixon if Wallace, who also appealed to hard-line opinion, had not been a candidate. Nixon had succeeded through an electoral strategy that shifted the allegiance of working-class whites, Franklin Delano Roosevelt's "forgotten men"—who had traditionally voted for the Democratic Party—to the Republicans, the party of blue bloods and big

---

[*] Two months later, the Walker Report issued by the Chicago Study Team, which was appointed by the U.S. National Commission on the Causes and Prevention of Violence to investigate the events of August 28, characterized what had taken place as a "police riot."

business. (These blue-collar conservatives would later come to be known as
Reagan Democrats.) It marked the beginning of a political realignment that
would ultimately pave the way for Republican presidencies from Ronald
Reagan to Donald Trump (whose Democratic opponent, Hillary Clinton,
won fewer working-class white votes than any major party presidential
candidate since World War II).

———

During 1969, the Vietnam War raged on. The number of Americans
killed rose to more than forty-two thousand; the number of Vietnamese to
nearly two million. The communists launched another series of attacks that
stretched through the spring and caused heavy U.S. casualties. American
forces fought one of the fiercest battles of the war to capture a mountain
in the Ashau Valley that was nicknamed "Hamburger Hill" because the
clash ground up so many GIs. The North Vietnamese reoccupied Hamburger Hill a month later, and what many came to view as a senseless
battle aroused even more antiwar feeling. Growing public pressure to end
the war led President Nixon to begin gradually withdrawing American
troops—twenty-five thousand in June, thirty-five thousand more in September, another fifty thousand in December—but at the close of the year
nearly 440,000 American troops remained in Vietnam.

Protests in 1969, meanwhile, became more frequent and aggressive.
Demonstrators at airports, train stations, and bus terminals confronted
soldiers returning from Vietnam with shouts of "Baby killers!" and spat
on them. On campuses, class disruptions, building takeovers, property
destruction, and even arson attacks occurred at a rate of two a day—twice
as many as the year before. At Berkeley in May, police opened fire with
buckshot on a crowd of militant protestors who had seized a plot of land
owned by the University of California and turned it into a "people's park,"
killing one and injuring dozens. In late June, *Life*, the largest-circulation
magazine in the country, devoted an entire issue to photographs of every
young American soldier, by name, killed in Vietnam the week before—
more than two hundred. "We must pause to look at the faces," said *Life*.

The effect was tremendous, bringing home the pain and cost of the war in an emotionally powerful way.* That same month, polls showed the public continued to back the war by a slim margin, 47 to 45 percent. By September, however, 57 percent of Americans opposed the war and only 35 percent supported it. A kind of tipping point had been reached.

The failure of nonviolent protests to end the war filled some antiwar activists with hopelessness and rage. Many had campaigned for Johnson against archconservative Barry Goldwater in 1964—and what had LBJ (then Nixon) done in Vietnam since? Disillusioned and increasingly desperate, they began to perceive Vietnam not as a tragic blunder but as a symptom of a deeper malaise. They began to view "the system"—the country's structure of wealth and power—as rotten, even sick: the "United States of Amnesia" ignoring its bloody history of conquest, genocide, and slavery. The system just kept rolling along and producing more atrocities.

What had marches and demonstrations accomplished? What had reason and moral suasion achieved? "They've got guns and bayonets. Where are our guns and bayonets?" The time had come to confront the grown-up world of power. It would be an eye for an eye, which they could not see eventually makes everyone blind. They began mockingly quoting Martin Luther King, Jr.'s, famous "Letter from Birmingham City Jail," in which the apostle of nonviolence rebuked the "moderate, who is more devoted to 'order' than to justice; who prefers a negative peace which is the absence of tension to a positive peace which is the presence of justice; who constantly says: 'I agree with you in the goal you seek, but I cannot agree with your methods of direct action.'" They had had enough. "I remember the rage setting in on me, and the frustration that we all felt because we couldn't stop the war," said one militant looking back. "What was in my mind was rage, pure rage." To him and others like him, nonviolence had become meaningless. The system would never yield. It was no longer about playing by the rules. It was now about resistance "by any means necessary" and

---

* More than fifty years later, I still remember the powerful effect seeing these photos in *Life* had on me as a young boy.

"shutting the motherfucker down!" "We are tired of asking for reform," said a frustrated activist. "We're ready to kick it in the balls." *That* would make the war makers of "Amerika" take notice.

The siren song that the end justified the means became very seductive. Initially, the New Left had been critical of totalitarian ethics. The 1962 manifesto of the Students for a Democratic Society (SDS), the Port Huron Statement, had declared that "the communist movement has failed, in every sense, to achieve its stated intentions of leading a worldwide movement for human emancipation" and that Soviet and Chinese collectivization efforts had been "brutal." By 1969, this had become "sissy talk." "The ruling class uses any means necessary to keep people in their place," went a declaration in SDS's *New Left Notes* that year, "and we must use any means necessary including people's violence to defeat them." Violence was now a "bourgeois hang-up" to be overcome. The moment to pick up the gun was *now*; that would show the world theirs was "a movement that fights, not just talks about fighting." "Doing nothing in an era of repressive violence," went their logic, "was violence." "I acquiesced to this terrible, demented logic," recalled one radical. "I cherished my hate as a badge of my moral superiority." They could not see, as Yale University psychologist Kenneth Keniston observed, "that the greatest danger which confronts those who struggle against violence is the danger that they themselves will become secretly contaminated by the violence they oppose."

The angriest, most aggressive among them—many, sons and daughters of the affluent—coalesced as a small but determined and media-savvy group of radicals. They took their name from the lyrics of folk icon Bob Dylan's 1965 song, "Subterranean Homesick Blues": "You don't need a weatherman to know which way the wind blows,"* which meant anyone could see that a world revolution loomed. They pointed to recent events such as China's Cultural Revolution, student revolts in Paris and Mexico

---

* These lyrics also became the title of their sixteen-thousand-word "manifesto of garbled Marxist doctrine" (as one Weatherman, Jeff Jones, later described it), published in *New Left Notes* in the spring of 1969. Thai Jones, *A Radical Line: From the Labor Movement to the Weather Underground, One Family's Century of Conscience* (Free Press, 2004), p. 195.

City, the Prague Spring,* and "ghetto rebellions" in America's poor African American neighborhoods as proof. They believed the world stood on the cusp of historic change and the morally bankrupt American government faced imminent collapse. "We actually believed there was going to be a revolution," recalled a Weatherman, "and we believed it was going to happen tomorrow, or maybe the day after tomorrow." All that was needed was a push. Overthrowing the U.S. government seemed lunacy, but a small cohort of revolutionaries had succeeded in Russia, China, and Cuba—why not in America? The idea was absurd yet intoxicating.

Fervently anti-American, the Weathermen were at the same time unconsciously America-centric, seeing nearly everything that happened in the world as a function of U.S. imperialism and the fight against it (which one could argue was an unconscious expression of imperialist thinking). "The main struggle going on in the world today is between U.S. imperialism and the national liberation struggles against it," they declared. Third-world people represented the vanguard and "set the terms for class struggle in America." The Weathermen would "open another battlefield of the revolution" through urban guerrilla actions in the United States. "They wanted a revolution," wrote a chronicler of the group, "and their anger made them want the violence that came with it."

Fired with the zealous intensity of Jesuits, Weathermen believed their fanaticism put them in the vanguard of revolution. There was no middle ground; if you weren't a Weatherman, you were a "Running Dog Pig." They, alone, knew what had to be done and would do it—the wind was blowing only where they pointed. It was ideological gangsterism straight from the pages of George Orwell. "You had to parrot the party line," a Weatherman remembered. "Woe unto you if you uttered some political formulation that sounded too much like what a rival faction—whose members might have been close friends a few months back—could have said. . . . You could be subjected to a 'criticism/self-criticism' session, in which you were expected to abase yourself, recant, and show reconstructed thought." Anyone who

---

* The Prague Spring was a liberalizing reform movement in Czechoslovakia that the Soviets violently suppressed in August 1968.

did not share Weatherman thinking and Weatherman methods—even
fellow leftists sympathetic to their goals—were "fools, unless they work
for the government and are [therefore] liars." "We were contemptuous of
others, convinced we had the answers, and willing to impose them through
violence. In other words, we were political terrorists." Another said, "We
turned against our closest friends. If you weren't willing to be with us,
you were counterrevolutionary. We did damage with that, both with the
arrogance and with the certainty." A third put it more bluntly. "A little
humility," he admitted, "would have gone a long way."

Weathermen detested liberals for recoiling from what they saw as necessary, fundamental change. They sneered at socialists for being trapped in
a "bourgeois stage" and not progressing into "a Marxist-Leninist perspective." "The dialectic is not like a pendulum swinging from right to left,"
opined one of their theorists. "It is a wrecking ball smashing through one
wall, then another wall, then another!" They saw themselves as *real* revolutionaries, the only ones with the guts to "do it." They weren't going to wait
around for peace marchers to prod the system into change. The only way
to do that was "to attack [the] monster at its heart and its head, to disarm it
and disable it." They hijacked the June 1969 SDS national election by stuff-
ing anti-Weatherman ballots in a brown grocery bag and dropping it in the
trash. Afterward, they occupied SDS's national office in Chicago, renamed
it "the Weather Bureau," and issued directives in the name of "democratic
centralism."* They even created their own logo—a triple rainbow with a
lightning bolt zig-zagging through it. The Weathermen would fight against
imperialism and in support of black liberation by "bringing the war home"†
and would "chaosify Amerika" through armed struggle against the fascist
state. They felt a powerful need to shuck "white skin privilege," which could
be done only by casting oneself into the fray. That would show weak-kneed

* When the University of Arkansas SDS chapter learned of the Weather Bureau coup, it
issued a statement: "All power to the people. No power to the Stalinists." Quoted in Thomas
Powers, *Diana: The Making of a Terrorist* (Houghton Mifflin, 1971), p. 151.

† The phrase also satirized the mainstream antiwar movement's slogan, "Bring the boys
home."

Leftists, who lacked the guts to break with nonviolence and hadn't shot even rubber bands at the police, what resistance really was.

Weathermen targeted working-class youth. If arrested or—better still—beaten and jailed, they would begin to hate the system and help tear it down. "America is in its death throes," declared one Weatherman, and "we have no time to lose organizing white kids to prepare for the oncoming struggle." They prowled inner-city streets "rapping" with teenagers about "kicking ass" and "getting us a few pigs" and inviting them to take part in "militant, out of sight destructive actions in every city in this country." In Seattle alone, Weathermen handed out almost a million leaflets in at least two hundred different locations. One declared, "The Man can't fight everywhere. He can't even beat the Vietnamese. And when other Vietnams start, he's just gonna fall apart. [We're] recruiting a *people's* army that's gonna fight against the pigs and win!!!" They assumed working-class kids would eagerly join them in droves. "We put our phone number on the leaflets for a while," a Weatherman in another city said, "but we got so many death threats that we eventually had to unplug the phone." "We were telling them to throw away any chance they got and fight, even though they were going to lose," recalled a Weatherman. "A kid who grows up on the street—he's gonna say you're crazy."

The Weathermen convinced one another there would be a "huge action." "Thousands upon thousands will be on hand, and the whole wide world will see what a radical fighting force in the mother country can look like. . . . The kids would come and join us, and we would march arm-in-arm in the service of the world revolution. Without a doubt." They were certain the government was on the verge of collapse—not in years, in months. "The mother was coming down," and all that was needed was a push from a small vanguard (like themselves) to finish it off. They were just a few hundred in a country of two hundred million, but Fidel Castro had begun his revolution in Cuba with only thirteen *compañeros*. Bold action—"propaganda of the deed" in their vernacular—would wake up the American people. This was heady stuff, and their mood was one of confidence—absurd, but confidence nonetheless. They had spent too much time listening to each other and had persuaded themselves, as one later wrote, "that if you talk about something enough, it will come true." "We were just stupid kids too in love with our ideas to realize they weren't real."

That autumn of 1969, Weathermen organized an "American Red Army" to confront "Pig Amerika" and "destroy the motherfucker from the inside." As the site for their "kick ass" anti-imperialist rampage they chose Chicago—which they referred to as Pig City—where police had brutally beaten and jailed antiwar demonstrators the year before. Their hatred would express itself through retribution. Weathermen plastered posters around the Windy City announcing, "During the 1960's, the Amerikan government was on trial for crimes against the people of the world. We now find the government guilty and sentence it to death in the streets." They called their plan the "National Action," but it would become known as the "Days of Rage."

On the chilly autumn night of October 8, a few hundred Weathermen gathered at the south end of Lincoln Park wearing army, football, and motorcycle helmets, "shit-kicker" steel-toed boots, gloves, and high-necked shirts taped at the wrists and pants taped at the ankles to protect against mace and tear gas. They came armed with baseball bats, blackjacks, chains, pipes, rolls of pennies as improvised brass knuckles, and spray cans of oven cleaner for use as homemade mace. The lake-fed wind blew hard, and they huddled around a bonfire made from nearby park benches and chanted, "The revolution has come! / Off the pig! / Time to pick up the gun! / Off the pig!" and "The only direction is insurrection / The only solution is revolution!" Behind them fluttered a large banner portrait of Che Guevara with "AVENGE" scrawled beneath it. Most of them were between the ages of eighteen and twenty-three. All but eleven were white. Where were all the revolutionary youth? One Weatherman looked around and nervously thought, "This is an awful small group to start a revolution." "We're in real trouble," another murmured to himself. "I had a secret wish that someone would rescue us from what we were about to do." A third thought the moment was like "showing up at the wedding knowing this is a terrible mistake but going through with it anyhow."

Around 10:30 p.m., off they started on their gladiatorial escapade,

whooping and whistling, moving south on Clark Street through the affluent Gold Coast neighborhood heaving bricks through bay windows of chan-
deliered townhouses, bashing car windshields with bats, and shoving aside
bystanders. "I don't know what your cause is," shouted one, "but you have
just set it back a hundred years!" On they went, chanting, "*Venceremos!**
Dare to struggle, dare to win! Off the pig! Ho-Ho-Ho Chi Minh!," breaking
more glass "with a mix of heartfelt conviction and thuggish righteousness."
Several blocks on, they encountered a barricade of police in light-blue uni-
forms and riot gear, waiting to pay them back for bombing a police monument in Haymarket Square three days earlier. The Weathermen charged,
swinging their blackjacks, bats, chains, and pipes. The police responded
with their nightsticks, ripping into necks, groins, and knees. A frantic
melee ensued during which police fired shotguns and pistols at the demonstrators and even drove squad cars into running crowds. Dozens on both
sides were injured, eight demonstrators were shot but survived, and more
than a hundred Weathermen were arrested.

Three days later, as National Guardsmen with live ammunition patrolled
Chicago's streets, remnants of the Weathermen regrouped at noon in
front of the blown-up police monument in Haymarket Square and started
another rampage through the downtown Loop. Once again, police cut them
off, beat them fiercely, and arrested another hundred and charged them
with aggravated battery and fomenting a riot. The next morning, survivors
recuperating in a church basement in nearby Evanston received a visit from
the Chicago Mafia, whose property had been damaged and who warned
that the Weathermen "would hear from them" if it happened again. Chicago Black Panther leader Fred Hampton, who feared racist policemen
would take out their anger at white radicals on black radicals like him,†
ridiculed the Days of Rage as "anarchistic, opportunistic, individualis-
tic, chauvinistic, [and] Custeristic." "That's nothing but child's play," said

---

* "We shall conquer!"—a popular slogan of the Cuban Revolution.

† Which, arguably, they did when Hampton was shot to death while asleep in his bed
during an early-morning police raid on his home on December 4, 1969.

Hampton. "It's folly." A young Puerto Rican immigrant in a poor Chicago neighborhood said, "Whoever heard of breaking windows and not taking anything?"

The paltry turnout demoralized the Weathermen, but they congratulated themselves for passing the "gut check" test: standing up to "the enemy." Smashing windows represented "material damage to imperialism" and made them feel their moral superiority even more keenly. A New Leftist who was not a Weatherman, on the other hand, summed up the Days of Rage as "a gigantic tantrum"—a lot of macho nonsense. Another New Leftist saw it as the expression of those who had a deep conviction that something had to be done, but who also "came from affluent backgrounds and suffered that insidious disease of Puritan culture which is guilt. They seemed like Puritans trying to prove they were saved" and thus relieve the psychological burden of their social and economic privilege. Still another looked upon it with a kind of horrified understanding. "Most of us working in the movement at that time were so heartbroken by the war that we didn't care too much what happened. . . . There was an existential agony that we all felt. . . . We lost our own way because of the psychic anxieties produced by the war. . . . A lot of the things that I think were stupid, against which I fought then, I was sympathetic to their being done anyway." Weatherman Bill Ayers put it best. "A lot of things that happened were quite nutty," he admitted in hindsight. "Some of the stuff was ridiculous. We made tremendous errors. Our sense of sparking something had really lost touch with both the moral vision and any kind of political base that might have been moved by that." "You can catch the very disease you're fighting—you want to stop war, you become warlike. You want to fight inhumanity, and you become inhumane."

———

Unlike the Weathermen, the vast majority of antiwar activists did not embrace violence as the solution to the violence in Vietnam. Far more numerous moderate opponents of the war believed the best way to end the war was not to rampage through the streets but to win over Americans who disliked the war *and* the Weathermen. That meant appealing to the middle class so that, in the words of twenty-five-year-old former divinity student Sam Brown, "the heartland folks felt it belonged to them." Brown and others organized a countrywide "Moratorium to End the War in Vietnam" that included not just college students but ministers, teachers, businessmen, housewives, and other ordinary Americans (though the great majority of congressmen and senators boycotted the event). On October 15, 1969, a week after the Weathermen's Days of Rage, millions of citizens participated in the moratorium in cities and towns across the nation. In Washington, fifty thousand people wearing black armbands proceeded ten abreast from the Capitol to the White House holding white candles against the dark sky in silent witness to their opposition to the war. In Vietnam, more than a few soldiers went out on patrol that day wearing black armbands.

The peaceful moratorium protest, happening virtually side by side with the violent Weathermen protests, added to the sense of cultural whiplash across the nation. Conservatives' reaction was voiced in the blue-collar *New York Daily News*, which labeled the moratorium "National Disgrace Day" and "National Aid-to-the-Enemy Day." The far-right John Birch Society termed it an "act of treason." But one moratorium organizer put it best: "We made our point without tearing things down." They had mobilized large numbers of Americans in a peaceful expression of grief and sorrow rather than anger and rage.

President Nixon could have sought calm and the middle ground. Instead, he chose to lump the moratorium and the Weathermen together. He viewed the entire antiwar movement as another enemy in a long line of political enemies out to get him and the moratorium as a threat to his goal of "peace with honor" in Vietnam. Antiwar activists made attractive enemies for Nixon. He recognized the antiwar movement's political impact—"the greatest social unrest in America in one hundred years," he privately called it—and responded in a nationwide television address on November 3. Using his prime-time speech as a counterattack, Nixon belittled antiwar protestors as a "vocal minority" that threatened the country's "future as a free society" and sought to "impose" its views on others "by mounting demonstrations in the street." He then appealed to "the great silent majority" of Americans for their support. "Let us be united against defeat," the president said, "because let us understand: North Vietnam cannot defeat or humiliate the United States. Only Americans can do that." By responding so forcefully against peaceful protestors, Nixon ratcheted up the social tension.

Conservatives reacted swiftly. Congratulatory phone calls, letters, and telegrams flooded the White House, and the president's approval ratings shot up. A poll taken shortly afterward showed that 69 percent of Americans considered antiwar protestors "harmful to public life." And although a majority (58 percent) of the country now considered the war a huge mistake, a Gallup poll in November showed that an even greater majority (65 percent) supported Nixon's strategy for getting out by gradually withdrawing U.S. troops and getting South Vietnam's army to take over the fighting. The next day, Nixon posed for photographs behind stacks of laudatory telegrams piled high on his Oval Office desk. "We've got those liberal bastards on the run now," he gloated, "and we're going to keep them on the run." To this end, Nixon unleashed Vice President Spiro Agnew, the administration's acid-tongued attack dog, to denounce antiwar activists as "candle-carrying peaceniks" and "pusillanimous pussyfoot[ers]" whose "course will ultimately weaken and erode the very fiber of America"—red meat rhetoric to aroused conservatives. Agnew quickly became the Republican Party's biggest fund-raiser.

On November 12, freelance journalist Seymour Hersh broke the story of the American massacre of hundreds of unarmed South Vietnamese civilians in the hamlet of My Lai and the U.S. Army's subsequent cover-up.[*] The story had an enormous impact, swelling the number of participants in a second and even bigger moratorium, known as the Mobilization ("the Mobe"), that began with a night-time "March Against Death" on November 13. Starting at Arlington National Cemetery, forty-six thousand people, each carrying a cardboard sign with the name of an American soldier killed in Vietnam, walked in silence with only a funereal drumroll breaking the

---

[*]   A military jury subsequently convicted U.S. Army lieutenant William Calley, Jr., of the murder of twenty-two civilians. Because of intervention in his case by President Nixon, Calley served a total of only three and a half years under house arrest for his crime. He did not publicly apologize until 2009.

quiet. They proceeded across Memorial Bridge down Constitution Avenue past the White House to the Capitol. When they reached their destination, they deposited their signs in coffins lined up across the Capitol steps. Two days later, five hundred thousand demonstrators gathered on the Mall, the largest such event ever held in the nation's capital. The District of Columbia opened its schools and the Smithsonian Institution its museums to shelter the vast number of peaceful protestors who had converged on Washington, DC. Parked buses and police surrounded the White House. The day ended on a discordant note. A hundred or so Weathermen wearing knapsacks to hide bottles, bricks, and rocks gathered in DuPont Circle and moved toward the Justice Department building on Pennsylvania Avenue, where they smashed windows, pulled down the American flag, and ran up the Vietcong flag in its place.* Police responded with tear gas. Attorney General John Mitchell, watching from his office, thought it looked like the storming of the Winter Palace in St. Petersburg in late 1917.

A kind of fever gripped the increasingly polarized country. This became clear at the Weathermen's "War Council" held in Flint, Michigan, on December 27–31, just before the group went underground into secret collectives or "tribes" in New York, San Francisco, and the Midwest to avoid the police and begin the "revolutionary armed struggle." They would become "tapeworm[s] in the belly of the monster, eating it up alive from the inside out." A flyer for the War Council featured a bandoliered Santa Claus toting a gift bag stuffed with weapons. The Weather Bureau's Liberation News Service advertised the event as an "outasight international youth culture freak show." And it was. The War Council took place in the Giant Ballroom, a dilapidated dance hall in the poor African American neighborhood of Flint. Behind the stage at the far end of the room hung a poster of a pig's head wearing a policeman's helmet. Off to the side stood a snack bar run by a local vendor who

---

* The night before, Bill Ayers and two other Weathermen had tried to shake down Mobe organizers, denouncing them as "peace creeps" and demanding $40,000 in return for refraining from violence. Mobe director Sam Brown refused, asking them what their objective was. "Kill all the rich people," said Ayers. "But aren't your parents rich?" "Yeah," Ayers replied. "Bring the revolution home, kill your parents, that's where it's really at." Quoted in *Washington Post*, November 18, 1969; *Village Voice*, November 20, 1969; and *Life*, November 28, 1969.

had no intention of sacrificing profit for the sake of the coming revolution. The ballroom's walls were decorated with posters of rifles labeled "Piece Now" and bullets bearing names such as "Daley" and "Johnson." From the ceiling hung a twenty-foot-long cardboard machine gun, its crooked barrel pointing at a photo of Nixon. The welcome packet handed out to the three hundred or so attendees stated, "Our strategy has to be geared toward forcing the disintegration of society, attacking at every level, from all directions and creating strategic 'armed chaos' where there is now pig order."

Discussions centered on terrorism and what would be required for Weathermen to continue their guerrilla war underground. It was all "deadly serious." To raise revolutionary consciousness, evening plenary meetings called "wargasms" began with group karate sessions (one led by Tom Hayden) followed by sing-a-longs to tunes such as the Beatles' "Nowhere Man": "He's a real Weatherman, / Ripping up the motherland." And Bob Dylan's "Lay, Lady, Lay": "Stay Elrod* stay / Stay in your iron lung." Then came speeches punctuated by bursts of cheers and applause. "That's what we're about, being crazy motherfuckers and scaring the shit out of honky America" (Bernardine Dohrn).† "It's a wonderful feeling to hit a pig. It must be a really

---

* Chicago Assistant Corporation Counsel Richard Elrod, a close friend of Mayor Daley, had been paralyzed from the neck down when he struck his head on a curb while attempting to tackle Weatherman Brian Flanagan during the Days of Rage.

† At this same gathering, Dohrn said about the "Manson Family's" August 9, 1969, murder of actress Sharon Tate and her friends: "Dig it: first they killed those pigs, then they ate dinner in the same room with them, then they even shoved a fork into pig Tate's stomach! Wild!" Tate was eight and a half months pregnant. Quoted in Powers, *Diana*, p. 168. Dohrn later claimed she meant to be satirical, but eyewitnesses, including Weathermen David Gilbert and Susan Stern, disagreed. "She may have meant to ridicule the American fascination with violence," wrote Gilbert, "but in the context of all our war talk it sounded like she was extolling these cruel murders." Added Stern, "The major thing that horrified me was the interest in, admiration for and concentration on Charlie Manson and his Family." David Gilbert, *Love and Struggle: My Life in SDS, the Weather Underground, and Beyond* (PM Press, 2012), p. 147; and Susan Stern, *With the Weathermen: The Personal Journey of a Revolutionary Woman* (Doubleday, 1975), p. 204. For the remainder of the War Council, Weathermen greeted one another by holding up three fingers to represent a fork and saying, "He [Manson] made people afraid, and that's what we have to do." Quoted in Jones, *A Radical Line*, p. 209.

wonderful feeling to kill a pig or blow up a building" (Mark Rudd).* "We're against everything that's 'good and decent' in honky America. We will burn and loot and destroy. We are the incubation of your mother's nightmare" (John Jacobs). The self-destructive nihilism reached a peak when participants denounced white American women as "pig mothers" and debated killing white babies so as not to bring more "oppressors" into the world. "Anything was applauded as long as it was against the American system, as long as it outraged middle-class morality, as long as it terrified the bourgeoisie, made them think they were next," explained one attendee. "We psyched ourselves up with a disgusting romanticization of violence," said another. But a third put it best: "Paranoia plus egotism plus a worldview that obliterated all subtlety combined to create an atmosphere that was insane."

The day before the War Council broke up, Weathermen leaders secretly met at the parish house of the Sacred Heart Church in Flint to lay plans for terrorist bombings in cities. In the following weeks, they traveled around the country visiting collectives and carrying out "the Consolidation"—purging those whom they judged lacked the strength and discipline to go underground and commit political violence. They also began planning "undiluted terrorist action" targeting not only symbols of power such as police stations and government buildings but also people. Weathermen had become the punitive fist of the revolution. "I remember talking with [fellow Weatherman] Teddy Gold about putting a bomb on the [Chicago railroad] tracks at rush hour, to blow up people coming home from work," recalled Jonathan Lerner. "That's what I was looking forward to." "As to causing damage, or literally killing people, we were prepared to do that," admitted Howie Machtinger. "It was agreed cops were legitimate targets. We didn't want to do things just around the war. We wanted to be seen targeting racism as well, so police were important." As were military personnel. "The sense was, if we could do something dramatic, people would follow us."

* But in his memoirs Rudd admitted, "Since I was a little kid, I'd been (and still am) afraid of violence. In my family, violence was for the goyim or the *trombeniks* (hoodlums)." Mark Rudd, *Underground: My Life with SDS and the Weathermen* (William Morrow, 2009), pp. 131–32.

They struck first on the night of February 12, 1970, at the Hall of Justice complex in Berkeley, California. Weathermen planted two pipe bombs filled with dynamite in the parking lot and timed them to go off just before midnight during a shift change when many policemen would be coming and going from their cars. "We wanted to do it at a shift change, frankly, to maximize deaths," said a Weatherman who took part that night. "They were cops, so anyone was fair game." They made no warning call. Both pipe bombs detonated, injuring more than half a dozen policemen but miraculously killing none. "It was seen as a successful action," added the same Weatherman, "but others were angry that a policeman didn't die." That happened four nights later, when another pipe bomb packed with dynamite and inch-long fence staples exploded on a window ledge outside the Park Police station in San Francisco's Upper Haight neighborhood, fatally wounding Sergeant Brian McDonnell and injuring eight other policemen.

Two weeks later, five Weathermen moved into a four-story, red-brick, federal-style townhouse at 18 West Eleventh Street, a quiet, tree-lined block just off Fifth Avenue near Washington Square Park in Manhattan's fashionable Greenwich Village. The townhouse belonged to James Wilkerson, a wealthy advertising executive on an extended Caribbean vacation whose daughter Cathy, a 1966 Swarthmore alumna and former editor of *New Left Notes*, belonged to a New York cell having the Manson-inspired name "The Fork" along with Kathy Boudin, 1965 valedictorian of Bryn Mawr College; Teddy Gold, a graduate of Columbia University who had participated in the 1968 student takeover; Diana Oughton, a 1963 Bryn Mawr graduate who had worked with poverty-stricken *Indígena* in the rural town of Chichicastenango, Guatemala; and Terry Robbins, an intense, angry, and pugnacious Kenyon College dropout from Long Island who had participated in the March on the Pentagon in October 1967 and the disruption of the Democratic National Convention in Chicago in August 1968 before becoming an SDS national political organizer and Economic Research and Action Project volunteer in Cleveland. The brown-haired, brown-eyed, bespectacled Robbins was The Fork's leader. He had recently told another Weatherman, "I'll be dead pretty soon—I know it. When I go down, I mean for it to stand for something, something no one can forget. Something big. I want to storm the heavens, and when I go down I want it to be in a fiery blaze of glory."

On Friday morning, March 6, a warm pre-spring day, a van pulled up in front of the townhouse and double-parked. Two fifty-pound cartons of dynamite, one hundred fifty blasting caps, and two seventy-five-foot rolls of orange wax fuse purchased four days earlier from the New England Explosives Corporation in Keene, New Hampshire,* by Weatherman Ron Fliegelman using a New York rabbi's stolen driver's license were quickly unloaded and carried into the sub-basement. Robbins, an English major in college with little technical training, had a copy of the DuPont Company's *Blaster's Handbook* and a notebook filled with lists of household equivalents to chemical ingredients (acetic acid = vinegar, carbonate carbon [a salt of carbonic acid]), and steps for making homemade bombs. "The pigs need a strong dose of their own medicine shoved down their throats," he had recently told another Weatherman.

Later that morning, Robbins and Oughton sat down at a workbench that Wilkerson's father had set up in the northeast corner of the unfinished sub-basement to refinish antique furniture. Using needle-nose pliers, they began running orange wax fuse from a screw drilled into a cheap alarm clock. The hour hand had been ripped off; the minute hand was to touch the screw and close the circuit from a dry-cell battery to a detonator cap set in a one-foot length of ordinary pipe stuffed with dynamite and sixteen-penny nails for shrapnel—with no safety switch. Nearby on the floor sat two cartons containing nearly two hundred additional sticks of dynamite. Just before noon, Robbins or Oughton attached the orange wax fuse in the wrong place, inadvertently completing the electrical circuit. A tremendous roar followed by a mighty explosion raised up the whole townhouse a foot or two as a shock wave shook the entire block. Two more blasts followed. These created a deep crater into which the structure collapsed, punched a two-story hole twenty feet wide through the sixteen-inch-thick wall of

---

* At that time, the purchase of dynamite—but not firecrackers—was legal in New Hampshire.

actor Dustin Hoffman's adjoining townhouse, and shattered windows up to the sixth floor of the apartment house across the street. The only things left of the townhouse were portions of the front and rear walls. On the street lay a tattered copy of Joseph Heller's *Catch-22* with a blasting cap as a page marker.

Kathy Boudin, naked and bleeding from her nose, and Cathy Wilkerson, hair singed and wearing only blue jeans—her blouse had been blown off by the blast—stumbled out of a broken front window, choking and covered with dust. Neighbor Susan Wagner, former wife of actor Henry Fonda, wrapped a coat around Boudin and led her and Wilkerson inside her townhouse to an upstairs bathroom, where the shaken women hurriedly showered and put on borrowed clothes. They then vanished without a trace. Inside the demolished townhouse, Teddy Gold's body was found crushed under the stone stairs leading up to the front door; he had been on his way out to the corner drugstore to buy cotton wadding to muffle the ticking of the alarm clock. Diana Oughton's nail-riddled torso was found four days later amid the rubble. She was identified a week later through a print taken from the severed tip of a little finger. Terry Robbins's remains were so thoroughly blown apart there was not enough of him left for identification. Another Weatherman's father had earlier warned him, "Son, I believe very strongly in your goals. But if you set out to hurt somebody, I would hope and pray that you are hurt first."

The Fork had planned to bomb an Officers' Club dance at Fort Dix, New Jersey, attended by dozens of young U.S. Army couples.[*] The cold and grisly logic that led to the townhouse explosion was expressed by Robbins and fellow Weathermen Bill Ayers, Jonathan Lerner, Susan Stern, and Brian Flanagan. "Collateral damage" was to be expected in any war, Robbins matter-of-factly observed. "We can't protect all the innocent people in the

---

[*] When another member of the New York collective learned of the bombing's intended target the night before the townhouse explosion, he confronted Teddy Gold and screamed, "What are we doing?! What are we doing?!" Gold replied, "You have been my best friend for ten years. But you gotta calm down. I wouldn't want to have to kill you." And "he was serious," the friend said. Quoted in Bryan Burrough, *Days of Rage: America's Radical Underground, the FBI, and the Forgotten Age of Revolutionary Violence* (Penguin Press, 2015), p. 104.

world," added Ayers around that time, "Some will get killed. . . . We have to accept that fact." "Innocent people were dying every day in Vietnam, so why not at home?" Lerner later wrote. "Do you really think all people with white skins should die, Susie, do you really?" a friend asked Stern. "If they're not going to do shit, well yes, I do. If people won't join us, then they are against us. It's as simple as that." "Everybody has to die?" "Everybody has to die." "If you think that you have the moral high-ground," observed Flanagan in hindsight, "that is a very dangerous position. You can do some really dreadful things."

The Greenwich Village explosion, like the Days of Rage, was a manifestation of New Left fury that inflamed conservative resentment, fear, and backlash. "It is not easy to shake the indifference of the quiet majority in this country," wrote James Reston of the *New York Times*, "but the militants have achieved it." *Time* magazine noted there was "a growing feeling throughout the nation that the rebels have at last gone too far." Working-class ethnic people and middle-class conservatives were fed up with smirking, obnoxious, and destructive "Commie-hippie-freaks." It made no sense to them that members of the most privileged group in the most privileged nation in the world would rise up against the society that had made them. They were trying to destroy Everything That Made This Country Great. "Everything I got, I worked for," said one working-class stiff. "It gets me sore when I see these kids, who been handed everything, pissing it away, talking like bums." They felt the America they had grown up in was being undermined and destroyed.

Blue-collar workers and middle-class conservatives saw nothing of themselves in the Weathermen, whose actions as reported in the media led conservatives to generalize about all antiwar protestors. Conservatives were not waiting to be enlightened by a radical vanguard. What moved them, what their attitudes were, could not have been more different. They decorated their hard hats with flag decals and the motto, "FOR GOD AND COUNTRY." They built the schools that protestors wanted to burn down. They felt deep antipathy toward elites, especially radical elites with college draft deferments. Many of them had served in World War II or Korea and viscerally despised antiwar protestors. They watched family, friends, and neighbors drafted to fight for America in a vicious and unpopular war, only to see such service demeaned by what they considered a bunch of pampered, overprivileged, flag-desecrating snotnoses. To working-class whites, antiwar protestors were poseurs who never toiled, just looked for trouble. "A working-class father who may have sacrificed for years in order to send his son to college cannot remotely comprehend why middle-class youths cry that 'the system' is rotten," observed *Time* magazine. "To him, they are all spoiled brats to whom everything has been offered and from whom nothing has been demanded." "All I can see," said one electrician, "is a lot of kids blowing the chance I never had."

To conservatives, the Days of Rage and the Greenwich Village explosion revealed a movement that had degenerated into nihilistic violence. They saw a crusade not to right wrongs but to terrorize citizens. Blue-collar Americans who proudly stood with hands over hearts during the playing of the national anthem at sporting events saw "longhairs" as unpatriotic draft dodgers, and to them draft dodging was nothing more than old-fashioned cowardice based on fear of facing enemy rifles in the jungles of Vietnam. They saw respect for the military replaced by contempt. They saw cherished symbols of patriotism such as the flag dismissed, desecrated, even burned at some protests. They saw militants not as equally patriotic citizens with very different politics but as bums, rotten apples, nihilistic anarchists— The Enemy. Like the radicals, conservatives created a divide between "Us" and "Them." Fear and demonization stiffened backs and intensified hostility. Calls for "law and order" grew louder and more insistent. Unnerved by the unprecedented challenge to their creedal values of family, religion, and patriotism and a growing sense of crisis in the nation, conservatives resolved to protect the status quo. "If it takes a bloodbath" to end New Left violence, conservative Republican California governor Ronald Reagan said in early April, then "let's get it over with." "No more appeasement." That same month, Vice President Agnew advised police and university administrators to "just imagine [student protestors] are wearing brown shirts or white sheets and act accordingly."

By the spring of 1970, America was divided into warring camps that spoke the same language and shared the same nationality but could not—and would not try to—understand each other. Each side refused to acknowledge the legitimacy of the other and believed that those who disagreed with them were acting in bad faith, if not part of a sinister conspiracy. It was a tense, suspicious, and combustible atmosphere that required only a spark to ignite a tragedy.

Chapter 2

THE SIXTIES COME
TO KENT STATE

I t was an ordinary university set in the rolling green hills of northeastern Ohio. Locals called it the largest unknown university in the country.
A carefully groomed, 1,850-acre campus dotted with mostly mustard-
brick buildings about thirty miles south of Cleveland and ten miles east
of Akron, it sat in America's industrial heartland not far from Amish and
Mennonite farmland to the south. From its beginning as a fifty-four-acre
teachers' college that opened with forty-seven students under a tent in
1910, Kent State had swelled in size after World War II to become the
second-biggest university in the state and to have the twenty-fourth-largest
enrollment in the country. Required by the state legislature to admit any
Ohio high school graduate, it had modest admission standards and charged
modest tuition fees. Its nearly twenty-two thousand students (more than
80 percent from Ohio and more than 60 percent from surrounding Ohio
counties) were mostly first-generation college students, sons and daughters of small businessmen and of blue-collar workers in the region's auto
plants, steel mills, and tire factories who saw education as the best way
for their children to get ahead. Many Kent State students had after-school
jobs delivering pizzas or flipping burgers to help pay tuition. The general
outlook was local. A professor asked a student from Youngstown, about

forty miles from the city of Kent, why she had come so far from home to attend school.

Kent State was no hotbed of campus unrest such as Berkeley, Columbia, or Wisconsin. Radicalism never gained much traction there. The school's nickname throughout the Midwest was Apathy U, characterized by career-ism and conformity. One Kent State student recalled talking with another while waiting in line at a campus cafeteria. "I remember one of us saying we were glad we were in Kent because [such extremism] wouldn't happen here." "This is a campus," noted a visiting New York journalist, "where you meet activists who have never heard of *The Nation* or read the *New Republic* and students who think themselves avant-garde because they read *Time* and *Newsweek*." It was a condescending remark that nonetheless accurately conveyed Kent State's quiet provincialism.

The mood on campus had been changing since the early 1960s even as students resisted the message of radicals such as the Weathermen. The civil rights movement attracted early support at Kent State. In October 1960, eleven African American students staged a sit-in protest at a bar in downtown Kent because it refused to serve drinks to black patrons. Other protests during this period focused on segregated housing and red-lining practices.* Kent State student Danny Thompson was arrested in Jackson, Mississippi, in June 1961 for joining Freedom Riders seeking to desegre-gate interstate bus travel. Other Kent State students registered voters during Mississippi's Freedom Summer of 1964 and marched at Bloody Selma in the spring of 1965.

Vietnam antiwar protests developed more slowly at Kent State. In late 1965, a small group of liberal activists founded the Kent Committee to End the War in Vietnam. It was "a puny little committee" in the words of one of its own organizers, whose membership paled in size compared with that of the vastly more popular and conservative Young Americans for Freedom. The Kent Committee to End the War in Vietnam held weekly demonstra-tions, usually at noon on Wednesdays, which attracted few students. When

---

* The practice of banks refusing to grant loans or insurance in minority areas or offering such services at prohibitively high rates.

it staged a protest in front of Bowman Hall in early 1966, thirteen students showed up. "The campus looked at us as if we were freaks," one of them recalled. "People threw things at us, reviled us, threatened us with bodily harm. Professors ridiculed us and the [campus] newspaper had a holiday."

"When I came to Kent State University in 1967," remembered Carole Barbato, "most of the female students wore skirts or dresses to class and the guys wore pants and loafers. The 'surfer' cut was in for the guys, with hair right below the ears. The girls were still wearing bouffant hairdos with just a slight upturned flip at the ends. I can remember one of the first projects of our dorm was 'Vittles for Vietnam.' After the cafeteria closed, girls in the dorm would go downstairs, bake cookies, and make packages for Vietnam soldiers. I only knew one person who was fighting in Vietnam. Most of my other high school friends had college deferments. . . . Without question, I accepted the fact that we needed to be in Vietnam."

At Kent State, opinion about the war slowly shifted during 1966 and 1967 as the fighting intensified and American casualties skyrocketed. Many students who had previously ignored the war now began to ponder its costs and, especially, its implications for them and their friends. Doubts about the war grew among Kent State students, but most remained reluctant to publicly express their doubts, preferring to share them in private conversations in dormitory rooms. In 1967, the Kent Committee to End the War in Vietnam began silent antiwar vigils in the center of campus largely because "there weren't enough of us to have a real demonstration," recalled one participant. The vigils gradually grew in size, but they also triggered "Back Our Boys" counterprotests, and the student newspaper, the *Daily Kent Stater*, gave the vigils little coverage. A campus poll that year revealed students supporting the war outnumbered those opposing it nearly four to one.

Then came the watershed year of 1968. The events of that tumultuous year—the Tet Offensive, the assassinations of Martin Luther King, Jr., and Robert F. Kennedy, riots in America's cities, violence in the streets of Chicago during the Democratic National Convention, the death of seventeen thousand more American soldiers and countless more Vietnamese, the election of Richard Nixon as president—transformed campus opinion about the war as they did national opinion about the war. These shocks

galvanized antiwar sentiment on campus. Many of those who had been
on the sidelines now began joining protests and chanting, "Hey, hey LBJ,
how many kids did you kill today?!" By the end of 1968, fewer than one
in four students still supported the war—a dramatic and telling reversal
from the year before.

One did not have to look far to understand why. Many Kent State students came from working-class families that supplied a large proportion
of the draftees fighting and dying in Vietnam. A growing number of them
were Vietnam veterans or had brothers, cousins, or friends serving there.
For them, the war was very real and very personal. Many had grown up in
labor families that had a tradition of political activism. Their outlook had
been shaped, in the words of one such student, "by familial influences [of]
unionism and a loyalty to New Deal politics, economic populism, Catholic
social gospel, Christian existentialism, secular Jewish radicalism, the Old
Left, a commitment to racial equality, and Cold War liberalism." They grew
up in communities with experience at organizing, a tradition of participation in sit-downs and strikes, and a willingness to confront issues of the
day head-on. In the 1940s, the typical Kent State student was a middle-class
boy or girl from a small town or farm who would be at home in a painting
by Norman Rockwell. By the late 1960s, the typical Kent State student was
a working-class boy or girl from an urban, industrial area who would be at
home in a painting by Ben Shahn.

A growing number of Kent State students opposed the Vietnam War, but
the vast majority remained committed to nonviolent protest. Radicalism
never gained much traction at Kent State, as illustrated by the campus fortunes of SDS and its extremist offshoot, the Weathermen. SDS's first meeting at Kent State in September 1968 attracted two hundred fifty curious
onlookers. Thereafter, its membership never exceeded three hundred—a
mere 1.4 percent of the school's population.[*] A campus informer for the

* This still made Kent State one of the largest SDS chapters in the country (which says
something about the limited popularity of SDS among college students nationwide). See the
interview with Bill Arthrell, Accession 1983-M-017, Box 1, Kent State Collection, Manuscripts
and Archives, Sterling Memorial Library, Yale University (hereafter cited as KSC, SML, YU).

FBI (whom student activists referred to as "the secret police") accurately reported, "All of the New Left organizations currently on the campus have very limited memberships and receive little sympathy or support from the student body."

On October 24, 1968, Mark Rudd, the public face of the student occupation of Columbia University the previous April, spoke on campus. He had become a minor national celebrity, having appeared on the cover of *Newsweek* the previous month. Since being expelled from Columbia, Rudd had become an SDS "regional traveler" who encouraged college students to develop a "revolutionary consciousness" and take "direct action" against their own universities. Slightly stooped, with thick and wavy sandy hair, a heavy jaw, and a small mouth, Rudd appeared before a packed audience of eight hundred paying students in University Auditorium wearing a rumpled button-down shirt. He began by screening a film documentary of the takeover of Columbia University featuring Mark Rudd. Afterward, Rudd sat on the front edge of the stage and delivered a rambling talk laced with profanity. Flippant and cocky, he spoke in a way that one witness described as "abusive, obscene, biased, and boring." Another member of the audience found his remarks "disgraceful and revolting," noting that Rudd "completely defeated his purpose in coming here." The longer Rudd spoke, the smaller the crowd got. During the question period, someone stood up and said, "I've been listening to you for two hours. I agree with everything you said about the problems in this system. And I know that the system is rotten. But what I need to know, now, is what do we do about it?" Rudd shrugged his shoulders and said, "Man, let it happen! After it's done, we'll work out something which will probably be better than what we had before." By the end, no more than twenty students were still listening. "It's a good thing Rudd didn't try to hold Columbia with the people in the Kent auditorium," said one of them, "because he wouldn't have lasted an hour." Later that night, Rudd got into a heated argument with Kent State SDS members over how to divide the admission fees, demanding and walking away with all of it.

The day before the November 1968 election, four members of Kent State SDS barged into Bowman Hall and disrupted the final minutes of

Professor Thomas Ung's Political Science 101 lecture. Carrying a coffin scrawled with the slogan "Elections Are Crap," they marched down one aisle, paraded in front of the lecture stage, and then exited up the other aisle as Professor Ung frowned and most of the students sat befuddled or booed. The next day the *Daily Kent Stater* editorialized, "One thing the Students for a Democratic Society have complained about has been students' rights on campus. Mainly, they want more of them. Therefore, it seems strange that some members of that group decided to show how well it can violate the rights of others with an inconsiderate and irresponsible act." Said one Kent State SDS protestor looking back, "The invasion of classrooms startled the professors and antagonized the students. It was a dreadful mistake, an action which lost us a lot of support."

On February 27, 1969, petite, fiery Joyce Cecora of Kent State SDS announced at a rally on the Commons, a ten-acre bowl-like grassy area in the center of campus, that unless the university administration stopped "repressing" SDS, it "would burn and level the campus." At a subsequent rally, Cecora stood before her audience with a little plastic gun and declared, "They used guns at Cornell* and got what they wanted and it will come to that here!" Later that semester, Cecora's father drove down from Cleveland and took her home.

Northern Ohio was an SDS stronghold. The first president of SDS was Stephen Ogilvie, a Kent State dropout. Carl Oglesby, elected SDS president in 1965, had been a Kent State student. Another past SDS president, Paul Potter, lived on Cleveland's Near West Side and helped run the organization's Economic Research and Action Project. SDS made Kent State the focus of its regional effort in the spring of 1969. The university appeared to possess all the necessary attributes of a "revolutionary vanguard": a strong leadership cadre, a predominantly working-class student body, and politically active African American students with an "anticolonial conscious-

* On April 19, 1969, protesting African American students took over Willard Straight Hall at Cornell University. The Cornell administration negotiated an end to the building takeover. Photos of the students marching out of Straight Hall toting rifles and wearing bandoliers made national news.

ness." The radical faction of SDS that would become the Weathermen aimed to spark an explosion at Kent State and other universities that would bring down "the American monster." SDS invested months of planning in the effort. Starting with thirty to fifty Kent State SDS members, it began trying to build a "radical consciousness" among the student body. SDS believed success could be achieved only by attracting large numbers of people to its cause, and that required getting attention.

Terry Robbins, the intense, volatile, and angry young radical who would die a year later in the Greenwich Village townhouse explosion, spent four months at Kent State in the spring of 1969. Robbins urged the Kent State chapter of SDS to become more provocative and confrontational. He and Kent State SDS members spelled out their plan in two detailed manifestos: "Time of the Furnace: An Organizers' Manual for the Spring Offensive" and "The War at Kent State." "The war is on at Kent State University," SDS declared. They demanded that Kent State's "pig-thug administration" ban the Reserve Officers' Training Corps (ROTC),[*] terminate a Defense Department grant to the school's Liquid Crystals Institute,[†] and close the state-affiliated Law Enforcement Training Program and Ohio Crime Laboratory on campus. They boasted that confrontation against "our primary enemy," the university administration, would build "revolutionary awareness" and force students to take sides. "Beginning with guerrilla theater, we can escalate to disrupting classes, street marches, quick assaults on buildings, etc., before moving to the major confrontation of the struggle."

---

[*] Established at Kent State in 1947, the voluntary ROTC program prepared students for commissioning as U.S. Army second lieutenants in return for scholarships that funded their tuition and expenses. Upon graduation, they served four years on active duty followed by two years in the Army Reserves (i.e., the National Guard). In 1969, there were 173 ROTC cadets at Kent State.

[†] Robbins and other SDS radicals erroneously presumed that liquid crystals—an intermediate state of matter between liquid and solid, having the flow properties of the former and the optical properties of the latter and which could be used to look for hot spots and to map heat flow—had been used by the CIA to help track down and kill Che Guevara in the Bolivian jungle in October 1967. Liquid crystals were used in GI night-vision goggles in Vietnam. The Liquid Crystals Institute's research largely focused, however, on early detection of cancers and development of liquid crystal display (LCD) technology.

On April 8, SDS militants gathered in front of the Student Union, read aloud the "non-negotiable" demands laid out in their manifestos, shouted "Pigs are going to catch hell!," and set out behind a Vietcong flag toward the administration building to post their demands, Luther-like, to the door of the board of trustees' meeting room. At the building entrance, they encountered jeering students and campus police, who blocked them from entering. Ernie Ames, a university police officer who had been a lineman for the Pittsburgh Steelers, held his position just inside the doors. An eyewitness stated that "Ames easily sustained the assaults on his huge frame by several members of the Kent SDS who had marched into the hallway and now were beating wildly on his chest, arms, legs, and whatever else they could reach—his privates." David Ambler, the balding, mild-mannered assistant vice president for student affairs, tried to calm things by telling protestors, "If you behave in an orderly fashion, three of you may enter the building and present your petition to whatever authorities you wish." To this reasoned appeal, SDS chapter president Ric Erickson, the son of a former Akron mayor, responded, "We all come in or none of us do!" SDS members then began shouting obscenities and resumed brawling with police. University police "were shoved and kicked, but they kept their cool. The police held their ground but never used their fists, clubs, mace, or guns."

The next day, the administration revoked SDS's campus charter and suspended Erickson and three other students and charged them with assault and battery.[*] A court injunction barred them from campus. But a few days later, the four appeared on campus to protest their suspension before several hundred students, adding another demand: "open and collective hearings for all those suspended." Some in the crowd heckled them so loudly that many could not hear what they said. SDS members again fought police who tried to arrest them. When they shouted "Pigs off campus!," anti-SDS students yelled "SDS go home!"

---

[*]   That autumn, a local jury found "the Kent State Four" guilty of assault and battery and inciting to riot. They served six months in the Portage County Jail and were released on April 29, 1970—two days before the events of May 1–4 began. None of them, however, participated in the events leading up to the shooting.

The university scheduled a suspension hearing on April 16 in the Music and Speech Building. Traditionally, conduct hearings were closed-door proceedings to protect student privacy. The hearing would be closed to everyone except witnesses *for* the suspended students. That afternoon, Terry Robbins led a rally on the Commons that drew about two hundred fifty students. Using a bullhorn atop an overturned fifty-five-gallon drum, his associate, Jim Mellen of the SDS national office, declared, "The revolution is on—and you better make a choice because the revolution is going to roll right over you if you get in the way!" He and the others then marched to the Music and Speech Building, determined to "open up bullshit hearings" and shouting, "Open it up or shut it down!" When they reached the building's portico, a fight broke out with counterprotestors. One of the militants discovered an unlocked side door, which they entered. They raced up a stairwell to the third floor, shoved their way past campus police, forced open the door to the hearing room, hung a Vietcong flag from the ceiling, and graffitied the walls with the slogans, "Revolution Now!" and "Up the Ass of the Ruling Class!" Ohio State Highway Patrol officers and Portage County sheriffs blocked the third-floor hallway at both ends, keeping the occupiers inside. The mayhem attracted the media, and so, that evening, the occupiers watched themselves on Cleveland television news stations. Later that night, Ohio State Highway Patrol officers arrested and charged fifty-eight, including Robbins,* with inciting to riot. The students among them were immediately suspended.

Just as it looked like the radicals were making inroads, Kent State's student government held a referendum on the Music and Speech Building incident that illustrated SDS's limited support on campus. More than 8,600 students participated in the voting—the largest such turnout in the school's history. The vote was 5,151 to 3,100 against ending the suspensions and 5,210 to 3,232 against reinstating SDS's campus charter. A substantial majority had rejected the radicals' message and methods. They had enough problems without looking for more trouble. Some students

---

* Robbins pled guilty and served a forty-five-day jail sentence at the end of the year, thus missing the Weathermen's notorious War Council in Flint, Michigan.

began circulating a cartoon booklet from Northwestern University called *New Laugh Notes* that lampooned the SDS newsletter *New Left Notes*. The cartoon booklet included a drawing of Bernardine Dohrn lolling around SDS's national office in Chicago saying, "Let's raise the dues, I want to go to the Riviera."

Dohrn spoke at Kent State on April 28, less than two months before she and others formed the Weathermen. Fewer than one hundred students attended her speech; even a glamorous radical couldn't get a foothold at Kent State. What she said that day illustrated SDS's growing extremism. A twenty-six-year-old Milwaukee native and University of Chicago Law School graduate who had been a social worker and an organizer for the National Lawyers Guild before becoming interorganizational secretary of SDS in June 1968,* Dohrn was attractive, strong-willed, articulate, charismatic— and arrogant. Jonathan Lerner, who would join her in the Weathermen leadership, said Dohrn combined "good looks, glib speech and daring posture." Everything about her was carefully calculated. Buxom, she usually appeared elegantly dressed—in a half-buttoned blouse. She was also very outspoken. When elected SDS's interorganizational secretary the previous year, someone asked Dohrn if she was a socialist. She replied, "I consider myself a revolutionary communist." During a speech at the University of Washington in January 1969 to celebrate the tenth anniversary of the Cuban Revolution, Dohrn observed that "a few well-placed bombs could stop a lot of institutions from functioning in this country."

Dohrn told her Kent State audience "there is a need for radical change through revolutionary action" and this entailed "carrying weapons in self-defense." She cited as an example the Black Panthers who had been charged with conspiracy to blow up Macy's Department Store in Manhattan. Macy's was a "stupid target," said Dohrn; the New York Police Department "made much more sense." When someone in the audience challenged her by saying that love, not violence, was the best way to bring about change, Dohrn replied, "I could murder in self-defense and murder in revenge." But she

---

* When questioned at the SDS national convention that summer about her qualifications for the post, Dohrn replied, "revolutionary communist."

also noted that "blacks had been killed on campuses"[*] and prophesied that whites "eventually would be" too.

On May 22, SDS disrupted a dress rehearsal on the Commons for the ROTC Honors Day Convocation. It began with a rally attended by fifteen students led by Rick Skirvin, one of those who had been arrested the month before for occupying the Music and Speech Building. Skirvin was angry and wanted his fifteen listeners to get angry, too. "We'll start blowing up buildings, we'll start buying guns, we'll do everything to bring this motherfucking school down!" screamed Skirvin. "When I was locked up [in] jail, I had one obsession: I wanted to take a machine gun and kill every bastard there!" He and six other Kent State SDS members then proceeded to the Commons, where they shouted "Off the pig!" at the assembled ROTC cadets, who ignored their screamed epithets.

The newly formed Weathermen held their first—and last—rally at Kent State in the autumn of 1969, again to protest ROTC's presence on campus. The featured speaker was Mark Real, a junior and former Catholic seminarian who wore a jacket and tie and was topped by a lock of black hair that fell neatly over his forehead. To his side stood another Weatherman holding a Vietcong flag. "We must attack the ruling class," declared Real, adding, "Hey, piggy wiggy / You gotta go now, / Oink oink / Bang bang / Off the pig!" Someone shouted that Real was the pig. His audience amounted to six other Weathermen and twenty-five students. Afterward, the administration banished Weathermen from campus.

Kent State SDS's behavior alienated many, if not most, students. They interrupted classes and disrespected the opinions of others. Instead of police brutality, there was SDS brutality. Tim DeFrange voiced a common opinion in 1969 when he later said, "I really believed the way [SDS] did, I was very angry about the war" but "there was a lack of dignity and respect in their anger. Their anger was just out of control. They really behaved radically . . . and it didn't do us any favors in terms of the cause." Another student observed: "I can't say that there was hate towards them, but there

* Three African American students had been killed during protests at South Carolina State University in Orangeburg on February 8, 1968.

was a lot of indifference—just didn't much care what happened to them because if they got themselves into trouble, then they deserved it. This was the consensus of a great majority of the student body at the time." "I was somewhat sympathetic to the SDS goal," recalled a third, "but I knew that wasn't the way to pursue the political struggle. There was a lot of anarchism in what those people were saying and doing, which I understand better now than I did then. But I knew instinctively that it wasn't the way to go. I couldn't see having a handful of people going off the deep end, doing some suicidal action, winding up either hurt or arrested."

———

SDS and the Weathermen did not radicalize Kent State students in the months leading up to May 1970—America's continued involvement in Vietnam did. Antiwar sentiment intensified at Kent State during the autumn of 1969 and the spring of 1970 as the conflict raged on, U.S. and Vietnamese deaths mounted, and an end to the war remained nowhere in sight despite President Nixon's promise to deliver just that. Antiwar demonstrations in 1970 increased in frequency and intensity throughout the country as well. At the University of California, Santa Barbara, in February, four days of protest resulted in one student killed, two shot, and more than one hundred fifty arrested. At the State University of New York at Buffalo in March, twelve students were shot and fifty-seven others injured during a clash with police. At the University of California, Berkeley, in April, four thousand students stormed the ROTC building and kept up an hours-long fight with police. That same month several thousand students occupied Harvard Square, battled police, burned cars, and vandalized local businesses. A poll conducted at Kent State revealed that students favored immediate U.S. withdrawal from Vietnam by a seven-to-one margin.

Not all Kent State students opposed the war, but the growing majority who did became increasingly alienated, frustrated, and resentful. Our "feeling of powerlessness was very strong," remembered a student. Eighteen-year-olds could be drafted to fight a war, but they couldn't vote in or out the politicians who led it. The counterculture now permeated campus. Male students began sporting beards and growing their hair longer. Bruce

Dzeda had the fourth pair of bell-bottom jeans at Kent State in the spring of 1969. "By the following autumn," Dzeda recalled, "everybody had them, they were like navels." Female students wore less makeup and also grew their hair longer. Both sexes abandoned traditional styles of dress for bell-bottom jeans, work shirts, and boots. "This is a different place than it was even two years ago," said student body president Frank Frisina that spring. On the day of the moratorium protest the previous October, five thousand students—vastly more than had ever attended an SDS rally—marched through downtown Kent behind a banner reading "Bring the Troops Home Now!" and boycotted classes. The *Daily Kent Stater* endorsed the boycott and began running an antiwar column. Such things would never have happened two years earlier.

On the surface, things remained calm. But the atmosphere grew tense and brittle. Republican governor Jim Rhodes declared that he would use whatever force necessary to maintain law and order. A tall, middle-aged man with graying hair, pudgy face, and squinty eyes behind large black glasses, Rhodes resembled "a football player turned mortician" in the words of Cleveland's Democratic mayor Carl Stokes. Rhodes was an up-by-the-bootstraps, rough-and-tumble politician who was "part hayseed and more than a little carnival barker." He was born into a poor coal-mining family in Appalachia, and his father died when he was eight. He worked odd jobs at night to support his mother and sisters until he enrolled at Ohio State University. After college, he rose through the ranks of the state Republican Party, becoming mayor of the capital, Columbus, and then governor in 1962.

Rhodes's instrument for maintaining law and order would be the Ohio National Guard.* Ohio ranked fifth among states in number of civil disturbances but first among states in mobilizing the guard to deal with those disturbances. The Ohio National Guard had been called out thirty-one

---

* One of fifty state militias under the command of state governors that can be federalized by the president during times of national emergency, the National Guard is also known as the Army Reserves and relies on training standards established by the Pentagon for the regular army. The Ohio National Guard had fought in every American conflict since the War of 1812.

Ohio Republican governor Jim Rhodes (in forefront at right), May 1970.

times in the two years since Rhodes had become governor. It had been called out five times during the preceding five years. Many guardsmen felt Governor Rhodes viewed them as his personal army and called them out too frequently. "If Rhodes's toilet wasn't working, he'd call out the Guard," they grumbled. The 145th Infantry Regiment was mobilized more frequently than any other guard unit in the state. It had never been mobilized to deal with campus protests before 1970.

The Ohio National Guard was commanded by Adjutant General Sylvester Anthony "Tough Tony" Del Corso. A self-made man of spartan habits from the working-class Berea section of Cleveland, Del Corso had joined the guard at fifteen by lying about his age. During World War II, the guard had deployed to the Western Pacific theater, where Del Corso earned two Silver Stars, three Bronze Stars, and a Purple Heart. By war's end, he was a full colonel with considerable combat experience. In 1960, he served as a senior U.S. military advisor to the South Vietnamese Army. Politically conservative, General Del Corso labeled the antiwar movement "part of the international Communist conspiracy" to destroy America and complained, "We have listened too much and too long to those who handle dissidents with permissiveness and tolerance." "I for one have no intention of standing back and letting them get away with it." He viewed anti–Vietnam War protestors as punks and intended to show them he meant business. He ordered guardsmen to carry loaded weapons while deployed on college campuses.

Even normally apathetic Kent State students began to question the Vietnam War and their own futures because they, like other college students, had lost their coveted 2-S draft-deferment status—"worth gold" to them—in 1969. Instead, a lottery system based on birth dates randomly drawn came into effect that year. Students huddled in front of televisions to watch the gruesome reality of Vietnam and thought, "I could be there soon if the war doesn't end." The Selective Service System set the draft quota for 1970 at a quarter million and held the first lottery on December 1, 1969. That night, millions of young men watched the proceedings on national television: blue plastic capsules containing slips of paper marked with numbers from 1 to 366 that represented birth dates (which included February 29) were drawn from a glass jar. The numerical order in which birth dates were drawn translated to the lottery numbers, or call-up numbers (the lower the number, the higher the likelihood of being drafted; e.g., the first date drawn, no. 258, which corresponded to September 14, became lottery number 1, and so forth). The randomness of the dates selected was unnerving and unsettling. "My birthday was April 23," recalled a student whose lottery number was drawn high—262. "The second [date] they drew was April 2[4]. I thought, 'Oh, my gosh.' They were drawing them at random, and I was one day away from having number 2 as opposed to 262." Asked by a passerby what he was majoring in, another Kent State student replied, "What does it matter when your number in the draft is 31?" It became all-consuming. "When two young men would meet each other on campus, you wouldn't say, 'Hello'—you greeted each other by saying, '263' and the other guy would say, '48,' and then you would start your conversation from there."* Steve Sharp spoke for many young men at Kent State at the time when he later said, "My major was staying out of the draft."

---

* The December 1969 draft lottery led to the induction of those with birth dates drawn up to lottery number 195.

Because the war dragged on, casualties continued to mount. The draft rules had been changed in a way that now exposed college students to the draft. Many at Kent State had come to loathe the war. To them, American involvement in Vietnam seemed the embodiment of militarism, racism, and dehumanization. One student remembered seeing a photo of "an American GI posing with a dead Vietcong, hanging by his feet, like he'd just shot a deer. And there were other scenes of them standing with their feet on piles of bodies of Vietnamese, posing proudly like they'd been out hunting." His brother serving in Vietnam had written him, "I cry every day. And I tell my men to cry. Because that's the only way we'll get through this thing without going crazy." He died only nineteen days after arriving in "Nam." Because of such things, many students felt little patriotism for their country. Few favored violence, but many had become deeply disillusioned and inclined toward angry, direct confrontation. They hated the war so passionately that any level of disruption now seemed justified to end it.

On April 10, 1970, Jerry Rubin* spoke to a large crowd on the Commons. Rubin was a social activist, antiwar leader, and counterculture icon who, along with Abbie Hoffman, led the Youth International Party (commonly called the Yippies), a radical political party that employed satirical theater to mock the status quo. A shrewd exhibitionist, Rubin saw "the revolution" as a series of headline-grabbing stunts. It was a windy, rainy evening. Some fifteen hundred students gathered to hear Rubin, who said, "The first part of the Yippie program is to kill your parents. And I mean that quite literally, because until you're prepared to kill your parents, you're not ready to change this country. Our parents are our first oppressors." Rubin also told his audience, "The American school system will be ended in two years. We are going to bring it down. Quit being students. Become criminals. We have to disrupt every institution and break every law. We should have more laws so we can break them, too. Everybody should have their own law to break." He told students to "burn all the books. It's quiet here now but things are going to start again."

---

* Within a decade, this counterculture icon and archcritic of materialism became a Wall Street stockbroker.

Many in the audience viewed Rubin as nothing more than a provocative entertainer. After a few minutes, according to one witness, "most of the kids walked away laughing." While many, if not most, Kent State students didn't take Rubin seriously, conservative town residents certainly did. His words caused them great anxiety.

A sense of foreboding set in. "The antiwar feelings were getting stronger and stronger," as was town residents' fear of antiwar protestors. About ten days after Rubin's appearance, astronaut-turned-Democratic politician John Glenn visited Kent State to speak. "When I finished the question-and-answer period," Glenn said, "a nice kid with bushy hair and a little beard followed me out to the car. He kept saying, 'People have got to listen to us. They've got to try to understand how we feel or everything will blow up.'" It seemed only a matter of time before some kind of explosion occurred.

———

Events in Washington ratcheted up the pressure. Support for the war was rapidly ebbing. The debate in the country had now become how fast to get out of Vietnam. Seeking to blunt growing disaffection with the war, President Nixon publicly pledged on April 20, 1970, to withdraw another 150,000 U.S. troops from Vietnam within a year, to be replaced by South Vietnamese troops in line with the policy of Vietnamization. War-weary Americans welcomed the announcement. The U.S. military commander in South Vietnam, General Creighton Abrams, warned Nixon that another large troop withdrawal would jeopardize remaining American forces unless communist sanctuaries in Cambodia were eliminated. Part of the Ho Chi Minh supply trail ran through Cambodia, and the communists used the neutral nation for staging attacks into South Vietnam. On the night of April 30, Nixon declared in a nationally televised address that U.S. troops had crossed into Cambodia. "This is not an invasion of Cambodia," Nixon told the nation. "Once enemy forces are driven out of these sanctuaries and their military supplies destroyed, we will withdraw." Privately, the president expected "a hell of an uproar at home."

Nixon saw attacking communist sanctuaries in Cambodia as a way to bring the boys home faster. But many Americans saw it far, far differently.

For opponents of the war, the Cambodia incursion seemed precisely what Nixon said it was not: a widening of the conflict by a president who had promised to end it. Although a large proportion of the American people supported the Cambodia incursion, Nixon's decision inflamed campus unrest. It enraged even conservative Kent State students such as U.S. Army veteran Ronald Arbaugh. "I didn't go for the war, but . . . I more or less accepted it," he said. "Then came Nixon's speech on Cambodia and I thought, 'Well for crying out loud, I voted for the guy because I wanted to get it over and then he goes and makes it bigger.' "

Kent State president Robert White did not watch Nixon's speech, but when he learned about it from his wife, he immediately had a "sinking feeling." Senior Paul Tople remembered friends saying, " 'Oh no, this is going to require more people, the chances of me getting drafted is going to increase and it's going to expand the war and this is going to last for a long time.' I think there was a fear in a lot of people's minds that they might get drafted, but I also think there was an anger that people were saying, 'What are we fighting for, what is the reason for this war?' " A sense of frustration, that their lives were being determined by events beyond their control, had become acute. Kent State students were angry and keyed up. Said one: "Everyone knew something was going to happen."

Chapter 3

THIRTEEN STUDENTS

Nearly twenty-two thousand students attended Kent State in the spring of 1970. The lives of thirteen of them would be changed forever by the tragedy about to unfold on campus. These thirteen students were a diverse group. One cluster of the thirteen was composed of antiwar activists. Alan Canfora, a 5'6", twenty-one-year-old junior business major with green eyes, long reddish-blond hair, and a Pancho Villa mustache, hailed from a working-class Italian American family in nearby Barberton, Ohio. His father, Al, was a high school dropout and disabled World War II veteran who worked at the Goodyear Tire factory, served as vice president of the local chapter of the United Auto Workers Union, and sat on the Barberton City Council as a Democrat. "Not many kids in Barberton at that time were politically minded, but I always was," remembered Alan, "because my father always talked about politics."

Many of Alan's high school classmates had entered the U.S. Army after graduating in the spring of 1967. If Alan had been drafted then, he, too, would have served. He arrived at Kent State that autumn with growing misgivings about the war based on the experiences of relatives and friends who had been to Vietnam and photos he had seen of napalmed Vietnamese children. The following summer, he watched Chicago police beat student antiwar demonstrators on live television during the 1968 Democratic National Convention. Although he initially supported the Democratic presidential candidate, Hubert Humphrey, he gravitated to Kent State SDS because Humphrey seemed "wishy-washy" on the war while Kent State SDS aggressively opposed it. "These people weren't willing to just stand around and give the peace sign. They had an understanding of what was going on, and they knew the situation was so drastically wrong. These people were determined to take militant action, and they did. It really affected me." He went to Washington, D.C., in October 1969 for the Vietnam moratorium protest.

Another campus activist was Alan's friend and apartment mate, Tom Grace, a twenty-year-old history and political science major from a working-class Catholic family in Syracuse, New York, whose father had been a committed New Dealer. Handsome, lanky, with long brown hair, Tom was a liberal Democrat who supported Hubert Humphrey and the war when he arrived at Kent State in the autumn of 1968 fresh out of the all-male Christian Brothers Academy in Syracuse. But Richard Nixon's election, the continuing carnage in Vietnam, and the end of college draft exemptions moved the former altar boy steadily leftward. He too attended the moratorium protest in Washington, D.C., and became an active member of Kent State SDS. By 1970, Tom no longer believed "in the two-party system or anything it represents" and viewed law enforcement officers as "not only dangerous" but as "my enemy." Yet he acknowledged that "serious errors" by SDS leaders "diminished their influence." "They went so far ahead," he later explained, "that they no longer led."

Alan Canfora and Tom Grace together began "a very antiwar evolution" in Alan's words—"a process of radicalization by being around these radical, militant, antiwar students in the SDS. We got more involved with the counterculture. We let our hair grow long, started smoking pot, stopped going to church, hanging out with wild hippy women from Cleveland—things like that. We went through our whole political metamorphosis together." One night in October 1968, the two caravanned with other Kent State Young Democrats for Humphrey to the University of Akron, where Richard Nixon planned to give a speech. They intended to heckle Nixon for refusing to

debate Humphrey (as Nixon had debated Kennedy in 1960). "In the top
bleachers was a section of SDS people, maybe two hundred of them," Alan
later recalled. "Tom and I had heard about SDS and seen things about
them in the newspapers. They weren't yelling 'Debate Humphrey!' They
were yelling antiwar slogans and 'Ho-Ho-Ho Chi Minh, the NLF is gonna
win!' Tom and I looked around at the liberal guys pulling for Humphrey.
I remember thinking, 'Maybe we should just go up with the SDS people.
They seem to have the right sentiments.' The Democrats appeared kind
of wishy-washy to us, so we walked away from them, and went up and sat
in the very top row. Some pretty heavy heckling followed, which Nixon's
people tried to shout down. Then, at one point, Nixon said something
ridiculous, and an SDS guy yelled, 'You asshole!' So the police came up
and threw him out. We all walked after him, everybody with their fists in
the air. Tom and I rode back to Kent with [the] SDS [students] and stuck
with them for the rest of the year."

In January 1969, Alan and Tom joined an SDS contingent that traveled
to Washington for the "Counter Inaugural," a left-wing demonstration
planned for the day before Nixon's swearing-in as president. Some ten
thousand protestors marched from the White House to the Capitol and
clashed with police. "These people weren't willing to just stand around and
give the peace sign," Alan remembered. "They knew the situation was so
drastically wrong and so serious that they had to shake the system to its
foundations to get some changes. These people were determined to take
militant action, and they did. It really affected me."

The next day, Alan and Tom joined militants along Pennsylvania Avenue who were wearing helmets, goggles, and gas masks. They pelted the
new president's motorcade with rocks and bottles as Nixon made his way
from his swearing-in at the Capitol to the White House. "When Nixon
came by," Alan later recalled, "he was looking out the window, he was
waving, and all of a sudden he realized he'd come upon our section. He
turned away and started waving to the other side. But people were screaming, real loud, and he definitely saw us. I've often thought back to that
day . . . and I remember [Nixon] had quite an introduction to the way we

felt." The militants then went on a rampage through downtown Washington, throwing bricks through store windows, overturning trash barrels, and assaulting police.

After returning to Kent, Alan and Tom started attending SDS meetings regularly. One featured Jim Mellen of the national office. "The first thing Mellen said," Alan remembered, "was 'We have to get down to the serious business of developing a Young Communist movement in this country.' Tom and I knew that the system was screwed up, that Democrats weren't the answer, we knew that the war and racism were wrong, but we didn't see Marxism provided any answer. So, when [Mellen] said that, I looked at Tom, Tom looked at me, and we thought, 'Uh, oh, what are we doing here?' At the earliest opportunity, during some pause in the meeting, we made up a convenient excuse, went up the stairs, and out the door." "For a week or two, we figured that if this is what SDS is all about, then we're not going to have anything to do with it. We went through a brief period where we were kind of confused. Then we remembered that SDS was the only group on campus that was coming out with any concrete analysis of things, especially the war, and they weren't afraid of action. As time went on, SDS brought down more and more of an analysis with class perspective, and they really pointed the brunt of their attacks at the ruling class. Gradually we became very sympathetic to those kinds of ideas. You might say we even started in the winter and spring of 1969 to consider ourselves to be socialists."

Then, in April 1970, Alan received news of the death of his best friend, Bill Caldwell. "I had known him since fifth grade," Alan later said. "I went to high school with him, played with him on the baseball team, shot pool with him." Bill's brother George shared an off-campus apartment with Alan and Tom Grace. Although a good student, Bill had decided not to go to college and thus had been drafted. He considered applying for conscientious objector status or fleeing to Canada but finally decided to be inducted; he'd take his chances and hope things turned out okay. He got sent to Vietnam. On the morning of April 10, Bill's sister phoned Alan and told him Bill had been killed—accidentally run over by an American tank. His funeral was held in Barberton on April 27. A U.S. Army officer accompanied the closed coffin and stood at attention during the burial. The officer's presence was meant as a gesture of respect, but it enraged Alan and Tom. They "had strong feelings of disdain for this guy because he was the living representative of the military, which directly caused our friend's death. We felt the U.S. Army should not even be at the funeral. A lot of us were disgusted that the Army would show up." "The war for us had come home."

Robby Stamps was a 5'8", nineteen-year-old sophomore Spanish major with a slender build, long face, narrow brown eyes, and long curly brown hair. He was from the white-collar Cleveland suburb of South Euclid, Ohio. He had Crohn's disease, which made him ineligible for the draft. Since graduating from high school the day Robert F. Kennedy was assassinated in June 1968, he had grown increasingly alienated from "the system." Unlike his father, a retired career U.S. Army officer who voted Republican, Robby was well known in the Tri-Towers dorms for his left-wing politics. He had attended the moratorium protest in Washington and often gathered with other activists to discuss politics. A conservative student living in Tri-Towers who disliked Robby's vocal antiwar stance had recently threatened him by smearing "You're Dead" in blood and black ink on his door, sticking a knife into it, and repeating the threat in a phone call before laughing and hanging up.

A self-styled "nonconformist," Robby loved political theater and had a flair for the dramatic, as when he played his trumpet at all hours of the day and night in his dorm hallway. Angered by the American military's widespread use of napalm* in Vietnam, he had recently announced in one of his classes that he and "a group of concerned citizens will napalm a dog to demonstrate scientifically the effects of this incendiary on a living organism." When the day arrived, Robby and the others did not sacrifice a dog, but they blasted students who turned out to stop them for being more concerned about cruelty to animals than to people. Robby vented his anger in a letter to his girlfriend Nancy. "I am really getting pissed," he wrote, "and i [sic] feel like burning this fucking country down."

* A flammable jellied gasoline used in incendiary bombs.

A second cluster of the thirteen was composed of Jewish students, who often got to know one another well. One was Allison Krause. "Al" to her closest friends, she was a 5'8", slender, strikingly attractive nineteen-year-old honors college student from an upper-middle-class suburb of Pittsburgh who had high cheekbones, a big white smile, and long wavy black hair. Her boyfriend was nineteen-year-old Barry Levine, a freckle-faced, goateed young man with long dark hair, a slight build, and a soft voice. He was from Valley Stream, New York, but dressed like a cavalier at King Charles's court. "Allison and Barry were constant companions, often listening together to the Beatles, Crosby Stills & Nash, Donovan, Jefferson Airplane, and the Rolling Stones," said a friend. "I remember them one night in J.B.'s when the James Gang was still playing there. They were sitting on the floor holding hands, smiling at each other. They looked so happy."

Outgoing, self-confident, and curious, Allison was unusually poised and mature for her age. A liberal, she nonetheless liked to study both sides of

Kent State student Allison Krause, autumn 1969.

issues—reading *Ramparts* and *National Review* every week. She was a bit of a rebel. She named her adopted alley cat Yossarian after the antihero of Joseph Heller's novel *Catch-22* and could often be seen carrying "Yo-Yo" around campus while barefoot. She opposed the war—and SDS. During her first days on campus, she attended an SDS meeting out of curiosity but left unimpressed. "They couldn't answer any of my questions, and they didn't know what they were talking about at all," she said. "I'm certainly not going to join up with that crowd!" She and Barry drove to Washington in October 1969 for the moratorium protest, where she had marched carrying a small American flag. Later that autumn, she led an antiwar protest through Kent.

Other students liked Allison, but some felt put off by what a friend described as her "natural tendency to tell anyone what she thought—in a very loud and forthright manner, without caring what they thought of her in return." "She was very headstrong, just like her father," remembered her mother. "They were two of a kind that way." Allison could be stubborn and quick to anger, but she also cared passionately about other people. She had interned the previous summer at St. Elizabeth's Hospital for the Insane in Washington, D.C., and got one of the patients who hadn't spoken in fifteen years to talk to her.

Jeff Miller was a twenty-year-old business major from Plainview, New York, who had transferred to Kent State the previous autumn. At 5'6", one hundred fifty pounds, and with long wavy black hair and dark-brown eyes, he bore a striking resemblance to the actor Dustin Hoffman, who portrayed the rebellious middle-class Benjamin Braddock in the 1967 hit movie *The Graduate*. His favorite book was J. D. Salinger's bible of youthful alienation, *Catcher in the Rye*. "When he was little," his mother recalled, "he wasn't easy to get along with because he had a strong will, but his saving grace was that he had a great sense of humor and great intelligence." He enjoyed goofing off and craved excitement, but his gregariousness masked insecurity intensified by his parents' recent divorce. "He was very upset and quiet" about it, remembered his mother. When his older brother called him with the news, Jeff phoned home, crying, and told his mother, "I'll hop the next plane to talk to you." On their way home from the airport, his mother explained things to Jeff. During the trip, he broke up with the girlfriend he had dated since they were fourteen.

In high school, Jeff had written a precocious poem about the Vietnam War titled "WHERE DOES IT END?":

The strife and fighting continue into the night.
The mechanical birds sound of death
As they buzz overhead spitting fire
Into the Doomed towns where women and children
Run and hide in the bushes and ask why,
Why are we not left to live our own lives?

In the pastures, converted into battlefields,
The small metal pellets speed through the air,
Pausing occasionally to claim another victim.
A teenager from a small Ohio farm
Clutches his side in pain, and,
As he feels his life ebbing away,
He, too, asks why,
Why is he dying here, thousands of miles from home,
Giving his life for those who did not even ask for
    his help.

The War Without a Purpose marches on relentlessly,
Not stopping to mourn for its dead,
Content to wait for its end.
But all that the frightened parents who still have
    their sons hear is:
"The end is not in sight."

—Jeff Miller, Feb. 14, 1966

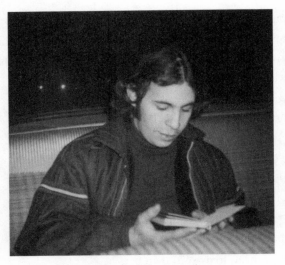

Kent State student Jeff Miller, March 1970.

After high school, Jeff enrolled at Michigan State University, where his older brother, Russ, was a student. Jeff joined Russ's fraternity, but they were very different. More of a straight arrow than his younger brother, "Russ would have gone to Vietnam," their mother said. "He would not have liked to, but he would have gone." Russ liked Friday night beer parties and serenading beneath women's dorm windows, but "it was not for Jeff," said their mother. All that seemed frivolous—even ridiculous—while some of his high school friends fought and died in Vietnam. Jeff saw how his friends had changed when they returned from Vietnam. It disturbed him that they seemed to have become less human. He gave up button-down shirts, grew his hair long, and embraced the counterculture. He attended the Woodstock Music Festival in upstate New York in the summer of 1969, began referring to himself as a citizen of Woodstock Nation, and spent long hours in the room of the off-campus apartment he shared with two friends practicing drums to Jefferson Airplane and Grateful Dead records. He painted his bedroom door with flowers—yet also proudly hung an American flag over his bed.

Like many college students of his generation, Jeff came to despise the military and everything associated with it. "I'm more into the peace thing than into the violence bit," he said. On a visit with his mother, they strolled around Greenwich Village and Washington Square Park, where he bought a small leather ring with a peace sign on it. He told his parents he would never go to Vietnam and kill. He opposed the war but, because he could not vote, he felt the only way he could express his opposition to it was through protest. He also opposed the draft—"for me, it's Canada or jail, nothing else," he told close friends—and considered applying for conscientious-objector status but changed his mind when he learned that if his application was rejected, he would immediately be drafted. "By the spring of 1970, we had migrated to opposite ends of the Vietnam spectrum," his brother Russ later recalled. "I lobbied [Jeff] that moving to Canada could potentially destroy his life. He saw no other option. I was still insulated from the war due to my employment in the medical device industry. Would he have actually headed north? I'll never know."

Jeff had attended the moratorium protest in October 1969. What he witnessed made him fear the antiwar movement was drifting toward violence. Weathermen asked him if he wanted to join them. "What are we supposed to do?" he said. "Start shooting people to end the war? Are we supposed to become violent to attain peace? That's what Nixon says he's doing—killing all these people so we can have peace." Afterward, he told his mother by phone that he might be taken for a "hippie radical" in the Midwest, but compared to extremists like the Weathermen, he'd be seen as conservative.

One of Jeff's closest female friends was Sandy Scheuer, a 5'5", outgoing and sensitive twenty-year-old junior and speech-therapy major who had a round face, freckled nose, brown eyes, and thick, shoulder-length, dark-brown hair. She was from a suburb of Youngstown, the gritty steel-manufacturing city forty miles east of Kent in Appalachian Ohio. The two met at the end of the winter quarter of 1970. They got along well and listened to each other's problems. Together they crafted a beautiful crayon drawing they titled "Who Is To Say?" Sandy also knew Robby Stamps. They often ate meals together in the Tri-Towers complex, shared many friends,

Kent State student Sandy Scheuer, May 3, 1970.

attended a few movies together, and had been in the same psychology class the previous quarter.

Sandy was a Conservative Orthodox Jew who attended synagogue often. Short and plump with a sweet disposition—her middle name, Gittel, means goodness, kindness, and joy in Hebrew—her warmth and humor made her "everybody's pal." "She had smooth, almost transparent skin and through it one could almost see her fine and gentle spirit," a friend observed. "She bubbled over, full of vitality, laughing all the time," her mother remembered. "She'd hug me so hard she'd give me a stiff neck. She'd say, 'Mother, I'm never going to get married because who's going to pester you?' then she'd chase me around the dinner table."

Sandy knew how to make others laugh and smile, often breaking into goofiness. Her playfulness and spontaneity charmed people. "I have never known anyone who loved life and people more than she," said a friend, who was equally impressed by her compassion. "We had a small argument over something. She cried because we had argued; and it wasn't a big argument at all. That is how tender and warm she was." "She had a quiet grace that penetrated even the hardest core and caused a smile from everyone she encountered," observed another friend. "She was an extremely kind person always willing to help anyone in trouble. She was a perfect listener." "She had a laugh like you haven't heard," said a third. "It made you feel good inside just to hear her. Within ten minutes, I guarantee, you'd be up on top again. There wasn't anything Sandy wouldn't do for you. She cared." "In a crowd you wouldn't pick her out as the best-looking chick," admitted a male acquaintance, "but when you talked to her, you knew she was different." "She was beautiful. She never, ever said a nasty thing about anyone."

Sandy spent her spare time volunteering at the university's Speech and Hearing Clinic. "Maybe I'm not going to set the world on fire through speech therapy," she explained, "but if I help a few people, that's good enough." A friend said that "her empathy and sensitivity, linked with her streak of insecurity, enabled her to understand human feelings." She was particularly interested in helping elderly people who had suffered strokes find their voices again. She liked to read about politics—Martin Ebon's *Che: The Making of a Legend* and Tom Wolfe's *The Electric Koolaid Acid Test* were on her bedroom dresser—but so, too, was a twenty-seventh anniversary card for her parents. She was not especially political. She thought it senseless to send young American soldiers to die in Vietnam, but she mostly kept those thoughts to herself. "Some of the guys who came over to the house would rap for hours about the economics of the war, U.S. imperialism—the standard topics," said one of her roommates. "But not Sandy. She'd just as soon be out in the kitchen fixing something for everyone to eat." When a campus radical activist lectured her, "We must oppose the oppressive fascist elements in our society," she replied, "Like what?" and teased him when he tried to explain. She had many antiwar friends, and in the words of one, "she was the proverbial Jewish mother, worrying that the rest would get in trouble."

"Sandy lived for what everyone else lived for—to find someone to love and someone who loved her," said her best friend. "I'm getting worried," she had confided to another friend. "I'm going to be an old maid. I want

someone special that I can care for and love the rest of my life, and what do
I have but millions of good friends?" Her mother, who wanted her to meet
and marry a nice Jewish boy, regularly mailed her local newspaper clip-
pings of her high school classmates' weddings. Her older sister Audrey's
wedding in February 1970 only intensified her anxiety. Babysitting others'
children reminded Sandy how desperately she wanted her own, but she had
a deep-seated insecurity about her adequacy in that role. "I am really scared
to have a child," she confessed to a teacher. "Even if the child is mentally
and physically sound, I could ruin the child's whole life by just trying to
be a mother. What a responsibility!"

A third cluster of the thirteen was composed of students who were bound
not by politics or religion but by a shared curiosity about the intensify-
ing antiwar demonstrations on campus. One, Dean Kahler, a six-foot-tall,
freckle-faced, soft-spoken twenty-year-old with carrot-red hair, blue eyes,
and black-rimmed glasses, was from a semirural area near Canton, Ohio.
His family belonged to the Church of the Brethren, a Quaker-like denom-
ination that preached nonviolence. The oldest of four children, Dean spent
his boyhood hunting, pitching hay on his uncle's farm, and participating
in Boy Scouts activities. He had been a prankster in high school but had
never smoked pot and didn't have enough facial hair to grow a beard. Lanky
but quick, he played offensive tackle and linebacker for three years on his
high school football team *and* ran the hundred-yard dash in ten seconds.
He liked to play backyard basketball nonstop for five or six hours, to run
five or six miles at a stretch, and dreamed of becoming a high school football coach after college.

Dean had aspired as a young boy to join the U.S. Navy and see the
world, but his attitude toward the military soured, and he developed a
strong commitment to nonviolence. With his minister's help, he sought
and received a conscientious objector (C.O.) exemption from the draft. "As
a C.O. I can think for myself," he said, assuming that "in the military, I will
be stripped of my mind only to become part of a machine." He agreed to
work as a medical orderly in a military hospital or in some civilian capac-

ity. His attitude was "I'd rather work with people than shoot them." After high school, he worked for a year at a gas station and in a steel mill to earn enough money to attend college, the first in his family to do so. In early May 1970, he had been at Kent State for just five weeks and had recently celebrated his twentieth birthday.

Bill Schroeder was a six-foot-tall, strikingly handsome nineteen-year-old sophomore from Lorain, Ohio, a steel town about sixty miles from Kent. Female students whisperingly referred to him as "a Nordic god" because of his dark-blond medium-length hair, ice-blue eyes, and muscular build. "He looked like the poster boy for Ralph Lauren," remembered another male student. "I mean he looked really good." He "could walk and talk at an earlier age than the average child," his mother recalled, "and his strong body, his thirst for knowledge, and his desire to make this country a better place to live were the keystones of his life." He had been a cross-country team captain and basketball star in high school, though he often played against taller opponents. Lorain's youngest Eagle Scout at age thirteen, he had graduated twenty-second in his high school class of 453. "I found him

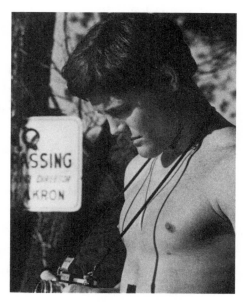

Kent State student Bill Schroeder, late April 1970.

to be an excellent student," recalled one of his teachers. "His intelligence, his perceptiveness, his leadership in the classroom, and his amiability made him one of the best students I have had the pleasure of teaching. What other words of praise do you give to someone you liked so much?" He never mentioned it to his friends, but he volunteered twice a week at a school for developmentally challenged children in nearby Ravenna, playing volleyball and checkers with them. He also wrote poetry, "but he'd always hide it," said a friend.

Although reserved, Bill drove a shiny Fiat sports car with a peace symbol on the window and loved the Rolling Stones, especially its lead singer, Mick Jagger, because "he lives as he wants to and doesn't take any shit from anybody." He thought Jagger "the coolest motherfucker in the world," hung a big poster of Jagger on the wall above his bed, and played Stones' songs—especially "Goin' Home"—every day. "The Stones symbolized something to him he admired but could never really be and I think that's why he was so hung up on them," said his best friend and roommate. He craved experiences, played sports aggressively, and liked taking risks. "He would have fondled a baby rattlesnake until it bit him," said one of his Kent State teachers. He was also fatalistic. "You know, I'm not gonna be around that long," he had recently told a friend. "I'll go fast and sudden, like Hemingway."

Bill started college at the Colorado School of Mines but transferred to Kent State after his freshman year because it was closer to home and allowed him to keep the ROTC scholarship that he needed to pay his way through college. He also took a job in the university cafeteria, where he earned extra money and received free meals. He switched his major from geology to psychology because, as his mother later wrote, "he decided that the presence of a trained psychologist on the military front could be as important as a soldier's rifle or a chaplain."

Bill was broad-minded. "He could argue both sides of a question," his mother remembered. "He would find out whatever side you were on and pick the other side just to stimulate the conversation." The previous summer, he had traveled to Guaymas, Mexico, with two conscientious objectors doing alternative service in a U.S. Army hospital and spent long hours walking the beach talking with them. He ranked the highest of any sophomore in Kent State's ROTC program and loved America but hated the mindless violence of war. He strongly disagreed with another ROTC student who, in discussing a hypothetical military operation, suggested the way to succeed was to "go in there and wipe them out." "Bill was just disgusted by that," a friend recalled. "He said, 'What kind of mentality is that?' He hated the thought of this kind of senseless killing."

Bill discussed the war often with one of his ROTC instructors who was a Vietnam veteran. "We disagree a lot," Bill wrote the instructor, "but there's an intangible mutual respect." They discussed everything from Che Guevara to current best sellers. "He wanted to understand the revolutionary movement," the instructor said, and "couldn't get over the fact they [the Vietnamese] were just like us." He had joined the moratorium march in Kent in October 1969 and attended a recent antiwar conference at Case Western Reserve University in Cleveland.

"When I first got the [ROTC] scholarship," Bill confided to close friends, "I thought it wouldn't be such a bad deal. But now I just can't justify our being in Vietnam, and I don't think I could ever fight there." "The worst part of it is having killing drilled into you day after day. I can take the military history part. I even like that. But when they start telling us the best way to kill peasants, I hate it. And what can I say when people are constantly hammering at you for being in ROTC? Like the other day when I happened to be in uniform, one of my professors said to me, 'What are you, some kind of fascist or something?' I know he was just kidding, but it really gets to you after a while." On the days he wore his uniform to ROTC class, afterward he would rush back to his rented house and change into regular clothing. "It bothered him that he might have to kill people someday," said one of his ROTC instructors. Two weeks earlier, he had told his mother, "I learned three more ways to kill in ROTC. Did you know you can kill a man with two sticks and a wire? I don't know how long I can take it." "Me and ROTC are sort of coexisting at separate levels." "Being an ROTC student and being as liberal minded as he was, I was aware of the conflict within him," his mother added. He had recently confided to a friend, "I just don't know if I can stay in ROTC." "Bill was totally opposed to the incursion of American troops into Cambodia and stated this in no uncertain terms," his best friend remembered. He "pelted the television screen with popcorn kernels as we listened to Nixon speak of the need to invade Cambodia and the benefits that would accrue from the invasion." "He hoped that by the time he was commissioned the war would be over," his mother later said, "but after Cambodia he more or less knew it wouldn't be over by the time" he graduated. He had recently expressed doubt about the place of ROTC on campus and had even considered fleeing to Canada.

Joe Lewis was a six-foot-tall, eighteen-year-old freshman from a large Catholic family in Massillon, Ohio, with a big build, brown eyes, and shoulder-length dark-brown hair. He had attended a Catholic high school, earned good grades, and won a partial scholarship to Notre Dame University. But his parents could not afford the remaining tuition, so Joe worked a summer job after high school to earn enough money to begin Kent State in the autumn of 1969. He found the febrile atmosphere on campus an exciting change from his strict and sheltered upbringing. He wasn't politically active but he participated in the moratorium and the Mobe marches through Kent in the autumn and listened to Jerry Rubin's speech on the Commons in April 1970. He went out of curiosity and was "not converted."

John Cleary was a 6'4", toothpick-thin, eighteen-year-old freshman architecture student from Scioto, New York, who had grown up in a very conservative family and had never questioned U.S. involvement in Vietnam before he arrived at Kent State the previous autumn. "I was in my own little shell" of studying hard to become an architect, he later said, and "Vietnam was something way over there." He didn't engage in any political activities, didn't belong to any political organizations, and didn't attend any antiwar rallies. "I had no strong views on American involvement in Southeast Asia," he said looking back, "but as I began to listen to the protests and what people were saying, it started to create some doubt and questions in my mind [about] what we were doing [in Vietnam] and should we really be there."

Doug Wrentmore, a 5'8", soft-spoken, blond-haired, twenty-year-old sophomore psychology major with a page-boy haircut, full lips, and wide-spaced blue eyes, was from rural Northfield, Ohio. His father was a past president of the Kent State Alumni Association and had been featured in a recruiting film for the university. Doug and his younger brother Hal, a freshman more opposed to the war, shared an off-campus house with two other students. Doug had drawn a low number in the December 1969 draft lottery and had applied for conscientious-objector status. His mother had recently phoned him with news that the local draft board had granted his request.

Scott MacKenzie was curious, too. A twenty-one-year-old junior business major with a sturdy build, curly collar-length brown hair, and a wispy beard, he had transferred to Kent State in the autumn of 1968 from Central College, a small Lutheran-affiliated school in Iowa whose "boxed-in social scene" left him wanting more. He thought Kent State would be less isolated and offer a more active social scene, and it was closer to his hometown of Richboro, Pennsylvania. He knew Robby Stamps. The two had lived in the same dormitory the previous year and had remained acquaintances since. "I was personally opposed to the war, I was morally opposed, I was spiritually opposed," he later said. "I thought it was a real bad idea for us to be there." "I didn't think the war made any sense, but I wouldn't classify myself as an activist." He moved around the edges of campus demonstrations, attended the November 1969 Mobe in Washington, and heard Jerry Rubin speak in April. He stayed for Rubin's entire speech because he thought it was funny. But like many other students in the audience, he thought Rubin said "ridiculous" things.

And then there was twenty-three-year-old fifth-year senior Jim Russell. A self-described "frat boy" from Pittsburgh, his primary goal when he arrived at Kent State in the autumn of 1965 was to enjoy himself. He was a member of the Republican Party and viewed the early campus antiwar rallies as occasions to have some fun by jeering the small number of protestors and deriding them as "commies" and "left-wingers." But his opposition to the Vietnam War intensified during his years at Kent State, and he grew his hair long and sported a beard. President Nixon's Cambodia announcement angered him deeply, and he wanted to express his opposition.

The lives of these thirteen students were about to be upended by events on campus.

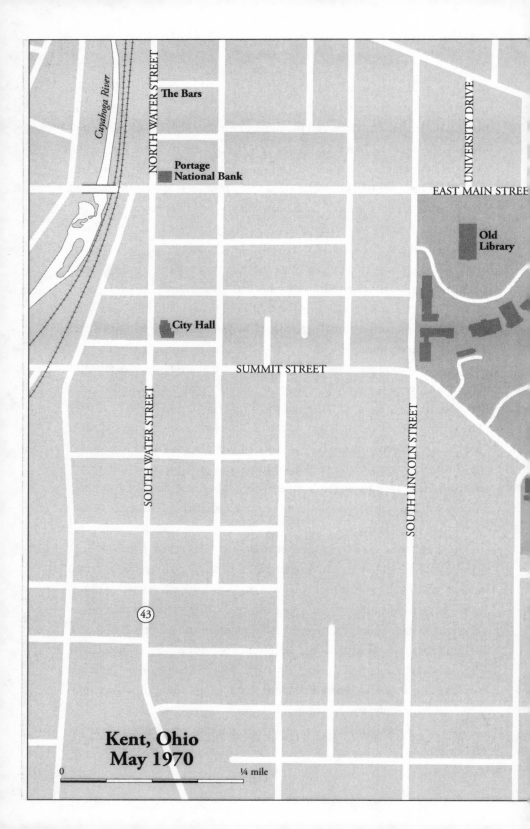

Kent, Ohio
May 1970

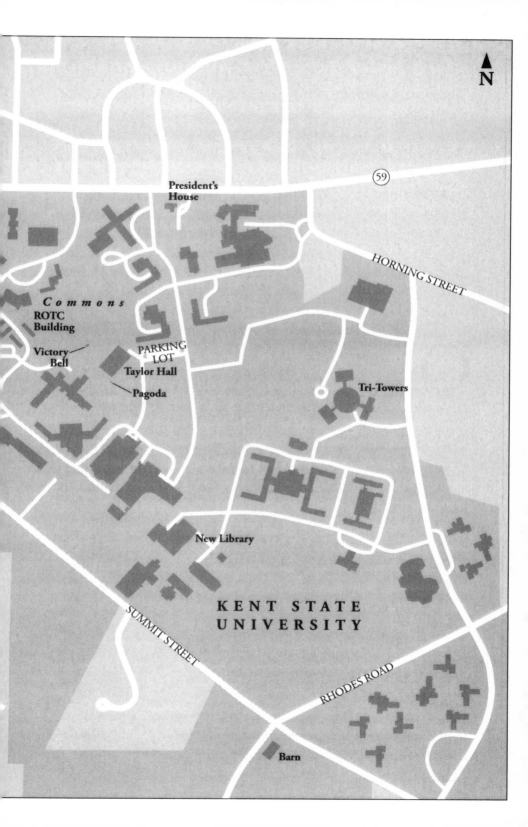

Chapter 4

MAY 1-3, 1970

On Friday, May 1, President Nixon fanned the flames of resentment at Kent State and campuses around the country when he uncorked a diatribe against antiwar students during a morning visit to the Pentagon. Unaware that his impromptu hallway remarks were being taped by a reporter, he contrasted "kids who are just doing their duty" in Vietnam with "these bums"—"the luckiest people in the world, going to the greatest universities"—"blowing up the campuses."

Antiwar activists at Kent State, who had come to view Nixon as "evil incarnate," reacted with swift fury. At noon that Friday, they held an antiwar rally on the Commons to blast Nixon's April 30 Cambodia decision. Before an audience of about five hundred including Tom Grace, Robby Stamps, Allison Krause, and Jim Russell, speakers assailed the president and the war. Tall, Custer-mustachioed graduate history student Steve Sharoff, son of the retired police chief of Monticello, New York, took a copy of the U.S. Constitution torn from a textbook and buried it in a shallow hole he dug with a shovel at the base of the Victory Bell[*] on the eastern edge of the Commons. "If a nation can launch a war on Cambodia without declaring it," he shouted into a bullhorn, "the Constitution as we knew it is really dead!" A

---

[*] Acquired from the Erie Railroad in 1947, the bell was normally used to celebrate school victories in football games.

student in the crowd tried to retrieve the copy of the Constitution from the hole, but Sharoff shoved him aside. Jim Geary, a 101st Airborne Division veteran of Vietnam with a Silver Star and a Good Conduct Medal, stood on the bell's brick encasement with his U.S. Army discharge papers in one hand and a Zippo lighter in the other. "I'm so disgusted with the behavior of my country in invading Cambodia!" shouted Geary. "I've earned the right to burn these papers and goddammit, I'm going to do it!" "Right on!" the crowd yelled back to him. "Burn, baby, burn!" Before things ended, protest leaders announced another rally on the Commons for noon on Monday, May 4. On a nearby tree hung a bedsheet scrawled with the words, "Why Is the ROTC Building Still Standing?" After the rally, Allison Krause told her boyfriend, Barry Levine, "Wow, that was a little too much, Barry."

Spring often comes late to northeastern Ohio—the month of March can seem endless—and it was the first weekend of warm weather after a particularly cold, gray winter. About 11:00 p.m. on Friday, several hundred alcohol-fueled students spilled out on The Strip, a section of North Water Street in Kent that hosted six bars, and started dancing in the street as a scruffy gang of helmeted bikers named the "Chosen Few" staged a loud rodeo on wheels at the main intersection, doing wheelies in interlocking circles. Other students gathered to watch, and a giant traffic jam formed. When an angry motorist tried to drive through the crowd, the mood suddenly turned ugly. Students jumped on the car, broke its windshield, started a bonfire in the middle of North Water Street, and began harassing other passing motorists. The crowd, swelling to about five hundred, then moved up Main Street toward campus, chanting "One, two, three, four, we don't want your fucking war!," "Fuck the pigs!," and "Fuck Nixon!" while smashing storefront windows and spray-painting buildings with slogans. Windows were broken in at least two dozen stores and offices; a jewelry store and a shoe store were looted.

Mayor LeRoy Satrom, a conservative Democrat who looked like a bespectacled Don Knotts* and had a nervous temperament, had been elected the

---

*   An actor best known for his role as Deputy Sheriff Barney Fife in the 1960s television series *The Andy Griffith Show*.

previous autumn on a get-tough platform against "long-haired students." Satrom declared a state of emergency, ordered municipal police in riot gear into the streets, and closed all the downtown bars. He then phoned the governor's office, said SDS members were rampaging through Kent, and asked the National Guard to be put on alert in the event of more trouble. Closing the bars brought a surge of more young people into the streets, who pelted police cruisers with rocks and bottles. The now sizeable crowd began to shout, "Sieg heil! Sieg heil!" It was the worst disturbance in the town's history.

Alan Canfora was in the crowd downtown that night. He later described "the musical sound of falling plate glass windows." "I think it's important to note," he added, "that, though some in Kent saw these actions only as violent and destructive, the students looked at them in political and historical perspective. We heard on the news that actions like these were happening across the country. The damage they did was insignificant compared to the death and destruction in Indochina during any one day. The way we saw it, these kinds of actions had to be taken to bring the war to a close. Nothing else was working." Jeff Miller didn't go downtown but discussed it afterward with his apartment mate. He had condemned violence in the past, but Nixon's Cambodia announcement changed his thinking. The president had turned a deaf ear to those protesting the war, he said, and students would have to turn to violence to make Nixon listen to them.

Not all students agreed with Alan Canfora and Jeff Miller. One female student said she "didn't see that the people [who owned] the shoe store and the butcher had anything to do with being the cause of the war." Tom Grace felt the destruction "was totally unfounded" because the merchants "weren't responsible for the war in Vietnam or the invasion of Cambodia." "I think it's crazy, what the kids did in smashing windows downtown," Allison Krause told a friend. "It's just not fair to make small businessmen suffer." Jim Russell, whose fraternity house was near downtown, joined a group of students that took brooms and shovels and swept up some of the broken glass in the street later that night.

The downtown riot highlighted the "town-and-gown" tension between residents of Kent and students at Kent State. In the early 1950s, the university had about five thousand students. Less than twenty years later, it had nearly quadrupled in size to just under twenty thousand. Business in town increased, but so did the number of students, many with long hair and headbands. Students nonchalantly and sometimes contemptuously gave townspeople their business, and townspeople silently and sometimes resentfully accepted it.

Kent was a conservative, middle-American town with brick streets and buildings, an old train depot, small shops, and a Rotarian spirit. "The university had grown in what seemed a few short years from the polite, sometimes rambunctious boy next door into a hulking, snarling teenage neighbor from hell," in the words of one long-timer. To many, it felt like living with an elephant—you had to be careful when it rolled over. On the surface, Kent remained quiet and peaceful. But "beneath that surface," said an observer, "lay a volatile, acidic subsoil of reaction." Long hair and beads bewildered residents who felt their values and way of life under siege. Those over age sixty were old enough to remember the 1917 Russian Revolution and associated beards with Bolshevism. Many townspeople were bitter, angry, and scared of students, who they saw as "anarchists," "hippies," and "outsiders" bent on wreaking havoc in a normally peaceful corner of Middle America. "You might as well call them what they are— Communists," said Bob Stratton, a clerk at Purcell's Department Store. "I have four kids and I thank God they're not old enough to go to college." Some locals began referring to Kent State as Chaos U. "I wish that Kent could become the peaceful old place it was, and that the university would go away and leave us alone," grumped one resident. How did destroying private property help stop the war? They feared anything could happen now. It felt like a revolution was brewing in their own backyard. Citizens of Kent would show the rest of the country how to preserve law and order.

Angry and fearful residents of Kent blamed Friday night's rioting on "outside agitators" and "subversive groups"—specifically the Weathermen, notorious for their "Days of Rage" in Chicago seven months earlier and the Greenwich Village townhouse explosion just eight weeks ago. The

Weathermen had become a spectral presence—a kind of bogeyman—in the minds of townspeople frightened by students' increasingly disruptive antiwar tactics. "They scared hell out of Middle America and small towns like Kent," explained a local journalist. "The Weathermen told people that Armageddon and revolution were imminent." The damage done by Friday night's rioting was limited compared with damage done in other university communities in 1970, but residents of Kent and surrounding conservative Portage County convinced themselves and state officials, without any concrete evidence,* that Weathermen were stalking their streets fomenting subversion and disorder. This was more comforting than pondering the fact that hundreds of Kent State students had become so infuriated by the war that they resorted to vandalism. Earlier in the year, Kent police chief Roy Thompson had said, "They got a lot of people over on that campus who I don't suppose are plain Communists, but an awful lot of them are pinkos." About reports of Weathermen on campus that first weekend in May, Kent State police chief Donald Schwartzmiller said, "As far as us seeing them, No. As far as us being able to identify them as Weathermen, No. Weathermen to us right now is faceless." Thompson warned the mayor that his force of twenty-one officers could not defend the town against the Weathermen, and the Ohio National Guard should be called in.

On Saturday morning May 2, Mayor Satrom set a citywide curfew for 8:00 p.m. Phone calls flooded into the police from anxious downtown merchants reporting anonymous threats that if they did not put up "Get Out of Cambodia" signs in their display windows, they would be firebombed. Jim

---

* "Rigorous research by various agencies failed to uncover any evidence proving that any SDS leaders engineered or participated in the riots." James A. Michener, *Kent State: What Happened and Why* (Random House, Reader's Digest Press, 1971), p. 154. No Weathermen were arrested during the four days of disturbances from May 1 to 4, no one saw Ric Erickson, Howie Emmer, Colin Neiberger, or Jeff Powell on campus that weekend, and the FBI uncovered no evidence to that effect. A Kent State administrator later recalled, "When I looked at all the surveillance pictures afterwards, I was sure I would find that we had been invaded by all kinds of SDS and Weathermen, but that wasn't the case. These were our own students." Quoted in Howard Means, *67 Shots: Kent State and the End of American Innocence* (Da Capo Press, 2016), p. 23.

Myers, whose pharmacy had been damaged the night before, felt "anger at the students who had caused it. There were rumors floating around that 'students were gonna come back and finish the job.'"* Everyone expected more trouble. Kent was going to be in for a long night. The local paper, the *Record-Courier,* announced that the National Guard had been put on standby alert if needed. If the guard came in, it would take "complete control" not only of the town but of the campus as well. University officials were nervous. Their riot contingency plan called for using university police, then county sheriff's deputies, then the Ohio State Highway Patrol as a last resort—not the National Guard. Later that afternoon, Chief Thompson informed Satrom that "guys with red headbands on, call 'em Weathermen or whatever you want to call them"—had been observed on campus. Rumors that a car with Illinois plates loaded with Weathermen armed with shotguns had been spotted in town and that they planned to poison the municipal water supply with LSD that night fueled fears and paranoia. "Feelings were strong and reason vague," recalled a town resident. Under pressure from constituents and feeling his police force ill equipped to deal with the potential unrest, Satrom called the governor's office about 5:30 p.m. and asked that the National Guard be sent to Kent.† Satrom did not inform university administrators of his request, perhaps because he knew they would oppose it.

———

At sunset on Saturday, about five hundred students gathered at the Victory Bell. They comprised a mix of antiwar activists, interested bystanders, and curious onlookers—among them Tom Grace, Joe Lewis, Scott MacKenzie, and Robby Stamps. Protest leaders handed out leaflets denouncing ROTC. One SDS pamphlet read:

* Other students helped clean up broken glass on the sidewalks and streets that day.

† Satrom later told the Scranton Commission that Kent's police department made the request for the National Guard.

MIND F.U.C.K.

At high schools and universities across the country sds is demanding an end to ROTC. The purpose of this demand is to cripple the use of the US military by the US ruling class. On college campuses the military is present in the forms of ROTC, recruiters and war research. ROTC is a key example of how all young people are used by the ruling class to support imperialism and racism.

Many young people become involved in ROTC only as an alternative to the draft—an everpresent reality from the time you sign up at 18. You really don't have too much of a choice. You just take what seems to be the best way out. Many guys are forced into certain jobs they don't dig so they can get an occupational deferment.

ROTC supplies the military with 85% of its 1st and 2nd lieutenants. They are used to giving leadership to enlisted men and draftees (Who can't get through college.) Besides giving leadership lieutenants are increasingly needed as their death rate in Vietnam is second only to that of Blacks. Lieutenants are necessary to the kind of army we have in the US. It is used solely to protect the interests of the US ruling class.

Orders in our army are handed down from a specially chosen elite group that uses heavy discipline on draftees and enlisted men— mostly blacks and white working-class guys—who don't necessarily support or understand the war. Guys in ROTC think the trip in the army will be better if they have that kind of control and authority. But they are just a messenger service for the ruling class. They are being used—and not really given any control . . .

National Liberation Front[*] officers in Vietnam are elected by the regular troops. Those officers determine strategy collectively.[†] If an offi-

---

[*] South Vietnamese communists.

[†] In reality, overall strategy was determined in Hanoi.

cer fucks up he is removed by the men. They can't afford to use this system in the US army. The Vietnamese are fighting for their own country, they understand why they are fighting. The mass media and education here do a mind fuck about communism. They portray it as a yellow and red plague to be fought against at any cost in human life and sanity in order to preserve "freedom" in the world.

END ROTC
POWER TO THE PEOPLE

By 7:30 p.m., the crowd at the Victory Bell had grown larger and angrier. "The point of discussion is past, the time for action is here!" shouted one participant. The crowd moved out from the Commons, picking up more protestors as it looped around the dormitories and spray-painted antiwar slogans on buildings, trees, and sidewalks. As the crowd crested Blanket Hill, a grassy knoll between Johnson Hall and Taylor Hall overlooking the Commons from the east where students sunned themselves in spring and summer, sledded on cafeteria trays in winter, and necked at night, the throng—which one eyewitness described as "a moving mob"—had grown to about sixteen hundred strong. They headed for the military science building on the southwestern edge of the Commons, shouting "Get it!," "Burn it!," and "ROTC has to go!" as they went. When they reached their destination, they formed a semicircle around it as daylight faded.

The one-story wooden barracks, formally known as East Hall, had housed Kent State's ROTC unit since its founding in 1947. The building had been a World War II field hospital that the university had purchased from the federal government as surplus after the war. Old and shabby, administrators considered its location prime campus real estate and a perfect site for a new building; faculty considered it a "sheep pen"; alumni considered it an embarrassing eyesore; and students considered it a symbol of the military-industrial complex they despised and a constant reminder of the war in Vietnam they hated. It seemed a convenient target. "It's symbolic. It's small, wooden, convenient and nobody in it at night," noted the student body president. Even ROTC officers understood this. "Everyone knew ROTC would go sometime or other," said a U.S. Army instructor, "and for some reason

I had a feeling it would be Saturday night. You could almost feel it in the air."* He was so sure the building would burn that he returned to campus later Saturday afternoon to retrieve his camera and radio from his office. The mood at Kent State was not unusual. The most visible symbol of the military on university campuses, nearly two hundred ROTC buildings around the country came under attack during the 1969–1970 academic year.

"Down with ROTC!" chanted the crowd as it hurled rocks and stones at the barracks. Someone shouted, "Six years of peaceful protest got us nowhere! They'll listen only when they see the flames, and tonight they're going to see them!" Sociology professor Jerry Lewis attempted to dissuade the protestors from burning down the building. Geology professor Glenn Frank, a popular campus figure and former marine who was still built like one and had gray flat-top hair, clear plastic horn-rimmed glasses, and wore a tie-clasped suit, told the angry protestors, "There's no need to condone violence." A young man with long hair shouted, "The point of discussion is past! The time for action is here! I don't want to hear anything a fucking pig like you has to say!" He then spit at Frank's face but missed. "I have never in seventeen years of teaching seen a group of students as threatening or as arrogant or as bent on destruction as I saw and talked to that night," Frank later said.

Protestors tried to use an empty fifty-gallon gasoline drum as a battering ram to smash in the front door of East Hall. They hit the side of the building instead and tumbled backward on the grass. Then they grabbed red safety flares from a box and threw them on the roof. Someone handed a flare to Robby Stamps and told to him to "chuck it" toward the building; Robby refused.† The flares that were thrown rolled off, fell to the ground,

---

* That afternoon, a student had shouted through a window to an ROTC officer, "This would be a good place for you and your men to be tonight because it is going to burn." Statement of ROTC officer, May 5, 1970, FBI Reports, Raw Inputs, FOIA January 1979, Box 64D, Folder 32, Charles Thomas Papers, May 4 Collection, Kent State University Library (hereafter cited as M4C, KSUL).

† Robby later confided to a Justice Department official that the individuals responsible for torching the ROTC building were not the ones indicted for doing so. He refused to identify who they were. William Gardner interview with Robert Stamps, November 26, 1973, MS 1800, Box 75, KSC, SML, YU.

and sputtered out. Someone ignited trash in a garbage can and threw it through a window, but the fire went out. Another flare was tossed through a broken window, which set afire the curtains, but the flames again petered out. Matches held to draperies squirted with lighter fluid failed to rekindle the fire. A protestor lit an American flag on a stick and knocked a photographer to the ground for taking his picture, beating and kicking the photographer. Freshman Peter Bliek and another protestor soaked a cloth rag in the gas tank of a motorcycle parked nearby, set the cloth rag on a windowsill, lit it, and tossed it through a broken window. This finally set the barracks ablaze. It was about 8:50 p.m. Someone in the crowd yelled, "You fuckers have got no right to do this!" He was drowned out by boos and jeers. "Burn, baby, burn!" shouted the crowd as rifle ammunition stored in the building popped off and gray smoke started billowing out.

Robby Stamps left before protestors set fire to the barracks and returned to his dorm. Scott MacKenzie moved to the hill in front of Taylor Hall. Joe Lewis wanted "no part" of the arson; he thought it was crazy. "It seemed futile to combat violence in Vietnam with violence of our own," he later explained. Joe and his girlfriend, Susan Tardiff, headed toward his dorm, where they watched from a little grassy hill by the parking lot in front of Johnson Hall. They then moved inside, where they looked out the window of his friend's room across the hall and saw flames billowing up. Joe's parents called later that night and warned him to be careful and stay out of trouble. He promised to heed their advice. John Cleary watched the ROTC building burn from the Commons. He saw people breaking windows, throwing flares on the roof, hurling Molotov cocktails against the building, and attempting to ignite the drapery. He understood the frustration fueling their behavior but "could not understand the destruction." Alan Canfora, Tom Grace, and Doug Wrentmore observed from atop Blanket Hill. Jeff Miller watched down on the Commons. He worried that everyone there would be arrested—so much so that he told friends they ought to leave before something happened. Sandy Scheuer, who had made dinner for Jeff earlier that evening, watched the burning ROTC building from Taylor Hall.

Earlier that day, Allison Krause had spoken on the phone with her father. He warned her to "stay away from trouble" and "be careful of the National

Guard." "I felt they'd be called in," he later explained. "I knew they had been on duty in Akron at a Teamsters strike and would probably be exhausted. And I told her so. 'They're probably frightened and nervous,' I said, 'so keep out of trouble and stay away from them.'" Allison assured him she "understood the danger." That night, she, Barry, and another of Allison's friends saw the anti-ROTC rally near the Victory Bell on their way to a movie. Allison and her friend wanted to stay and see what would happen. "Look," Barry said, "somebody's going to say, 'Let's do this' and everybody will yell, 'Yeh, Yeh!' and then they'll go off and do it, no matter what it is. We shouldn't stay here because the whole thing is just going to be a mess." Allison and her friend prevailed on Barry to stay. They watched the ROTC building ignited from atop Blanket Hill, then watched it burn from Johnson Hall when instructed to move indoors. "We both wanted to see it burn and get ROTC off campus," Barry later admitted.

A small number of university officials stood off to the side watching; they feared for their safety if they tried to intervene. The campus police were not present because they had been sent to guard the university president's house. A municipal fire truck arrived just before 9:00 p.m. Firefighters started unrolling a water hose. Protestors were "grabbing the hose, pulling it, and getting in the way—not letting them hook the nozzle up to the hydrant and run the hose to the building. There certainly was a concerted effort to not let the Fire Department put the fire out," a witness recalled. Other protestors punctured the hose with pocketknives and ice picks until someone severed it with a machete. When a fireman tried to stop them, protestors clubbed him. He and other firemen gave up trying to fight the spreading blaze and left shortly before 9:30 p.m. About that time, campus police in riot gear arrived and drove off the protestors with tear gas.

Dean Kahler learned of the fire on the radio back home near Canton and thought, "Gee, that's crazy." "The burning of the ROTC building was symbolic, but [I] didn't condone it," he later said. Bill Schroeder was also away from Kent that night. He, too, was shocked by the news. "I'd heard rumors and I'd seen the demonstrations against ROTC," Bill told a friend, "But I just couldn't believe they'd actually burn it. ROTC may not be the greatest thing, but you can't just go around burning up things you don't like." He abhorred "violence for the sake of violence," his friend remembered, and he didn't see how burning buildings would help end the war any sooner. Jim Russell, staying at a roommate's home in Fairport, saw a brief story about the fire on the Cleveland television news Saturday night. He also disapproved.

A student's letter to a friend summed up the feelings of many that night. "We watched the building burn. I was glad it burned. I'm against the war in Vietnam. We've been trying to end ROTC for a year, and burning down the building was a reasonable answer to an administration that doesn't listen to students." "I'm surprised it wasn't burned earlier," said another student. They overlooked the fact that Kent State's student government had held a referendum the previous autumn on the question, "Do you want ROTC on campus?," and students had voted overwhelmingly to keep it. Later that night, a dorm resident director remembered, "this rather crazed student saw me and said, 'Man, this is it—the revolution is beginning!' I just looked at him and said, 'You're insane! Do you know what you've done?'"

Around 9:30 p.m., a long line of armored personnel carriers, jeeps, and trucks carrying Ohio National Guardsmen from Companies A and C of the 145th Infantry Regiment based in Wooster and Troop G of the 107th Armored Cavalry Regiment based in Ravenna rumbled into Kent. The guardsmen hailed from cities, towns, and rural areas across north-central Ohio and varied widely in class and occupation. They included an architectural draftsman, auto mechanic, building contractor, carpenters, construction workers, farmers, a floor installer, forklift operator, laborer, lawyer, locksmith, machinist, managers, office workers, policemen, postal workers, a production foreman, saddle maker, salesmen, a shoe buyer, teacher, trucker, and a welder. Most enlistees were in their twenties, a few in their late teens or early thirties—the officers being generally older. Their education ranged from high school to graduate study at the London School of Economics.

Some joined the Ohio National Guard because they wanted to serve their communities. Many others joined for the same reason that many students attended Kent State—to avoid the draft. Pentagon surveys confirmed that more than 80 percent enlisted in the National Guard to escape conscription. Enlistment had increased substantially in 1969, when the Pentagon lifted the freeze imposed five years earlier to keep the National Guard from becoming a refuge from the war. One Ohio National Guardsman was very candid: "I joined the guard instead of being drafted into the Vietnam War."

The commitment period was six years. During this time, guardsmen strived to avoid accumulating five "unsats" (unsatisfactory performance ratings), which made them eligible for active duty; that is, a tour in Vietnam. "If we were unsat, it was on a plane and you were over there—that was the sword," recalled a guardsman. Many would readily admit they'd much rather be sent to inner-city Cleveland than to the jungles of Southeast Asia. Vietnam veterans were aware of this, and it made many of them very negative toward the guard.

Service in the National Guard began with eight weeks of basic training at Fort Knox, Kentucky, followed by ten weeks of advanced instruction elsewhere. Thereafter, they drilled each weekend at their local National Guard armory (thus the label "weekend warriors") and spent two weeks each summer on active duty at the National Guard training site at Camp Grayling in northern Michigan. First and foremost, they learned to follow orders. "When you're in the military, you do as you're told," said guardsman B. J. Long looking back. "That's the way the military trained you: 'It's an order.'" They didn't challenge things. They did their job.

They were taught the following Rules of Engagement, which were read verbatim to guardsmen by an officer immediately prior to every deployment in a civil disturbance: "In any action that you are required to take, use only the minimum force necessary"; "If people do not respond to request, direction, and order, you have the rifle butt and bayonet which may be used in that order, using only such force as necessary"; and "Indiscriminate firing of weapons is forbidden." "Regardless of the actions and taunts of the rioters, you must remain the well-disciplined soldier," "exercise soldierly restraint under all conditions," and "the temptation to use high-handed methods may be great, but you must remain calm and retain your good judgment in order that you may act wisely regardless of personal feelings or beliefs," "using only the minimum force necessary." The message was clear: "Good judgment may prevent [a] situation from getting completely out of hand" and "Use common sense and do only what is necessary to do and can be justified *afterwards*."* Yet guardsmen were also taught to use their rifles as lethal weapons, not as nonlethal control instruments, and that "in any instance where human life is endangered by the forcible, violent actions of a rioter, or when rioters to whom the Riot Act has been read cannot be dispersed by any other reasonable means, then shooting is justified." One guardsman said in hindsight: "We didn't have training in how to deal with student protests. We had training in how to kill people."

Guardsmen received sixteen hours of riot-control training a year, which included watching films, studying manuals, receiving classroom instruction, and practicing formations. An officer candidly conceded, however, that "if they had sixteen hours a month, they wouldn't have sufficient training." Efforts were made to ensure everyone's participation, but a U.S. Army inspector had recently reported that more than a quarter of all guardsmen in the 145th Infantry Regiment had received no riot training at all. They received no instruction about what to do if they heard other guardsmen firing in a crowd-control situation. One sergeant later noted that "I was not taught anything about firing warning shots into the air" and "I was not taught anything about the circumstances under which it was permissible to fire live rounds in crowd-control situations." "I don't remember any discussion about how to use my weapon in crowd-control situations," a private admitted. In simulated riots, "agitators" figured prominently: guardsmen were taught to expect "verbal abuse, taunts, jeers, obscenities, yelling, and thrown objects" and demonstrators attempting to grab their

---

* Another Army National Guard directive elaborated, "The use of deadly force . . . in effect involves the power of summary execution and can therefore be justified only by extreme necessity. . . . Use of deadly force is authorized where: (1) Lesser means have been exhausted or are unavailable. (2) The risk of death or serious bodily harm to innocent persons is not increased by its use." Appendix 9 (Special Instructions) to Annex C (Concept of Operations to United States Continental Army Command) Civil Disturbance Plan (Garden Plot), May 1, 1969, Series 2062, Box 2842, Ohio Historical Society, State Archives, Columbus, Ohio (hereafter cited as OHSSA).

rifles. When practice riots got rough, tempers flared on both sides. The 145th Infantry Regiment staged a mock riot with Wooster College students at the Wooster County Fairground, and "they got totally out of hand." The danger of instinctual, emotional reactions was *the* lesson of riot training, but Ohio National Guard leadership did not internalize and operationalize this crucial insight.

Guardsmen had considerable experience dealing with urban riots but very little experience dealing with campus protests. This became apparent to one guardsman who had served on active duty in the U.S. Army. "When you're trying to do crowd control," he said, "you do it in an orderly fashion. They were not orderly. They were not trained properly. You could tell they weren't trained just by what they were doing." Unlike many police departments, Ohio guardsmen had no riot-control gear such as plastic face shields and nightsticks. "There was [tear] gas and bullets and nothing in between," noted an officer. "We were only equipped for basic combat," said another. In the spring of 1970, the Ohio National Guard introduced new training for dealing with campus demonstrations, but the 145th Infantry Regiment had received only one training session in the new techniques and had not really learned them.* In their combat gear with high-powered rifles and fixed bayonets, guardsmen knew how to project force but not how to perform what amounted to policing work. "We [were] virtually untrained in the discipline and personal restraint so necessary for critical civil duty," a guardsman wrote looking back.

The guardsmen arrived in Kent on Saturday night from nearby Akron, where they had spent the past four days protecting non-union truckers from violent assaults by striking Teamsters and had slept in tents on wet, cold ground in an outdoor stadium called the Rubber Bowl. "It was miserable," one of them recalled. During the strike, the guard requested nonlethal equipment such as nightsticks, riot batons, and face shields from the

---

* The group that *did* learn these more restrained riot-control techniques was the Ohio State Highway Patrol. "They'd had time to practice with it. We didn't." Author's interview with Mathew McManus, October 24, 2020. The Ohio State Highway Patrol had handled the Music and Speech Building disturbance in April 1969 without any serious injuries.

army, but the request was denied. It was a fateful refusal. "Had we had this equipment at Kent State," said two guardsmen looking back, "we probably would have been accused of being brutal, but that would have been better than the alternatives that would eventually come into play." The tension of the four-day Teamsters' strike had worn down the National Guardsmen. Most had gotten only a few hours of sleep the previous four nights, and several were sick with the flu. On Saturday morning, when they thought they were going home, they received orders for another deployment.

The guardsmen's first sight of Kent was an orange glow on the horizon from the burning ROTC barracks. "It was just one building, but it lit up the sky something fierce," recalled a guardsman. The orange glow could be seen by county residents more than a dozen miles away. One trooper thought, "My God, the whole town is burning, the whole campus." "It was like something out of *Gone with the Wind*, with Atlanta burning," remembered another. Guardsman Jim Pierce described their arrival:

> I was driving a jeep into the city of Kent in a convoy. . . . The streets were lined with [students] . . . chanting obscenities. As we proceeded, in my headlights I saw what appeared to be a hailstorm of rocks, bottles, concrete chunks and bricks. They were hitting the vehicles ahead of me with a dull thud, making dents in the vehicles. . . . Our vehicle's windshield was busted. The guy next to me watched a brick bounce off my helmet. . . . No one could believe what was happening.

Kent city police told the guard: "We can't control them anymore, we've lost control, they're all yours." "It was just so surreal."

Once the guard reached campus, Adjutant General "Tough Tony" Del Corso took command on the scene. He ordered guardsmen to fix bayonets on their rifles, which they had not done during the four-day Teamsters' strike in Akron. The bayonet "doesn't look like a deadly weapon," one of the guardsmen later explained, but its ten-inch blade "is as sharp as a razor and very strong metal. You were taught to insert it and rip it, and it would do just that. You could charge into a group with a fixed bayonet and kill somebody." "I was shocked that we used fixed bayonets in Kent." Del Corso also ordered guardsmen to don gas masks. It was a muggy night, and the gas masks' goggles quickly fogged up. He also deployed guardsmen around the burning ROTC barracks to protect firemen who had returned to put out the flames. "That night I saw some of my friends in the crowd," recalled a guardsman and former Kent State student, "only they didn't know it was me because I had a gas mask on." He told his commanding officer, "I live here. I don't really want to be involved in this."

Protestors regrouped on Blanket Hill on the far side of the Commons to watch firemen extinguish the flames. Some threw rocks at the guardsmen. One hit General Del Corso on the shoulder. "If these little bastards can throw rocks," Tough Tony yelled, "I can too!" He reached down, picked up the rock, and hurled it back, but hit a guardsman's helmet instead. Del Corso then ordered the guardsmen to disperse the crowd of students. "Go back to your dormitories. If you remain outside, you will be arrested! We do not want to arrest you!" they warned over bullhorns as they approached Blanket Hill. Guardsmen drove off those who refused to scatter. Three students suffered lacerations from bayonets. A professor saw a female student

Ohio National Guardsmen deploy at burning Kent State ROTC building, May 2, 1970.

explode in anger at a guardsman. "She was slapping at his face. She spit on him, and he was pushing her back with his rifle until she got to the edge of the hill. As steep as it was, it caused her to stumble, and she had to turn around to get herself down the hill." When she did, the guardsman kicked her hard in the rear end with his heavy boot.

Later that night, as Alan Canfora crossed campus on the way back to his apartment in town, he encountered a group of guardsmen. "I said to one of them, 'Hey, soldier, where are you from?' He hit me with the [butt] of his gun, pushed me, and said, 'Get over there and be quiet.'" Allison Krause called her parents a second time that day just before midnight. She told them the ROTC fire was "a terrible way to destroy property" but added, "This is the boys' way of telling President Nixon they didn't want to go to Cambodia."

At night's end, guardsmen who were deployed around the burned-out ROTC barracks returned to the Wall Elementary School gymnasium where they were billeted and fell, exhausted, into their two-man pup tents. Because the gymnasium's lights were kept on and guardsmen constantly came and went, few of the guardsmen got much sleep. "I got about five and a half hours' sleep out of [the] seventy-two hours we were in Kent," remembered one.

Sunday, May 3, dawned warm, clear, and quiet. Acrid smoke rising from the charred remains of the ROTC building wafted over the dewy grass of the Commons. Platoon sergeant Matt McManus of Company A, 145th Infantry Regiment, had been asleep for only an hour when a runner summoned him to meet with Captain John Martin, a farmer from near Wooster who commanded Company A. Martin told McManus his platoon would guard the burned-out barracks again that night. McManus briefed his squad leaders.

When McManus finished, Corporal Dale Antram came up to him. "Sergeant McManus, we've got a euchre game going on out on the [Commons] with some of the students. Can you come and join us? We need a fourth person." McManus agreed. He, Antram, and two female students played game after game of euchre sitting on the grass beneath oak and maple trees from late morning to late afternoon while, nearby, other guardsmen joined touch-football games with students. "It was a nice day," recalled McManus. "Just young people having fun—not keeping score or worrying about who won or lost." They played cards, watched the touch-football game, and talked. The female students asked McManus and Antram about the clips of eight .30 caliber bullets* prominently displayed on their lapels. The female students touched the bullets and asked if they were real. Very real. The brass-jacketed, .30 caliber, 5½-inch high-velocity bullets could kill at a range of one thousand yards. At two hundred yards, they could pierce a steel helmet and pass straight through a human head. McManus and Antram had never loaded live ammunition in their rifles during earlier urban riots.

The female students asked about their M-1 rifles. Standard U.S. Army issue during World War II and the early years of the Korean War, the M-1 was a military weapon designed for one purpose: to kill. Ohio National Guard brass realized as early as 1965 that the M-1 "was a more powerful weapon than was necessary for civil disturbances" and had petitioned the army for more appropriate substitutes such as shotguns, but the army was slow to respond, and Ohio National Guard leadership did not press the issue. The few shotguns in the Ohio National Guard's possession had been provided by the state.

The mood on the Commons that afternoon was relaxed and tranquil. Matt McManus later remembered thinking, "What are we doing here? It's so calm, quiet, and peaceful. Very peaceful." The clean-cut, short-haired guardsmen looked very different from most Kent State students, but many had ties to the university. One had joined the guard to pay his tuition and was headed for class when the call came in to report to his unit. Another was the son of a professor. Major Arthur Wallach had attended graduate school there. Lieutenant Stephen Gagnon had gone to Kent State before attending Officer Candidate School. Captain Roger Gardner's daughter was a student. Lieutenant Colonel Charles Fassinger's wife was an alumna. Sev-

---

*   It was later learned that some of the guardsmen's bullets at Kent State were armor-piercing ones.

eral guardsmen sympathized with the students and resented being called out against them. "I'd been told when I entered the National Guard that I would not be called out for an action against my own home," complained one guardsman. They saw themselves as reluctant participants. Students perceived them far differently, however. For them, the Ohio National Guard symbolized a militaristic system that had led the nation into the debacle of Vietnam and now was abusing its power at home and repressing them—taking over *their* campus. "We looked upon them as an occupation army that had invaded our campus, and we wanted them gone," one student recalled.

Guardsmen's attitudes toward the antiwar movement and the counterculture varied widely. Some guardsmen sympathized with the "long-hairs." "God—He had long hair," said one. "To me, how you wear your hair is unimportant." Many younger guardsmen wanted to wear their hair longer. "It's altogether possible that some men in this guard unit have smoked pot," another matter-of-factly observed. A greater number shared the antipathy to antiwar protestors characteristic of small-town Ohio. "They brought with them to Kent not only their fatigue but also their envy and anger against people of their own age who enjoyed social and educational advantages they lacked." Lieutenant Roy Dew said, "These kids just don't understand. They're 19-20-21-year-old kids and they just want to run the country."

Most guardsmen strongly supported the constitutional right to dissent. "I believe in dissent," said one, "because it's healthy for society." Sergeant Mike Delaney had attended the moratorium protest and didn't "think I should change what I think because I'm wearing a uniform." Another sergeant, Jim Thomas, knew a man in his outfit who, "if he wasn't in uniform, would have been out there on the other side of the line." Even those who supported the war, such as Private Don Cozant, said, "I'd like to sit down and talk with [protestors] to try to understand what they're doing."

Many guardsmen felt they had more in common with the students than they knew. One guardsman was a student himself, had been to an antiwar rally in Akron, and only joined the guard to keep from going to Vietnam. Robby Stamps recognized another guardsman, Robin Hefflefinger, as his geology classmate the year before and shared a sandwich with him. Hefflefinger said he wasn't happy to be on campus in uniform—he wanted to get back to his classes—but it was his duty.

When a male student in long curls and velvet jacket passed a guardsman, the guardsman remarked, "You sure got some wild-looking people on this campus." "We feel the same about you," replied the student, not missing a beat. "I remember how relaxed things seemed," said a visitor. "Students in shorts and short skirts were walking around, picking dandelions and putting them in the rifle barrels." When a student flashed a guardsman the peace sign, the guardsman winked, opened his tunic, and displayed a T-shirt with a peace symbol. Another guardsman talking to students quickly glanced left and right then turned back one of his collar points to reveal a button that read: DOWN WITH REPRESSION. A student told a guardsman, "We're all fed up with having military on our campus." "From the way the trooper laughed," said someone who witnessed the exchange, "I got the idea that maybe he was fed up being there." Student Terri West spoke with many guardsmen that afternoon on the Commons. "The majority of them said, 'We don't want to be here either.'" "They seemed like normal guys, not much different from us," recalled junior Richard Watkins. "They probably preferred being about anywhere else."

What had happened Friday and Saturday nights—"it seemed as if it was all over," said a student. Many eyewitnesses described the atmosphere as carnival-like—"no fear, no anxiety, no animosity." Joe Lewis remembered it felt like a "circus" or "sailors in port," everyone "chatting, smiling, laughing." Sandy Scheuer toured the burned-out ROTC building holding a piece of ribbon as a leash attached to a stray dog she and her housemates had adopted. Doug Wrentmore played Frisbee with and talked to guardsmen standing around the ROTC building. "People [said] 'Hey, how ya doin'?' Wavin' to ya," remembered a guardsman. Female students in miniskirts and baggy blue jeans flirted, feeling the muscles of blushing guardsmen. Guardsmen talked openly with students, winking and laughing with them. The burned-out ROTC barracks drew curious sightseers from as far away as Cleveland. They gawked at guardsmen and had photos taken with them in front of the building like tourists posing with Beefeaters in front of the

Ohio National Guardsmen socialize with
Kent State students, May 3, 1970

Tower of London. John Cleary called home and told his parents "that things
had calmed down and if they were worried, not to worry."

But there were ominous portents as well. Guardsmen patrolling in jeeps
through town encountered residents who came out of their houses to offer
them homemade cookies but who were followed by students who threw
bags of feces at them from car windows. Some students wanted to have
their photos taken with guardsmen; others called them "pigs," spat in their
faces, and taunted, "Who is fucking your wife while you are here?" "Don't
you think a guy like me gets disgusted when co-eds scream at him and
curse him as an imperialist?" asked a guardsman. "It so happens that I'm
against the war in Vietnam as strongly as the girls who curse me. I believe
it's a waste and a sad error. I'd get out tomorrow if I could, and I sure as
hell don't want to be flying over there. But I also believe that a man like me
can honorably serve his country in uniform." Joe Lewis's parents visited

him that afternoon on their way to Cleveland. The cafeteria in Johnson
Hall where Joe lived was closed on Sunday afternoons, so they brought
him a sandwich. "If there's trouble" again, his mother warned, "stay in
your dorm." "I will," he replied.

Wandering the Commons that afternoon, Allison Krause and Barry
Levine made their way to the burned-out barracks, where they encountered
B. J. Long of Company A. "Why are you guarding a burned-out building?"
she asked him. "We just talked," Long later said, "Nothing significant."
Another young guardsman smiled at Allison and sheepishly flashed her
the peace sign. "He stood quietly alone," Barry remembered, "a lilac [blos-
som] in his gun barrel. Taking me by the arm, Allison walked over to him."
He was Ronnie Myers, a young farmer from Ravenna whose little sister
was a Kent State student. "Unlike many of the soldiers we had met that
day," Barry went on, "Myers wore a pleasant smile, and when he spoke, he
did so with a gentle compassion. He said he did not want to be guarding
the campus, but when asked why he didn't leave, he looked to the ground
and shyly said he couldn't." An officer standing nearby "was not too happy
about what was going on. You could see it in his face." The officer "slowly
strolled over and placed his arm around Myers's shoulder. As we watched
inquisitively, Myers's face tightened up, his back straightened, and his
smile completely disappeared. The officer, yelling in Myers's ear, ordered
him to identify himself and his division. Myers did so, and as we watched
the fear swell in the young guardsman's eyes, the officer began: 'Doesn't
your division have target practice next week, Myers?' 'Yes, sir.' 'Are you
going there with that silly flower?' 'No, sir.' 'Then what is it doing in your
rifle barrel?' 'It was a gift, sir.' 'Do you always accept gifts, Myers?' 'No, sir.'
'Then why did you accept this one?' No answer. 'What are you going to do
with it, Myers?' Myers feebly began to remove the lilac. 'Now, that's better,
Myers. Now, straighten up and start acting like a soldier and forget all this
peace stuff.' Realizing the officer would merely throw the lilac away, Allison
grabbed it from his hand and gave him a look of disgust." The officer glared
at Allison, turned his back, and walked away. "As the officer walked away,
Allison called after him, 'What's the matter with peace? Flowers are better
than bullets!'" The officer turned and glared at her. "Pig!" she yelled at him.

Guardsman Ronnie Myers with lilac
placed in his rifle barrel by a student.

Elsewhere on the Commons there was this exchange:

STUDENT: "You have live ammunition in there?"

GUARDSMAN: "Yup."

STUDENT: "You going to shoot?"

GUARDSMAN: "I'm not going to shoot anyone. They can tell me all day and
    I'm not going to do it. All I want to do is go home. You kids going to
    cause trouble?"

STUDENT: "Are you kidding? The trouble is over."

Captain John Martin appeared on the Commons at about five o'clock.
"He was definitely not happy with me," remembered McManus. "He didn't
seem to like the idea that a touch-football game was going on and that we
were playing cards with students." Martin said, "Sergeant McManus, I want
[your] people in formation and back at the school building. We have to get
ready to move out." McManus returned to the Walls Elementary School

gymnasium, gathered his men, and marched across campus to the burned-out ROTC barracks to take up their watch for the night. McManus didn't understand why they had been sent back to guard the barracks because there was almost nothing left of the now roped-off barracks except the charred remains of the front entrance.

———

Earlier that afternoon, Governor Rhodes met at Kent Firehouse Number 1—which was being used as the temporary city hall—with Mayor Satrom, General Del Corso, Ohio State Highway Patrol chief Robert Chiaramonte, and Portage County prosecutor Ron Kane to discuss next steps. Rhodes was in the final year of his second four-year term, barred by the state constitution from running again,* and was seeking the Republican nomination for a U.S. Senate seat in an election just forty-eight hours away. He was behind his rival Robert Taft, Jr., in the polls. He had positioned himself as the "law and order" candidate who would use "all the force that was necessary" to end campus disturbances throughout the state.

Kent State officials† were invited to the meeting, but Rhodes shunted them aside. He viewed academics as arrogant naïfs living in ivory towers. "You university people stay out of this," he snapped. "We're taking over now." Those who understood the students' temper and attitude best had effectively been told to shut up. At this meeting, Rhodes changed the guard's mission from protecting lives and property to using "whatever force necessary to break up a protest on the campus." When someone asked Rhodes to define a protest, the governor replied, "Two students walking together." "There was no discussion," one of those present later said, "because it wouldn't have done any good. The governor had made up his mind."

---

* After a four-year hiatus, Rhodes would once again be elected governor in 1974 and a fourth time in 1978.

† University president Robert White had left Kent at 5:30 p.m. on Friday (before the disturbances began) for Mason, Iowa, to attend a meeting of the American College Testing Program, which he chaired. Poor weather delayed his return flight to Kent until Sunday afternoon. White preferred that the Ohio State Highway Patrol be called to the campus in the event of any trouble, but civil authorities did not seek his opinion.

At this point, reporters entered the room, flashbulbs popping and tape recorders turning. The situation in Kent seemed an exploitable moment. Trailing in the pending Republican primary,* Rhodes struck the pose of a take-charge leader who wasn't going to be pushed around by a long-haired rabble. Red faced, he spoke in a loud and angry voice and pounded his fists on the conference table. "We've seen here in the city of Kent probably the most vicious form of campus-oriented violence yet perpetrated by dissident groups," he declared. "We're going to put a stop to this." "We're going to use every part of law enforcement in Ohio to drive them out of Kent. We are going to eradicate the problem." He paused a moment, then added, "They're worse than the Brown Shirts† and Communist element and also the night riders and the vigilantes. They're the worst type of people that we harbor in America." "No one is safe in Portage County. It's just that simple. *No one* is safe." Instead of exerting a calming influence, Rhodes's table-thumping theatrics added fuel to the fire. Students felt he had equated them with Nazis and the Ku Klux Klan.

General Del Corso reinforced Rhodes's hard line: "As the Ohio law says, use any force that's necessary, even to the point of shooting." Ohio State Highway Patrol chief Chiaramonte made a comment intended to deter violence by antiwar protestors but instead planted fear in the minds of guardsmen. "The next phase that we have encountered elsewhere," Chiaramonte told the press, is when agitators "start sniping." He paused for effect, then said, "They can expect us to return fire." For guardsmen already anxious about protestors' intentions, these comments only heightened tension and fear among tired young men. As one worried observer put it, "What conclusions could the guardsmen reach but that the students were an evil lot against whom they would have to defend themselves, perhaps with bullets?"

As the meeting ended, Portage County prosecutor Kane, a blunt-

---

* Rhodes narrowed his opponent Robert Taft, Jr.'s, lead by 90 percent between Sunday and election day. Rhodes lost the primary on May 5 by 5,270 votes out of 939,934 votes cast.

† The reference is to the *Sturm Abteilung* (SA), shock troops of the early Nazi Party who wore brown uniform shirts and leather boots.

speaking man who understood the mood in Kent as well as anyone, followed the governor into the men's room for a private talk away from reporters. He thought of the old criminal law proverb, "The situation can come under control when the heat of the blood is cooled and reason resumes control." "That was my thought [about] Kent State University: students were not happy with the guard being present and the guard were not happy with the students. You had one hell of a horrible god-damned confrontation of hostility." "The guard were tired because they had just come off of [the] truck strike and the students had been worked and lathered up over the last two nights." "You knew something was going to happen." "It just seemed logical to me—and it should have been logical to anybody else—that the best way to eliminate any future problems was to get everybody the fuck out of there." Kane begged Rhodes to close the university until things quieted down. "I told the governor we were sitting on a keg of dynamite that could blow at any minute. I was afraid of what might happen." "You ought to close this fuckin' place before somebody gets hurt!" he implored the governor. "Get everybody the fuck out of here!" "No—we mustn't do that!" snapped Rhodes. "We'd be playing right into the hands of the Weathermen and the SDS and other dissident groups." "I'm determined to keep it open. We must not knuckle under." Later that afternoon, the university printed 12,000 leaflets announcing that "all forms of outdoor demonstrations and rallies" had been banned. Many students did not receive the leaflet because of distribution problems. The guard believed it had been authorized to break up any protests the following day.

As dusk set in, things took an ominous turn. A majority of Kent State students opposed the war but had not rioted downtown on Friday night nor participated in torching the ROTC barracks on Saturday night. But in the past three days, Nixon had labeled them bums, Rhodes had equated them with Nazis, and the National Guard had occupied their campus. Governor Rhodes's remarks "really, really inflamed the students very, very much," Robby Stamps recalled. "They were very, very upset." "If the president thinks I'm a bum and the governor thinks I'm a Nazi," said a female student, "what does it matter how I act?"

As darkness fell, McManus and his men watched about one hundred students gather on the tennis courts on the north side of the Commons. The students, angry at the occupation of their campus, began baiting the guardsmen, shouting epithets at them. Some students climbed the thirteen-foot-high cyclone fence around the courts, swinging forward and backward until it gave way. They then merged with an even larger group of students strung out on the rise overlooking the Commons near Taylor Hall and Blanket Hill. Together they moved toward the burned-out barracks, chanting, "Here . . . We . . . Come!"

"It was sort of spooky," a guardsman recalled. "You could hear the rocks falling all around you, but you couldn't see them." Another guardsman thought, "What are we gonna do now?" McManus ordered, "Present arms!"—lowering rifles into firing position but not aiming them, in an effort to deter the crowd from coming closer. The crowd kept coming. Just at that moment, an Ohio State Highway Patrol helicopter with a high-intensity searchlight swooped in and hovered low over the Commons. The loud wop-wop of rotor blades—familiar to Vietnam veterans on campus—created a downdraft of air that pushed several students to the grass. A man sitting next to the pilot shouted through a bullhorn, "This is an illegal assembly, you must disperse, go to your dorms!" When the students did not disperse, the voice said, "You're being photographed right now—do you want your parents to see you on live television?" That did it. "They ran in every which direction, except toward us," said McManus, adding: "If that helicopter had landed, I would have kissed the pilot." McManus and his men spent the next several hours escorting hundreds of students from the nearest dormitories into which they had fled to their own. Other guardsmen picked up and hurled stones through dormitory windows at students taunting them.

As the students scattered, a group of them peeled off and headed toward Prentice Gate, the main entrance to campus. Guardsmen hurried down the heavily treed slope behind the ROTC barracks to cut them off and prevent them from going downtown, where they knew residents were sitting by their windows and on their rooftops with loaded shotguns, deer rifles, and whatever weapons they could get their hands on to prevent a repetition of Friday's night rampage. A Kent resident later recalled that "people were loading their guns, pulling down their shades and locking their doors. I heard one neighbor say, 'If that armed mob comes down this street, I'm shooting.' There was no armed mob, but he apparently believed there was." Earlier that evening, residents told guardsmen who were patrolling downtown, "Kill those SOBs if they cause any more trouble. Get tough with them." "We thought these remarks were stupid," said a guardsman.

Students and guardsmen collided in the shadows of Rockwell Hall, the old library near the intersection of East Main and Lincoln Streets. Guardsmen were accustomed to people fleeing at the sight of fixed bayonets. They expected students to do the same, but the students did not. Things quickly got rough. A guardsman recalled:

> A demonstrator crept up on us at a blind point, carrying a long pipe, and he bent down, winding up like a batter on a baseball team and swung at a guardsman's legs. I yelled just as he swung, but it was too late. He connected and the guardsman went down. I smashed him with the butt of my rifle.
>
> Suddenly a part from an automobile motor came flying through the air and hit a guardsman in the mouth, knocking out his teeth. When we saw the blood flow from his mouth, some of us charged at them, knocking them to the ground and stabbing them with bayonets.

One student spit in a guardsman's face. The guardsman butted him in the face with his rifle. A second student was cut on his left bicep when he refused to do as he was told. A third was bayoneted in the back. A female student suffered puncture wounds to her abdomen and right leg. A guardsman wearing a gas mask pinned a student against the library wall, put his bayonet to the student's nose, and said, "I know your face, but you don't know mine. If I ever see you again, this is gonna go in your head." The student urinated himself on the spot. "I'm not saying we were right or we were wrong," the guardsman later said, "but you have to realize the situation you get into emotionally." Protestors shouted, "Cut off their fucking balls!," "Cock sucker!," and "Fucking pigs off campus!" Three students, one holding up a white flag, approached the guard and said they wanted to talk. "Maybe we can calm this crowd down," thought an officer. The three students got within twenty-five feet, reached into their pockets, and unloaded a handful of rocks. "They threw rocks, railroad spikes, bottles—anything they could get their hands on." Nearby, a guardsman hit by a wrench fell to the ground. A female student came up and kicked him in the groin and then in the face. Other female students opened their blouses or lifted their skirts, wearing nothing underneath, and shouted, "Wouldn't you rather be sleeping with me than doing what you're doing?"

About three hundred students including Dean Kahler, Jeff Miller, Scott MacKenzie, and Jim Russell staged a sit-in at the intersection of East Main and Lincoln Streets just south of the main entrance to campus. A few nights before, Dean had gone to a downtown bar. "I was sitting in the bar watching TV and all of a sudden [President Nixon] came on," he later said. "I couldn't believe what he was saying. I thought, 'Is this a dream?'" On Friday, he had gone home for the weekend, where he talked with his father "about staying out of trouble and not getting too involved with groups of people doing violent things." He told his father he "wasn't going to get involved." When they drove back to Kent late Sunday afternoon, they were surprised to find guardsmen occupying campus. His father asked Dean if he wanted to stay. "I reasoned that I would not get into trouble if I stayed out of the way of the National Guard, and that I would be safe," he remembered. "Dean, mind your business," warned his father. "Keep away from stuff. Watch from the edges." After saying goodbye to his father, he strolled around campus, chatting with students and guardsmen and taking snapshots of both. He decided to join that night's sit-in. "I'd seen demonstrations on TV, in *Life, Time,* and *Newsweek* magazines, talked about it all through high school, and knew friends who were killed in Vietnam," Dean later recalled. "As a farm boy, you don't get the chance to go to protests because cows have to be milked, taken care of, and nurtured twenty-four hours a day. This was probably my only chance to get to an antiwar demonstration." It would give him something exciting to tell his children. "Just as my father talked about World War II, I would talk about having been to an antiwar protest." And besides, he was confident that he could outrun any guardsman if he had to.

The demonstrators had three demands: withdraw the National Guard, lift the curfew, and grant amnesty to arrested students. Dean Kahler and Scott MacKenzie heard a policeman announce, "If you get off the street, Satrom and White will come." "The next thing I heard," said Dean, "they were making an announcement to disperse and shooting tear gas" while students sang John Lennon's "Give Peace a Chance," an Ohio State Highway Patrol helicopter with a searchlight circled overhead, and a stereo in a nearby house window blasted the Rolling Stones' "Street Fighting Man."* "I remember hearing the sound of bayonets clicking on to the rifles," said an eyewitness. Then, guardsmen stomping their boots "charged right into the crowd without any warning whatsoever." "I was walking quickly away from the area when a National Guardsman ran after me to get into striking range and hit me in the back," a protestor recalled. "I really nailed some kid's head with a rifle butt," bragged a guardsman. "That'll teach those damn hippies to run faster," boasted another. A different guardsman ordered a student to get up. When he didn't move fast enough, the guardsman bayoneted him in the back. The student stumbled across the street to a house, where he collapsed, bleeding, and later went to the hospital.

These ugly confrontations embittered students and guardsmen alike. Protestors screamed "Lying Pigs!," "Fucking Pigs!" and gave troopers the finger. Guardsmen grumbled, "We don't have to take this stuff," "they're not going to get away with it," and "they got us good tonight, but that's not the end of it." Demonstrators resented what they viewed as broken promises made by the police and excessive force used by guardsmen. Guardsmen saw demonstrators as foul-mouthed, rock-throwing radicals, threatening their safety as well as town and campus security. Attitudes hardened on both sides.

---

* Sergeant Joseph Myers of the Kent Police Department later said he notified Mayor Satrom of the students' request and that the mayor was on his way to the intersection when the crowd was dispersed. "It was the guard's decision to move," said Myers. "Tragedy in Our Midst—A Special Report," *Akron Beacon Journal*, May 24, 1970.

The ugly way the sit-in ended enraged Jeff Miller. "We have a right to have rallies and be on the street," he told a friend. "It's our campus—and they'd better not try that stuff again tomorrow! Our rally is going to be peaceful because that's the way we want it." "Maybe that's the way you want it," his friend replied, "but that's not the way it's going to be."

The situation remained tense the rest of the night. A student returning at the end of the weekend "came up over the hills that overlooked Kent and w[as] astonished to see a scene out of a war movie—a scene of flashing police lights all over the city and helicopters hovering and crisscrossing the city." "It was a night that none of us will ever forget," recalled another. Said a third, "We would be in our rooms and the helicopters would come swooping down, only a few feet from our windows. You could have looked out and waved at the pilots, except that if you tried, the man with the bull-horn sitting beside the pilot would shout at you, 'Get back indoors, turn out that light, this is an order!' It was a voice from the sky. And when the helicopter had gone, a National Guard jeep would come slowly cruising down your street, flashing its spotlight up through the trees, and some-one with a bullhorn would bellow, 'Turn out those lights!' And when you were sickened by this, they really got you—tear gas. Even though we were on the second floor of our rooming house, one of the canisters they threw contained so much gas it filled our room, and we had to leave. Then the helicopters zoomed down and the voice form the sky shouted, 'Get back inside!' It gave you the feeling that you were living in a police state." Joe Lewis watched guardsmen "eagerly" forcing students into Johnson Hall at bayonet point. It reminded him of something out of George Orwell's dystopian novel, *1984*.

The wind carried tear gas into John Cleary's dorm. "We had to leave the building," he recalled later, "and as we went out the front, they ordered us back in the building. We were trying to explain to them that we couldn't go back in because of all the tear gas. And they said, 'We don't care, you're not allowed to be out here.'" "It was almost like you were in the middle of a war zone."

Dean Kahler ran back to his own dorm and found the door locked. A counselor saw him and let him in. He went to a friend's room. "I want to go to tomorrow's rally," Dean told him, "But I don't want to get into any trouble. What should I do?" A veteran of earlier campus demonstrations, his friend told Dean that if he went, he should "keep his eyes on me at all times" because he had "a sixth sense of knowing when to get out before the conflict got too out of hand." They agreed to attend the antiwar rally at noon together. Dean called his mother at one o'clock in the morning. She could tell he was "all upset." "They lied to us!" he told her. "Why do they lie to us?!" "I don't know why they lied to you," she said. "It must be a communication gap—Did you do anything?" "No," insisted Dean.

Scott MacKenzie made his way from Lincoln and Main Streets to Franklin Hall behind Rockwell Library, where he saw a female student hit in the stomach with a tear-gas canister. He felt scared as he made his way back to his apartment on the edge of campus as a helicopter buzzed overhead. He sensed guardsmen's hostility toward "long-hairs" like him and bitterly resented the National Guard as an occupation force that prevented him from going where he liked.

Jim Russell hustled back to his fraternity house on Lincoln Street on the western border of campus. He found his way blocked by several guardsmen. Jim told them he had a right to proceed. An officer told him he was an insult to the army fatigue jacket he was wearing and swung a baton at his stomach and left knee.

Allison Krause and Barry Levine got caught up in the mayhem too. "When we heard that the guard was pushing kids back from Main Street, and that we were all to go directly to the dorms, we set off for Tri-Towers," Barry later said. "We were walking across the football practice field when the shit hit the fan. Out of nowhere, about twenty to thirty guardsmen appeared and started running with their bayonets lowered. We panicked and started running too. We were so relieved when we got to Tri-Towers. Allison and I had both been scared out there. It felt like a war zone, with the guard, and the helicopters flying overhead." Allison screamed obscenities at Tri-Towers staff when they wouldn't allow her and others into the dorm to escape the tear gas. "Her face was ashen white and her hair was matted," remembered the dorm counselor. "She seemed completely distraught, out of control, and rather pitiful so I let her in." Allison phoned her parents again and told them what happened. Her father again warned her to be careful. John Cleary also called his parents late that night. He told them not to worry if they heard about what had happened. "The problem is over," he assured them.

Bill Schroeder got a call from a friend who had been in the crowd that had confronted the guardsmen. "That asshole," he said after hanging up, "that stupid asshole." Later that night, Bill called his mother. He was very disturbed by the events on campus. He criticized the guard's presence at Kent State and the burning of the ROTC building, but he told her he understood why it happened. "They've got to end this war." "Will you stand by me no matter what I do?" he asked his mother. "Yes," she said. Before turning out the lights, Bill leaned out of his bunk and told his roommate, Lou Cusella, "Christ, Louie, I don't like all this: the cops, the trouble, the guard—God, it scares me. It really scares me."

"I'm afraid of what's going to happen on this campus tomorrow," a female student said to her roommate as she turned out the lights in their dorm room—"too many guns, too many people mad at each other." "Anyone could see that the way the situation was developing, it had to end in tragedy," said another student. "I went back to my dorm room and wanted to cry. Instead, I got mad and said, 'What the hell? Tomorrow there'll be shooting.'"

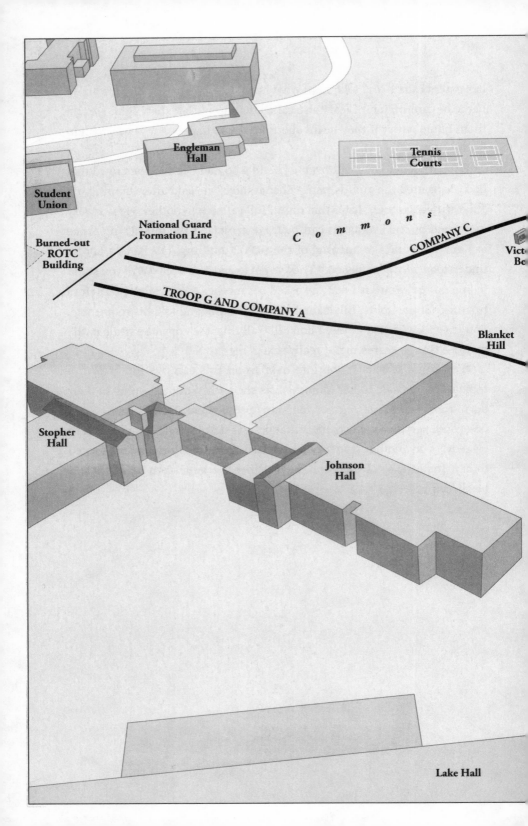

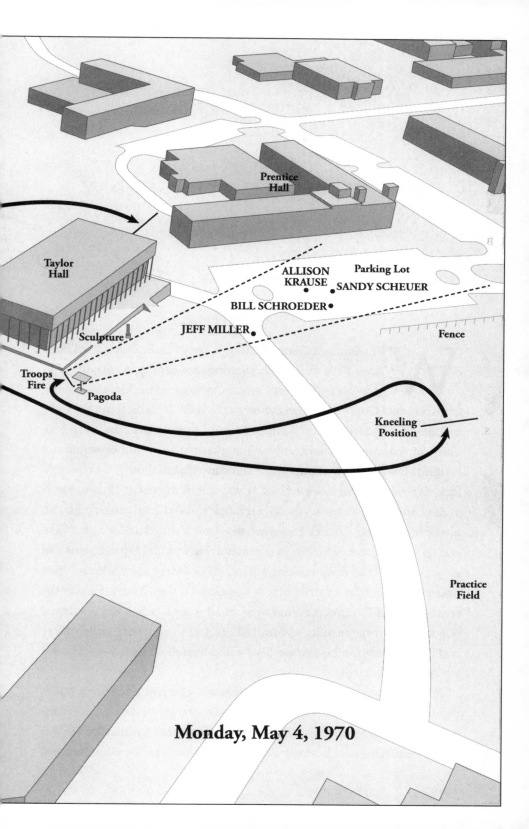

Monday, May 4, 1970

Chapter 5

MAY 4, 1970—THE TRAGIC DAY

Part I

With Adjutant General "Tough Tony" Del Corso's departure from Kent on Sunday evening, his deputy, Assistant Adjutant General Robert Canterbury, became the highest-ranking Ohio National Guard officer on the scene. This made Canterbury the commander of all guardsmen at Kent State, with the authority and responsibility for making decisions on how the guardsmen would or would not be used. It was his most important and consequential duty. Despite that fact, Canterbury later asserted that "I was not in the chain of command" at Kent State—an assertion directly refuted by the second-ranking officer, Lieutenant Colonel Charles Fassinger, who later testified under oath, "General Canterbury was definitely in command. He was making decisions and giving orders." The third-ranking officer, Major Harry Jones, also testified under oath that "the superior officer was General Canterbury. He was the commander of the troops at that time, of all troops." Canterbury's denial of command responsibility epitomized his gross negligence as an officer and his failure to exercise proper leadership the following day—a day that would end in tragedy.

Robert Canterbury was fifty-five years old and had a medium build, thinning salt-and-pepper crew-cut hair, and a weather-beaten face. Guardsmen viewed Canterbury as a "desk officer" not a field commander. He was an administrator who held the second-highest rank in the Ohio National

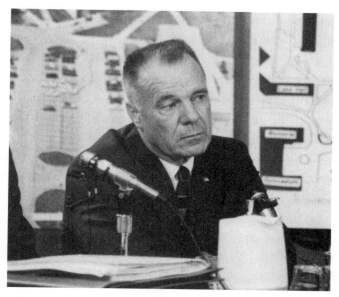

Ohio National Guard assistant adjutant general Robert
Canterbury, commanding officer at Kent State, May 4, 1970.

Guard, had twenty-three years of experience—including combat in the
Pacific during World War II and considerable experience dealing with
urban riots—but precious little experience dealing with student protests.
More fatefully, he lacked the understanding and empathy that are antidotes
to tunnel vision and awareness of one's limitations. He had the authority,
as he later acknowledged, to refuse any mission that was "clearly illogical,
out of bounds [and] impossible to accomplish," but he could not see that
this applied at Kent State. Looking back, a guardsman under his command summarized the situation painfully well: "The general led us like
a blind fool."

The morning of Monday, May 4, 1970, was sunny in Kent, with a nearly
cloudless, enamel-blue sky and a mild fourteen-mile-an-hour southwesterly
breeze. There was a bit of a chill in the air, and a thin shroud of dew blan-
keted the Commons. Students began moving across campus. Despite all

that had happened since Friday night, the university remained open with classes as usual with midterm exams beginning that day.* Many guardsmen were anxious to go home. "It's almost over with," one said hopefully to another. Another thought it was too peaceful for anything to happen and it was going to be a relatively quiet day. But to one student, "there was an air of expectation. It was this energy that you could really truly feel, you could physically feel it." "I had an uneasy feeling," said another looking back. "As I slowly passed by the patrols of National Guard, my uneasiness increased." Guardsmen and students "both felt they had a legitimate right to be there and to act as they did, and people who had no desire for a direct and fatal confrontation moved inexorably toward one."

Joe Lewis woke up with "a feeling" that he should "stay in the dorm." His mother had the "same feeling" and called Joe. "Aren't you worried?" she said. "No," answered Joe, whose trepidation had passed. He would attend the antiwar rally on campus that day after all. Robby Stamps, wearing ankle boots, bell-bottom jeans, blue T-shirt, and denim jacket, headed to his 9:55 a.m. Spanish class when he heard someone yell, "Hey Stamps!" Two guardsmen ran over to him. One was Robin Hefflefinger, the guardsman Robby had shared a sandwich with the previous afternoon. "This is ridiculous, you standing here in your uniform and me standing here in mine," Robby told Hefflefinger. "It *is* sort of ridiculous for me to be on campus in this gear," Hefflefinger replied, "and I sure want to leave." "We want you to leave, too." They shook hands and parted.

Shortly after 10:30 a.m., guardsmen who were bivouacked in the Wall Elementary School gymnasium received the order, "Get it on!"—to put on their gear, get in formation, and head back to campus. Students were gathering on the Commons in defiance of the governor's ban on any more protests on campus. "We said, 'Oh, not this shit again,'" recalled a guardsman. "We'd been through this, we're tired, why don't these kids go to school where they belong? A lot of us started thinking, 'Why aren't they in class? What's goin' on with these people?'" Sergeant Matt McManus asked that

---

* Kent State was then on the quarter, rather than the current semester, system. Classes did not end until late June.

his platoon be excused—they had gotten off all-night duty only four and a half hours earlier and were exhausted. McManus himself had had no sleep between Saturday morning and 6:00 a.m. that morning. "Captain Martin slammed down his fist, looked me right in the eye, and said, 'I said all men, no exceptions!'" McManus went back to his platoon, woke up the squad leaders, and told them to make sure each guardsman donned his field jacket, "steel pot" helmet, web belt with ammunition pockets, canteen, bayonet, and gas mask. Rifles were then handed out, not signed out. "They weren't too happy about it, I wasn't too happy about it, but we formed up." They received no briefing from officers about the use of weapons. Just then, Captain Martin pulled up in a jeep. "Sergeant McManus, those men look sloppy. Get them straight and march them down to the Commons." "I thought if ever there was a time I'd like to protest, it was then," said McManus looking back, "but I didn't." Martin left. McManus, as ordered, led his platoon to the Commons. "I didn't care if they were out of step or not. It seemed to take a long time because we were so tired." On the way to the Commons, the guardsmen saw bedsheets hanging from dorm windows with obscenities scrawled on them. One read, "Fuck Weekend Warrior Pigs!" Students standing in the windows jeered as they passed.

At that hour, Ohio National Guard officers and university officials met again with local and state officials at Kent Firehouse Number 1. Most of those present believed a student antiwar rally scheduled for noon would be unlawful because Governor Rhodes had signed a special proclamation declaring martial law when he mobilized the Ohio National Guard and ordered it to Kent on Saturday night.* At this meeting, according to General Canterbury, he asked university president Robert White, "You want this assembly permitted?," and White replied that it would be highly dangerous. "I took that to mean I was to break it up." White later denied making such

---

* The martial law statute had been illegally applied because civil courts, which must be incapacitated before martial law can be imposed, remained in operation in Kent and elsewhere throughout Portage County. Rhodes later admitted in a sworn deposition that he signed the proclamation (drafted by his top aide and chief legal advisor, John McElroy) without carefully reading it.

a statement, and other guard officers at the meeting told investigators that Canterbury, not White, decided the rally would not be held.

Canterbury returned to the temporary command post on the second floor of the administration building and told the assembled officers that the noon rally would not be permitted. Captain James Fletcher, Captain Roger Hinton, and Major John Simons all expressed concern that there were not enough guardsmen for the task and that students had not been informed. A university official said the campus radio station and the school's intercom system would spread the word that "all outdoor demonstrations and gatherings are banned by order of the governor."* Canterbury headed out the door. Walking down the hall, he turned to Simons. "John, Del [Corso] and I had a great time chasing these students around [last] night, even throwing rocks back at them," he said with a lazy little smirk curving around the corners of his mouth.† "Canterbury was an aggressive guy," recalled forty-year-old, stocky, blond-haired Lieutenant Colonel Charles Fassinger, a combat veteran of the Korean War and the 107th Armored Cavalry's senior officer. "Otherwise, he wouldn't have been there." It was highly unusual for a guard general to be in the field.

Canterbury ordered guardsmen to the burned-out ROTC building on the western edge of the Commons. When they arrived, they encountered Alan Canfora dressed in blue jeans, T-shirt, and waist-length denim jacket, his long hair wreathed in a bandana headband. "Hey, boy, what's that you're carrying there?" a guardsman asked him. "Just a couple of flags," Alan replied. "I did this to signify the sad turn of events in the city and on our campus," he later explained. "I was sad and angry." The one-foot by two-foot black flags, with the word "KENT" spray-painted in green, were tacked to shortened broom handles. "We're going to make you eat those flags today," the guardsman told him. "I kind of mouthed off to him," recalled Alan.

---

* The announcement reached only a limited number of students, however, because the intercom system did not operate in all classrooms and in none of the dormitories. Others understood the rally had been banned but considered it an illegitimate exercise of arbitrary military power.

† Canterbury later denied under oath throwing any rocks. Deposition of Robert Canterbury, November 21, 1974, pp. 118–20, MS 804, Accession 1989-M-048, Box 35, KSC, SML, YU.

" 'Just don't get too close, motherfucker,' I said, 'or I'm going to stick them down your throat.' It was an arrogant remark. I didn't like being threatened, but I figured as long as I kept my distance there wouldn't be any problem."

———

Word of the noontime rally, posted on outdoor bulletin boards and chalked on classroom blackboards, spread quickly that morning. But the original purpose of the rally had changed. What had begun as anger over the invasion of Cambodia and reescalation of the war had turned to outrage of a different sort. "Vietnam had receded. Cambodia had receded. It was clear that the issue [now] was the guard's occupation of the Kent State campus," said a student. "It wasn't an antiwar rally; it was a National Guard get-the-hell-off-our-campus rally," said another. "We were very angry." Students simmered with frustration and anger over guardsmen, tear gas, and curfews—restless on that edge where everything was just about to happen—but they lacked leadership and organizational discipline, creating the potential for chaos and tragedy. "Excitement was in the air," wrote an eyewitness. "There was an unnatural mood on the campus, like a contest going on. The students wanted to express themselves, but they did not know how." A student noticed some demonstrators carried bags filled with rocks and other projectiles in anticipation of a confrontation.[*]

By 11:45 a.m., the crest of the bowl surrounding the Commons was covered with students. About five hundred protestors had gathered at the Victory Bell. One was Joe Lewis, wearing a blue sport shirt, jeans, wide black leather belt, fatigue jacket, and black leather moccasins. "My main reason for participating in the noon rally was to object to the invasion and occupation of our campus by the Ohio National Guard when I had worked all through high school to save money to afford one year of

---

[*] "I saw objects the size of half bricks down to golf ball size," Captain Raymond Srp said later. "Most were between the size of a baseball and a golf ball." Statement of Captain Raymond Srp to Ohio State Highway Patrol, June 4, 1970, Case No. 400-67A-132, Accession 1989-M-048, Box 29, KSC, SML, YU.

Kent State," Joe later said. Someone handed him a piece of wetted cloth
to protect his face against tear gas. Tom Grace was also there, dressed
in bell-bottom pants, blue work shirt over dark T-shirt, spring jacket,
and light-brown desert boots. He had spoken with his mother by phone
over the weekend. "Be careful, Tommy," she said. "Don't worry Mom,
I'm careful," he replied. He remembered "experiencing a deep feeling
of apprehension" as he neared the bell. "Hearing their antiwar chants—
'Pigs off campus!,' 'We don't want your fucking war!'—and seeing black
flags waving in the breeze, I drew closer. When I reached the crowd
assembled around the bell, I discovered that the flags were being borne
aloft by two of my roommates," one being Canfora. "Anxiety began to
leave me, for the presence of friends and the size of the crowd provided
a sense of safety in numbers." Robby Stamps stood between the tennis
courts and the Victory Bell with a hamburger and pretzels in his hands.
He was near-sighted and didn't have his glasses on, so he couldn't see
very well at a distance. Unlike many students, he assumed the guardsmen had live ammunition in their rifles.

Student protestors gathered on Kent State Commons, May 4, 1970.

Dean Kahler, wearing a green varsity-letter jacket, medium-gray button-up sport shirt, blue jeans, and light-colored high-top work boots, stood near the Victory Bell with his hands in his pockets. He also assumed the guardsmen were carrying loaded rifles. "I'd been hunting since I was sixteen years old," he later said. "I took the NRA* safety course. I learned there was only one time you could assume and not make an ass out of you and me, and that's when you see a weapon. You see a weapon, and you always assume it's loaded. *Always.* I had no naïveté, no illusions that these weapons were not loaded." Angered by what had happened at the previous night's sit-in, Dean decided to attend the noon rally even though, as he left his dorm room, he heard the loudspeaker announcement warning students to stay away from the noontime event. "I went primarily to see what would go on and to lend my voice if I could," he remembered. He had phoned one of his professors that morning to tell him he wouldn't be in class. He "told me not to get too close to the guard and not do anything stupid." Shortly before noon, Dean and a friend headed for the scheduled rally. Dean reached into his green jacket and pulled out a plastic bag with two blue bandanas soaked in water and handed one to his friend. They would use them to mitigate the effect of tear gas. They laughed and mocked "the Establishment" as they neared the Commons but soon joined the chorus of students chanting "No More War!" and "Pigs Off Campus!" "Dean had a smile on his face as he was yelling and taunting the National Guard to get off our campus," his friend remembered. "This was like a game of dare, and he showed none of the anxieties of the night before."

Nearby on Blanket Hill stood Allison Krause. Early that morning, she called her parents again to tell them "everything is all right" on campus. Her boyfriend, Barry Levine, "noticed an enormous amount of light and joy in her eyes despite the anger and terror of the previous night. We had resolved a personal problem earlier in the morning and ironically this morning, Allison was happier than I had ever seen her. We contin-

* National Rifle Association.

ued laughing and joking as we walked, unaware that the exact path we were walking would minutes later be traveled by marching soldiers. As we climbed the path toward the Pagoda, we agreed to meet after lunch on Blanket Hill to participate in the scheduled rally. Upon reaching the Pagoda, we stopped and spoke a while before going our separate ways to each lunch."

"After lunch I walked to where we agreed to meet and waited standing at the top of Blanket Hill. I watched angered students gather and one hundred yards from them I saw men armed with rifles standing and waiting across the Commons. Allison left the dorm and crossed the field to the gathering students. She walked in front of the crowd, her eyes searching the top of the hill to see if I had arrived. She stopped for a minute to say hi to a friend of ours, Jeff Miller. They exchanged a few words but what she said will never be known."

"She continued on her way, her eyes fixed on the top of the hill, [and] never once looked around to see the soldiers. It was almost as if she was oblivious to them. As she approached, I noticed she had changed her clothing during lunch. She now wore bell-bottom jeans, her favorite blue sneakers, and a tan safari jacket open at the front to expose one word, "Kennedy"[*] [on her gray T-shirt]. Her hair had been pinned up, accentuating her prominent cheek bones and baring her neck. Finally, her eyes met mine and as a smile stretched across her face, she quickly ascended the hill to my side." In her left jacket pocket she carried a moistened cloth for protection against tear gas. In her right jacket pocket she carried small rocks and pieces of concrete.

Atop Blanket Hill sat Taylor Hall, a modern building of light stone and dark windows that housed the Schools of Architecture and Journalism.[†] It was surrounded by big rectangular columns extending three floors from ground to roof and was set on a wraparound terrace edged by a black-iron railing. A large number of students clustered on the western slope of Blan-

---

[*]   She graduated in the top quarter of her class at John F. Kennedy High School, an experimental education school in Wheaton, Maryland.

[†]   Today, Taylor Hall's ground floor houses the May 4 Visitors Center.

ket Hill, with a commanding view of the Commons. They included John Cleary, who was dressed in white shirt, purple vest, dark three-quarter-length jacket, gray pants, and brown loafers and had attended an architectural design class in Taylor Hall that morning. "Out of curiosity, I decided to be in the area of the rally to see what the hell would happen," he later said. "It was not every day that guard [was] on campus." He had his roommate's Kodak Instamatic Camera because he wanted to take photos. "At that time I felt it was a peaceful gathering, this was my college, I felt I had a right to be there, classes were in session, and college was open."

There, too, were Alan Canfora and Bill Schroeder, standing near each other. Alan carried one of his black flags with the word "KENT" spray-painted in green. Bill was there "because he was curious to see it," a friend later said. "He went there to observe." Walking to campus that morning, Bill had told one of his roommates, "It feels like we're walking through a war zone rather than going to class." Although he had an ROTC exam at 11:00 a.m. in North Hall next to the burned-out ROTC barracks, he wasn't required to wear his uniform to the test. Instead, he wore an old denim jacket his grandfather had given him that was adorned with an enamel flower—one yellow, the other purple*—in each lapel, a black-and-red striped T-shirt, his "Brian Jones" orange corduroy bell-bottom pants cinched with a belt he had hand-painted with peace symbols, and light-brown cowboy boots. Finishing the exam shortly before noon, he decided to go to the rally, telling an acquaintance, "I just want to see what happens." On his way to Blanket Hill, he ran into a friend. "I hope there aren't any trigger-happy reactionaries with guns out there," the friend said nervously. "Naw," Bill reassured him. "Lots of these guys don't even have clips in their guns."

Scott MacKenzie sat on the north slope of the Commons near Robby Stamps and was clad in a maroon wool plaid shirt, blue jeans, and brown boots. Sandy Scheuer, wearing a tan leather coat, long-sleeve red blouse,

---

* "You know what these are, don't you?," Bill frequently kidded his close friends. "My purple heart."

wide green, red, and white beaded belt, bell-bottom jeans, and closed-toe brown leather sandals with a buckle across the top, stood on the edge of the Commons, watching. The last thing her mother had told her was, "If there's trouble on Monday, Sandy, I don't want you going to class." That morning, a student living around the corner from Sandy ran into her on the way to campus. "I told [Sandy], 'Too much tear gas has been thrown for this to continue as a game. It's going to come down to a life-death situation.' She shook her head as if this were impossible." Jim Russell, wearing sunglasses, a tie-dyed T-shirt, fatigue jacket, bell-bottom jeans, boots, and a headband to keep his long hair out of his eyes, stood near the parking lot by Stopher Hall. "I was interested in what was happening but I wasn't going to be right in the middle of it."

About a thousand other students stood in the general vicinity, shouting encouragement. Another thousand or so—some headed to their dorms after morning classes or to the Student Union for lunch—milled about on the walkways, the grass, and nearby buildings like spectators awaiting the kickoff of a football game. An eyewitness remembered "the building tops, stairways, and dorm windows crowded with people trying to get a glimpse of the confrontation they knew was soon to come." "I wanted to see what was going to happen," a student recalled, "and there were many, many people that were like that. I didn't think it was going to be that serious— they'd shoot some tear gas, chase the students off, [the students would] get tired of it and go to class." "It struck me as a carnival-like atmosphere with a lot of curiosity-seekers and passersby stopping to take in the spectacle," said another. A third remembered seeing someone "running around telling people to leave, that there was going to be a lot of trouble, and a lot of people were laughing at him." There was an edge of confrontation in the air, but no expectation of violence. The Commons was buzzing, waiting for the moment for things to kick off.

"There were people all around the rim" of the Commons, said another eyewitness. "You had super-straight Joe Fraternity and ultra-radical Joe Freak out there." The National Guardsmen could not see these distinctions. All they saw were "a couple thousand pissed-off people." "You never knew who was a spectator and who was a rioter," said a guardsman looking back. The crowd, moreover, was growing by the minute.

Many students, frightened by the previous night's events, looked on anxiously from the safe distance of dorm windows and building roofs. Conspicuously absent were nearly all of Kent State's six hundred African American students,* many of whom belonged to Black United Students (BUS) and had previously encountered the guard during disturbances in Cleveland. BUS official Rudy Perry explained their thinking. "Sure, we wanted a piece of the action. But not with those guns on campus. Because we're black, and we know that when a white man has a gun and he sees a black, he gets uptight. He has a compulsion to shoot. And the black man gets shot, no matter what he's done. Portage County is filled with immigrants from the South. To us, Portage County is Mississippi, and in Mississippi it's easy for a black to stay indoors when whites are running around with rifles." An incident the night before lent credence to their fear. Student body vice president and BUS leader Bob Pickett had been stopped on campus by two National Guardsmen. "You better get out of here, nigger," said one, pointing a pistol at Pickett's head. "If you don't turn around and run," the other said, "I will put the butt of this gun up your ass." Pickett slowly backed away with his arms up.

An African American professor sat in his office that morning waiting for his weekly conferences with students. One of Rudy Perry's lieutenants entered and abruptly said, "Professor, you've got to get off this campus right now." "What are you talking about?" "Off. Get off." "Why?" "There are guardsmen out there. They have loaded rifles." "What have they to do with me?" "They like to shoot blacks." "What are you talking about?" "Professor, you may be an intelligent man. But there are some things you don't

---

* African Americans composed 13 percent of Ohio's population, but only 2.9 percent of Kent State's student body. Unlike most Ohio universities in 1970, however, Kent State had a Center of African American Culture headed by a black professor and a Human Relations Center directed by an African American dean.

know. I'm from Newark, New Jersey. And I do know. You get the hell off this campus." The professor left.

———

As morning classes ended at 11:50, protestors began ringing the Victory Bell. A loud, incessant clanging in G-sharp rolled across the campus. "I'll never forget the sound of that bell," a guardsman later wrote. "There was a lot going on," recalled Matt McManus. "The press had arrived. It seemed like mass confusion. I couldn't understand why the press was [there]—we'd never had the press before.* I did not know Canterbury was coming, so of course that changed the whole picture—the general was there." "Oh my God, that's General Canterbury!" gasped a young guardsman as Canterbury arrived at the burned-out ROTC barracks. Dressed in a single-breasted, dark-brown business suit with a gas mask atop his head, he was immediately surrounded by the press. He behaved "like he owned Kent State University," remembered McManus. "He was the man." "They were sticking mics in front of his face and the cameras were rolling. I thought, 'Wow, this is unusual. This isn't like any riot situation I've ever seen.'"

Canterbury's presence on the Commons "instilled a little bit of fear into the guys because you've got the big guy—the general—leading you, where before we'd only had captains or lieutenants, at the most a colonel," explained McManus looking back. It signaled to already nervous troopers that the situation was dangerous enough to require the presence of a general in the field—a highly unusual occurrence. "It gave the men a certain inner fear they did not need to have," McManus explained. "They thought, 'Wow, this is a whole lot worse than what we are seeing ourselves.'" And Canterbury was dressed in civilian clothes, which made things even more confusing. "Did you have any understanding of who was in charge?" a guardsman was later asked. "No." "Of who was giving orders?" "No," he

---

* It is quite possible that Canterbury invited members of the press because they knew exactly where to be when he arrived.

again replied. Another said he remembered seeing an older man in civilian clothes, but "I didn't even know who he was at the time."

Canterbury had learned of the noon rally less than two hours earlier and had had little time to devise a plan. He looked at the reporters and cameramen around him, then turned and stared at the students surrounding the Commons, as if taking the measure of what he was dealing with. "What are you gonna do now, general?" the reporters demanded of him. "What are you gonna do now?" Canterbury "was overtaken by the attention he was getting from the press," concluded McManus looking back. "The mixture was there to make him a hero," to make a desk general think "it was his moment of glory" as a field commander.

Canterbury later told the FBI that the assembled students "seemed much more hostile than the crowd [on] Saturday night." They "seemed to consist primarily of extremely vociferous agitators." Several of Canterbury's officers and guardsmen contradicted his assessment. Lieutenant Colonel Charles Fassinger said, "It was a crowd, not a mob." "There was no violent activity going on." Major John Simons perceived "a kind of picnic, a festive atmosphere." "The students who were assembled were entirely peaceful and orderly" and "unarmed." Sergeant Mike Delaney saw "a totally peaceful assembly—as far as I was concerned, a lawful assembly. There was no move by the crowd toward the guard." "There didn't appear to be any physical threat to property or persons." Sergeant Lloyd Thomas "didn't see any physically aggressive, unlawful behavior on the part of the crowd." "They weren't doing much of anything, just screaming." Private Rodney Biddle, whose brother was a Kent State student, said, "All I saw was sign language and verbal abuse; I didn't see any rock throwing or destruction of property." "There was just noise," said Private Larry Mowrer, adding: "I think our movements provoked the crowd." And then there was Donald Schwartzmiller, chief of the Kent State Police Department, who later recalled that "prior to the attempt to disperse this group, the gathering was peaceful; there were some jesterings and catcalls, but I was familiar with this harmless behavior from previous occasions. To my knowledge, peaceful gatherings had not been banned on campus. No Ohio National

Guard official consulted with me concerning the breakup of this gathering. I saw no reason to disperse the gathering."

"We're going to clear this field!" barked General Canterbury.[*] By issuing this order, Canterbury unequivocally transitioned from being an observer to being the commander. Major Harry Jones, a forty-three-year-old Tennessean and fourteen-year Ohio National Guard veteran who had a long, equine face and a lazy eye and was wearing a soft fatigue cap, had written the Ohio National Guard training manual for dealing with student disturbances and questioned the propriety of breaking up a peaceful gathering, but, as he later said, "I was a staff officer, not a commander. A staff officer does not have the right or the responsibility to make any decision."

University policeman Harold Rice handed Canterbury a bullhorn. "I asked him if he wanted to use it," Rice later said. "His answer was 'Hell no, I'm too busy. I want you to call up to those people and try to disperse them. I have my hands full right here.'" Rice leaned on the roof of a university

---

[*] Canterbury later denied—under oath—issuing this order: "I didn't understand the mission to be one of dispersing [the] assembly, whether tumultuous or not." Testimony of Robert Canterbury, Federal Civil Trial, p. 8348, MS 1800, Box 61, KSC, SML, YU. The U.S. Justice Department concluded that Canterbury's "order to disperse the crowd appears to have been illegal and in violation of the demonstrators' rights to peacefully assemble. The First Amendment guarantees 'the right of the people peaceably to assemble, and to petition the Government for a redress of grievances.' The assembly on May 4th was, prior to the order to disperse, a peaceful one which was called to protest certain aspects of American foreign policy and the presence of the National Guard on the campus. Surely only extraordinary circumstances could justify the Government's refusal to allow such an assembly." "The theory which is most often advanced to justify the dispersal order is that the assembly was in violation of O.R.C. [Ohio Revised Code] 2923.51, which provides, in pertinent part: 'Where five or more persons are engaged in violent or tumultuous conduct which creates a clear and present danger to the safety of persons or property, a law enforcement officer, or commissioned officer of the organized militia or armed forces of the United States called to duty to protect against domestic violence, shall, forthwith upon view or as soon as may be on information, and unless prevented by such persons, order such persons to desist and disperse.' The facts of this case, however, do not justify the conclusion that any of the persons were engaged in 'violent or tumultuous conduct' at the time the dispersal order was given. All of our evidence indicates that prior to the dispersal order the crowd was entirely peaceful, and that the first rocks were not thrown at the guard until after the dispersal order was given." Robert Murphy to Stanley Pottinger, December 5, 1973, U.S. Department of Justice 144-57-338, Box 122, M4C, KSUL.

police department patrol car, turned up the volume on his bullhorn all the way, and "I begged [the students] to please disperse and leave the Commons immediately. The plea was made four or five times." The wind and noise drowned out the metallic voice of the bullhorn. Canterbury ordered Rice to go out on the Commons in a jeep with three guardsmen to repeat the order. The jeep proceeded slowly, a media soundman following behind it with a handheld wooly microphone. Sitting in the right front seat, Rice announced, "Please leave the area! Please leave the area! This is an illegal gathering! Leave before someone is hurt!" Scott MacKenzie yelled, "Forget it!" Several other students shouted they *were* home and the guardsmen should go home. The jeep made three circuits as Rice repeatedly ordered the crowd to disperse. A stone hit the face shield of Rice's helmet.

"He had the best of intentions," said an observer, "but it did nothing but whip the crowd into a further frenzy." Resentment quickly turned to defiance. Each time Rice spoke, the crowd chanted, "Fuck the pigs! Fuck the Vietnam rejects! One, two, three, four, we don't want your fucking war!" It was "so loud and so clear that it seemed it would be heard for miles." "We just couldn't believe they could tell us to leave," recalled a student, thinking "this is *our* campus." "If anyone ought to leave, it's them, not us," thought another. It "was like waving a cape at a bull," added Dean Kahler. Joe Lewis remembered thinking, "My dorm is right here. Where did you come from?" at the same time that he felt a knot in the pit of his stomach. Robby Stamps gave the guardsmen the finger. Some protestors laughed. Some booed. Some began throwing rocks. Some shouted, "Off the pigs! Sieg heil! Two, four, six, eight, we don't want your fascist state!" Some raised their middle fingers. Watching students ignore repeated orders to disperse, a guardsman thought, "How stupid is this?"

One of those shouting epithets was Jeff Miller, wearing an untucked maroon-and-white western shirt, bell-bottom jeans cinched with a wide brown belt, dirty white sneakers, and a red headband around his long wavy black hair. Jeff raised both his middle fingers and yelled, "Pigs off campus, you motherfuckers!" He had called his mother that morning, told her another rally was planned for noon, and he planned to attend. "Is that okay?" "I assured him that I had faith in his judgment," she remembered, "but asked if he thought attending could accomplish anything. He said it probably couldn't, but sometimes, if you felt strongly enough, you had to take a stand." "All people your age have ideals—you won't have them when you're forty," his mother said. "Then I don't want to be forty," replied Jeff. "I love your ideals," she said, but begged him to be careful. "Don't worry, Ma," he reassured her. "I may get arrested but won't get my head busted." Then he hung up.

At this point on Monday, "the guardsmen were taking it much more seriously than the students were," recalled Allison Krause's boyfriend, Barry Levine. A guardsman looking back agreed. "Generally speaking, the students were enjoying a bit of a party atmosphere," he said. "It seemed to me they were totally unaware of the danger they were spawning. We all, at that age, pushed the boundaries to test the water. The students at Kent were no different." One of them bumped into a friend near Taylor Hall. "She had this bandana around her face, for the tear gas. She said, 'Come on. Join us. This is fun.' I said, 'No, I think I'll just watch.' It was one of the best decisions I ever made in my life."

Because students resented the guardsmen's presence on campus, they felt no qualms about harassing them. Guardsmen, in turn, had grown increasingly resentful about the harassment they encountered. They anticipated today's crowd would be like the one they had encountered the night before. The students were saying, "The guard should get off campus." The guardsmen heard, "They are all determined to get us off campus." Tension between students and guardsmen had built up to a dangerous point.

———

General Canterbury decided to disperse the crowd of two thousand to three thousand students* with ninety-six guardsmen and eight officers—a ratio of nearly 30 to 1. He ordered the guardsmen into a line, shoulder to shoulder, with bayonets unsheathed. They lined up slowly. "The mood was tense," remembered a guardsman. "We were definitely the bad guys.

* This meant 80 to 90 percent of Kent State students *did not* attend the rally that fateful day.

I could tell [it] wasn't going to turn out well." University policeman Harold Rice "look[ed] into the faces of the men in the front line. I could see that they were frightened." "It was just mass confusion," another guardsman recalled. "I didn't know who I was standing next to." (They had taped over their name tags because the night before protestors had taunted them, "I see your name, I'm gonna get you.") "It was so unorganized," confirmed a guardsman. "I was not in my own platoon. I was not even in my own company."

"[We] had no understanding as to the amount of force we were supposed to use to accomplish that mission," remembered a sergeant. "There had not been a briefing before we moved out to explain what to do and how to do it." "We had never been anywhere that had not been under the control of the local police," added another guardsman. "When we were in Akron and Cleveland for the riots, we were riding around with policemen and they were the ones in charge. Kent State was the first time we were the main enforcer." "Loaded rifles and fixed bayonets are pretty harsh solutions for students exercising free speech on an American campus," noted a third. Looking back years later, a fourth guardsman groaned, "Why would you put soldiers trained to kill on a university campus to serve a police function?"

Many guardsmen had no desire to be there. "Someone had put you on the front line and you're facing people similar to you," one later said. Another guardsman, who was enrolled at Kent State, saw students walking across the Commons with textbooks under their arms and thought, " 'I wish I could go to class.' I had a class I wanted to go [to], I wanted to graduate, I needed to get out of there and move on with my life." "You take the military uniform off, you're one of them," explained a third. "There was a strong identification not with the protestors but the students." A fourth turned to the guardsman next to him and said, "This looks bad. Where are all the rest of the guardsmen? What the hell are we doing here alone?" Unverified reports that came in that morning of snipers on rooftops intensified their anxiety.

"We were beat, dead tired," remembered a guardsman. They had been on twelve-hour shifts for days. Troop G had turned in at 1:00 a.m., only to be roused at 4:00 a.m. for watch. Company C had been relieved at 2:30

a.m., then awakened at 5:30 a.m. to patrol downtown Kent. Company A had been on duty all night, did not get to bed until 9:00 a.m., then got called back to campus at 11:30 a.m. "The only thing I saw among the guys was fatigue and nerves," said a guard officer. "I personally didn't think my life was in danger," a guardsman remarked looking back, "but there were young guys there who were afraid of what would happen to them."

Jim Pierce, a big blond former track star at Kent High School who was then attending night classes at the university, seemed "nervous as a hawk" to eyewitness and friend Charles Madonio. Pierce's fear stemmed from two incidents in his past—one distant and one recent. In 1965, while spending a semester at the University of Hawaii, he had been severely beaten by native Hawaiians angry that a *haole* like Pierce was dating one of their young women. Then, on the night the guard arrived in Kent, protestors had hurled bricks and chunks of concrete at his jeep, shattering his windshield, denting his helmet, and just missing the guardsman seated next to him. These incidents made Pierce fear groups of hostile strangers. Madonio had run into Pierce the previous afternoon:

> I decided to walk up to see the remains of the ROTC building. Jim was guarding one entrance to the campus. We chatted. He expressed great fear to me, much more than the other guardsmen he was with. . . . Pierce said that the action Saturday night at the scene of the fire was more dangerous than the week he had spent in Hough, the area ravaged by race riots in Cleveland. He said he was more fearful for his life the night before than at any time in Hough. . . . He also said he was tired, because he had been on duty all week with the truckers' strike.

University policeman Harold Rice turned to a fellow officer and said, "Somebody is going to get killed."

The guardsmen got into line carrying their rifles loaded with live ammunition. Ohio was one of few states that allowed guardsmen to carry loaded rifles, but Ohio National Guard regulations stressed that "rifles will be carried with a round in the chamber" only "when all other things failed."

"Some in my platoon," said a guardsman, "have never handled a rifle and hardly know how to load it." One private had never even fired an M-1. Another was so unfamiliar with how to operate his rifle that he had to have another guardsman load it for him.

When Lieutenant General John Throckmorton took command of federalized Michigan National Guard troops during the 1967 Detroit riots, his first order to guardsmen was to unload their rifles and pocket their bullets. Asked later at a congressional hearing why he had issued this order, Throckmorton explained, "I was confronted with a group of trigger-happy, nervous soldiers." A congressman who questioned unloading weapons amidst an urban riot asked Throckmorton how many disarmed guardsmen had subsequently been wounded. "None," the general replied. Eight Michigan guardsmen had later been injured—seven carrying loaded rifles and another who shot himself in the foot while loading his weapon.

Surveying the crowd of students, Matt McManus "saw no weapons—none." "It was no different than any other riot situation where you just had people with things in their hands that they shouldn't have, but no guns." Looking back, McManus firmly believed that if guard officers with more riot-control experience such as Lieutenant Colonel Fassinger and Major Jones had been in charge, their "first order would have been, 'Leave the weapons back' or 'Don't load them, for God's sake.'" They "would've eventually talked [Canterbury] out of the idea"—if he had been willing to listen. "But he was not going to listen. That was obvious from the time that that first cameraman ran up to him with the camera rolling." "If only he'd listen. If only—."

Canterbury failed to inform the crowd of students that the guardsmen had live ammunition in their weapons, even though Ohio National Guard regulations required this to be done as part of crowd-control strategy. "These weapons weren't play toys. We were very aware of that, the students were not," reflected a guardsman looking back. Many students doubted the rifles were loaded because "it didn't make sense" to them. "I thought it was against the law," Joe Lewis later said. Canterbury's failure to announce that the guardsmen's rifles were loaded with live ammunition was a reckless judgment made by a man whose hubris, stubbornness, and

narrow-mindedness blinded him to the foolishness of his actions and esca-
lated the risk of tragedy. "If that general had had his head out of his ass,"
one guardsman later said, "he never would have put us in that situation."

Canterbury then ordered guardsmen to "Mask up!"—to put on their
rubber, charcoal-filter gas masks. Those in Company A had masks with
breathing canisters on the left; those in Troop G had masks with breathing canisters in front. Near-sighted troopers wearing glasses had to pocket
them. A private said, "Half of [my] company wore corrective lenses." One
guardsman was so near-sighted that without glasses on, he couldn't count
the number of fingers held up on his hand. A third tried to put his gas
mask on over his glasses. "The gas mask wouldn't seal over the frames
of the glasses," he later said, and "with the mask pushing down on the
glasses, the frames were blocking my view." A corporal broke off the tem-
ples of his eyeglasses and wedged the bridged lenses inside his mask so he
could see. Without his glasses on, all that one private could see out of his
gas mask was "a blur." (His vision was 20/200.) "Had the man beside me
been wearing anything but green," he later told investigators, "I wouldn't
have been able to tell who he was." Nevertheless, he was permitted to carry

Guardsmen prepare to disperse the crowd of students.

a loaded rifle. Ohio National Guard headquarters had ordered gas masks with corrective lenses, but they were never made because the guard lacked funds to pay for them.

It was difficult for officers to communicate with, and therefore control, guardsmen wearing gas masks. What is more, "the gas masks were heavy," a guardsman recalled, "and as soon as you put yours on, you were hemmed in and sweating. Your vision was restricted to a narrow field and sometimes you couldn't even see the man next to you. It was like being tucked away in a corner, sweating." "It's impossible" to accurately aim a rifle "with a gas mask on," a guardsman later explained. "You can't get the weapon close enough" to your eyes. The gas masks also distorted their hearing, making it difficult to hear anything clearly. "For crying out loud, they weren't no good!," Matt McManus later moaned. "They weren't doing anything but obstructing our view," which made the guardsmen even more fearful. With gas masks on, guardsmen felt alone and appeared like extraterrestrial creatures, which meant protestors could no longer see the human faces beneath them. Whatever empathy that still existed between students and troopers dissipated further.

General Canterbury had hoped the dispersal order would prompt students "to get out of there" and "that actual dispersal by the troops wouldn't be necessary." But they didn't leave. So, at 12:05 p.m., Canterbury turned to Lieutenant Colonel Fassinger and said, "Move 'em out, Charlie." "I stood there looking at the odds as the general told us to move up the hill," recalled Matt McManus. "I could tell we were in a predicament and we would soon regret it. It was obvious that when he told us to go up that hill with no other troops behind us that the students were going to be able to surround us."

Shoulder to shoulder with their rifles at "high port" arms, the guardsmen started out from the burned-out ROTC building in a ragged line across the Commons, trailed by photographers, cameramen, soundmen, and reporters. Some guardsmen threw red tear-gas canisters shaped like lightbulbs, which they carried on their lapels, while others shot gray tear-gas cylinders shaped like soda cans from M-79 grenade launchers, which made popping sounds as they fired, followed by a high-pitched whistle as the cylinders arced through the air. Unlike red tear-gas "lightbulbs" that burned hot at both ends, gray tear-gas "soda cans" burned hot at only one end—and therefore could be picked up and thrown back at the guard. The "lightbulbs" and "soda cans" exploded like firecrackers as they fell, streaming trails of smoke. "A tear-gas canister landed at my feet, and I got a whiff right in the face," Robby Stamps later said. The wind carried away most of the tear gas before it settled to the ground, affecting spectators watching from a distance more than those surrounding the Commons. McManus thought, "We're not going to move them with that." "The tear gas didn't have much of an impact," recalled Lieutenant Colonel Fassinger. "In fact, it emboldened them and they started to throw back some of them." More-daring protestors ran out, picked up the "soda cans," and threw them back at the advancing guardsmen. Female students leaned out of dorm windows to toss down jars of Noxzema and Vaseline for protestors to smear on their skin as protection against the burning chemical. Students clapped and cheered. "It was like a game—like a serious game of Frisbee," said an eyewitness. "They were having fun with the guard. The circus was in town,"

Guardsmen begin advancing toward students.

said another. Others threw rocks and hurled invectives, calling National Guardsmen "shit-heels," "motherfuckers," "half-ass pigs," "toy soldiers," "weekend warriors," and "fascists." A student watched and thought, "Why are they doing that? You're only going to get into trouble."

Doug Wrentmore, wearing a plaid madras short-sleeve shirt and blue jeans, arrived near the Victory Bell as the National Guard jeep carrying Officer Rice and three troopers started pulling back from the Commons. He then witnessed the exchange of tear gas and guardsmen driving protestors back. A shifting haze of tear gas hung over the emptying Commons, the stench fouling the warming spring air. Students scattered in various directions as the line of guardsmen approached the Victory Bell and the western slope of Taylor Hall. Some students ran into the Taylor Hall and Prentice Hall restrooms to dampen paper towels and flush out stinging tear gas from their eyes. One protestor ran toward a guardsman and attempted to grab his rifle. The guardsman clutched his weapon tighter as the student tried to tear it away. Three other guardsmen, afraid they might be attacked too, aimed their rifles at the attacker. Captain Ron Snyder ran up, struck the student with a baton, and drove him off.

Students pulled back up the hill and around both ends of Taylor Hall. Tom Grace, Robby Stamps, and Scott MacKenzie hurried to the left, through the gap between the north end of Taylor Hall and the southwest corner of Prentice Hall, a girls' dormitory where female students passed out wet paper towels through first-floor restroom windows to relieve the effects of tear gas. Alan Canfora, Dean Kahler, Allison Krause, Joe Lewis, and Bill Schroeder hurried to the right, through the gap at the top of Blanket Hill between the south end of Taylor Hall and the north end of Johnson Hall. Looking over his shoulder, Dean watched the line of guardsmen moving uphill. "Why are they doing this to us?," Allison sobbed to Barry. "Why don't they let us be?" Seconds later, a tear-gas canister landed at their feet and exploded. Allison stomped her feet and with tears streaming down her cheeks screamed at the top of her lungs, "You motherfuckers, get off our campus!" Barry pulled her along as she continued shouting obscenities at the advancing guardsmen. She was one of the last students over the top of Blanket Hill. Holding the wet cloth to her face with one hand

and Barry's hand with the other, the two made their way down the eastern slope of Taylor Hall to the parking lot. Alan Canfora and Bill Schroeder also headed there. Doug Wrentmore slowly crossed the Commons and ascended Blanket Hill. "I can't convey the feeling I had seeing these men come across the hill with rifles, gas masks, and in uniform," another student later said. "I just kept thinking, 'This isn't happening, we are civilized in Ohio. This isn't happening!'"

"I remember breathing very hard with all that junk on as we walked up" Blanket Hill, recalled a private. The guardsmen had to inhale through dual charcoal-filter gas masks, which created resistance to inhaling and made it necessary to draw in deep breaths. Exhaling also required effort. The lenses of the masks fogged up from perspiration and heat. "We halted momentarily, gasping for air," recalled a guardsman. "I personally could not breathe because of the gas mask. The lenses of the masks were steamed up from the heat. I lifted the mask and took a deep breath—of gas!"

A corporal in Sergeant McManus's platoon, Charlie Dodson, came up to McManus and coughed, "Sergeant—." "You're out of formation, get back in line," snapped McManus. "Sergeant, I forgot my gas mask," Dodson sheepishly said. Dodson "was the Gomer Pyle[*] of the platoon," McManus later said. "I wanted to chew him up one side and down the other. But I couldn't because we were in formation. So, I reached down and handed him my gas mask." Meanwhile the line of guardsmen continued forward. "I hurried to catch up to the line," said McManus, but "my intention was to stay as far away from Captain Martin as I possibly could" because Martin "was not in a good mood" and had already been "on me something fierce." "I definitely did not want him to see that I didn't have a mask on" because he had given his to Dodson—they would both "get a royal chewing."

At this point, General Canterbury directed Lieutenant Colonel Fassinger to split the line. Guardsmen on the left—two officers and thirty-four

---

[*] The lead character portrayed by Jim Nabors in the 1960s CBS-TV comedy series *Gomer Pyle, U.S.M.C.* Gomer was the goofy foil to the tough drill instructor Gunnery Sergeant Vince Carter, played by Frank Sutton.

enlisted men of Company C under Captain Ron Snyder—moved toward the gap between the north end of Taylor Hall and the southwest corner of Prentice Hall through which some students had passed. Guardsmen in the center and right—eighteen enlisted men from Troop G, two enlisted men from Company C, and five officers and fifty-three enlisted men from Company A—moved toward the gap between the south end of Taylor Hall and the north end of Johnson Hall through which a larger group of students had passed. The intent was to continue moving and dispersing the crowd beyond Prentice and Taylor Halls.

Major John Simons watched from the center of the Commons. A thirty-nine-year-old with an ash-colored crew cut, Simons was the rector of St. Philip's Episcopal Church in Cleveland Heights and a chaplain for the guard. The son of a retired career U.S. Army colonel, he had served three years as a military policeman at a U.S. Army base in West Germany. Simons was blunt and outspoken. He had had a run-in with top brass the year before, when Tough Tony Del Corso pressured guardsmen under his command to support Nixon's Vietnam policy and sent them form letters to sign and send to the White House. Simons felt Del Corso had no right to do this and confronted the general. "I asked him why did he use guard stationery and guard letterheads? He said he wasn't ordering anybody to do it, he was just giving the men an opportunity to show their support. Then why, I asked, weren't the men given an opportunity to show their dislike for the war, too? Why weren't antiwar forms provided as well? The general didn't have much to say. Our dialogue had ended."

Now, Simons believed Canterbury was crossing a line, too. He thought, "That silly Canterbury; they're supposed to disperse the crowd, the crowd is dispersed, where in the hell is he leading those men?" Simons would later say that Ohio National Guard leaders "apparently feel that every campus disorder is another Normandy invasion, so you go in with the weapons loaded with rounds." "Kent State is not Iwo Jima." He added: "Canterbury is a general—yeah. But he is no more general material than I am." He was a "paper soldier."

The guardsmen under Canterbury soon reached the Pagoda, a square bench of wooden beams shaded by a concrete shelter[*] at the crest of Blanket Hill thirty-one feet off the southeast corner railing of Taylor Hall. Looking down, from left to right they could see, 77 yards away, a 250-foot rectangular concrete, 89-space "Faculty Only" parking lot paralleling the southern side of Prentice Hall; directly below them, across Midway Drive (a narrow access road connecting the parking lot and Memorial Gymnasium), a patchy (because well used) grass-covered sports practice field with a soccer goal at the south end and a baseball diamond at the north end; and to the right, Memorial Gymnasium. Expecting Company C to come around the far side of Taylor Hall at any moment, Canterbury and the guardsmen of Company A and Troop G continued down the hill toward the practice field.[†] John Cleary photographed the guardsmen as they passed close by him. The right flank came within two or three feet of Jim Russell, who fell in behind the guardsmen and followed them as they went over and down the east side of Blanket Hill.

Protestors who had come around the eastern side of Taylor Hall in "groups of five, ten, twenty, spread out in all directions" in the words of an eyewitness. The largest group—"at least two hundred people," according to one student protestor—gathered in the Prentice Hall parking lot, "with another one hundred fifty to two hundred" milling about a construction site that ran along the far edge of the parking lot and the far edge of the practice field and was littered with rocks, bricks, cement building blocks, lumber, and other scattered debris.

Company C was nowhere to be seen. As Captain Snyder led the company through the gap between Taylor and Prentice Halls, a protestor perched in a tree repeatedly shouted, "Fuck you!" at Snyder and other guardsmen. Rather than continuing to the far side of Taylor Hall as he had been ordered

---

[*]   The Pagoda had recently been installed by five architecture students, who labeled it an "inverted hyperbolic paraboloid umbrella-like structure."

[†]   Canterbury later claimed, "We needed to move down to the practice field to re-form and have room to re-form." Deposition of Robert Canterbury, p. 172, MS 804, Accession 1989-M-048, Box 35, KSC, SML, YU.

to do, Snyder became distracted and stopped. He grabbed the protestor by his leg, pulled him out of the tree, and "proceeded to beat the crap outta the kid" using an unauthorized[*] nightstick he carried. "There was no reason to do it—none whatsoever," said Matt McManus looking back. "The kid called him names—that's it."[†]

———

After reaching the bottom of Blanket Hill and crossing Midway Drive, the guardsmen under Canterbury were at the sports practice field. They found it surrounded by a six-foot-high chain-link fence on three sides—to their left [north] toward the parking lot filled with protestors;[‡] in front of them [east], where other protestors had gathered beyond the fence by jumping the fence or passing through a gate to the construction area for the planned new Student Union; and to their right [south], toward Memorial Gymnasium. The only open side lay behind them [west], where protestors were regathering on Blanket Hill. If the guard headed back where they came from, they would have to march up toward a large crowd of students. Instead of linking up with Company C under Snyder's command—which was supposed to be coming around the northern side of Taylor Hall— "they were caught in a box in which they felt trapped," said a guard officer looking back.

"The students began to realize the guard had maneuvered themselves

---

[*]   Guardsmen were supposed to carry only guard-issued equipment.

[†]   Students John Hayes and Dennis Taruben corroborated McManus's account. See Stanley Pottinger to J. Edgar Hoover, October 10, 1973, DJ 144-57-338, Box 122, M4C, KSUL. Snyder told a different story to explain why he halted Company C at this location. "I stopped between Prentice and Taylor Hall[s] as I realized that we may have eliminated their avenue of escape. I then moved the troops back and to the right, about twenty yards, thus creating an opening between the two buildings and giving them an avenue of escape. The reason I thought they needed this avenue was because I believed I could see A Company and G Troop ahead of us, and out on the practice field." Quoted in Ed Grant and Mike Hill, *I Was There: What Really Went on at Kent State* (C. S. S. Publishing, 1974), p. 78.

[‡]   This northern portion of the chain-link fence was half as long as the other two sides of the fence.

into a partially enclosed area and were, in a sense, encircled," said an eye-witness. "Let's surround them!" a protestor shouted. "The students started gaining the upper hand for the first time and they knew it," another eye-witness observed. A third remembered "people laughing and going, 'Boy, are they stupid, advancing into an area like that and getting trapped!'" Lieutenant Colonel Fassinger ordered guardsmen to face in alternate directions—one toward the fence, the guardsman next to him back toward Blanket Hill. Some protestors in the parking lot shouted, "Kill the pigs!" "It was terribly loud," a guardsman on the practice field later said. "All I remember is 'Kill the pigs!'" Jeff Miller and others on the eastern slope of Taylor Hall lobbed tear gas canisters back at the troopers.

One protestor in the parking lot wore a soft brown Vietcong cap, a white handkerchief over his mouth, and a fatigue jacket stuffed with rocks. When interviewed by a Kent State oral historian forty years later, he insisted on remaining anonymous. Looking back, he said, "it seems silly throwing

A crowd of protestors in the Prentice Hall parking lot.

rocks at them, but I did. It was kind of crazy." What had brought him to this moment? He had transferred to Kent State from a university in the South, where he had been in the Airborne Ranger ROTC program—"the most gung-ho ROTC group" on campus. But his brother's experiences in Vietnam changed his outlook. The brother came home with two Bronze Stars, two Purple Hearts, and a cap he had taken off the body of a dead Vietcong soldier. What he had seen and done in Vietnam had changed him for the worse. He became addicted to heroin and, fifteen months after he got back, died of an overdose. Then the protestor's best friend's brother was killed in Vietnam. "These two close deaths" led to "a lot of soul searching," he later said. "I had my brother's jacket on" and the cap "my brother took off a Vietcong that he killed," "so I was living something personal for me, against the war and everything it stood for."

Radicals invited him to participate in the Days of Rage in Chicago in October 1969, but he declined. Instead, he befriended more moderate opponents of the war such as Allison Krause and Barry Levine. He, Allison, Barry, and four others carpooled to Washington in November for the Mobe. The candle he carried during the vigil past the White House that night "to give peace a chance" carried the name of a high school classmate who had lied about his age to enlist in the U.S. Marines and then been killed in Vietnam.

His antiwar rage intensified when he received a low number in the December draft lottery and, soon after, a letter from his local board ordering him to take a physical exam prior to induction. He knew that falling below a certain weight would exempt him from the draft, so he went on a thirty-day starvation diet. Although he was tall and had been a well-muscled wrestler in high school, he showed up for his physical two weeks before May 4 weighing just one hundred eighteen pounds. Others present that day were "dressed like Jesus, acting crazy" to get a psychological exemption from the draft. "The poor young lieutenant" in charge "was taking abuse and it was getting kind of ugly in there." He did not participate in the rioting in downtown Kent on Friday night. On Saturday night he smashed windows of the ROTC barracks and threw a long stick with a burning American flag tied to it into the building to accelerate the fire. "I had gone from wanting to go to Vietnam a few years before to being totally opposed to it with the same amount of vehemence."

An Ashland College student-journalist covering events at Kent State for his school newspaper saw two protestors with a bucket "large enough that it took two of them to carry it" containing "rocks and broken pieces of concrete bricks" from the construction site close to the parking lot, which they passed out to the crowd. He saw more than a hundred rocks thrown.[*] Many fell short, but some hit home. "Two of my men came up to me and said, 'We're getting hit pretty bad by stones and loose construction stuff,'" recalled Matt McManus. An observer on the Taylor Hall terrace saw a brick hit a guardsman on the shoulder and knock him down. Others saw a stone bounce off a guardsman's helmet. Another brick struck Sergeant Larry Shafer's right forearm, which he thought had been broken. Acting Sergeant Bill Herschler was struck twice on the lower right leg and once on the left forearm. A brick hit Corporal Jim Pierce and knocked him down. A rock struck Private Phil Raber in the face and broke a rear tooth. Guardsmen on the practice field wondered what Canterbury would do next. "The guard was rattled," said an eyewitness. Some felt angry. Some felt vulnerable. Some felt humiliated. "It started all closing in so quickly," remembered McManus.

About two dozen students in or near the parking lot and the construction site—including Alan Canfora, Dean Kahler, and Barry Levine—hurled rocks and epithets at the guardsmen forty to fifty yards away. "I was very upset," Dean Kahler later said. "I was frustrated. I had to release something in me, and this was the way to get rid of it," adding: "After I did it and up to this day, I still feel I shouldn't have thrown stones that day." Tom Grace

---

[*] After the shooting, university police, guardsmen, and the FBI collected about 340 rocks weighing approximately 175 pounds from the practice field and Blanket Hill. The rocks ranged in weight up to 7.5 pounds. William W. Scranton, chairman, *Report of the President's Commission on Campus Unrest* (Avon Books, 1971). They also found paper cups filled with cement, rail spikes, baseballs and golf balls studded with nails, and coat hangers clipped off and sharpened at both ends.

didn't think throwing rocks was right "because a lot of the guardsmen only joined the guard to stay out of Vietnam" and "throwing rocks at them just antagonized the guard." Joe Lewis watched a protestor throw a stone and shouted, "Don't be an idiot!"

Atop Blanket Hill, Doug Wrentmore watched and thought, "If I was in the position that the [guard] were in at the practice field, it might be somewhat volatile. But there were seventy-five [guardsmen] with loaded guns and tear gas against perhaps hundreds of people. It wasn't like they were our enemy. Because they are us. They are just people."

Those watching from dorm windows and rooftops cheered. A student photographer atop Blanket Hill described the scene:

> Somebody would come running up, usually with a wet towel or something on their face, pick up the tear-gas canister and throw it back right in the middle of the guardsmen. . . . It would land in the middle of them, they would pick it up, throw it back. Sometimes the same canister would go back three, four, six times. And there were some rocks being thrown. . . . One of the guardsmen would pick up [a] rock, throw it back into the parking lot of the students, who would see it coming and they would sidestep it. And so sometimes the same rock went back and forth several times.

Alan Canfora moved from the parking lot onto the edge of the practice field, waving his black flag at troopers about thirty-five yards away and shouting, "Kill the pigs! The pigggs!!" "We know you can't shoot!"[*] Thirty-nine-year-old First Sergeant Myron "Pappy" Pryor, Troop G's senior noncommissioned officer (NCO), relayed an order from General Canterbury to guardsmen to kneel and point their rifles at Canfora and other protestors in

---

[*] Canfora later told the FBI, "I did not hear any violent language from the crowd and did not see anyone carrying black flags." Statement of Alan Canfora to FBI, May 8, 1970, p. 5, MS 804, Accession 1989-M-048, Box 35, KSC, SML, YU. He testified at trial, "I never heard 'Kill the pigs.'" Testimony of Alan Canfora, June 19, 1975, p. 3777, MS 1800, Box 60, KSC, SML, YU.

Protestor Alan Canfora jeering guardsmen, some kneeling on the practice field.

the parking lot to deter them from coming any closer.[*] It was "meant to be a 'scare tactic.'" Safety locks were kept on and guardsmen were told, "Don't fire, just aim." Canterbury's order went against standard guard practice, which Lieutenant Colonel Fassinger later summarized as "you don't point a weapon at a person unless you intend to shoot."

Eight guardsmen dropped to one knee and aimed their rifles in the direction of Canfora and those in the parking lot. John Cleary watched them point their weapons. "Keep your cool and don't shoot unless they try to overrun you," First Sergeant Pryor instructed those kneeling. It was "a bluff to push the students back," explained one who pointed his rifle. They were trying to signal, "The games are over, don't come closer." "Maybe this will deter them from coming forward,'" thought Sergeant Larry Shafer.

---

* Canterbury later said: "I didn't know why they were doing it. . . . I saw no reason at that point for such." Deposition of Robert Canterbury, November 21, 1974, p. 176, MS 1800, Box 11, KSC, SML, YU; and MS 804, Accession 1989-M-048, Box 35, KSC, SML, YU. See also Testimony of Robert Canterbury, Federal Civil Trial, pp. 8383–85, MS 1800, Box 61, KSC, SML, YU; and Engdahl Memorandum I, Kent State Civil Cases, January 16, 1975, Charles A. Thomas Papers (hereafter cited as CTP), Box 64C, M4C, KSUL.

"If you're in a position where it looks like you're going to fire," he later explained, "people are less apt to charge." But another sergeant looking back thought "that was not a good move to make because [it was like] crying fire when there wasn't necessarily a fire."[*]

Protestors and students interpreted the move far differently. "Here was this symbol of what everybody was angry about, kneeling, aiming rifles not just at protestors or rock throwers in a parking lot, but at a dormitory [Prentice Hall] full of big glass windows filled with students," recalled one observer. "I'm thinking . . . if they're trying to defuse the situation, they're doing the exact opposite." Some students on the eastern slope of Taylor Hall yelled, "Shoot! Shoot! Shoot!" Most believed the guardsmen would not—but if they did, the bullets would be rubber or blanks. "People were saying, 'They don't have live ammunition in their weapons. It's just to scare us. Don't worry about it." Allison Krause turned to Barry Levine and said, "They can't possibly shoot." Barry agreed. "If they had fired a warning shot, it'd be a different story, but this is nothing."

Further back on the practice field, Sergeant McManus heard chatter on a guard radio. "They were talking to [Captain] Snyder because he was supposed to be there," he remembered. "Where're you at?! Where're you at?!," the officers kept asking. "I'm not going to move until I know where Snyder is," said Canterbury. "I'm not going to move." "We couldn't see Snyder," explained McManus, "because there was just a little enough of a knoll that you couldn't see over it." Major Jones, who had walked through the crowd of students down to the practice field, gathered other officers and NCOs in a huddle in the middle of the practice field. Barry Levine watched them huddle and thought they were probably asking each other, "Now what do

---

[*]   One guardsman who knelt and aimed his rifle later said that another guardsman elsewhere on the practice field fired a warning shot straight up in the air with a .45 caliber pistol. Statement of James Farriss to Ohio State Highway Patrol, June 13, 1970, MS 1800, Box 64, KSC, SML, YU. Another guardsman and two students corroborated Farriss's account. See Statement to Ohio State Highway Patrol, June 10, 1970, 12:54 a.m., in Ohio State Highway Patrol, Report of Investigation, June 13, 1970, p. 4, Case No. 400-67A-132, Series 2062, Box 2823, OHSSA; and student statements, May 4 and 22, 1970, in Ohio State Highway Patrol, Reports of Investigation, May 22 and 23, 1970, Case No. 400-67A-132, Series 2062, Box 2823, OHSSA.

we do?" He was spot on. "How in the hell did we get here?" Major Jones and the other officers said to one another. "We're in a vulnerable position. What is it that we've gotta do to get outta here?" Major Jones suggested to Canterbury that the guardsmen return to the burned-out ROTC building. "That's a good idea, major," Canterbury said. "Let's get the troops formed up into a wedge formation and move out." Canterbury, Fassinger, and Jones ordered the guardsmen to "line up, form a wedge, and get moving." They would retrace their march. "My purpose," Canterbury later testified, "was to make it clear beyond any doubt to the mob that our purpose was now defensive and that we were turning to the Commons, thus reducing the possibility of injury either to soldiers or students."

The guardsmen formed a ragged line and started back up toward Blanket Hill. They moved "quick time," a very fast walk, with General Canterbury at the front and Major Jones at the rear. The line was a jumble of officers and troopers from three different companies—"a confused mixture of guys who didn't know" each other, in the words of one. They jostled and bumped into each other on the way. Watching nearby, a student and former marine silently called cadence as they returned up the hill. "I thought it was humorous because they had a hard time keeping formation," he said. "There was no control." More ominously, there was no leadership. "I was aware of the officers," remembered a guardsman, "but at that moment it didn't mean much. I was on my own and everyone else was too." "No one knew who was in charge," recalled another. Canterbury's failure of leadership and of the fire-control discipline that was an integral part of it would encourage frightened guardsmen to take matters into their own hands with tragic consequences.

Cheers went up among those on Blanket Hill, the eastern slope of Taylor Hall, and in the parking lot. Allison Krause and Barry Levine exchanged smiles and Barry yelled, "They ran out of [tear] gas! The whole thing's over!" "The crowd sensed a turn in their favor and started to get bolder," observed lanky, long-sideburned Captain Raymond Srp. "Everybody started screaming because it was like we'd won," said a protestor. "The guard had failed and they were going back." "That's when a great number of people in the parking lot began to fall in behind them," said an eyewitness. "We sort of closed in behind, yelling Indian war-whoops," said a protestor. One of them shouted, "Let's surround them!" Some walked, others began trotting up the hill. A faculty member watched some throw stones and others cheer "like children in a chase." To a guardsman, it seemed like it was "as if you had just cut dogs loose that were charging their victim."

Student James Dawson, standing in the middle of the parking lot, watched the guardsmen leave the practice field and head back up Blanket Hill. "As they were walking off the football field, the students began throwing rocks and bottles and stones more heavily. It seemed to almost panic the National Guardsmen. They almost seemed to start running, which I thought did nothing but give more impetus to the students to move more quickly toward them." As "we started to move out," recalled Matt McManus, "the first thing I heard from the students was, 'The guards are retreating! Let's get them!' A couple of guys chanted, 'Kill, kill, kill!'" Major Jones heard, "Get the weapons! We've got them! Take them! Kill the green pigs! Get them off the campus!" As the guardsmen neared Midway Drive, Jim Russell, about ten feet from their left flank, moved aside in the direction of Memorial Gymnasium as the guard passed. Alan Canfora, Jeff Miller, and a handful of others moved closer, within about twenty-five yards. Half a dozen guardsmen on the right end of the line turned toward them. "It was hard to see through the [mask]," said a guardsman. "To look behind you, you had to turn your head around." The lack of peripheral vision made them more fearful. A few guardsmen kept their eyes on Canfora and Miller as they ascended the hill. Another cluster of protestors standing to their right on Midway Drive and the eastern slope of Taylor Hall moved closer still, within about twenty yards. More guardsmen turned to look at them—a few pointing their rifles—and continued watching them as they climbed the hill. Tom Grace started up the eastern slope of Taylor Hall. Dean Kahler ran along the border of the parking lot and the practice field in the direction of the guardsmen shouting, "Get out of here! Get off our campus!" Scott MacKenzie crossed the parking lot away from the troopers but watched their movement.

"The intensity continued to increase and increase as we started up the hill," Major Jones said, "and I knew we [had] a problem." As the guardsmen proceeded, the crowd of students ahead of them gave way as the rock-throwing behind them and to their lower right increased. John Cleary, who moved from the wooded area on the lower eastern slope of Taylor Hall toward the Don Drumm steel sculpture *Solar Totem #1* just off the Taylor Hall terrace, described a "shower of rocks coming from behind me." "As the rock-throwing group advanced up the hill, they were hitting the National Guardsmen very badly with rocks up to the size of softballs." Another photographer saw the rear-most guardsmen flinch. "I can remember the chills running up and down my back when I started up that hill," a guardsman later said. "As we were climbing the hill, I thought we were going to be rushed," said another. "I figured I wouldn't be able to defend myself and I was really thinking that they were going to rush us, too." "Most of the men were looking back and saw how close they were and how fast they were coming," recalled one sergeant. "We were thinking behind us," said another. "We were glancing over our shoulders and guys were saying, 'Back there—watch it!' 'Here comes a rock!' " "I could see a kid run close behind the guard," said an eyewitness. "He had a rock and he threw it." A chunk of concrete hit a guardsman in the leg. A golf-ball-sized rock made a pinging sound as it hit another guardsmen on his helmet. A piece of brick hit a third guardsman's steel helmet hard enough to dent it and crack the fiberglass liner inside it. Half a brick narrowly missed a private's head. One protestor, twenty-two-year-old Vietnam veteran Jim Minard, who had long, curly dark-brown hair and a neatly trimmed beard and was wearing a white headband, field jacket, and bell-bottom blue jeans, threw another chunk of brick at Major Jones. "It hit me in the [right] kidney and I went down on my knee," Jones later said. He drew a .22 caliber Baretta pistol[*] from a holster behind his right hip, pointed it at Minard, and told him to back off, but did not fire. "I said, 'Hey, buddy, don't be throwing them bricks and rocks—go!' He looked at me and laughed, and I said, 'Get out of here!' He went trucking off toward the parking lot." "I was hit no less than six times," Lieutenant Colonel Fassinger recalled, "with one rock hitting me

---

[*]   Captain Snyder had loaned the pistol to Major Jones, who did not have a weapon. It was against guard regulations to carry a private weapon while on duty.

in the left shoulder hard enough to make me lose my balance" and almost fall down. About seventy-five feet from the crest of Blanket Hill, Sergeant McManus heard a voice yell, "Look out!" "I turned around just in time," and he saw a protestor throw a two-foot log at him. "I saw it coming toward me. It landed about five feet in front of me, took a high bounce, and came down on my leg right at the top of my boot." "It didn't hurt," recalled McManus, but "it stopped my forward motion as the line kept going. I was now maybe twenty-five, thirty feet behind" the rest of the guardsmen.

Students quickened their pace as the guardsmen ascended the hill. One student started trotting "just to keep up" with others climbing the eastern slope of Taylor Hall. "Some students were running towards the National Guard," recalled Tom Grace. "The crowd grew increasingly hostile and ugly, and the noise level was very intense." "It reached kind of a deafening roar." "The distance [between students and guardsmen] was steadily decreasing." "Almost all of us were in movement toward the National Guard," another protestor later said. "Kids were running up the hill chasing them." As the guardsmen neared the top of the hill, a female student on the sidewalk near the Taylor Hall terrace watched as "about ten people broke away from the main body of the crowd. These ten ran toward the guard and started throwing sticks and rocks at the guardsmen. The closest one of the small group was approximately thirty feet from the guard." "I was pretty close" to the guardsmen, a protestor later admitted. "I was way too close to them at that point." "I was about thirty to forty feet away." Jim Minard, in his own words, was only "about fifteen feet away."

"At first, they were just walking kind of fast behind us," remembered a guardsman. "As we quickened our pace, they started running. At that point, it just seemed that they were set on overtaking us." "I was scared to death." Major Jones waved his riot baton as a signal for guardsmen to quicken their pace up the hill. "I was hollering, 'Move it up!' 'Close it up!' to keep the formation [as] best I could." People screamed, "Get them! Kill them! Kill the pigs!" "Charge! Charge!" "Lay down your guns!" "You're surrounded!" "Those students were controlled by emotion rather than reason," a guardsman concluded. "The closer they got, the worse it got." "It didn't exactly make you feel easy," recalled Matt McManus.

Cheers, whistles, and jeers, combined with the incessant clanging of the Victory Bell, produced terrific noise and confusion. One guardsman remembered "a lot of yelling, a lot of confusion, a lot of things being thrown, and they stepped up their pace." "It was a real fast pace." "They were actually chasing us." "You couldn't hardly hear anything," said another. A third recalled "yelling at the top of my lungs at Sergeant Shafer and he was three feet away from me. He couldn't hear what I was saying, and I couldn't hear what he was saying." The "chanting, cheering, screaming was reaching a crescendo at that point," recalled Jim Pierce. Major Jones felt the crowd "closing in" as they neared the top of Blanket Hill. Some students on the Taylor Hall terrace joined those moving up the slope. Others heading toward their first afternoon classes added to the general mayhem.

The guardsmen had grown very edgy. "We were tensed up and keyed up," remembered one. "I was nervous and scared to death," said another. A third guardsman was so frightened that he was in tears. When later asked what he felt at that moment, a fourth simply replied, "Fear." The protestors "kept getting closer to us. Everybody on that line was scared as to what was gonna happen." Many felt vulnerable despite being armed unlike the students. They were outnumbered, and protestors continued surging toward them, shouting, "Get them!" "Kill them!" "Stick the pigs!" "I figured we were going to have bodily contact with them and someone was going to get hurt. I was very concerned for my men," First Sergeant Pryor later said. "They had hate in them and I feel were trying to kill us," said another guardsman. "The mob was in a frenzied state." "In my mind, they just weren't going to stop at anything." "It would be all I could do to keep my cool," thought a student eyewitness. "I would not want to be armed with a [rifle] at a time like that." Lieutenant Colonel Fassinger summed up the situation well in retrospect: "it was volatile and something was bound to happen."

To one protestor, the guardsmen looked like a bunch of "scared little boys." "At first, they were just walking kind of fast behind us because we were walking at a quick pace," a guardsman recalled. "As we quickened our pace, they started running, and, at that point, it seemed that they were set on overtaking us. I was scared to death." Another thought that he and others "would not have made it down that steep incline back to the ROTC area without being overrun." "You didn't have protestors in a line in front of you, you had them around you," recalled a third. "You had a gas mask on and you had a loaded rifle with bayonet which might be grabbed and used against you. We were scared stiff." "I was very frightened. The only thing I could think of was being shot with my own rifle," said a fourth. "Man, how are we going to get out of here?" a private thought to himself. "They were getting closer and closer. If they would have overtaken us," they would have "taken our bayonets and started sticking us with [them]." Such a prospect seems far-fetched—even absurd—in hindsight. But something like that had nearly happened earlier on the western slope of Taylor Hall. "In a crisis," admitted a guardsman looking back, "you forget everything but self-preservation." "You think only of the immediate thing, and that is when self-preservation kicks in." One guardsman gripped his M-79 grenade launcher like a baseball bat to protect himself. Another "was literally praying that I would make it alive to the top of the hill. That's how scared I was." A third prayed to God to take his life because he felt "the shock of one of us dying would stop the riot." "I was shaking like a leaf," said a fourth. "I think everyone else was too."

Matt McManus, who had stopped momentarily to help Major Jones during his confrontation with protestor Jim Minard, now lagged about forty feet behind the jumbled line of guardsmen topping Blanket Hill. He was wearing green fatigues, heavy field jacket, and steel helmet and was armed with a holstered, loaded .45 caliber pistol attached to his belt and a 12-gauge Remington pump-action shotgun loaded with three shells filled with no. 5 birdshot. He had never before carried a pistol or a shotgun on duty. He had been issued the shotgun during the Teamsters' strike but had no training in its use. "I felt out there by myself," he remembered. "I had students on one side of me [to the right], I had this student who insisted on throwing this stick at anybody he could aim it at, and my troops were already at the top of the hill. Running would've been the worst thing to do, so I was walking as fast as I could toward my troops."

At 12:23 p.m., the guardsmen reached the Pagoda. An eyewitness "estimate[d] that there were about one hundred to two hundred students close to the walk of Taylor Hall to the right rear of the troops and another two hundred students" on the terrace "in front of Taylor Hall where I stood." To the guardsmen's left, students watched from Johnson Hall and Lake Hall. The students ahead of them were backing down the hill to the Commons. To their upper right, students on the top floor of Taylor Hall pressed their faces against the windows, watching, as did those on the nearby Taylor Hall terrace. Those spread down the eastern slope of Taylor Hall were moving up quickly toward them, expecting the guardsmen to continue their retreat over Blanket Hill. One protestor reached a tree about ten yards from them. About a dozen students got within about twenty-five yards, but most remained further back. Many guardsmen could not see well enough through their gas masks to accurately judge how close—or far—the approaching students were from them. "All I saw was a blur of bodies coming after us," said one guardsman. "It seemed to me that they were only fifteen feet away," said another. "I'm sure they were farther than that, but that's how close they seemed."

Joe Lewis was about twenty yards away, standing a few feet off the Taylor Hall terrace, angry at the guardsmen's "presence in a place where I lived and went to school, because I didn't see any need for them to be there, herding us around." "I was frustrated, but I didn't think I had any right to resort to violence," so "I was giving them the finger" with his right hand. "That was the most obvious expression of my disgust." John Cleary stood thirty-seven yards away next to the fifteen-foot-high steel sculpture, *Solar Totem #1*, just off the Taylor Hall terrace. "I wanted to get one last picture of them before they went over the crest of the hill, so I was winding the camera, getting it ready to take another shot." Jeff Miller was a short distance down the slope, about forty yards from the guardsmen, hurling the last of several rocks that day. Nearby were Tom Grace and Alan Canfora. Dean Kahler was jogging parallel to the guard along the border of the parking lot and the practice field. Doug Wrentmore, telling himself, "I'll be a lot safer if I'm not in the middle of a crowd," moved down to the near corner of the parking lot. He kept looking over his shoulder, charting the guardsmen's movement as they neared the Pagoda where he had been. Behind Doug, Allison Krause looked up toward the Pagoda. To her left, halfway down the parking lot along its border with the practice field, Bill Schroeder turned partway around to leave. Nearby Sandy Scheuer talked with her friend, Ellis Burns, as they crossed the middle of the parking lot away from the commotion, headed for afternoon class. At the far end of the parking lot, Robby Stamps was going back to his dorm room before his 1:10 p.m. psychology course; his classmates in that course included Allison Krause, Barry Levine, Jeff Miller, and Bill Schroeder. Still further away, Scott MacKenzie was in the construction area beyond the parking lot. Far from all the others, Jim Russell made his way from the eastern slope of Taylor Hall to the southern end of the practice field near Memorial Gymnasium.

John Cleary watched the troopers cross just over the crest of Blanket Hill back toward the Commons. "They seemed to be very scared and panicky," he later said. Looking up from the parking lot, James Dawson believed "the National Guardsmen had to do something at the time or they would have gotten run right over by the mob," which was "spurred on by the fact that they [were] beating [the guard] at their own game—they had them on the run." "They were moving in very fast on them." "As we got to the top of the hill," a guardsman later said, "I heard somebody yell, 'Get them!'" "It seemed like they all started to rush us from behind because you could hear them yelling. Out of the corner of my eye I could see them coming, so at that point that's when we turned."

First Sergeant Pryor tapped several guardsmen on their backs, helmets, and shoulders, and shouted over the noise, "Halt, turn, stand your ground and use bayonets and rifle butts if necessary!"* About a dozen guardsmen

---

* Three other guardsmen recalled Pryor also yelling words to the effect, "If they rush us, shoot them" or "Fire if they continue towards you." Statements of Corporal James Farriss, Corporal Jim Pierce, and Sergeant Dale Sholl, CTP, Box 64D, Folder 1, M4C, KSUL; and Sholl to Scranton Commission, "Kent State: Scranton Commission Files: Wrap-up," CTP, Box 64D, Folder 38, M4C, KSUL. Pryor later denied issuing any order. He told the Ohio State Highway Patrol, "at the crest of the hill the men turned and faced down the hill. I have no idea why they turned. I turned because they did." Myron Pryor statement to Ohio State Highway Patrol, July 10, 1970, in Ohio State Highway Patrol, Report of Investigation, July 13, 1970, Case No. 400-67A-132, Series 2062, Box 2823, OHSSA. And Pryor testified under oath at trial that he gave no such order: 1975 Federal Civil Trial Transcript, vol. 14, pp. 3283–84, 3293–94, KSC, SML, YU.

just over the crest of Blanket Hill between the Pagoda and the Taylor Hall terrace stopped, took four or five steps back uphill, wheeled in unison 135 degrees to their right, kneeled, and lowered their rifles at the approaching students to deter them from coming closer—similar to what they had done down on the practice field. "When we were down on the practice football field, we had turned toward the advancing crowd and they stopped," said Jim Pierce. "This was tried on the hill, but they just kept coming. When we turned out, they didn't stop. I thought the crowd was going to run us over and beat us to death." "We tried to stop them by kneeling [i]n line and pretending to be ready to fire," added another guardsman. "They laughed and after hesitating only a moment moved forward again. They really began to charge." Seeing what was happening, other guardsmen standing behind those kneeling stopped, pivoted right as well, and pointed their rifles down the hill toward the approaching students.

"All of a sudden," said a student nearby, "I saw one of the guardsmen [First Sergeant Pryor] turn around with a sweeping motion of his hand which held a [.45 caliber pistol] and this guardsman pointed it at the approaching students.* Almost immediately six or eight guardsmen with rifles turned around." "They just turned," said another student, "and I

---

* The FBI determined after extensive investigation that Pryor did not fire his pistol. See Robert A. Murphy and Robert Hocutt to Jerris Leonard, "Summary of the Kent State Incident," June 18, 1970, Box 22, M4C, KSUL. A controversy arose over the different slide positions of Pryor's pistol in various photos. (When the weapon is fired, the slide moves back and the tip of the barrel is exposed. The barrel is not exposed when the weapon is not being fired or when the slide hasn't been manually pulled back.) "Prior to hearing the shots, I attempted to withdraw my .45 caliber automatic pistol from the shoulder holster. I had to withdraw my pistol with my left hand although I am right-handed [because] I had injured the palm, thumb, and first finger on my right hand in the course of firing tear gas shells by hand the previous evening. . . . I was successful in drawing the pistol and was able to cradle it against my body with my right hand and arm for the purpose of pushing the slide into lock position using my left hand. At this time my pistol was not loaded. I then unsnapped my ammo pouch using my right hand while holding my pistol in my left hand with my body in a half-crouched position with arm extended. Just as I laid my hand on one of the magazines to withdraw it from the ammo pouch was when I heard the rapid series of shots . . . so I released the slide of the pistol with my left hand, the hand in which I was holding it, and returned it to the holster and snapped the holster shut." Statement of Myron Pryor to FBI, May 14, 1970, MS 804, Accession 1989-M-048, Box 37, Folder 483, KSC, SML, YU.

Guardsmen aim toward approaching students. Major Harry Jones (at far left) reacts. General Canterbury (upper row of guardsmen, far right) turns to look.

thought, 'They're going to scare us or something.'" Dean Kahler "saw them turn with their deliberate motion." Joe Lewis interpreted the turn as a "threatening gesture" like their lowering of rifles on the practice field, "and so, being eighteen and foolish, I gestured back at them by raising the middle finger of my right hand." "This is from me to you," he thought to himself.

Matt McManus, about forty feet behind the guardsmen at the Pagoda with no gas mask on to block his peripheral vision, saw the right end of the line stop and turn in unison. It was 12:24 p.m. "When the line suddenly turned, I looked to my right. The weapons were coming down almost like dominoes from left to right. It was uncanny—one right after the other, coming down in firing position." "Out of the corner of my eye I could see Major Jones by the Pagoda." Jones also saw what was happening because he, too, wasn't wearing a gas mask. "Troops on the right flank [were] starting to turn around to the rear and get into a kneeling position," Jones said shortly after the shooting. I started toward these troops." "I had the feeling that something was wrong." "I knew we had a problem, things were going to happen."* "I could see Major Jones," McManus later said. "That told me that whatever was going on wasn't supposed to be going on. At that point, I felt I had to get some control over it, so I yelled at the top of my lungs, 'Get the weapons up! Get them up!' "

McManus's voice thickened and his eyes teared up as he recalled what he did next:

> I wanted to demonstrate for them, so I placed the shotgun directly in my belly and I yelled, "Fire one round in the air! Fire in the air!" I turned, wheeled around, and fired one round with my weapon. I remember the butt of the shotgun hitting my belly so hard and the weapon pointing directly up. . . . I was thinking at the time that it wouldn't hit anybody. If you fire directly at somebody, you're going to put a hole in them, but to shoot up in the air, birdshot just splatters. I fired one round and hit the ground.†

McManus had never before fired a weapon during a civil disturbance. And his fellow guardsmen were utterly unfamiliar with warning shots. "I had no training with respect to firing of warning shots," one of them later said. "I had no understanding . . . whether the firing of warning shots was

---

* John Darnell's photo no. 52 in Peter Davies, *The Truth About Kent State: A Challenge to the American Conscience* (Farrar, Straus and Giroux, 1973), captures Jones at this moment.

† Eighteen-year-old freshman Terry Strubbe audiotaped the shooting by using a small Craig "Campus Pet" reel-to-reel tape recorder attached to a mike on the outer windowsill of his first-floor dorm window in Johnson Hall next to Blanket Hill. Strubbe was outside at the time of the shooting but left his tape recorder on. His recording was the only one that captured the moments before the shooting started. (A WKYC-TV soundman also taped a portion of the shooting—but only after it started.) A 1974 spectral analysis of Strubbe's recording concluded that the first shot was fired by an M-1 rifle rather than a shotgun. "Analysis of Recorded Sounds from the 1970 Shooting Episode at KSU," Bolt, Beranek and Newman, Cambridge, Massachusetts, February 28, 1974. A more recent, 2012 U.S. Department of Justice spectral analysis of the audio recording utilizing more sophisticated technology concluded that it was "unintelligible with no consensus." As Howard Means wrote, "the acoustics of gunfire echoing off nearby buildings can be confusing at best." Howard Means, *67 Shots: Kent State and the End of American Innocence* (Da Capo Press, 2016), p. 81.

a proper thing to do. I had never fired a warning shot before. I don't know any other men in my unit who had." In fact, National Guard regulations prohibited warning shots. "In order to avoid firing which creates a hazard to innocent persons," the relevant regulation stated, "warning shots will not be employed."

Recalling what he had done fifty years earlier brought Matt McManus to tears, surfacing the grief looming inside him for so long. But in 1970, McManus told a different story to investigators and attorneys: that he shouted an order to fire in the air *after* the shooting started. To the FBI, McManus said, "I heard firing to my immediate left flank. Realizing that we were completely surrounded, I turned to my right, facing a large crowd, and fired one round over the heads of the crowd."* To the Ohio State Highway Patrol, he said his order to fire in the air followed "a good sound volley of shots." "I naturally assumed that an order had been given when the fire began." To a special state grand jury, he said, "I saw three National Guardsmen down in kneeling position firing their weapons. . . . I assumed there was a command given. I turned, positioned a 12-gauge shotgun that I had in the center of my belt, aimed it in the air, and fired. Then I turned to my men and ordered [them] to fire in the air over the heads of the crowd." When asked in a sworn deposition to describe "the sound of the first shots that you heard when you were on the hill," he said, "It was a burst of shots." "Did you hear one shot or did you hear them all in a group?" "I did not hear one single shot. I heard a group." Then "at the top of my voice, I said, 'For Christ's sake, if you are going to fire, fire into the air!'" "I threw my arms up in the air, which I hoped signaled for them to raise their weapons." Under oath at the 1975 federal civil trial, he testified that he "initially heard a burst of shots," "heard no order to shoot," and "some had already started firing when I shouted, 'Fire into the air!'"

Why did McManus mislead investigators, grand jurors, and courts about

---

* In a second interview with the FBI, McManus said he "noticed members of the 107th in kneeling position firing their weapons. . . . Although he did not hear any order to fire, [he] fired one shot with his shotgun over the advancing crowd. He stated he ordered several of his men to fire their weapons into the air." FBI Memorandum, May 9, 1970, CV-44-703, Accession 1989-M-048, Box 3, KSC, SML, YU.

the true sequence of events? To admit the whole truth meant admitting to the victims, their bereaved families, the nation, the world, and posterity that he had unintentionally triggered a shooting that killed four students and wounded nine others—a crushing admission for anyone to make, and one that would have exposed him to serious legal jeopardy. McManus could not bring himself to admit the whole truth at the time—doing so was simply too burdensome and problematic. So he kept the whole truth—and the grief and guilt that went with it—tightly locked up for half a century. "The truth about Kent State has never been printed," he cryptically told a reporter in 1974. "I believe that eventually the truth will come out," he said to the Ohio State Highway Patrol investigator who interviewed him after the shooting. The whole truth did come out, more than half a century later, when McManus finally explained what actually happened.

McManus's belated confession solved the central mystery of the shooting. The enduring questions—"Was an order to fire given and if so by whom?" and "Who fired the first shot and why?"—had been answered at last. It was like a jigsaw puzzle in which every jagged edge suddenly slid smoothly into place.

Several eyewitnesses—guardsmen and protestors alike—corroborate McManus's belated confession. Sergeant Richard Love recalled "the shots did not immediately follow the order to halt and turn; seconds elapsed." At that moment, Scott MacKenzie "noticed one guardsman turn to his right and fire his weapon. It was held at his hip, rather than at his shoulder." Sergeant Lloyd Thomas said that "the order was given—'Fire above their heads!' Whoever made that statement wanted to make sure where those bullets went." "The order to fire seemed like it came from in back of me." Sergeant Dale Sholl "heard someone yell 'Fire over their heads!' At this point, I heard rifle fire." "I did not hear the order, 'Fire!' given," Sergeant Jim Case later said, "but I did hear someone say, 'Not at them, over their heads!' Then the flank started firing." Corporal Richard Lutey "heard somebody yell, 'Warning shots!'" but "didn't know who it was." Lieutenant Dwight Cline thought he saw someone fire a shotgun. Major Harry Jones saw "troops on the right flank starting to turn around to the rear and get into the kneeling position. I started to the right flank toward these troops.

The next sound I heard was a single round being fired from a weapon, immediately more rounds were fired." Jones described the initial shot as "a muffled explosion. It seemed not to be a rifle." Protestor Carol Mirman, moving up the eastern slope of Taylor Hall toward the guardsmen as they neared the Pagoda, said: "I distinctly remember a single shot. That single first shot that preceded the volley had a different sound quality. And there was a space of silence between it [and] the volley. It's not to be denied—I was in the middle of it." Private Richard Shade heard a command to fire. "It came from behind me," he said. "It didn't have the [sound] of an M-1." "There was something said before the word, 'Fire!' "* Nearly two dozen other eyewitnesses further substantiate McManus's confession.

In fact, Matt McManus had no authority to issue an order to fire. Major Harry Jones later testified there were only two circumstances in which guardsmen could discharge a weapon in a civil disturbance: if an order was given by an officer or, if an officer was absent, by a key NCO. Sergeant McManus was such a key NCO—but officers were present at or near the Pagoda. Given their presence, Lieutenant Colonel Charles Fassinger later explained that other guardsmen would not have followed a key NCO's order "if they recognized his voice." But the noise was tremendous and no one was in charge at that fateful moment because of General Canterbury's dismal failure of leadership. "Who was the senior officer on the Kent State campus on May 4, 1970?," Canterbury was later asked. "I was," he answered. "Did you consider yourself in command?" "No." "I was there, but I was not in command of any unit." Canterbury's devastating admission—his gross dereliction of duty—enabled unit integrity to break down, fire-control discipline to disintegrate, and the likelihood of each guardsman

---

* Two other guardsmen, whose names were redacted when their statements to the Ohio State Highway Patrol after the shooting were released by the Ohio State Archives in August 2023, provided further corroboration. The first: "I heard someone say, 'Fire—above their heads.'" Statement to Ohio State Highway Patrol, May 27, 1970, 3:25 p.m., in Ohio State Highway Patrol, Report of Investigation, June 2, 1970, Case No. 400-67A-132, Series 2062, Box 2823, OHSSA. The second: "I think I heard, 'Over their heads.'" Statement to Ohio State Highway Patrol, May 27, 1970, 10:35 a.m., in Ohio State Highway Patrol, Report of Investigation, June 2, 1970, Case No. 400-67A-132, Series 2062, Box 2823, OHSSA.

acting on his own to increase. Control of troops under one's command is an officer's most fundamental and important task. Canterbury failed miserably at this task. In doing so, he violated a cardinal principle that he had promulgated: "It is necessary that a force at the scene act as a unit and the idea of individual actions by members is to be discarded."

Matt McManus shouted his "Fire in the air!" order in a desperate attempt *to prevent bloodshed*. A young man under tremendous strain and pressure, he tried to do the right thing but ended up making things much, much worse—in large part because of General Canterbury's failure of leadership, which allowed the situation to get out of control. McManus's "Fire in the air!" order inadvertently triggered a tragedy.

Chapter 6

MAY 4, 1970—THE TRAGIC DAY

Part II

"I yelled as loud as I could," Matt McManus remembered, "but I didn't think they'd hear"—the muffling effect of the gas masks and crowd noise made it very difficult. Some guardsmen heard him shout, "Fire in the air!" "Even before I fell," McManus said, "I saw some of their weapons going up." Some guardsmen did not hear him. And some guardsmen heard or listened to only his first word and reacted. "They had been trained to react to an order," a guardsman there that day soberly noted later. "One shot was all it took," another said ruefully. "Under the pressure of the moment," as Howard Means later wrote, other guardsmen "might have heard the same word ["Fire!"] and taken it as a simple imperative: squeeze the trigger." They could not see the man next to them because of their gas masks, as McManus later noted, but they "were shoulder to shoulder, practically touching each other"—"so close that they could feel" that first squeezed trigger. And in the National Guard, another guardsman noted, "you learn to do what the guy next to you does."

Two guardsmen at Kent State that day—but not at the Pagoda—explained the mind-set. "The military trains you to shoot. Suddenly, when you feel like your life is in jeopardy, you do what you're trained to do," said Second Lieutenant William Herthneck. "'God, someone else is shooting. Did I miss an order?' I would assume that when others are firing, they were firing for a reason. I probably would have fired," admitted another.

Major Harry Jones, who was at the Pagoda, later said: "Everyone—students and guardsmen—were on edge and when [the first] explosion occurred, something was bound to happen."

One guardsman pushed the lever at the front of his trigger guard forward, off "Safe," and squeezed the trigger with his index finger.

"Someone just snapped," surmised Corporal Keith Crilow, who was nearby. "Somebody lost their temper, let those insults get to them [because of] lack of sleep and being on edge, and just said, 'You son of a bitch, I'm going to shoot your ass,' and that started it." "They were in a position where someone, or some, could act out their fear and anger in a very lethal way," explained 107th Armored Cavalry chaplain Major John Simons. "What do you think caused the firing?" an investigator asked one of the victims, Robby Stamps. "A bunch of scared, ill-prepared guardsmen with live ammunition—period," Robby replied. "In the end," said Matt McManus, "it was emotions that took command." "Anger and fear short-circuited rational behavior," said another eyewitness. "That is a formula for tragedy."

A fusillade of gunfire roared down the eastern slope of Taylor Hall toward the Prentice Hall parking lot.

Within 12.53 seconds, approximately thirty of the seventy-eight guardsmen on Blanket Hill fired sixty-seven shots. "It was indiscriminate shooting," Major Jones later said. "They were firing in the trees, in the ground, all over the place." Some fired at the students. Many more fired in the air or at the ground.* "I thought that any rounds fired into the air would scare the crowd and they would retreat," explained Sergeant Lloyd Thomas. "That is why I fired into the air." Private Lonnie Hinton did the same. Corporal Robert James said, "I felt firing a shot in the air was sufficient to protect my life." Yet this may have created unexpected peril, depending on the angle of the shot. "The pagoda on Blanket Hill [was] on the high point of the area," an analyst later noted, which meant "shots fired over the heads of people twenty or thirty yards away would [travel] on a downward trajectory

---

* During the 1975 federal civil trial, a ballistics expert testified that four to six of the high-velocity bullets "tunneled"—that is, entered the ground and then exited—before possibly continuing to inflict damage.

and inflict mortal wounds hundreds of feet away to people [in the Prentice Hall parking lot] at whom the guardsmen weren't aiming." Some of the guardsmen "who thought they were safely aiming over the heads of people near them may have inflicted wounds on others quite some distance away."* Most of the guardsmen fired reflexively. "Everything happened so fast, it was like a car wreck," said one. "Your sergeant's shooting, then everyone else shoots—it's just confusion," lamented another in hindsight.

The retrospective accounts of eleven guardsman who fired convey soberly the tragedy of those terrible 12.53 seconds when rocks, obscenities, and verbal threats were answered with high-velocity bullets:

Private Bob Hatfield fired one shot in the air "because of hearing firing on my right."

"Why did you fire?" Sergeant Robert James, who shot once over the heads of students, was later asked. "I thought I heard an order to fire. But I still didn't fire until I heard others firing. I fired to scare the crowd. That's what I thought we were all doing."

"I thought we were under order—especially when I heard the other shots," said Corporal Richard Lutey, who fired once at the ground.

Corporal Jim McGee "never thought about firing my weapon. It never dawned on me until the time, let's say, two seconds before I did." He fired two shots in the air and one at the knee of an approaching student because he worried about "having [my] rifle taken away and being stabbed" with his own bayonet. McGee was not wearing his glasses. His vision was 20/80 without them.

"A lieutenant to my left stepped out and started firing," said Staff Sergeant Barry Morris. "Since I couldn't hear very well because of a gas mask possibly muffling the sound, [I assumed] that an order had been given and that I hadn't heard it."

---

* The Ohio Bureau of Criminal Identification and Investigation concluded "at least twenty-eight rounds of ammunition [were] fired in a direction below the horizontal from the elevation of the firing point; the total rounds [were] probably thirty, since two victims were shot twice." "Charts of Movements and Shooting Incident, May 4, 1970, 400-67A-132, Appendix III, B-9," MS 804, Accession 1989-M-048, Box 30, Folder 363, KSC, SML, YU.

Private Larry Mowrer said the firing moved down the line of guardsmen like "a chain reaction" and that he fired twice in the air after the shooting started "on a reflex." When asked in a later sworn deposition, "What caused that reflex?," Mowrer replied, "Probably my training, even if it wasn't good training." "Did you feel your life was in danger when you discharged the weapon?" "No, I didn't." "I fired instinctively when I heard the others."

Corporal Bill Perkins "realize[d] that [other guardsmen] were shooting at the crowd, so I followed suit."

"When the men around me were firing," said Corporal Jim Pierce, "I assumed the command *had* been given and I fired over their heads with one round. My rifle jammed and while I re-cocked it, I saw everyone was shooting directly into them. . . . I then began firing into them—three more rounds—until I heard the command to "Cease fire!" All the while, "there was sweat running down [my] forehead into [my] eyes and steaming up [my] mask from the inside." "I couldn't aim because of the gas mask."

"The man beside me had opened fire before me and then I started firing," said Sergeant Larry Shafer, who shot Joe Lewis.

"I heard shots," said Corporal Ralph Zoller, who also targeted Joe Lewis. "I turned around. Guardsmen began firing on both sides of me. I fired."

"I heard the first shot," said an anonymous guardsman. "Right after that first shot—only a couple of seconds—it sounded like everyone squeezed off one round." "I had my finger on the trigger and fired when the others did. I just didn't think about it. It just happened. How can you think at a time like that?" "I fired once, just closed my eyes and shot. I didn't aim at anyone in particular. I just shot at shoulder-level toward the crowd. . . . It was like an automatic thing." As he related his story to reporters a few days after the shooting at a diner, the guardsman kept nervously rolling and unrolling his paper napkin.

"A great deal of them didn't know exactly where they were firing, they were just firing," said Keith Crilow.

The staccato of gunfire sounded like rapidly popping popcorn, only much, much louder. It stunned the crowd. "I and the boy standing next to me started to laugh," recalled student Judy Cox, standing near Taylor Hall. "We thought, 'What are they trying to prove, scaring us with blanks?'" On the Taylor Hall terrace, philosophy professor Bob Dyal likewise shouted, "They are using blanks, aren't they?!" "Of course they are!" answered history professor Ken Calkins. "They never use real bullets in a crowd!" Freshman Ron Steel thought the same "until I saw bullets kicking up the dirt in front of me." So, too, did photographer John Filo—up to the moment he saw dust fly off the nearby steel sculpture and a bullet gouge bark off a tree. Thuds and splintering noise continued as more bullets hit trees. Other bullets hit cars in the Prentice Hall parking lot, shattering windshields.

Students approaching the guardsmen stopped, frozen, for a few moments then turned and ran, fanning out as they fled down the eastern slope of Taylor Hall toward the parking lot and the practice field. "Everyone was running, screaming, and shouting and gasping," recalled one. Others dove behind trees and parked cars or dropped to the ground and hugged the earth. "There were people trying to hide behind a curb," an eyewitness later said. "If you could dig a hole that fast you would if you realized you were being shot at." A guardsman on the far side of Taylor Hall saw "one kid standing and saying, 'They're firing blanks. They don't have any bullets in those guns.' All the while, people [were] dropping around him." A female student started screaming, "They're shooting their guns! They're shooting their guns! They're trying to kill us!" Lorrie Accettola remembered "the sound of bullets flying through the air. They sizzled and hissed as they flew by my head." Jim Minard lying on the ground felt four or five bullets hit around him. Graduate student Joseph Carter looked out a Prentice Hall window and thought, "Where am I? Is this a battlefield? Is this a campus? Is this America?" Junior Jerry Geiger, a Vietnam vet, thought, "There are people bleeding all around. I'm back in Vietnam." Photographer Dan Smith felt numb, but the tears wouldn't come. A freshman ran into Taylor Hall, crawled under a desk, and sobbed.

Hearing the first shot, Major Harry Jones thought, "Who would discharge a firearm in as intense a situation as this?" "Who would be so stupid?" He then frantically tried to stop what quickly became "indiscriminate

Students run and duck for cover in the Prentice Hall parking lot as firing begins.

firing." "I had my stick in my right hand and I started beating my men over their helmets. I hit so hard I cracked it." "The major hit me so hard it made my ears ring," said Corporal David Rogers. Jones struck Sergeant Pryor on the head and told him, "Put that damn thing [.45 caliber pistol] away and help me get this firing stopped!" Pryor shouted at guardsmen, "High port—get your Safeties on!" Jones shoved his way in front of the firing line, hitting rifles with his cracked swagger stick, pushing some up, others down, screaming, "What the hell do you think you're doing!?" "The major really risked his life. He was out there waving like crazy," said Rogers. "I yelled, 'Cease fire! Cease fire! Cease fire!'" Jones said later. "If I wouldn't have, they never would have stopped." He had to grab one guardsman by the collar to stop him from firing. Another officer hit a guardsman with the butt of his pistol to stop him from shooting. First Lieutenant Ralph Tucker knocked one rifle into the air. Many guardsmen had to be shaken by the shoulders to make them stop. Once the firing ceased, Jones demanded to know, "Who gave you men the order to fire?!" "Major Jones was shaking his head like he was knocking his head on something," said a guardsman. Captain Raymond Srp "was shocked" some had fired. Further back from the Pagoda, General Canterbury and Lieutenant Colonel Fassinger turned in surprise when the shooting started as if thinking, "What the hell is going on here?!" and rushed toward the Pagoda. Fassinger shouted at the top of his lungs, "Cease fire!" as he grabbed guardsmen, pushing weapons to get their attention. Many could not hear him because of the terrific noise and the gas masks they wore. "For Christ's sake, stop shooting!" he and Canterbury shouted as guardsmen continued to fire. Canterbury, who saw two students hit and later said he was "horrified" by what had happened, grabbed two guardsmen by the shoulders and screamed, "Put the weapons down!"

When the shooting finally ceased, an awful hush hung in the air for four or five seconds—a "deathly silence" of disbelief. "The quiet felt like gravity pulling us to the ground," remembered Chrissie Hynde, a Kent State student and future lead singer of the British-American rock band The Pretenders. "Everything slowed down and the silence got heavier." "It was almost like time stood still for a while," said another eyewitness. A thin cloud of haze from rifle smoke hung in the air around the Pagoda. Then shrieks and moans pierced the air, shouts of "Oh, my God!," "Murderers!," "Look what you did!" and anguished cries for help. One protestor, livid with rage, approached Staff Sergeant Rudy Morris with his rifle still lowered and screamed, "Shoot me, motherfucker! Shoot me too!"

The sixty-seven high-velocity bullets traveled fast and far, inflicting fearsome damage. Nearly a mile away, a bullet smashed through a second-floor window of the Silver Oak Apartments (where Corporal Jim Pierce lived), tore through a wall, and ended up on a living room floor. Five hundred seventy yards away—nearly six football fields—another bullet crashed through a sixth-floor window of Leebrick Hall in the Tri-Towers complex and struck a concrete wall near the elevator. Several bullets glanced off the fifteen-foot-high steel sculpture, *Solar Totem #1*, making pinging sounds as they struck at an angle. One bullet passed clean through one of the lower steel panels, leaving a well-defined hole; the panel was five-sixteenths of an inch thick.* Another bullet drilled through the trunk of a large elm tree and sped on. The force of a bullet fired from an M-1 rifle was enough to move a five-hundred-pound object four feet on impact.

Joe Lewis, twenty yards from the guardsmen, froze in a moment of disbelief. "I thought they were firing blanks, because nobody in his right mind is going to kill somebody for giving him the finger." "My God," he then told himself as the grass around him kicked up, "they really are bullets." Then Sergeant Larry Shafer's rifle fire struck him in the lower right abdomen. The bullet exited through his left buttock. Corporal Ralph Zoller's rifle fire hit him a second time, the bullet passing through his lower left leg four inches above the ankle. Joe screamed, "Oh my God, they shot me!" fell backward, and collapsed on the ground, clutching his gut. He began to convulse as blood seeped from beneath his arms. "I didn't lose consciousness, I was in a state of shock." He thought the bullets must have been warning shots gone astray. But how could he have been shot twice by accident? He screamed, "Oh my God!" said eighteen-year-old Kent State University High School senior Ellen Mann, who dropped to her knees by his head. "He was all white and looked like he had a three-inch hole in his hip. He said it hurt, and he asked how bad it was." "He had such a grip on my hands," she said, "his knuckles were turning purple." "Well, this could be it," thought Joe. "I was afraid I was going to die, so I made an act of contrition to say that I was sorry for my sins."

John Cleary, thirty-seven yards from the Pagoda and standing next to the *Solar Totem #1* steel sculpture, caught a bullet in his upper right chest. "I was facing directly toward the group of National Guardsmen when I got shot. The impact of the bullet did not knock me down. It did not hurt very badly. It felt as if I had been hit with rock salt." "I covered my head with my hands and "crawled behind the metal sculpture to protect myself until the firing stopped." "I didn't know I was seriously wounded until I tried

---

*   The bullet hole is plainly visible to this day.

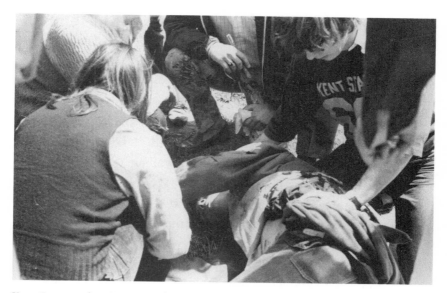

Kent State student Joe Lewis lies wounded off the Taylor Hall terrace.

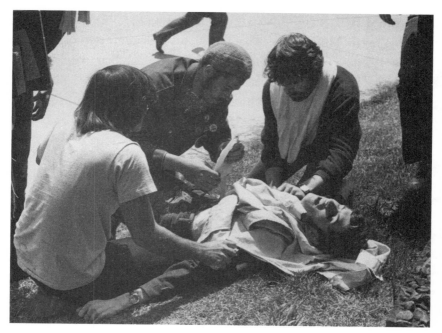

Injured Kent State student John Cleary is administered first aid.

to stand up and saw blood gushing out. A blond-headed male student [Joe Cullum] then helped me lay down." At that point John passed out. A second student came over to assist. Nineteen-year-old Denny Herman pressed his tear-gas rag against John's chest to stanch the bleeding.[*] The wound was the size of a half-dollar coin. After a few moments, Herman leapt to his feet, jabbed his finger repeatedly at the guardsmen, and screamed, "Look what you did!" "I wanted help," he later explained. "I didn't care who shot him—they were there, and I wanted them down here."

Jeff Miller, standing on the eastern slope of Taylor Hall about fifty yards down from the guardsmen, released the last of a dozen or so rocks he had thrown at the guardsmen that day. Freshman Eldon Fender had been watching him. Jeff's "intent, in my opinion, was that he was definitely trying to hurt somebody." As Jeff released the rock, he started to turn. The first shots rang out. A bullet slammed into the left side of his mouth. The student standing next to him "saw Miller's mouth explode outward with fragments of blood and skin." A girl spattered with his blood screamed. Sergeant Matt McManus also witnessed the moment. "I saw what happened to Jeffrey Miller. I wish I hadn't, but my eye caught part of his flesh coming off." The bullet fractured Jeff's lower teeth and jaw, lacerated his carotid artery, shattered the base of his skull, and severed his spinal cord before exiting the right side of his neck. Jeff "jerk[ed] like a puppet." The velocity of the bullet was so great that he pirouetted with his head bowed and one shoulder higher than the other, with a look of "utter disbelief" on his face. Eldon Fender watched him "stumble a good fifty feet" down the slope before he fell onto Midway Drive near the entrance to the parking lot, a few feet from the automatic gate and thirteen feet from a yellow sign that read, "Dead End." His red headband landed two feet from his body. Jerry Persky watched Jeff fall face down. "I looked over to him and I saw this blood dripping down the street." "He was bleeding to death and I started to scream." "His face was a sickening mess," said another eyewitness. "The

---

[*] Howard Ruffner's photo of this tableau appeared on the cover of the May 15, 1970, issue of *Life* magazine.

Kent State student Jeff Miller, shot dead, lies on Midway Drive.

right side of his face was all swollen out and you could see blood running out of his eyes, his nose, and his mouth. It was a very sickening sight."

Carol Mirman had run down the eastern slope of Taylor Hall with other fleeing protestors, bullets whizzing past her ears, and dove behind a yellow Volkswagen near the parking lot entrance. When the firing stopped, Mirman got up and saw Jeff's body. "I'd never seen blood like that. It was a complete shock. I wanted to touch him. I remember wanting to hold him, but I was afraid of the blood. I did touch him and hold his hand because I didn't want him to feel alone." She shook her head and thought, "How can anybody live with his life running down the sidewalk?" "It just kept flowing. And there was nothing that I felt I could do." Protestor Tom Miller, an apartment mate of Alan Canfora and Tom Grace and who was wearing an unbuttoned dark vest over a white shirt, dipped his black flag in Jeff's blood and jumped up and down in a kind of war dance, shouting "Look!" again and again. Moments later, Mary Ann Vecchio, a fourteen-year-old runaway from Opa-locka, Florida, who had long, flowing dark hair, was wearing jeans, a white scarf, and sandals, and had spoken with Jeff a few minutes earlier, knelt over his lifeless body. "I'll never forget how I felt when I looked down and saw Jeff lying in this pool of blood," she later said. "I was scared. . . . I knew he was dead because his face was blown off. . . . It looked like a river of blood." Shaking and sobbing with her arms outstretched, Vecchio screamed, "They shot him! They shot him! They shot him!" Student photographer John Filo captured the instant in what became the iconic image of the Kent State tragedy—what some have called the "Kent State Pieta."* Mirman put her arms around the sobbing Vecchio. "She felt like a block of ice. She was frozen. She was stone. She couldn't move." Another student stood over Jeff's body fingering her rosary beads, moaning and crying. Junior Jerry Persky and a friend turned Jeff over onto his back and saw the hideous wound to his face. His left eye was askance and his right eye was closed.

Tom Grace, who "was very excited and very eager to be after" the guardsmen according to eyewitness Ben Parsons, was near Jeff Miller when the firing started. He saw Jeff "being shot, doing a spin, and fall [in a] pool of blood." "I thought, 'Oh, my God!,' turned, and started running as fast as I could." "Seized with fear" in his own words, he got about ten yards when a bullet tore into the back of his left boot. He screamed when it hit him. "All of a sudden I was on the ground" on his stomach. "It was just like somebody had come over and given me a body blow and knocked me right down." The bullet entered his Achilles tendon, shattered his left heel, and passed through his ankle, shredding several bones and creating a gaping hole on the inside of his foot. The bullet fragmented as it traveled, scattering three dozen tiny metal splinters. His foot didn't hurt at first; it felt numb and bled profusely. "I tried to raise myself, and I heard someone yelling, 'Stay down, stay down!' I looked up, and about five or ten feet away from me, behind a tree, was my roommate Alan Canfora. I threw myself back to the ground and lay as prone as possible to shield myself as much as I could, although like most people I was caught right in the open. I couldn't run because I

* Filo's Pulitzer Prize–winning photo ran three columns wide on the front page of the next morning's *New York Times*.

had already been hit. There was no cover. I just hugged the ground so as to expose as little of my body as possible to the gunfire." "Digging my fingers into the ground, I could hear the bullets over my head." "It seemed like the bullets were going by within inches of my head. I can remember seeing people in the parking lot dropping. I didn't know if they were being hit by bullets or they were just hugging the ground. It seemed like [the shooting] kept going and going and going. And I remember thinking, 'When is this going to stop?'" "It was the loneliest and sickest experience you can imagine."

As Alan Canfora moved up the eastern slope of Taylor Hall with other protestors, he saw guardsmen stop at the Pagoda and a group of them turn in unison. "I had my flag in my hand," he later said. "They were aiming their guns into the crowd. I turned and started to run." He passed a tall pin-oak tree. "I heard bullets cracking by me." "I thought to myself, 'Surely, they must be firing blanks,' because nobody was doing anything deserving to be killed. Then I thought I'm going to make it behind this tree. So, I took a couple of real quick steps and, as I swung around, my right wrist was protruding and I was hit." A bullet penetrated the top front of his right wrist and exited on the underside of his right forearm. "I felt a stinging pain in my right arm and noticed trickles of blood on my wrist." He thought, "This is a nightmare but it's real! I've been shot!" "It felt as if someone had taped a powerful firecracker on my wrist and lit it. There was a sharp feeling of pain and a stinging sensation. Then numbness." "Another student was standing behind the same tree. I knelt on the ground, about two feet behind him."

Dean Kahler, near where the practice field, Midway Drive, and the parking lot intersected, about eighty yards from the Pagoda, saw Joe Lewis give guardsmen the finger and thought the confrontation was over when the guardsmen crested Blanket Hill. "I remember looking at my watch and thinking, 'Well, it's almost 12:30. I'll get a cup of coffee at the student union and go to my class.' Then, the next thing I knew I hear rounds hitting the ground around me and I said, 'Oh my God, they're shooting at me!'" Dean fell onto his stomach and shielded his head with his arms, squirming in fright at the gunfire and "praying that I wouldn't get hit" "because there was no place to run to, no cover for me." "Blacktop was being ripped by bullets all around me." "It seemed like it went on forever."

About halfway through the shooting, a bullet slammed into Dean's back just below his left shoulder blade. "I knew I had gotten shot because it felt like a bee sting on my back." "I felt a stinging sensation through my legs." "Immediately my legs got real tight and then they relaxed." He could feel nothing below his waist. "I knew I had a spinal cord injury. I just tried to stay calm until the shooting stopped." The bullet disintegrated as it tore through his thorax, shattering three vertebrae, destroying part of his left lung, and punching holes in his diaphragm. Because of his first-aid training as a Boy Scout and a zoology course he was taking that quarter, he understood what a damaged spinal cord meant: he would probably never walk again. "The only thought that came into my head was, 'If I turn over, will I bleed more internally than externally? It's a 50-50 chance. You're going to die one way or the other.' I wanted to see the sky and the sun and the leaves and the people's faces. I didn't want to be eating grass when I died." "Someone roll me over," he said, feeling nauseous. "The one thing

Kent State student Dean Kahler lies paralyzed on the practice field.

I'll never forget about that day is seeing the looks on the faces of the students who were standing over me, not knowing that there were twelve other people out there shot, four of them bleeding profusely, lying dying on the ground."

Doug Wrentmore was in the near corner of the parking lot, about eighty-five yards from the Pagoda. "I was walking away because it didn't look like it was going to get good and I didn't especially want anything to happen between the guard and myself." He glanced over his right shoulder when he heard something. At first "I thought they were firecrackers, then I thought they were shooting blanks. Then I got shot and I knew they weren't." He felt a sharp, stabbing pain just below and to the side of his right kneecap. "I took a couple of steps and then I couldn't walk anymore." His right leg gave way, he fell to the ground, and he crawled behind a blue Chevrolet in the first row, third space of the parking lot. After a few seconds he braced himself up against the car to see what was happening. "Get down!" someone nearby shouted. "Those are live bullets!" Doug quickly sank back to the pavement. Just then a bullet shattered a window of the car behind him. "They're shooting at *me*!" he thought. When the shooting finally stopped, he peered at his trousers and saw a hole outlined by dark red below his right knee. A bullet had fractured his right tibia and exited the back of his right leg. Someone shouted, "Doug, you're shot and it's going to hurt!" "I felt a tremendous wave of pain through my body," he recalled.

Allison Krause and Barry Levine were about ten yards behind Doug in the parking lot. "I had my back to the guard when I heard the barrage," said Barry. "I thought they were shooting blanks." "I just couldn't believe they would shoot bullets." "By instinct, I pulled Allison behind a car for cover. While we were falling behind the car, the pop, pop, pop continued." Barry felt relieved they were safe. "As I looked at her to see if she was okay, she didn't respond. Then I heard her whisper to me, 'Barry, I'm hit.'" "I said, 'Where?' I didn't see any blood." "Barry, I'm hit," she whispered again. "It couldn't be. It's impossible. 'What do you mean you're hit?'" "She never said another word." "As I stroked her cheek, I saw a smudge of blood. It had come from my hand underneath her. I realized at that point she had been shot in the back and was bleeding." "When I saw the blood coming from under her left armpit I started screaming." A bullet had penetrated her upper left arm and then entered her left chest. It fragmented as it tore through her lower left lung, spleen, stomach, duodenum, liver, and vena cava, the large vein leading to the heart, and left a gaping hole where it exited. "I had gloves on that day," Barry remembered. "When I pulled my hands out, the gloves were all bloody. Then she slipped into shock and turned white. Her breathing became labored, and she was drooling. She started to lose consciousness. Something was seriously wrong." But "I never dreamed she'd die." A group huddled around Allison. One was graduate student Marion Stroud. "We tried to put enough scarves and handkerchiefs into the hole to stop the bleeding. She was breathing a little bit but as we waited for the ambulance, I saw her lips go white and her eyes glaze over, and I realized she wouldn't make it."

Halfway down the parking lot where it abutted the practice field about one hundred twenty yards from the Pagoda, Bill Schroeder was turning away and ducking when a bullet pierced the left side of his back. "The impact of the bullet picked him up off the ground and thrust him backwards," remembered an eyewitness. "It's burnt into my mind and my memory." The bullet entered his seventh rib, traveled upward fracturing five left ribs, deflected inward puncturing his left lung, and exploded out his left shoulder. "I saw him fall," the eyewitness added. "I was in total disbelief of what I witnessed and what had happened. I went over to Schroeder and by the time I got there, there was a group of people around him." Bill had fallen face down, but students turned him over onto his back to try to help him. "Stand back to give him room to breathe!" someone yelled. "You could [see a] big bloodstain in his chest, and he was having a hard time breathing." Those around him saw the agony on his face. "His eyes were open, and he was looking up at a very blue sky," recalled Chic Canfora. "He had blood all over his shoulder." "It was all very messy," said senior John Barilla. Bill remained conscious and occasionally moved his leg a bit. Someone used a shirt as a pillow under his back. Despite this, "the blood was soaking into the grass," remembered senior Jim Nichols.

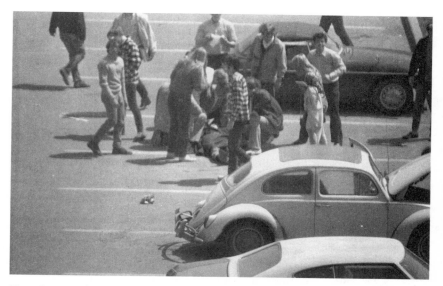

Kent State student Bill Schroeder lies mortally wounded in the parking lot.

About ten yards behind Bill Schroeder and an equal distance to Allison Krause's left—almost exactly in the middle of the parking lot—was Sandy Scheuer. Student Ellis Berns remembered: "I happened to see Sandy Scheuer. She'd come to a demonstration where there's bound to be a lot of tear gas, and what does she have? A little corner of Kleenex. So I tore my rag in half and gave it to her to wipe the tear gas off her face, because her eyes were still streaming. She had a class. We started walking away, just talking about the morning. Then we heard a noise as the guard retreated up the hill, and for some reason we half-turned toward [them] to see what was happening and when we did so, we faced right into the volley of shots." "I grabbed her and tried to get her to the ground as fast as possible," said Berns, who put his arm around her waist. She and Berns fell on their stomachs. "I remember there was muscle tension" in Sandy's back, "then all of a sudden, it relaxed."

After the shooting stopped, Berns said, " 'Sandy, it's over. Let's go.' There was no response. And then I looked. I realized she had been hit." A bullet had entered the left side of Sandy's neck, shattered her larynx, and severed

her jugular vein before exiting the right side of her neck. She was unconscious and "her face was distorted." "The bleeding was bad," remembered
Berns. "It was spurting up like water out of a hose." "I remember trying to
stop the bleeding in her neck, because you could just see where the bullet
had penetrated her carotid artery [sic]. There was blood all over and she was
unconscious." Freshman Bill James cradled her head. "There was a huge
hole in her neck—it looked like it had been ripped away," he said. Fellow
student Ben Parsons heard Berns scream for help. "I had a yellow towel
for the tear gas," said Parsons, and "we put it around her neck." Michael
Erwin watched as Parsons and Berns held the towel to her throat, "only
there wasn't much of her throat left." Parsons checked her heartbeat and
kept shouting, "She's still breathing!" "She wasn't talking, she wasn't suffering, she was unconscious," observed her friend Sharon Swanson.

Several people running in panic nearly trampled the dying Sandy before
Berns and Parsons moved her to the practice field as broken glass crunched
underfoot. "We couldn't carry her any further, she couldn't take it," said
Parsons. Berns propped her head on his coat so she could breathe. Her
mouth and eyes were wide open. "She convulsed three times while I was
giving her mouth-to-mouth resuscitation. She was very white. I remember trying to lift her feet so we could keep blood going to her brain, but it
seemed totally unsuccessful." Berns looked at his coat. "The left side was
covered with blood. It had skin tissue on it." Chic Canfora—a friend of
Sandy's—came over. "She was so blue and gray that I didn't even recognize her." A third friend, Larry Raines, knelt down, cradled her motion-
less head, and cried, "Why Sandy!? She was one of the most non-political
students I knew." "I wiped away my tears and used my jacket to dry my
hands of her blood."

At the far end of the parking lot—more than one hundred fifty yards
from the Pagoda—Robby Stamps had his back to the guard and was hand-
ing his friend Kathy Kovac a pretzel. "I thought the rally had dispersed, that
it was all over." "I turned my head and saw smoke coming out of the guns.
I thought to myself, 'Jesus Christ, I'm getting out of here!' I immediately
started running. I took about three or four steps and 'Boom!' [the bullet]

hit me and picked me up about a foot in the air. I was hit right in the rear end." A bullet ricocheted off the parking lot, struck Robby in the upper part of his right buttock an inch and a half from his spinal cord, and traveled down his leg where it was stopped by his right femur bone, just missing the femoral artery. The wound felt "like sticking your finger in a live electrical socket," he remembered. "I felt intense pain and tingling. I put my hand back there and felt warm blood running down my leg. I thought to myself, 'I'd better get down. If another bullet hits me, I'm gonna be dead.' I jumped on two girls lying face up in the parking lot. They would cushion my fall and I wanted to protect them from getting shot. I remember putting my body over both their heads."

Scott MacKenzie was in the middle of the parking lot. "When I heard the volley, I began to get out of there. I was just loping. I wasn't running very fast." He reached the construction site adjacent to the parking lot, more than two hundred yards from the Pagoda—the farthest away of any shooting victim—when "I felt a snap in my neck and I fell." "My initial reaction was that something exploded next to my head." He fell to his knees. "I got up and there was blood running out of my cheek." "I remember thinking, 'Holy shit, I got shot!'" He ran in a crouching position into a ditch for cover, where he remained until the shooting stopped, dazed and frightened by the blood pouring from his neck. Then he got up and walked around in circles as he yelled, "Help, help, I've been shot, I need help!" A bullet had entered the back of Scott's neck an inch to the left of his spinal cord, shattered his lower left jaw and exited his left cheek, leaving a hole the size of a nickel.

Jim Russell, heading through the trees on the lower slope of Blanket Hill near Memorial Gymnasium, far from the other shooting victims—all of whom were in the "cone of fire" down the eastern slope of Taylor Hall toward the Prentice Hall parking lot—heard a shot ring out followed by a volley and started running. Birdshot from Sergeant McManus's shotgun, discharged at a 50-degree angle from the horizontal of his belt, ricocheted off one of the trees below McManus and struck Jim when he was about one hundred sixty feet downhill from the guardsmen and facing Lake

Hall perpendicular to the guardsmen. "I didn't know what had hit me."
"It felt like somebody hitting me in the head and the leg with a hammer,"
Jim later said. "It knocked me to my knees." One pellet hit his right thigh,
sliced into his bell-bottom jeans, and created a half-dollar-size gash. More
dangerous, another pellet struck his upper right temple, lodged between
his skin and skull, and created a peanut-size lump that spurted blood into
his eyes. An Ohio State Highway Patrol investigator later told McManus
that if the pellet had hit a bit lower, it would have killed Jim. "You nearly
took a person's life," the investigator said. "It struck me so hard to be told
that," McManus later admitted. "I had terrible dreams."

———

A graduate student surveyed the grisly scene from the top floor of Taylor
Hall, a huge open space with wraparound glass windows that was used as
a drafting area by architecture students. "I could not believe it." "There
was complete confusion. No one knew what to do. I was never so shaken
in my life. I just stood there in shock. What actions could have justified
such reaction?" "I saw people scurrying from one injured student to
another, but they really did not know what to do. I saw some trying to
administer first aid. I saw some trying to form human fences around the
wounded to protect them, but they did not know who they were trying to
protect them from. I saw girls crying and guys trying to keep back tears.
There were no longer any obscenities, but now cries of help. I saw a football player motioning people away from [Jeff Miller] as another student
covered his face with a handkerchief. He was dead! I looked in disbelief. I
thought, 'Death on my campus—how could that be? How could a demonstration end so tragically?'" Student Jerry Casale* heard "a distinctive
wailing and screaming. You turn[ed] around and [saw] people down, and
it was the old heart, stomach, shit-in-the-pants" feeling. "I felt like I was
going to pass out. I was so undone I couldn't stand up." Another student
who was a Vietnam veteran said, "Hell, I was in Nam for a full tour and

* Later a member of the rock band Devo.

never saw anyone shot down. I had to come back to my own campus to see kids killed."

Most of the firing had been random. Fifteen guardsmen in Company A, two in Company C, and seven in Troop G admitted firing up in the air or down at the ground. Five guardsmen in Troop G acknowledged firing twenty-two rounds into the crowd or at individual students.* "Some [rifles] were pointed at the ground and I could see the dirt flying," said Corporal Dale Antram. "I could see some were pointed in the air, and I could see a couple that were level." A man with poor eyesight, Antram thought, "I am not going to fire a weapon when I can't see thirty feet. That's ridiculous."

Private Larry Mowrer "was sick" and "praying that no one was killed or injured." Sergeant Richard Love fired once in the air and "could not believe" others were shooting at students. Staff Sergeant Barry Morris crouched against the post of the Pagoda and fired his .45 caliber automatic pistol "about knee level straight ahead of me toward the crowd."† Sergeant Larry Shafer and Corporal Ralph Zoller deliberately aimed at Joe Lewis.‡ Another

---

* The five were Jim McGee, Barry Morris, Jim Pierce, Larry Shafer, and Ralph Zoller. The Justice Department later determined "that from one to three National Guardsmen, carrying .45s, fired their weapons and have not admitted it. In fact, we know that one National Guardsman used another guardsman's .45 and fired it four times and has not admitted doing so. An analysis of the statements given by guardsmen to agencies other than the FBI indicates that two guardsmen fired at persons and did not tell the FBI that they had. Two more guardsmen told their superiors that they had fired more shots into the crowd than they had admitted to the FBI." Robert Murphy to J. Stanley Pottinger, December 5, 1973, Box 122, M4C, KSUL. Private Larry Mowrer admitted under oath, "I felt I had to justify what happened, so I said [to the FBI that] I fired in the air; I felt ashamed." He fired two shots toward the practice field. Testimony of Larry Mowrer, June 30, 1975, p. 2699, MS 1800, Box 70, p. 2699, KSC, SML, YU. Lieutenant Alexander Stevenson testified that Mowrer did not fire; Captain Raymond Srp testified that he did. Testimony of Alexander Stevenson, 1975 Federal Civil Trial, pp. 6365–66, Box 75, KSC, SML, YU; and Testimony of Raymond Srp, p. 4599, Box 75, KSC, SML, YU.

† At the 1975 civil trial, this exchange occurred: Plaintiffs' attorney: "You intended to hit someone, didn't you?" Morris: "Yes." Plaintiffs' attorney: "Did your bullets strike any students?" Morris: "I don't know." Quoted in *Cleveland Press*, June 13, 1975.

‡ "Where did you sight in on when you fired at [Joe Lewis]?," a state investigator later asked Shafer. "I just aimed and fired," he replied. "I couldn't sight in because of the gas mask." Larry

guardsman probably targeted Jeff Miller as he threw his final stone. (Eyewitness Eldon Fender "firmly believed" Miller "nailed somebody with a rock and was shot instantaneously.")* Platoon sergeant Matt McManus said he saw Acting Sergeant Bill Herschler empty his clip of eight bullets in the direction of the practice field (though Herschler later strenuously denied doing so to the FBI and under oath at trial). Corporal Bill Perkins, who fired three times† into the crowd, later said, "I don't know if I hit anyone and I really don't want to know." "Most of the guardsmen shot over the students' heads," concluded an eyewitness. "Had they shot directly into the crowd, many more students would have been killed."

Company C under the command of Captain Ron Snyder, which had halted between Taylor and Prentice Halls during the shooting, reached Jeff Miller's body lying face down on Midway Drive, blood streaming from his mangled mouth. Carol Mirman remembered the guardsmen "were as shocked as I was. I remember the looks on their faces. They didn't know what to do. And they didn't know what to say." Captain Snyder would later claim that he shoved his laced-up boot under Miller and rolled him over. "As I bent down to assure myself he was dead, I saw protruding from under his chest the handle of a revolver.‡ Quickly I snatched it up and stuck it inside my blouse."§

Shafer statement to Ohio State Highway Patrol, May 28, 1970, in Ohio State Highway Patrol, Report of Investigation, June 4, 1970, Case No. 400-67A-132, Series 2062, Box 2823, OHSSA.

* Corporal Jim Pierce acknowledged firing at "a white male" who "was standing out of the crowd with his arm drawn back and getting ready to heave another stone or rock." "My vision was impeded by the gas mask which was steamed up." Testimony of James Pierce, June 25, 1975, pp. 4345 and 4356, MS 1800, Box 71, KSC, SML, YU. A guardsman told a reporter, "As we were coming back up the hill, I saw Jeff Miller running at me and taunting me. How did I know it was Jeff Miller? Because of the unusual cowboy shirt which I had become familiar with that day." Background Notes, James A. Michener Papers (hereafter cited as JAMP), Container II: 29, Manuscript Division, Library of Congress (hereafter cited as MD, LOC).

† Lieutenant Alexander Stevenson later testified that Perkins told him he emptied his clip. Testimony of Alexander Stevenson to Federal Grand Jury, p. 6252, MS 1800, Box 75, KSC, SML, YU.

‡ A rusted, inoperable .32 caliber revolver with no hammer or bullets.

§ Snyder repeated this falsehood about the "throw down" weapon to Major Harry Jones, the Ohio National Guard inspector general, federal and state investigators, and under oath to the special state grand jury. He subsequently admitted in a sworn deposition and in federal civil trial testimony to planting the revolver on Miller and perjuring himself before the state

Enraged students surrounded the guardsmen, screamed, "Pigs! Murderers! Motherfuckers!" and tried to beat them with their hands. "As [the guardsmen] were backing up," said an eyewitness, a guardsman reached for a drab-olive stun grenade, "pulled the pin, and threw it high in the air over the heads of the students. It exploded with a loud noise but no one was apparently hurt." Snyder then withdrew his unit and led them back across the Commons.

Up at the Pagoda, "we were pretty much in shock," remembered Matt McManus. "I felt sick." "I couldn't believe it," Ron Gammell later said. "It was just shock and awe." "I was stunned," Gabe Brachna recalled. "My mind was racing," said Rudy Morris. It "was telling me, 'This is not right, this is not right, this is not right.'" Some guardsmen "shook their heads in disbelief," recalled B. J. Long. "They couldn't believe it had happened." "I couldn't believe what was happening," remembered Robert James. "It scared me, frightened me. I didn't want anything to do with it." "I saw tears in a lot of men's eyes," said Lieutenant Alexander Stevenson. Another officer tried to talk but couldn't, his throat was too dry; he'd never seen anyone gunned down before.

After a few long moments, the guardsmen of Company A and Troop G, who had been retreating before opening fire, continued their way down Blanket Hill, west across the Commons, and back to the burned-out ROTC barracks. A student following them overheard one say, "Now they'll know we mean business." "It's about time we showed the bastards who's in charge," said another. Most guardsmen felt far differently, however. "We had no idea how many people had been hurt," Rudy Morris recalled. "Our fear was that it was awful." "Coming back down the hill, I was honestly in a complete daze," said Jim Case, who walked straight into a tree. "I couldn't and can't get the things that happened out of my mind." University employee Bill Barrett watched the guardsmen. "The closest guardsman was about five yards away from me, and through their gas masks, you could just see the looks of horror on the faces of these guys coming

---

grand jury. Snyder was never prosecuted. Why did Snyder tell this falsehood? "Everybody was quite concerned about legal action against them. I told them I have the answers to that problem; it was self-defense." Quoted in *New York Times*, July 1, 1975.

down. And I thought, 'Thank God I'm not out there.'" Photographer John Filo "noticed that one guardsman was very nervous, the students were shouting obscenities at him, and other guardsmen beside him calmed him down." To student Chrissie Hynde, the guardsmen "looked stunned." "They were just kids, nineteen years old, like us. But in uniform. Like our boys in Vietnam."

Once back at the burned-out ROTC barracks, General Canterbury asked Major Jones who had given the order to fire. "I told him I didn't know," Major Jones later said, and "I don't know if anybody asked [McManus] at that time whether he had given an order." McManus didn't volunteer that crucial information. Canterbury then instructed Chaplain Simons to find out why some guardsmen had fired and in what direction. Many could not explain why they fired. But the first guardsman that Simons approached said, "I fired right down the gulley." "There was hate on the guy's face," said Simons, who thought, "You just can't get away from it. This guy placed one exactly where he wanted to." "I think this guy was tired and angry and disgusted and when the occasion arose, he just acted out his anger and disgust in a very lethal way." "He had put it where it hurt." "I could see the kids fall," said Corporal David Rogers, who was at the Pagoda but did not fire. He added, "I don't think anybody wants to know who hit anyone." Looking back, Sergeant Terry Lucas said, "Only that person who looked down the sight and squeezed the trigger, who watched someone fall, only he'll know." Charles Madonio said of his friend Jim Pierce:

The next time I saw Jim was the day after he got off duty. He was nervous and scared, and refused to talk about it other than to admit to me that he was on the hill in the firing line. "They were going to kill us," was all he could say. He meant it. He also expressed fear for his family, said he planned to move out of Kent, not go back to school. I tried later to get a statement from him, but he refused to talk about it, saying he was sworn to secrecy. He, in my opinion, had no grudge against the students, no ax to grind. . . . He was just plain scared.

Pierce felt "sorry it happened" but "felt no remorse because it seemed to be the only way to defend myself."[*]

Most of the guardsmen "weren't talking," remembered Matt McManus. "We were just stunned at what did happen, what some of us saw." "Everybody was in a daze," recalled another. Many of those who fired knew they were in hot water. "After it happened, they were in shock. They realized what they had done," said a guardsman. General Canterbury walked down the line and said, "Don't worry about it. You did what you had to do."

"The fact that someone was killed had a great emotional impact on the whole troop," said an officer. "The degree depended on each person." Acting Sergeant Bill Herschler broke out in a cold sweat. Private Rodney Biddle, who had fired once in the air and felt "pretty shook up," watched as Herschler "took off his helmet, put it on the ground, put his head down, and sobbed, 'Oh, God!'" "I got a terrible headache, my hands went numb, and I started to cry," Herschler later told investigators. He handed his rifle to a fellow guardsman and said, "I'm not going to shoot anyone." "If we [have] to go out again, I'm not up to it . . . and I should be taken off the line." Herschler began crying uncontrollably and kept repeating in an ambulance that carried him to Ravenna Memorial Hospital, "I shot two teenagers! I shot two teenagers!" Sergeant Dennis Breckenridge, who had fired in the air, fainted. Another guardsman vomited. A third "was in a state of shock," said Captain Raymond Srp. A fourth felt sick and "ashamed." A fifth, Sergeant Jim Case, knelt and prayed. "I was praying for everyone up on that hill because I knew that was live ammunition. I was praying for anybody who possibly got hit." "Until we came off the hill, I didn't know that anyone had been killed," said another sergeant. "It numbed me sick. The day before I had talked to many students. They were good people. We got along. I thought about the shooting and I thought, 'No, they were just wounded, not killed, please not killed.'" "I just wanted to get away from

---

[*] Pierce's reaction softened over time. Five years later, he said, "I felt remorse when I saw what happened." "I felt remorse that people had been hurt [but] I didn't feel that there was an alternative to the situation that had been created. . . . As far as the people being injured and seeing them on the ground, I felt bad." Testimony of James Pierce, 1975 Federal Civil Trial, pp. 4392–93, MS 804, Accession 1989-M-048, Box 37, Folder 482, KSC, SML, YU.

there," said Staff Sergeant Barry Morris, who had fired into the crowd. Corporal Ralph Zoller, who fired at Joe Lewis, felt "all messed up inside." Corporal Bill Perkins "really [didn't] want to know" if he hit anybody when he fired. Staff Sergeant Rudy Morris, who had not fired, cried. "The only thing going through my mind," said Private John Backlawski, who also hadn't fired, "was, 'Are they hurt or shot?'" Corporal Dale Antram, another who hadn't fired, threw off his gas mask. "I couldn't believe it. My first thought was, 'I'm getting out of the guard. I'm a C.O. [conscientious objector], baby, and I don't care who knows it.'" Two guardsmen laid down their rifles and started to walk away.

"They were already withdrawing," Chaplain Simons said. "They were shaken, they were shocked, they were all broken up." An eyewitness saw some "throw down their weapons and start to bawl." Captain Bill Reinhardt, chaplain of the 145th Infantry Regiment, tried to console those tormented by what had been done. There is "a time to weep," he said, and "a time to mourn. This is the time." To one agitated guardsman, he recited a psalm: "Relieve the troubles of my heart / And bring me out of my distress." Private Richard Shade told his mother that night that he wished he'd been drafted, served his time in Vietnam, and gotten out than been at Kent State that day. "I talked to one guard," said photographer Howard Ruffner, "and he was really upset. He kept saying he hadn't wanted to kill anybody." Sergeant Jim Case, who fired one shot over the heads of approaching students, said, "Only God can take lives and only by his order. I didn't get the order from him to aim at any human. No matter how hard they threw the rocks. I just couldn't shoot at them." Afterward he was so shaken that he couldn't unload his gun. Private Ray Shook believed "taking another person's life is futile. Because every person has something to give—because life is so precious. I feel that the Kent incident changed my life, but it reinforced my belief about killing. I think some people came out of this more emotionally battered than most people realize." Captain Raymond Srp said many of his men "wanted to throw their weapons away, and some said they felt like they had to vomit." "People don't realize the hurt was on the other side too," said Ron Gammell.

Around this time, Terry Norman, a twenty-one-year-old junior law-enforcement major from Akron clad in a yellow shirt, tan jacket, and laced-up boots with a camera around his neck, came running toward the line of guardsmen back in front of the burned-out ROTC barracks. Norman had been photographing protestors for the campus police and the FBI. He had pointed his camera at a protestor about to throw a rock. The protestor, who didn't want his photo taken, had grabbed Norman's gas mask with one hand and his camera with the other. Another person tripped Norman from behind. Norman drew a nickel-plated, snub-nose .38 caliber Smith & Wesson Model 36 revolver from a concealed shoulder-holster and struck the protestor across the face with it. A third protestor then chased Norman down the hill toward the ROTC area. "I took the gun from him," said campus patrolman Harold Rice, "opening the cylinder to see if any of the cartridges had been fired. The cartridges were fully loaded. I smelled the end of the barrel to see if I could smell burnt powder, which I could not."

General Canterbury ordered officers to get a "hands-on" ammunition count to determine who had fired how many rounds. Initially there was some hesitation. One of the officers said, "Look, no one is going to be interrogated. We just want you to tell whether you fired or not." Each guardsman unloaded his rifle, and his ammunition was counted. As each guardsman's clip contained eight bullets, those with fewer than eight bullets were considered to have fired that number of rounds.* Junior officers performed this chore with their respective platoons. "I took out my notebook and started

---

* The next day, FBI agents collected those rifles fired by members of Company A and a list of the serial numbers of rifles fired by members of Troop G. FBI agents instructed the guardsmen to write their names on ID tags and for each trooper to fasten his tag to the rifle he had been issued, but guardsmen often swapped rifles after individually signing them out. "The rifle issued to me," said one trooper—"I didn't have it, someone else did. They were mixed up in the rush when we were called out" the morning of May 4. Statement to Ohio State Highway Patrol, June 19, 1970, 6:15 p.m., in Ohio State Highway Patrol, Report of Investigation, June 25, 1970, Case no. 400-67A-132, Series 2062, Box 2823, OHSSA. This meant FBI ballistics experts were unable to establish which guardsman fired which weapon at which demonstrator. See J. Stanley Pottinger to FBI Director, June 21, 1974, Box 122, M4C, KSUL; Motions Hearing, Kent State Criminal Trial, received by ACLU of Ohio, October 23, 1974, Box 64D, Folder 9, M4C, KSUL; and William O'Connor memo, November 25, 1970, cited in *Akron Beacon Journal*, May 20, 1975.

to ask the men," recalled Second Lieutenant Alexander Stevenson. "I saw tears in a number of eyes. It was like swallowing dry lumps. I thought the men could not take asking those questions." First Lieutenant Ralph Tucker could not bring himself to look at the faces of his men.

Later that afternoon, those who had fired were ordered to Wills Gymnasium in Kent Hall behind the Student Union and told to provide written statements to a judge advocate general (JAG)* officer. "No one briefed us as to what we should put in our statements," Jim Pierce later testified, "and there was no discussion amongst us as to what we should put in our statements." They were simply told, "Sit down and write what you saw." Upon entering the gymnasium, they were confronted by tough, crusty Cleveland television commentator Dorothy Fuldheim, who had slipped into the restricted area. Fuldheim was the first woman in the country to anchor a television news broadcast and host her own television talk show. Outspoken with fiery red hair, Fuldheim screamed at the top of her lungs, "Murderers! Killers! You killed! You murdered!"† "I'll never forget it," McManus later said, "and a lot of them won't" either.

———

Down in the parking lot near Prentice Hall, "the scene was grotesque, blood gushing out from the wounded and dead students"—"incredible hys-

* JAG officers are U.S. Army lawyers.

† That evening, Fuldheim reported live from Kent State, "What is wrong with our country? We're killing our own children!" Callers flooded WEWS-TV's switchboard demanding Fuldheim's resignation, some even threatening to kill her. Thousands of letters came into the station in the days and weeks that followed, three-quarters of them criticizing her for criticizing the guard. Many said they would never watch her again. "In my twenty-four years on television, nothing I ever said drew such an avalanche of disapproval and some of it couched in savage and brutal words." (Statement on WEWS-TV, December 8, 1970.) Fuldheim could be equally searing with antiwar radicals. During an interview a month earlier with Yippie Jerry Rubin about his book, Do It, Rubin called the police "pigs." Fuldheim replied, "I've got a shock for you. Some of my friends are policemen." "Well, I've got a shock for you," retorted Rubin. "I'm good friends with the Black Panthers." Fuldheim's face reddened, she threw the book at Rubin, and shouted, "Out! Stop the interview! Get the hell out of here!" as cameras rolled.

teria." There was fear, hate, and confusion all around. "When I saw fellow students bleeding and writhing in pain," wrote David Wolfson many years later, "I felt intense anger. And helplessness. So helpless." People screamed, "We need a doctor!" "We need an ambulance!" Others locked arms in rings around the students. The first ambulances arrived about fifteen minutes later, sirens screaming. As the ambulances screeched to a stop, attendants jumped out with metal stretchers. Students pointed and cried, "Here! Here!" They helped the attendants load the wounded onto litters and carry them to the ambulances as the shocked and curious looked on. "I remember the ambulance driver's face when he picked [Sandy Scheuer] up and saw her neck. He knew damned well she was dead." Afterward, the only physical traces of what had happened were bloodstains. The psychological scars would last a lifetime.

Doug Wrentmore tried to stand up but couldn't. He called out for help. Two students helped him into a green Chevrolet driven by a couple who took him to Robinson Memorial Hospital six miles away in Ravenna (where many of the guardsmen of Troop G lived and worked). He held his knee in the car and at one point blacked out. He was the first shooting victim to reach the hospital. Emergency room physician Dr. Castaldi examined his wound. He had a compound fracture of his right upper tibia caused by the wound. "You won't be taking part in any more demonstrations for a while," Castaldi clinically said. He sewed up Doug's wound, put a big cast on his right leg, and parked him in a wheelchair in the admitting room. "I watched the [other shooting victims] come in after that, stretchers and stuff," Doug later said. "Most of them were a lot worse off than I was." The wounded moaned in pain while the dead lay silent beneath sheets. Shocked and stunned nurses cried as they worked. Doug saw Allison Krause's and Sandy Scheuer's lifeless bodies. It was his first encounter with death. "It is really something when you see a girl lying on a stretcher, her face all contorted and swollen and then they pick up a sheet and lay it slow over her. That does something to you." It had a "profound effect" on him.

A friend phoned Don Wrentmore at Ohio Bell Telephone Company and said a radio report identified Doug among the wounded. Jan Wrentmore was in the kitchen of their home baking a lemon meringue pie when she heard the news on the radio. She immediately called the rented house in Kent where Doug and Hal lived. Hal told her he had a "terrible gut" feeling. He had also heard the news but didn't know where Doug was. Within the hour, Don and Jan were on their way to Robinson Memorial Hospital, not knowing the extent of their son's injuries. When they arrived, a policeman told them they couldn't go in. Don shoved the policeman aside. They were relieved to learn that Doug's injury was relatively minor. "All Doug wanted was to leave the hospital," Jan later said.

The next day, Doug went home with his entire right leg in a cast. Unable to climb and descend stairs, he convalesced in a ground-floor room, unsure whether his right knee would ever work again. A constant stream of reporters and investigators rang the doorbell—so many that "I got tired of seeing anyone enter," he later said. His family received numerous phone calls from well-wishers but also anonymous calls that were vicious.

Joe Lewis opened his eyes as attendants lifted him into the same ambulance as John Cleary. On the way to the hospital, he screamed in pain each time the ambulance hit a bump or a pothole. In the emergency room of Robinson Memorial Hospital, he felt a strange calm as nurses cut away his bloodied clothes. He thought he was dying. About this time, his mother, Betty, heard about the shooting on the radio while gardening. "Betty, are you worried?" a neighbor asked. "No," she replied—the initial report said four guardsmen had been shot. She waited for Joe to come pick up his father and take him to the hospital for tests. Her oldest daughter, sixteen-year-old Mary, came outside. "Mom, you're so calm. Haven't you heard? Joe's been hit." "You're kidding. If he was shot, they would have called us." Betty went inside and told her husband to call the Ohio State Highway Patrol, which proved no help. About 6:00 p.m. the Massillon police phoned and told them Joe had been shot.

She and her husband hurried to the hospital. When they arrived, reporters rushed them like a "swarm of bees." A nurse led them to the head emergency room physician. They asked him about Joe. "There're so many, I don't remember," he said. He pulled Joe's chart, scanned it for a few moments, then said, "Don't get your hopes up." Joe had lost six pints of blood, the surgeon had removed more than fifteen feet of his intestines, and peritonitis had set in. Several of the attending doctors didn't expect him to live. He remained in critical condition for forty-eight hours. The surgery left him with a nine-inch vertical incision scar on his right abdomen. The exit wound tore out an eight-inch piece of flesh in the shape of a half-moon on his left buttock that required a skin graft. When he regained consciousness two days later in intensive care, he saw his parents looking down at him. "What did you do?!" his mother said. Joe closed his eyes. He kept wondering why he had been shot.

Joe's steady improvement in the days that followed relieved his parents, but their world had been upended. Many relatives, neighbors, and friends thought Joe had disgraced the family. "How's Joe?," Mary asked her parents when they returned from the hospital one day. "He's still in intensive care." "That's too bad," said Mary. "That S.O.B. should have died." Joe Sr.'s sister said her nephew deserved what he got—he should not have given guardsmen the finger. Betty's brother told her, "What did these guys expect when guardsmen have loaded guns?" She and Joe Sr. wavered between suspicion that Joe wasn't telling them everything and disbelief that he had been shot by guardsmen. Betty, in particular, argued with Joe about what happened. "What good do such protests do for the country?" she asked. Joe said there was "something wrong with the country." "Go to Russia or stay here and make it a better country!" she countered.

John Cleary was hit in the left chest. The bullet fragmented inside him, leaving several small exit wounds. The impact "put me into a numbing shock," and he soon passed out. He and Joe Lewis rode in the same ambulance. He regained consciousness briefly on the way to the hospital, murmured, "I can't believe they had live ammunition," and passed out again. He came to on a stretcher in a corner of the hospital corridor. "I remember being afraid that someone was going to leave me there, that they were going to forget about me. It was very chaotic. There were a lot of people running around." "Then I started to feel the pain." "That's the last thing I remember before waking up the next day" with three tubes coming out one side of his body, two tubes out the other, another tube down his throat, more tubes in his arms, and water draining from one of his lungs. "When they opened me up, they took pieces [of bullet] out. I was very lucky [they] did not hit any of my vital organs." A portion of his lungs was removed. John remained in intensive care for four days and in the hospital for ten. He and Joe Lewis ended up in the same room. He returned home to upstate New York that summer. "I promised [my parents] if there were any more rallies or confrontations, I wouldn't be anywhere near them."

Tom Grace writhed in pain on the ground when "all of a sudden, this real husky, well-built guy* ran to me, picked me up like I was a sack of potatoes, threw me over his shoulder," and carried him into Prentice Hall. "Students were screaming as I was placed on a couch, bleeding all over the place. A nursing student† applied a tourniquet to my leg." "The bullet blew the shoe right off my foot, and there was a bone sticking through my green sock. It looked like somebody had put my foot through a meat grinder." The right side of his left foot was gone. A student wanted to pour alcohol on it. "No, no, no!," Tom screamed. Ambulance attendants eventually arrived. "I remember my foot hitting the edge of the ambulance as I went in." He felt "the most intense pain that I've ever experienced in my life." The attendants put him on the top berth. He looked down and saw Sandy Scheuer. He had met her a week before. "She had a gaping bullet wound in the neck, and the ambulance attendants were tearing away the top two buttons of her blouse and then doing a heart massage. I remember [them] saying, 'It's no use, she's dead.' Then they just pulled up the sheet over her head." That moment "will never leave me," he later said. "That was, and remains, the toughest memory from the whole day." "The full impact of what had occurred did not touch me until two or three days later. It was an awful, awful thing."

Once he reached the hospital, Tom was parked in the hallway as doctors treated the more seriously wounded while he screamed, "Please give me something—the pain is horrible!" Nurses eventually wheeled him into an elevator, took him to an upper floor, and finally gave him anesthesia. He woke up later in a hospital bed. A surgeon had cleaned his wound and

*   Mike Brock. The two became lifelong friends.

†   Kathy Hill.

put on a plaster cast from his toes to his hip. "I looked down to see if my foot was still there. I could see the tips of my toes sticking out of a cast. I just lay back and breathed a big sigh of relief." One nurse remembered him being "shaken up," "pretty edgy all night and talking a lot about the incident." Gangrene set in, and doctors concluded they had to amputate. Tom's mother, Collette, a nurse, beseeched doctors to save her son's foot. "If not for my mother, I likely would have been strapping on a prosthesis every morning," he later said. Nurses gave him antibiotics as well as morphine and Demerol for pain. Staff and visitors had to wear masks and gowns when entering his hospital room. The gangrene eventually cleared up, and he was transferred to a hospital in Syracuse. Multiple skin graft surgeries followed, with operations every four or five days. That was when the pain was at its worst. Tom was eventually able to have his foot reconstructed, but he spent six months on crutches and would feel pain in his foot for the rest of his life.

"It was kind of an eerie calm just for a split second," remembered Alan Canfora. "We waited to hear if there were any more bullets that were going to be fired and there were none." Alan stumbled into the Home Economics Building, rinsed his wound in a drinking fountain, wrapped his wrist in a hand towel, went back outside, and flagged down a car driven by a graduate student and his wife, who took him to the hospital. As he walked into the emergency room, he looked in the back of an ambulance and saw Jeff Miller on a blood-smeared stretcher, lying face up, a gaping hole in his left cheek. Inside the hospital, he saw Tom Grace lying on a stretcher in the hallway "not being treated by anyone. He was in extreme agony. The bones were protruding out of the bottom of his foot. He was crying and screaming and asking for something to kill the pain. I tried to calm him. They were treating the others who were dying and who were wounded more severely."

Al Canfora was on the Goodyear Tire factory floor when someone shouted that National Guardsmen had shot student protesters at Kent State. Al rushed to a phone and called his wife, Anna, who "was hysterical." When Al learned that Alan was one of the wounded, "my heart started beating fast." He knew his daughter Chic also had been on campus but didn't know if she, too, had been shot. It took Al and Anna forty-five long minutes to get to Robinson Memorial Hospital in Ravenna. When they arrived, they learned to their relief that Alan was only slightly wounded and had already been treated. Chic was there, too. When she saw her father, she ran up to him in tears and said, "Daddy, you should have seen how they treated me when I came to the hospital! The policemen said, 'Get the hell out of here!' My brother is hurt!" she shouted. A policeman grabbed his billy club and seemed about to strike her when a photographer took out his camera and the policeman turned away. Al and Anna drove Chic back to her Kent State dorm. She took her parents over to Blanket Hill. They could still see spent shells on the ground. Chic suddenly screamed at guardsmen nearby, "You goddamned pigs! You goddamned pigs!" When they went to Alan's off-campus apartment, a sheriff "told us to get out of town."

Dean Kahler tried to stay calm as he lay paralyzed on his back on the practice field. "Someone came to me and asked who I was and who my parents were. I gave them their phone numbers and they carried me away in an ambulance. I had been in an automobile accident about six months before, so I knew what was going to happen to me when I got to the emergency room." "A friend of mine who was a minister[*] showed up, so we had a little time together before I went into the operating room." "We talked about life in general, about the fact that I might not make it, and to tell my mother and father it would be all right." They prayed, then the minister told Dean "Good luck" as nurses wheeled him into the operating room. Surgeons examined his X-rays before beginning. One of them said, "The bullet is lodged in this boy's spine. He's never going to walk again. In all my years of medicine, this is the most senseless thing I've ever seen," and wept.

Elaine Kahler got a call at work at the K-Mart in Canton from the student who had spoken to Dean. He told her, "There's been trouble. Dean was shot." "Is he alive?" she asked. "He's conscious. He gave me your telephone number and told me to call you." Elaine took her three other children to

---

[*]   Reverend Gordon Bucher of the Church of the Brethren. Dean's mother called Bucher immediately after hearing the news. Bucher reached the hospital before the ambulance carrying Dean arrived.

a niece's house and rushed with her husband, John, an inspector in an engine assembly plant, to Robinson Memorial Hospital. They reached Dean just before he went into surgery. He was conscious, but to his mother "he looked bad with no color."

Dean regained consciousness three days later in the intensive care unit. "I woke up in tremendous pain. God, I just couldn't understand all that pain." During the first weeks of hospitalization, when he could not be given pills to ease the pain, his constant thought was, "Why me?" The pain was so huge and diffuse that it felt like it would never go away. "There were tubes in my throat, nose, in my sides, and intravenous needles in my hands, elbows, and feet. I could not move and was hooked to machines." "They had opened me up from just below my armpit, across my chest, down my stomach to about three inches below my navel. They broke three ribs and man-handled my insides looking for shrapnel." They didn't try to remove all the fragments "because I was in such danger that they figured if they did any more probing around, I would probably bleed to death." "I don't remember much except my mother crying and my father looking like he was ready to cry." Though heavily sedated, he lamented to his parents, "Man, I'll be in a wheelchair for the rest of my life." "Later that day, I felt like going through my mail. The first letter I opened was a hate letter. 'Dear Communist Hippie Radical, I hope by the time you read this, you are dead.'" At that moment, his friend Kensey Paulus was lunching in the Ohio National Guard's Ravenna arsenal, and Dean's name came up. "He's no radical," Paulus told fellow guardsmen. For ten days, doctors told the Kahlers it was touch and go—their son might or might not live. Dean remained hospitalized for nearly six months, much of the time with a steel brace around his head, consuming only liquids through a straw, his weight dropping to one hundred twenty pounds. Holes remained in his diaphragm, and bullet fragments remained in his lower abdomen. He was eventually transferred to a rehabilitation clinic in Canton, then to a hospital in Cleveland, where he remained until October 25. He would spend the rest of his life in a wheelchair as a paraplegic.

"Ambulance! Ambulance!," Barry Levine screamed hysterically as he cradled Allison Krause in his arms. A fellow student nearby watched. "After the shooting stopped, I heard screams and turned and saw a guy kneeling, holding a girl's head in his hands. I ran to them and was the first to reach them. The guy with her was getting hysterical, crying, yelling, shouting, 'Those fucking pigs, they shot you!' First, I got him to lay her head on a coat and had to yell at him several times to get him to control himself. I treated her for shock and immediately applied direct pressure to her wound with my handkerchief. She was shot just below the left armpit and her shirt was ripped apart and soaked with blood. She began to salivate. She seemed to be trying to swallow her tongue. I gave her mouth-to-mouth [resuscitation], but only for an instant. The bleeding slowed down, and I thought she would be all right." He and Barry placed Allison on a metal stretcher and carried her up the hill to a waiting ambulance, but it was already full. They hurried back down to the parking lot and loaded her into a second ambulance. "Don't worry, she'll be all right," a medic said as they lifted her into the back of the vehicle. Barry climbed in with her and held the stretcher still. Allison's breathing became labored as the ambulance

Fatally wounded Kent State student Allison Krause is carried to an ambulance.

raced to the hospital. She gasped for air while a medic kept saying, "She'll be okay, she'll be okay." On the bunk above her lay the lifeless body of Jeff Miller, unrecognizable to Barry because part of his face was gone, even though Barry, a fellow Long Islander, knew him well. When the ambulance screeched to a stop outside the emergency room entrance, Barry pleaded, "C'mon, Allison, just hang on a little longer." As medics removed her from the ambulance, her eyes rolled back in their sockets and her arms fell off the stretcher. She died.

Assistant county prosecutor Charles Kirkwood was in the hospital morgue. "The door to the morgue opened, and they rolled in the first body with a sheet over it. I went over and picked up the sheet and saw a young girl whom I later learned was Allison Krause. I could see that she had been very beautiful in life. I turned her over and could see both the entrance and exit wounds; all you had to do was look at it to realize that it had come from some military type of weapon. That's when I realized that guardsmen had shot the other people." Kirkwood felt "sadness more than anything else, at the waste of life."

Bill Schroeder, lying on the edge of the practice field, remained conscious and kept whispering, "Where the hell is the ambulance? Where the hell is the ambulance?" An ambulance was nearby, but it took another wounded student away. A second ambulance arrived about ten minutes later. As attendants lifted him on a stretcher, Bill moved his leg up to help them. He was the second victim to arrive at Robinson Memorial Hospital. He was barely conscious as orderlies wheeled him into the emergency room. He had no ID on him. He whispered his name, which an orderly caught as "William Schneider." Five minutes later, before he could be rushed into surgery, he died of massive internal hemorrhaging.

Robby Stamps heard the shooting die down, isolated shots continuing here and there. "I could hear them cracking as I was getting up. I ran right into some guy,[*] put my arms around him, and said, 'Brother, I've been shot. Help me!' He thought I was joking. He looked down at my wound and said, 'Oh, my God!'" He and another student carried Robby

---

[*]   Jim Minard. See Transcripts of Tape No. 2, Scheuer Family Papers, Box 2, OHSSA.

into nearby Dunbar Hall, put him on a couch in the lobby, and examined his wound. One of them poured rubbing alcohol on it. "It hurt so much that I bit his arm." "Four of them then carried me out" to an ambulance. "Two grabbed my legs and I put my arms around the other two." "As I was going out, a kid shouted right into my face; he said he hoped I died." They put him in the back of the ambulance. A minute later, attendants loaded the body of Jeff Miller. Robby gazed at him in horror. "His head was blown off, literally. His cheek was puffed out and it was blue." "The idea that he was dead really didn't register."

The attendants told Robby he had to get out so they could load a second stretcher carrying Allison Krause. "I didn't see a lot of blood and so I thought that she would be okay, even though she wasn't moving at all." Robby sat in the front passenger seat. "That's when it started to hurt," he said. "The drive to the hospital was unbelievable. Guard jeeps on the highway were not getting over for us to go by and cars were not getting over." "[Our] siren was right behind them, but they kept going down the road, not moving one bit."

When Robby reached the hospital, staff laughed at his misfortune and called him dirty names. "They carried me into the emergency room. A nurse ripped off my pants with obvious maliciousness. She didn't take off my shoes, she just pulled. It really hurt. Two doctors walked in and they just stared at me. One of them said, 'I don't know why you students are causing all this trouble.' Another doctor came in and [examined] me." They gave him no painkillers. After X-rays, the doctor decided to leave the bullet in place and put in a drain. The wound eventually left a scar five inches long and half an inch wide. "They took me to a double room. My roommate was some redneck who looked at me and said, 'Well, when I was a janitor in a school, the students had more respect for law and order than you hippies do now. They should have shot a few more of you.'" He asked Robby if he was a Christian. "As a matter of fact, I am not." The roommate responded: "You refused to take the Lord Jesus into your heart as your savior."

Floyd Stamps was sitting in his Cleveland office when the phone rang. It was Robby's seventy-five-year-old grandmother. She had been watching the television when a reporter broke in with news that Robert Stamps, among others, had been shot and was in guarded condition at Robinson Memorial Hospital. She was hysterical. Floyd got in his car and raced to Ravenna at one hundred miles per hour. "I didn't feel I had actually gained my sanity back until he walked in the hospital," said Robby. When he saw his father, he cried and said, "I wasn't doing a thing, so help me!" "It doesn't matter," Floyd said, "the important thing is you're all right."

A Good Samaritan drove Scott MacKenzie to the campus health center. Its staff did their best to stop the bleeding. From there an ambulance took him to St. Thomas Hospital in Akron.

Jim Russell made his way to Lake Hall to wash the blood off his face. The dorm counselor mocked his wounds and said, "We're going to hold you for the police." Fearful that he would be arrested, he fled, and with the help of two nursing students he crossed the campus to the health center, where an attendant washed and dressed his wounds. From there, he went by ambulance to St. Thomas Hospital. A physician performed exploratory surgery but decided it was too dangerous to remove the pellet lodged near his temple. It would remain inside his head for the rest of his life.

A middle-aged woman who had been sleeping on a couch outside Robinson Memorial Hospital's intensive care unit for a month as she tended to her slowly dying husband, Nick, who had passed away that afternoon, took it all in. She walked to a window, looked out, and said, "Lord, Nick has had fifty-five good years. All this time, all this month, I've been praying that you would spare him. But how can I ask for that when these kids haven't even had twenty years?"

Instead of scattering after the shooting, students shadowed the guardsmen down Blanket Hill, screaming, "Get the guard!" "Murderers!" "Killers!" Most had never witnessed killing before—the blood, the screams, the horror. "We didn't know what we were going to do," said one. "We were just walking down the hill to confront them." "Anything could have happened," Charles Fassinger said later. Now "they knew the guns were loaded and they were willing to charge the guard." Once the guardsmen reached the burned-out ROTC barracks, about five hundred students gathered on the Commons and refused to move, re-creating the scene from that morning—except now the students were angrier and closer to the guard. "There was horror and there was sadness," recalled John Darnell, "but there was also the feeling of revenge that surfaced there." The guardsmen stood nervously in a circle in front of the remnants of the ROTC building, rifles on their shoulders, facing an increasingly hostile crowd. "Some came right up face to face with us, talking dirty," recalled guardsman Keith Crilow. A female student assailed the troopers as murderers. "If you don't watch it sweetheart," a guardsman shot back, "you may be next." Another guardsman, Larry Raines, "could feel the grief, could see the disbelief on [people's] faces. Everyone was stunned. No one knew what to do, the shock was just too much to overcome."

Fellow student Ronald Arbaugh "felt like tearing up the damn [place] and grabbing the first guardsman I could find and beating the guy's head in. I knew I wasn't going to do it but if a couple of others had tried, I might have gone across there with them." Other students stood up and moved toward the guardsmen. General Canterbury heard some students shout, "Let's go get them!" He grabbed a bullhorn and declared, "If you move any closer, I will give an order to shoot!" Canterbury later described his emotional state at that moment. "I certainly wasn't the calmest person in the world. I was trying my best to hold myself under control."

The bloodshed of a few minutes earlier seemed as though it might be but a prelude.

"There was tremendous hostility, tremendous anger, absolutely unbelievable," remembered psychology professor Sy Baron. "The girls were crying. Some of the boys started crying. They told me they'd rather die right here, now, than in Vietnam. It terrified me. They were defiant as hell." "There wasn't any rational thought," recalled one student. "People were ready to die now." "We were really pissed but didn't know what to do with that anger." "The crowd became one in its sullen, numbed defiance," another remembered. "We would not be moved." Young men stripped to the waist, scrawled Xs on their chests, backs, and foreheads. Wild with rage, they yelled, "Pig! Pig! Pig! This is it—let's go! The revolution starts here!" "Let's drive these fuckers right off our campus!" "Let's finish it here and now!" "Let them shoot us too, if they want to!" "You felt like you were invincible because you were so angry [about] what had happened," remembered Rob Fox. "Everybody was in shock," explained another student. "The feeling was they killed four of us. What the hell? Might as well make it a couple of hundred."

A spectator watching thought, "God, again? Is it going to happen again?"

Ellis Berns, who had been with Sandy Scheuer when she was shot and bled to death, stumbled in a daze along the path north of Taylor Hall running from the Prentice Hall parking lot to the Commons. He encountered a group of guardsmen in Company C. "The guard was not letting anybody [pass] and they were pointing guns," remembered Burns. "I ripped my jacket off, this green fatigue jacket with Sandra's blood, and I threw it at them. And I told them to go fuck themselves. I was just livid. I didn't know what to do. I could have been killed right there—I had no clue. I was completely shocked."

Back on the Commons, Steve Sharoff pleaded with the protestors to calm down. A guard officer came over and loudly said, "Move them out or else!" Then another guardsman came over and told Sharoff, "General Canterbury wants to speak with you." Sharoff approached the general, "who wasn't done playing the part of an idiot," said Matt McManus later. Canterbury told Sharoff, "You need to move these students out of here because this is an illegal gathering." "You can't be serious," replied Sharoff. "These students just watched their friends being killed." "I am serious," Canterbury said. "You have to tell them they need to leave. They don't have a choice, and I don't have a choice either." "I remember him saying to me very directly, 'These are my orders and they have to move.'" "As a historian it reminded me of Nazi Germany," Sharoff later recalled, 'These are my orders.'"

Sy Baron feared a massacre. Wearing sunglasses and holding a bull-horn, the bearded, balding Baron struggled to calm the students. "What does retaliation mean? Retaliation means escalation," he explained. "If

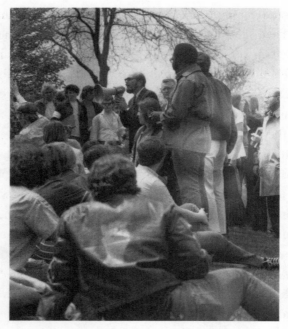

Kent State professor Sy Baron struggles to calm
students after the shooting.

they want to kill us all, let them do it now!" someone shouted. "They killed
somebody," Baron acknowledged, then quickly added, "I'm sure the guy
who did it—I wouldn't want to have his conscience." "If you walk down the
hill, they're going to *shoot!*" "Don't go down there, they'll *kill* you!" They
weren't listening.

Baron approached the guardsmen. "They were a bunch of young men
with dry mouths whose fists were clenched up so tight to their rifles that
their knuckles were white. They were benumbed." "Who's in command
here?" Baron asked. "Talk with the man in the suit," said an officer, pointing to Canterbury. Baron pleaded with the general to diffuse the situation.
Canterbury told Baron he still had a job to do—disperse the students—and
he didn't want the professor telling him how to do it. "General, you've got
to stop this—this is going to result in a slaughter! You say you're unmoved
by it? It's a horrible thing—these are college kids! I was in the military, I
know about this killing stuff." Canterbury walked away as he spoke.

Baron would not give up. He confronted the general again. "Tell your men to put down their guns. For heaven's sake, do something! You've got to give those kids some kind of sign." "Sign of what?" Canterbury asked. "That you're not going to shoot. That we can quiet this thing down. Isn't there some kind of order like 'Parade rest!'?" Hearing these words, several guardsmen immediately dropped their rifles. "Shoulder those guns!" barked Canterbury. The professor begged, "General, can't you make them stop pointing those guns as if they were going to fire?" Canterbury reflected a moment, shrugged his shoulders, and declared, "Parade rest!" Down went the guns. He told a guardsman standing nearby, "Take this man away." Canterbury then ordered officers to go around to each guardsman and ask, "How many bullets have you got? How many do you need?"

Baron went back and pleaded again with the students. "If you walk down toward them, I promise you they'll kill you. The reason they'll kill you is because they're scared to death. These guys are scared stiff. It's a dumb thing to put live ammo in the guns of scared kids. There is only one way you're going to stay alive, and that is to stay here. The only way to stay alive is to stay here. I don't want you going down there. Some of you guys feel you have to be heroes, but there are people here who don't want to get shot and killed. That includes me. All I can say is don't go down. They've got guns and live ammo." "Who ordered them to shoot?!" someone shouted. "My answer is I don't know. I can tell you this: you put live ammunition in a gun with a scared and untrained kid behind it and you've had it. And we've had it; we've had blood shed. It's a terrible thing that's happened here today. This campus will never forget it. Don't start chasing across this field again! . . . For heaven's sake, cool it! I don't want you to die! It won't help! You're going to get a bullet in the belly if you stay!"

Professor Glenn Frank, the former marine and self-described "flag-waver" who had confronted protestors at the ROTC burning on Saturday night, also sensed an impending calamity. He had been eating lunch at the Student Union when the shooting occurred, but afterward had guided ambulances to the Prentice Hall parking lot and witnessed the carnage firsthand. Now, an even greater threat loomed. Frank later described his feelings at that moment. "I felt the anger of the shopkeepers who had their

Kent State professor Glenn Frank (in coat and tie), May 4, 1970.

life's work partially destroyed by a mob who lashed out at a distant but 'decadent' government. I felt the horror of an escalating war in Vietnam and that my son might be called. I felt the frustration of the police in trying unsuccessfully to cope with the mob. I felt the need to maintain a semblance of order in a chaotic situation. I felt the anguish and hopelessness of moving a group of students who would not move after the shootings."

Feeling "like a chicken with my head cut off," Frank ran toward the guard and told Major Jones, "For God's sake, don't come any closer!" "My orders are to move ahead," Jones nervously replied. "Over my dead body!" "I was beginning to get hysterical," Frank said later. "This whole thing was just beyond reason, nobody seemed to be using their head." He walked over to General Canterbury. "Give me some time! I'll get these students out of here, give me some time!," Frank begged the general. "If you don't get the kids out of here in the next five minutes," snapped Canterbury, "we'll move on them too."* "You'll what?!," Matt McManus thought as he watched.

* Canterbury later stated in a sworn deposition, "After the shooting, while I was in the area of the ROTC building, there was never any consideration given to moving out on the

"How could he have seen what I just saw and say something like that?" "I didn't want to go through the same thing again in any way, shape, or form." "We were in no condition to be ordered to lock and load to be put in firing position again. We were in no position for that at all. We couldn't have taken another stand, we couldn't have." "If there was any time I would've refused an order, it would've been then and I think I would have been followed by about ninety men who would've just laid their weapons down."

Tears streaming down his cheeks, Frank rushed back to address the students as a thin line of guardsmen with rifles in hand and bayonets fixed slipped into position on the high ground behind them. "Please listen to me!" he shouted through a bullhorn. "I don't care whether you've never listened to anyone before in your lives! I am *begging* you right now! If you don't disburse, right now, they're going to move in and *it can only be a slaughter*! Would you *please* listen to me?! *Jesus Christ—I don't want to be a part of this*! Please!" "Join us, man!" a student shouted back at him. Others started screaming, "Fuck you!" as a distant public announcement told them to immediately clear the area. Unbeknownst to Frank, his freshman son Alan was in the crowd.

General Canterbury "got all cranked up to clear the area," said 107th Armored Cavalry chaplain Major John Simons. "He wanted to start the sweep again." Major Simons thought, "No, no, no!" Canterbury picked up a bullhorn and prepared to tell the students to disperse. Simons tapped the general on the shoulder. "Come on," said Simons, "you told him five minutes." "Oh, all right," Canterbury said, shrugging his shoulders. Another guard officer heard Canterbury say the students might be shot if they didn't leave. First Lieutenant Ralph Tucker heard an officer say, "Break it up or we're coming through again."

Just then, buses pulled up and 181 Ohio State Highway Patrol officers wearing Smoky Bear hats or protective helmets filed out. "I was so glad to

---

students again." Captain John Martin "asked me specifically not to disperse the crowd again." "I don't know why he would think that." "I had no intention of ordering people to disperse that crowd at that point again." Deposition of Robert Canterbury, November 21, 1974, pp. 179–80, MS 804, Accession 1989-M-048, Box 35, KSC, SML, YU.

see them," remembered Matt McManus. Unlike the Ohio National Guard, the Ohio State Highway Patrol had considerable experience dealing with student protests. "The difference between those [Ohio State Highway Patrol officers] and the [Ohio National Guard] was striking," said an eyewitness. "When the state police arrived, you could see a total difference in how they reacted to being assigned to a riot situation where violence had occurred," another eyewitness later said. "They didn't carry rifles, their pistols were holstered, the only thing they carried were two-foot hickory batons. They took over the campus without any violence, without any bloodshed. They made sure people got situated. If they saw somebody doing something radical, they didn't shoot him, they put him in a holding area and just kept him surrounded." Their commander, Major Donald Manly, who had written the Ohio State Highway Patrol manual for riot-control procedures and taught civil-disturbance control at its academy, walked up to General Canterbury and said, "You're no longer in control. My men are taking over now." Manly then walked over to Professor Frank and calmly said, "You take all the time you want."

Ohio State Highway Patrol officers arrive at Kent State on the afternoon of May 4, 1970.

Frank, crying openly, raced back to the students and again begged them to leave. "Glenn Frank made us realize that it was a bad situation, that if we didn't leave we might be shot," recalled Laura Davis. "Finally, the sense that something terrible had happened to these other people could happen to us got through."* The students slowly began to disperse. Ohio State Highway Patrol officers, who had cordoned off the Commons, made openings for them. They walked off in different directions because they believed that way the guard couldn't shoot all of them. "I could barely walk I was so weak," said Frank. "I could hardly see because of the tears in my eyes." He had to be led off the Commons with the help of his son and another friend. Over by the burned-out ROTC building, a newspaper reporter saw a guardsman sitting in a jeep with his helmet pulled down over his face to hide his tears. "My God," the guardsman wept, "they were just kids." "Yeah," the reporter thought, "and you're just a kid too."

———

News of the four students' deaths reached their families at different times in different ways, but always with the same stabbing pain. Elaine Miller worked as secretary to the principal of John F. Kennedy High School in Hicksville, Long Island. Four feet, eleven inches tall and having straight blond hair, a round face, and glasses, colleagues looked on her as the office pixie. She left work on May 4 at 4:00 p.m. headed for her apartment in Queens. Hearing about the shooting on the car radio, she decided "I better call Jeff" once she got home "and tell him to get out of there—that he [shouldn't] hang around during all that trouble." "I called his number. It rang and rang. Then a young man answered. I said, 'Let me speak to Jeff.'" It was Bruce, one of Jeff's roommates. "He said, 'Who is this?' I said, 'It's his mother.' Bruce said, 'Oh, Mrs. Miller, you don't know? He's dead.'" Elaine screamed, refusing to believe her youngest son was dead. "I thought maybe somebody had borrowed Jeff's wallet; this doesn't happen to people

* That summer, another student on the Commons after the shooting, Diane Schempp of Cleveland, wrote Frank a letter thanking him for saving her life. "Notes on Kent State Shooting Story," Container No. II: 29, JAMP, MD, LOC.

you know." Her second husband, Artie, called the hospital in Ravenna and learned that one of the slain students was wearing a leather ring with a peace sign on it. "Then I knew it was Jeff," she said. "The rifle bullet that entered Jeff's mouth and exited at the base of his skull changed my life as surely as it ended his," she later wrote. "Before May 4, 1970, I was naïve. I believed—if I thought about it at all—that . . . no one would ever deliberately hurt me or anyone I loved." She later told a friend that she woke up on May 4, 1970, as one person, but by the time she went to sleep that night, she had become someone else entirely.

In the months that followed, she received hundreds of letters of support. Along with this outpouring of sympathy came letters—some with return addresses—that threatened her life, that contained feces, that said, "People of your ilk who raise their children to be Communists should have expected this." Everywhere she turned she saw a newspaper or a magazine with John Filo's iconic photo of Mary Ann Vecchio hunched screaming over her son's body. "It was like darts going into my head. I told myself this is how Jeff looked when he was asleep. That's what got me through it." She went to see a psychologist, who praised her for coping well. She felt he didn't understand—she coped with what had happened to her youngest son by "shutting it out."

A stout, mustachioed, middle-aged man, Jeff's father, Bernie, had divorced Elaine the previous summer. His ex-wife called him the afternoon of May 4 at the *New York Times*, where he worked as a linotype operator, and told him Jeff had been killed. Bernie immediately flew to Cleveland and drove down to Ravenna. Upon arrival at Robinson Memorial Hospital, he was taken to the morgue and shown his son's body. He stared at it in sorrowful horror. For a few moments he didn't even recognize Jeff because the left side of his face was completely gone. Bernie's grief led him to say, "My life is worthless."

Two days after the shooting, a school board meeting at Jeff Miller's alma mater, Plainview-Bethpage High School, opened with a minute of silence. Students asked the school board to issue a proclamation condemning American involvement in the Vietnam War. The school board refused. "Jeff was killed for practicing the beliefs and principles and freedom that he

was taught right here in this school," protested his roommate Steve Druckner, "and you won't take a stand. After seeing you people here tonight, I
am sick." As Druckner spoke, an older man rushed up and tried to grab
the microphone away from him. The two began to scuffle. Police led them
and several others from the auditorium.

The next day, a memorial service and vigil for Jeff were held at Riverside
Memorial Chapel on Manhattan's Upper West Side. "Numb and sure I
could not survive," Elaine later wrote, "I looked out the car window on my
way to Riverside Memorial Chapel and saw a seemingly endless stream
of young people, walking slowly and silently toward the chapel, all carrying flowers." It was a cool, sunny, windy day, and by eleven o'clock, half
an hour before the service, a crowd of nearly four thousand mourners—
mostly young people wearing blue jeans, fatigue jackets, buckskin coats,
and floppy hats—had gathered behind police barricades along Seventy-
Sixth Street between Amsterdam Avenue and Broadway. "Hushed and
solemn," an observer wrote, "they stood or sat and, like a silent, accusing
chorus, stared impassively at a crowd of policemen, photographers, television cameramen, and reporters milling about." A police helicopter circled
overhead. One mourner carried a placard that read, "WE ARE ALL BUMS."
Another carried a large photo of Jeff lying face down on Midway Drive with
the word "AVENGE" scrawled in red across it.

"Jeff was no radical," his father Bernie said during the service. "He only
wanted to end the war, to end the killing." "Jeff was a war casualty, the same
as if he was shot in Cambodia, or Vietnam, or Laos, and he didn't even have
a gun." "I have no bitterness about the guardsmen. They were young, just
as Jeff was young, but there shouldn't have been bullets in their chambers."
Nothing Bernie nor anyone else said lessened Elaine's pain. At the end
of the service, Rabbi Julius Goldberg intoned the Kaddish as pallbearers
wearing black yarmulkes carried the plain wood coffin out of the chapel.
Behind the coffin was Elaine, barely able to walk, supported by Bernie and
Jeff's older brother, Russ. The sea of mourners watched silently. Across
the street, a large blue banner hanging over a police barricade displayed a
white dove of peace carrying the peace symbol above a field of white stars.
Young people flashing peace signs followed the funeral cortege as it made

its way up Amsterdam Avenue to Eighty-Sixth Street, where the hearse left for Ferncliff Cemetery in Hartsdale, where Jeff's remains were cremated and buried. That Sunday, Mother's Day, New York Republican governor Nelson Rockefeller paid a secret condolence call on Elaine. Rockefeller put his arm around Elaine and told her that he, too, had lost a son.[*]

Doris Krause, a part-time accountant, was at work when the awful news came. "My younger daughter [fifteen-year-old Laurel] called to say that some reporters were trying to get me—that something had happened. I drove home as quickly as I could. When I got home, someone from [a local] TV station called to say that Allison was in the hospital in Ravenna, Ohio. I called the hospital. At first, I couldn't get through. Finally, I got hold of an operator and told her who I was and that I wanted to speak to somebody in the hospital. I was put through to the hospital administrator. He came on the phone and said very casually, 'Oh, yes, Mrs. Krause, she arrived DOA [dead on arrival].'" She heard laughter in the background. "That's how I found out my daughter was dead. I just couldn't believe it. Who would think that this could happen? Be shot by representatives of your government for speaking your mind? That doesn't happen in the United States, does it?"

Her husband, Art, a big, intense, forty-six-year-old Westinghouse executive and World War II veteran with a Purple Heart who had relocated from Maryland to corporate headquarters in Pittsburgh less than a year earlier, was in a meeting when he was paged for a call from his younger brother Jack, who lived in Cleveland. Jack had heard on the radio that Allison had been shot. Art was stunned—it couldn't be true. He frantically tried to reach university officials. He eventually got through to the Kent police, who told him not to worry: "just a couple of kids shot in the leg." He learned the truth at 5:00 p.m. when he walked in the front door of his home as Doris put down the phone. A friend drove them to Ravenna. They reached the hospital at 7:00 p.m. A surly policeman confronted them at the doorway,

---

[*] Twenty-three-year-old Michael Rockefeller disappeared on November 19, 1961, while on an expedition to collect Dani tribal art in the remote Asmat region of southwestern New Guinea (now part of Indonesia). His body was never found. Many of the artifacts Rockefeller collected are today displayed in the Michael C. Rockefeller Wing of the Metropolitan Museum of Art in New York City.

then escorted them to the morgue. "We went in and uncovered her face and shoulders. She looked as though she were asleep. I kissed her on the forehead and cried out in anguish. My wife, who has more strength than I, held my arm." The coroner told them a guardsman's bullet had killed their daughter. Art staggered out in the hallway, where reporters surrounded him. "Any comments, Mr. Krause, any comments?" "All I know is that my daughter is dead!" he sobbed, his dark eyes filling with tears behind large black-frame glasses. "We were so glad we had two daughters so they could stay out of Vietnam. Now she's dead. What a waste—what a horrible waste . . . ," his voice trailing off. Sorrow turned to anger. "I'd like to know who the boys were who shot my daughter," he said loudly. "I'd like to meet [the] young, immature guys who joined the National Guard to stay out of Vietnam. They've got a miserable job to do." The next morning, Art read a statement to reporters gathered on the front lawn of the Krause's split-level brick home. His face contorted because he was fighting back tears. He said Allison "resented being called a bum because she disagreed with someone else's opinion. She felt that war in Cambodia was wrong." "Is dissent a crime?" he asked, his voice quivering as it rose. "Is this a reason for killing her? Have we come to such a state in this country that a young girl must be shot because she disagrees deeply with the actions of her government?!" Later he said: "Some people said to me, 'She wasn't a child.' Well, she was my child. And bullets took her away because she was out there hollering at the brave National Guard. You butchers!"

Art's anguish was compounded by his violent quarrels with Allison over Vietnam in the months before her death. "My daughter would say things, and being older with my dogmatic approach, I would say, 'You're wrong.' And because I said it was wrong, it just had to be wrong. I'm a very dogmatic person. She was a very dogmatic person. And when we had discussions on these subjects, I would shut her off." Allison told friends that she locked herself in her bedroom during visits home to escape her father's anger. She even confided to another friend "that if her father beat her one time, she [would] never go home again."

Art "loved, cherished, and understood [Allison] much better in death than in life," admitted a family friend. This truth cut Art to the bone.

It—and his remorse—devastated and changed him. A year after Allison's death, he picked up a student hitchhiker who'd been having trouble with drugs. "I told him that I had some difficulties with my daughter, that she had smoked some pot and stuff. I talked to him straight. I wish I could have talked to Allison like that." The unresolved tension in his relationship with Allison would haunt Art for the rest of his days.

The Krauses also received hate mail within days of Allison's death. Rumors circulated that Allison's "body was so filthy and dirty that the undertaker wouldn't accept it." Teachers of her younger sister, Laurel, told her that Allison was a traitor. At her former high school, one group of students urged lowering the flag to commemorate her death. Another group of students protested vehemently. "Everybody's out mourning her death and wanting us to lower the flag. Two GIs from this school have been killed in Vietnam. Why didn't we lower the flag for them? They're fighting there to keep the flag up." School principal John Dorn decided to raise two flags—one to the top of its pole, the other at half-mast on a second flagpole. Dorn thought his compromise would solve the problem and please everybody. It only infuriated both groups. Those opposed to the half-masted flag hauled it down and burned it in a trash can.

Allison was buried in a small Jewish cemetery in Wilkins Township, Pennsylvania, just over a hill from her parents' home in Churchill. "I do not think there is a God," Art said, "but the myth haunted me." Barry Levine came. Art took Barry's hand in his and thanked him for coming and sharing their grief. Art and Doris inscribed Allison's headstone with the words she had spoken to a guard officer the day before being shot: "FLOWERS ARE BETTER THAN BULLETS." Afterward, Barry wrote Allison's family: "This part in such sorrow / I do here impart. / No words of mine can ease / This awful time. / But perhaps these lines I borrow: / Say not with sadness: she is gone; / But say with gratitude: she was."

At the little white house on Missouri Avenue in Lorain, Ohio, with an American flag hanging on its front porch, Florence Schroeder, a heavy-set woman with a determined expression, called Bill's number every ten minutes after learning of the shooting on the radio. She couldn't get through because the lines were jammed. Her fear rose when she learned one of the dead students had been identified as William Schneider. Surely the authorities would have notified her, she thought. At four o'clock, a reporter from Cleveland's *Plain Dealer* called and asked if he could have a photo of Bill. "Why do you want it?" she asked with a tremor in her voice. "Oh sorry, must have the wrong Schroeder" the reporter said and hung up. When her husband, Lou, came home, she sent him across the street to Lorain's chief inspector, who was mowing his lawn. A quiet, fifty-four-year-old World War II veteran with a square jaw and ice-blue eyes like his son, Lou worked as superintendent at the Fruehauf Trucking Terminal in Avon Lake. The neighbor assured him that they would have been notified if something had happened to Bill. At six o'clock, the *Plain Dealer* reporter called back and told Florence her son had been hurt. Beside herself, Florence called the Lorain Police Department, which told her to call Robinson Memorial Hospital. After fifteen minutes, she finally got through. An administrator answered. When she heard the word "expired," she collapsed on the floor.

Florence and Lou did not go to Ravenna to identify their eldest son's body. That grim duty fell to Bill's roommate Lou Cusella, who had known him since junior high school. A deputy sheriff drove Cusella to the hospital. On the way he thought, "It won't be so bad, you've seen him asleep on the bunk a hundred times." When he arrived, he met the coroner, who was wearing white gloves. Cusella reached into his pocket, took out a handkerchief, and began wringing it. "Was he wearing a belt that had peace symbols scrawled on it?," Cusella asked. The coroner nodded. "Let me see him, let's get it over with." The window curtains were drawn back. A bright light illuminated the body. It was Bill, lying open-mouthed, his blood-soaked shirt pillowing his pale head. "Oh God, Oh God, it's him, it's him!," sobbed Cusella in a guttural voice. He began trembling, his face twitching uncontrollably. After regaining his composure, Cusella phoned the Schroeders. When he returned to the rented house in Kent that night, he sat alone in the room he had shared with Bill and cried for an hour. The following day, Lou Schroeder, normally a man with a keen sense of humor but this day with a tired and pained expression on his face, went to the Akron morgue to claim Bill's body. Three days later, he and Florence, shaking visibly, buried their "extra-special son" at Ridge Hill Memorial Park on the outskirts of Lorain.

The afternoon of the shooting, Sarah Scheuer, forty-five years old, was painting the exterior of her house in the middle-class Youngstown suburb of Boardman. It was the Scheuer's twenty-seventh wedding anniversary. The phone rang. "I had paint all over me. I ran in." It was her husband. Fifty-nine-year-old Martin Scheuer, a native German Jew who spoke with a thick accent, had fled his homeland when the Nazis came to power in 1933. He first went to British-occupied Palestine, where he lived on a kibbutz and served in the Haganah, the Zionist underground army, before immigrating to the United States in 1937 and settling in Youngstown. He had voted for Richard Nixon and had supported the president's Vietnam policy, even arguing with Sandy about the war. Martin told his wife there had been trouble at Kent State. Sarah hung up and immediately phoned her younger daughter. "Finally, I got her apartment. The roommate said, 'You had better come—Sandy's been hurt.'" "Where is she?," Sarah asked, her fear rising. "I don't know, Mrs. Scheuer." Sarah frantically tried to call the university, then Robinson Memorial Hospital. It took a long time to get through because the lines were jammed, but she finally reached the hospital director. "A girl with a red shirt has been hurt. Maybe you had better come" was all he said. Her heart sank. Martin drove them the thirty-four miles from Youngstown to Ravenna in twenty minutes. Sarah still had paint all over her fingers and clothes. The whole time they feared turning on the car radio. "I expected the worst," Martin later said. They reached the hospital in Ravenna at 4:30 p.m. A policeman—assuming they had already been informed—said, "Do you want to identify the body now?" "Is she wearing a gold ring with a blue stone?," Sarah asked. Yes, he said softly. She collapsed into a wheelchair. Martin cried on a Catholic priest's shoulder. "Dear God, Dear God. She's our daughter," he sobbed. His brother came and drove them back to Youngstown. It rained but "there was a rainbow all the way home," remembered Martin. "We drove right towards this rainbow like it was created by God to show he was over us, like a sign from heaven." Sandy was buried the following rainy afternoon in the Jewish cemetery in Youngstown.

The Scheuers covered the mirror over the mantle of their living room with a cloth, a Jewish custom when death occurs, and lit a red candle, a symbol of mourning, on a table. Sandy's death crushed her parents. "What greater anguish is there, than the thought that [life] should lead her into the path of a bullet, shot thru her lovely neck?," Martin wrote. "We are heartbroken," he told a friend six weeks after the shooting, "and it is still as bad as the first day when it happened." Sarah could only stare down at the living room carpet and mumble, "I just don't understand."

She and Martin were convinced a guardsman deliberately targeted Sandy. "We were so embittered," he said. They even wondered if anti-Semitism was somehow involved. "Maybe 1 percent of the crowd was Jewish," said Martin. "Why were 75 percent of those killed Jewish?" Hard, too, were the hate letters they received. The writers' cold cruelty shocked and deeply wounded them: "Now you know what kind of a daughter you had—just a plain *communist*, destructive, riot-making person. *Nothing American* about her. . . . You should be happy & glad that she is gone." "You want to KNOW who really killed your girl?" another asked. "GO TAKE A LONG, LONG LOOK in the mirror. . . . BLAME yourself, lousy parents, YOU KILLED THAT GIRL. I dare you to deny it."

Vicious gossip and rumors swirled around Youngstown in the weeks that followed. "Heard the Scheuer girl organized all the trouble at Kent State," went the talk at a local barbershop. "Yeah, she traveled around the state, sold drugs, and stirred up the kids. She deserved to be shot." A city councilman announced at a public meeting that "instead of four people getting shot down, if 4,004 got shot down a lot of this bullshit would stop." Sarah went to confront the city councilman, but he wasn't in. The clerk told her all the students should have been killed. "My daughter was a special person who was not involved in any of the demonstrations," Martin told a reporter, "yet in the press, she was called a communist. I left Germany to guarantee that my daughters could live in a country with freedom. It doesn't make sense. The pain will always be there." When the local newspaper published a story sympathetic to Sandy, hundreds of people canceled their subscriptions. "The grief in my chest is like a rock," Sarah lamented to friends. "What is the matter with people?"

Chapter 7

AFTERMATH AND
INVESTIGATIONS

News of the Kent State shooting spread rapidly across the country and around the world. In London, the British Broadcasting Corporation interrupted its regular evening television programming with an announcement of the shooting, and the next morning British newspapers made it the headline story. In New York, the Wall Street stock market suffered its worst daily loss since the assassination of President Kennedy. In Washington, D.C., "grim-faced White House aides, haunted by memories of the domestic violence that erupted after the assassination of Martin Luther King, Jr., two years earlier, clustered around the chattering ticker-tape machines in [press secretary] Ron Ziegler's office as the ugly story unfolded," recounted presidential special counsel Charles Colson. In the oak-paneled West Wing mess that evening, "I looked around the crowded room," Colson wrote. "Like a scene from a stop-action camera nothing was moving" as officials stared at a color television displaying images of the tragedy. "Dinner plates were untouched, red-jacketed stewards stood frozen in place, White House staffers sat in stunned silence." Their boss, National Security Advisor Henry Kissinger, later wrote that the shooting left Washington "shell-shocked" and created "a shock wave that brought the nation and its leadership close to psychological exhaustion." Attorney General John Mitchell felt "sickened and saddened" by the shooting but refrained from public comment for fear it would prejudice the rights of those potentially indicted.

President Nixon was "very disturbed" when his chief of staff, Bob Haldeman, brought him the news. He was "afraid his [Cambodia] decision set it off and that is the cause of the demonstration there," Haldeman wrote in his diary. The White House issued a statement. "The president shares the sadness of the parents involved and that of all Americans over their unnecessary deaths. This should remind us all that when dissent turns to violence, it invites tragedy." Nixon "kept after me all the rest of the day for more facts," noted Haldeman.

Privately, Nixon was deeply shaken. An aide "had never seen him appear so physically exhausted." "I could not get the photographs out of my mind," Nixon later wrote. "I could not help thinking about the families, suddenly receiving the news that their children were dead because they had been shot in a campus demonstration." "I thought of my own daughters," of them "learning to talk and to walk, and their first birthdays, and the trips we took together, getting them through college and then—whoosh—all gone." "Those few days after Kent State were among the darkest of my presidency. I felt utterly dejected."

On May 6, the president sat down in the family quarters of the White House and handwrote letters of condolence on light-green stationary with the presidential seal to the parents of each of the slain students. To Art and Doris Krause, he hoped they could "take comfort from the sympathy the entire nation feels." To Martin and Sarah Scheuer, he stressed that "as parents of two daughters, Mrs. Nixon and I feel especially keenly the loss of one so young, so happy, so much a source of joy to her friends and so full of promises of life ahead." To Lou and Florence Schroeder, he acknowledged that "certainly nothing can lessen the extent of your tragic loss, but I hope that the heartfelt sympathy of so many across the nation can in some measure ease it. . . . You have been, and will be, continually in our thoughts and prayers." To Elaine Miller Holstein, his words of condolence rang hollow. "Nixon acts as if the kids had it coming. But shooting into a crowd of students—*that* is violence," she told the press.

Nixon's domestic policy chief, John Ehrlichman, phoned Art Krause and told him that "there will be a complete investigation" by a blue-ribbon commission. "Are you sure about that?" asked Art. "Mr. Krause, I promise you there will be no whitewash," Ehrlichman replied. Yet Nixon had helped set the stage for the tragedy. Labeling protestors "bums" had been "foolish rhetorical self-indulgence," as *The Economist* noted. His inflammatory words, combined with his repeated "assurances that peace was on the way," had contributed to the "outburst of rage" at Kent State. According to Bob Haldeman, Nixon "obviously realize[d]—but won't openly admit—that his 'bums' remark [was] very harmful."

Nixon told a press conference on May 8 that he understood how student protestors felt. "They are trying to say they want peace," he said. "They are trying to say they want to stop the killing. They are trying to say that they want an end to the draft. They are trying to say that we ought to get out of Vietnam. I agree with everything that they are trying to accomplish." That night, "agitated and uneasy as the events of the last few weeks raced through my mind" and unable to sleep, Nixon decided to talk with protestors gathering on the Mall for a national day of protest—his way of reaching out to close the gap with the young. Nixon left the White House in the early morning hours for a short drive to the Lincoln Memorial. He struggled to connect with the drowsy but astonished students he encountered there. "They were not unfriendly," he later wrote. He wanted to tell them not to let their hatred of the war—which "I could well understand"—become hatred of their country and everything it stood for. Instead, the socially awkward Nixon rambled on about subjects like sports and international travel. "I hope it was because he was tired, but most of what he was saying was absurd," a Syracuse University student who talked with him told a reporter. "Here we had come from a university that's completely uptight, on strike, and when we told him where we were from, he talked about the football team."

Nixon instructed his acid-tongued vice president, Spiro Agnew, to "avoid any remarks regarding students." But three days after the shooting, Agnew spoke about the shooting with uncharacteristic thoughtfulness in a television interview. Agnew maintained that the guardsmen's youth helped to explain their actions. He added that "one or two may have lost control" and "responded with far more force than they should have." What happened had been murder, "but not first degree" murder, because there was "no premeditation but simply an over-response in the heat of anger."

Democrats reacted much more critically. "Four American students lie dead, slain in the heart of middle America by the violent temper of our society," declared Senator Edward Kennedy of Massachusetts. "Who of us," he asked, "seeing American troops in Ohio fire wildly into a crowd of students, does not also see My Lai, with its defenseless Vietnamese civilians cut down by American troops?" Kennedy's Democratic colleague, Senator Stephen Young of Ohio, was even more outspoken. A longtime, vocal critic of the Ohio National Guard, Young chastised "trigger-happy" guardsmen for "murder[ing]" four students. Guard commander "Tough Tony" Del Corso responded by calling Young "a senile old liar," to which Young replied, "My father told me, 'Never get into a spraying contest with a skunk.'"

Beyond the Washington Beltway, popular reaction split between the America of "Love It or Leave It" bumper stickers and the "Amerika" spray-painted on campus walls by student radicals. The former viewed the shooting as a predictable and justifiable consequence of disobeying a lawful order. The latter viewed it as deliberate, murderous repression of dissent. These differing reactions reflected a country torn between opposing outlooks, a profound dislocation in the American system. Predictably and regrettably, both sides rushed to judgment.

To those on the Right, the shooting represented a grimly satisfying, overdue "law and order" response to years of student unrest. They blamed the victims and believed the guardsmen had not reacted harshly enough. Four students dead in Ohio? More than a dozen young American servicemen who hadn't dodged the draft died in Vietnam every day. A Gallup poll found that 58 percent of Americans blamed the students; only 11 percent blamed the National Guard. Ohio National Guard headquarters received 10,089 letters in the weeks after the shooting; only 454 were critical—a ratio of 22 to 1. Conservative Kent State students spread malicious rumors that Allison Krause had been "the campus whore," that her body had been found ravaged by syphilis, that "when they got her to the hospital, they found she was carrying hand grenades," and that she had met with Communists a week before the shooting. One student's mother "had a neighbor who actually said to her that if the National Guard could shoot into a crowd of three hundred people and only kill four, they should be on a target range." When another student returned home after the shooting, his mother told him that "it would have been a good thing if all of them had been shot." "Mom," said the student, "that's me you're talking about." "It would still have been better for the country if they had all been mowed down," she again replied.

"You can't believe the atmosphere in this town right now—pure, unadulterated HATE," observed a resident of Kent. "The general opinion is that they had it coming and it's too bad there were only four." One middle-aged woman interviewed at random on the street said, "I'm sorry they didn't kill more. They were warned. They knew what was happening and they should have moved out." Some townspeople raised four fingers when they passed each other, a silent signal that meant "At least we got four of them." The local *Record-Courier* received one hundred eighty-eight letters in the weeks following the shooting; all but two condemned the protestors or praised the guard; eleven openly approved the killings. Attorney Guy Showalter spoke for many Kent residents when he said, "We feel that the guard did exactly what they were sent to do: to keep law and order. Frankly, if I'd been faced with the same situation and had a submachine gun, there would not have been fourteen [sic] shot, there probably would have been one hundred forty of them dead and that's what they need." And then there was the middle-aged woman whom guardsman Mike Delany encountered downtown just hours after the shooting. "How are things going?" she said. "Haven't you heard?" Delany said. "Oh yes. How did it go?" "Well, you know that four kids were killed up there today." "Yes," she said. "You should have killed one hundred fifty of them. That would show the little bastards."

When the 107th Armored Cavalry chaplain Major John Simons visited guard headquarters in Columbus the morning after the shooting, a guardsman told him "a lot of callers are telling us to go ahead and kill four more kids today." That afternoon (it was primary election day in Ohio), Simons was leaving a voting booth in his fatigues when a big, beefy Teamster came up, slapped him on the back, and said, "As far as I'm concerned, you guys can go back to Kent and kill some more students, that's what the country needs."

A week later, Simons spoke to a Kiwanis Club luncheon in the conservative Cleveland suburb of Parma (where 1968 right-wing populist presidential candidate George Wallace had gotten his largest vote in the state). Simons did not mince his words. They resonate powerfully across the years:

> I am sure that some of you in this room wanted us to kill more. . . . The younger generation is naïve, life is not that simple, but [their] elders run from change by placing the responsibility for every rocky event on some Communist conspiracy. The older generation that wields power now has sold out to its fear of Communism. Perhaps the middle generation can gain the power and achieve the maturity which is not afraid of criticism or change. If we do not, life will go on as usual— there will be more Kents and Jacksons and Vietnams and Cambodias and with each new horror the solid middle America will become smaller and smaller until there is nothing left but two unspeaking and unspeakable extremes tearing the guts out of this great country. If you are part of those extremes, get lost. I hope you see Kent as an avoidable tragedy, not something you secretly longed for. Four young lives were lost that day. . . . Those lives were irretrievable.

Even before Simons finished speaking, people in the audience stood up and walked out. Around this time, a CBS reporter overheard General Robert Canterbury tell someone that Simons needed to be "shut up."

Nothing revealed the vicious hatred that the shooting evoked among those on the Right more vividly than a letter the Schroeders received in the weeks after their son Bill's death:

> Mr. and Mrs. Schroeder,
> There's nothing better than a *dead*, destructive, riot-making *communist*, and that's what your son was, if not he would have stayed away

like a good *American* would do. Now you know what a goody-goody son you had. They should all be shot, then we'd have a better U.S.A. to live in. Be thankful he is gone. Just another *communist.*

To those on the Left, the shooting stirred demands for revenge. When Alan Canfora returned to his off-campus apartment in Kent with a bandaged wrist, one of his roommates, Whitey Ward—a Vietnam vet—opened his buckskin jacket to reveal a loaded Luger pistol in a concealed shoulder holster. Ward said, "Uncle Sam taught me how to kill. They got four of us and I'm going to get four of them." Canfora told Ward to calm down. Another Kent State student, former Green Beret Ron Arbaugh, told a reporter that "I felt like grabbing the first guardsman I could find and beating the guy's head in."

After the shooting, vengeful antiwar activists publicly threatened National Guardsmen and promised to "even the score." "I tried to think of scenarios that we could come up with that would get four National Guardsmen shot," remembered one Kent State student enraged by May 4. A group of students tailed guardsman B. J. Long, who had been on Blanket Hill but had not fired, one night with their high-beam headlights trained on him. "I carried a pistol and a sawed-off, double-barrel shotgun in my car," Long said. Fed up with the intimidation and harassment, Long stopped his car, got out, and confronted those who had been following him. They backed off and he never saw them again. When Long returned to work the week after the shooting, his supervisor said, "You ain't got a job here. You're fired." Barry Morris, one of the guardsmen who fired into the crowd, received telephoned threats to burn down his house, blow up his car, run him over in the street, shoot him, and burn down his workplace. Another guardsman who fired into the crowd, Jim Pierce, had his family members' lives threatened and had to move several times as a result of the threats.

Across the country, the shooting radicalized moderate students and moved radicals toward violence. Alienation from "the system" intensified. "The overflow of emotion seems barely containable," observed the *Washington Post* on May 6. Students began to wonder if open season had been declared on them. This led to the first nationwide student strike in U.S.

history, with nearly 4,500,000 participants representing every state of the Union, many of them carrying banners that read, "REMEMBER KENT." The strike forced the closure of more than five hundred schools. California governor Ronald Reagan ordered the shutdown of all twenty-eight state colleges and universities. Demonstrations broke out at four out of five campuses that remained open, many marked by brutal clashes between students and law enforcement. Militants occupied buildings and bombed ROTC facilities from coast to coast at such a rate that governors in Kentucky, Michigan, Ohio—even conservative South Carolina—declared all campuses within their state in a state of emergency.* On May 10, George Winne, Jr., a former ROTC member and son of a U.S. Navy captain, ignited a pile of gasoline-soaked rags in his lap as he sat in the main plaza of the University of California, San Diego, next to a sign that read, "In God's name, end this war!" Winne died ten hours later in the hospital. On May 14, white policemen and state troopers in Mississippi opened fire on unarmed African American students at Jackson State University, killing two and injuring twelve. The New Yorker called it "the most critical week this nation has endured in more than a century." In Boston, twenty thousand angry students forced the lowering of the statehouse flag on the Common. In New York, militants threatened to bring the city to a stop by blocking bridges, tunnels, and highways.

In Washington, D.C., more than one hundred thousand protestors gathered on the fifty-two-acre Ellipse south of the White House grounds. Five thousand six hundred soldiers in combat gear took up position in government buildings. The 82nd Airborne Division deployed in the basement of the Old Executive Office Building next to the White House. "I went down

* ROTC buildings damaged or destroyed after the Kent State shooting included those at Brooklyn Polytechnic, SUNY Buffalo, University of California (Berkeley and Davis), Case Western Reserve, City College of New York, Colorado College, DePauw, Hobart, Idaho, Indiana, Kentucky, Loyola (Chicago), Maryland, Michigan, Michigan State, Missouri, Nevada, North Carolina, Ohio, Oregon State, Princeton, Rutgers, San Francisco State, Seton Hall, Southern Illinois, Virginia, Washington, Wisconsin, and Yale. On August 24, 1970, an explosion tore through Wisconsin's Army Mathematics Research Center, the site of frequent antiwar protests, killing graduate student Robert Fassnacht.

just to talk to some of the guys and walk among them," recalled Charles
Colson. "They were lying on the floor leaning on their packs and their helmets and their cartridge belts and their rifles cocked and you're thinking,
'This can't be the United States of America. This is not the greatest free
democracy in the world. This is a nation at war with itself.'" Unlike guard
commanders at Kent State, the Pentagon ordered that soldiers' use of force
be kept to "the absolute minimum" and "all efforts should be nonlethal."
The Secret Service parked a double ring of District of Columbia Transit
buses around the White House grounds to prevent them from being overrun. Helmeted riot police stood behind the buses. A young woman on the
Ellipse spit at a cop and screamed, "Fucking pig! Filthy swine!" Later she
handed a flower to another cop and said, "It's not your fault, but what do
you expect us to do?" After nightfall, some of the demonstrators took to
the streets, breaking windows, blocking traffic, and confronting police,
resulting in more than four hundred arrests.

Nixon's advisor on campus unrest, Vanderbilt University chancellor
Alexander Heard, said, "The general effect of May was one of radicalizing
as well as politicizing student opinion across the board." Columbia University president William McGill called it "the most disastrous month of
May in the history of American higher education." After seeing photos
of the shooting in *Life* magazine, Neil Young wrote the lyrics to a new
song that began "Tin soldiers and Nixon coming" and had the refrain
"Four dead in Ohio." When Crosby, Stills, Nash & Young recorded "Ohio"
a few weeks later, David Crosby broke down in tears at the end of the session. Rush-released, the song got heavy radio play and became a protest
anthem. A Harris survey found 58 percent of students believed the United
States had become a highly repressive society, intolerant of dissent.

These conflicting reactions collided head-on in lower Manhattan on Friday, May 8—the day after Jeff Miller's memorial service—in what became
known as the Hard-Hat Riot. Federal Hall, an imposing nineteenth-century
Greek Revival building fronting a large plaza in the narrow corridors of
the Wall Street district, was the site of an antiwar demonstration early
that afternoon and drew more than a thousand student protestors, many
of whom had attended Jeff Miller's memorial service on Thursday. They

waved Black Panther, Cuban, and Vietcong flags, carried placards that read "I'M A BUM FOR PEACE," "KENT-BODIA," and "IS MY LAI IN OHIO?," and shouted "One-two-three-four, we don't want your fucking war!" "Two-four-six-eight, we don't want your fascist state!" "We're gonna stop Wall Street tomorrow," one speaker screamed through a bullhorn. "We're gonna stop New York City on Monday. And we're going to bring the whole country down with us next week!"

Longshoremen and hard-hat workers at the nearby World Trade Center under construction had grown fed up with antiwar protests. Many had sons or their neighbors had sons who had been wounded or killed in Vietnam. They were short-tempered when it came to reverence for the American flag. To them, "one could disapprove of the war but feel duty-bound, because citizenship was not only about what it gave you, but also about what you gave it. And that meant in wartime, to the old-fashioned, a willingness to give everything." Family, flag, and country—that is what mattered. U.S.

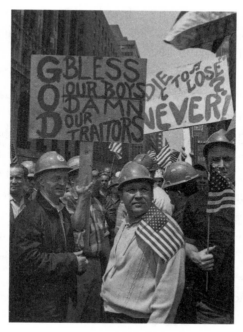

Hard-hat workers confront antiwar
demonstrators, New York City, May 8, 1970.

Army veteran Joe Kelly lived in a modest house on Staten Island and built elevators at the World Trade Center. During his lunch break, Kelly joined hundreds of others wearing steel-toed boots and hard hats decaled with American flags and waving hammers and wrenches. They marched in light rain over to Federal Hall chanting, "U-S-A, all the way! U-S-A, all the way!" "Love it or leave it! Love it or leave it!" They would take care of those "long-hairs." "There was a swagger to the crowd, built of a kind of joy at being what participants saw as the first counter-response from a long-suffering middle America. And this joy could quickly shift to anger at the sight of a long-haired dissenter."

When the hard hats reached Federal Hall, they set upon protestors, who screamed, "Mother-fucking fascists!" Fists and lead pipes started to fly. Policemen in baby-blue helmets looked on impassively from Federal Hall's marble steps as broad-shouldered tradesmen savagely punched and kicked student protestors. When an elderly woman near the steps shouted at a worker to stop kicking a young man on the ground, she was knocked down and spat on. The hard hats chased youths through the canyons of the Financial District in a wild melee that left more than seventy people seriously injured.

Encouraged by the crowd and the pointedly disinterested police, the hard hats then stormed City Hall, where liberal Republican mayor John Lindsay had ordered the flag lowered to half-mast in honor of the four killed at Kent State. One group of rampaging hard hats headed for the mayor's office to force city employees to raise the flag back up. The other group headed for nearby Pace College. Shouting "Kill those long-haired bastards!," they stormed into a campus building with a huge white banner draped out of a window that read "VIETNAM? CAMBODIA? KENT STATE? WHAT NEXT?," smashed windows with crowbars, overturned desks, and clubbed any student they could get their hands on. As students fled in panic, the hard hats grabbed two professors, whom they beat with their fists. The wail of ambulances continued long after the hard hats had disbanded for celebrations and back slapping. Nixon later invited the riot's organizer, construction trade union leader William Brennan, to the White House, where Brennan gifted the smiling president with a hard hat. Brennan was later appointed secretary of Labor.

Polls revealed that 40 percent of Americans sympathized with the hard hats compared with 24 percent who took the side of the antiwar protestors, though a significant 23 percent supported neither. But when asked if it was right or wrong for the hard hats to attack the antiwar protestors, the public thought it wrong by a margin of 53 percent to 31 percent.

The Kent State shooting led to five different investigations—by the FBI, the Ohio State Highway Patrol, the Ohio Bureau of Criminal Identification and Investigation, the Ohio National Guard's inspector general, and the presidentially appointed Scranton Commission.

The morning after the shooting, senior Justice Department officials directed the FBI to begin an investigation. FBI director J. Edgar Hoover assigned more than three hundred agents to the task. The White House urged Hoover to move quickly because Kent State was "awfully hot." Hoover personally believed "the students invited and got what they deserved," but he did not interfere with or obstruct the bureau's investigation. An army of FBI agents descended on Kent State, filling Memorial Gymnasium with clerks and typists as agents interviewed students and town residents. Other agents fanned out across Ohio and states as far away as California and Florida, seeking out anyone associated with the events of May 1–4. President Nixon instructed Hoover to send him "same-day copies of all field reports relative to the Kent State investigation." He wanted the reports to be "unabridged—not boiled down or condensed."

General Canterbury ordered guardsmen to cooperate with investigators but not to discuss the shooting with anyone else. Those who fired on May 4 were interviewed by FBI agents without a lawyer present, though the guardsmen were advised of their rights and none of them asked for legal representation. The agents did not tell the guardsmen they were investigating possible civil rights violations and knew prosecutions could result from the interviews; they told the guardsmen they were only trying to find out what happened and how to deal better with a similar situation in the future. Two young FBI agents interviewed Matt McManus in a small room at guard headquarters in Columbus. McManus arrived carrying his M-1 rifle and .45 caliber pistol. FBI agents were unaccustomed to interrogating people with weapons. One "was a young guy who acted very nervous," McManus remembered. "About halfway through the interrogation, he looked at me and said, 'Could you possibly take off your .45 and stand your rifle in the corner over there?' He was probably thinking, 'If this guy loses his temper and both weapons are loaded, . . .' I knew what he meant. I thought, 'I'd be nervous too.'" McManus quickly complied. Thereafter, guardsmen were ordered to leave their weapons at the barracks before being interviewed.

After six weeks, FBI field agents' findings were collected in a massive report totaling more than eight thousand pages divided into eight sections. The first section presented a detailed chronology of events. The second section focused on the burning of the ROTC building on Saturday night, May 2. The third section contained background information on the students killed and wounded—mostly interviews regarding the character and activities of the thirteen victims, much of it hearsay and rumor. The fourth section included autopsy and medical information such as statements from doctors who treated the injured students, the pathologists who conducted autopsies on those killed,[*] and autopsy photographs.[†] The fifth section consisted of hospital records. The sixth section contained statements of law enforcement officers concerning events in Kent from May 1 to 4, particularly the downtown rioting on Friday night. The seventh section listed information about "subversive organizations" at Kent State, including the identity of FBI informers and intelligence-gathering techniques.[‡] The eighth and final section focused on the "Kent

---

[*]   Robinson Memorial Hospital coroner Dr. Robert Arnold (Krause); Dr. Robert Glasgow (Scheuer); and Summit County pathologist Dr. A. H. Kyriakides (Miller and Schroeder).

[†]   "The autopsy photos hit one with a deep tragic feeling," said Joseph Rhodes, a member of the Scranton Commission who saw them. "Allison Krause was such a beautiful girl and she is dead with a gaping hole in her left side." Notes of interview with Joseph Rhodes, CTP, Box 64B, M4C, KSUL.

[‡]   This section of the FBI report remains largely classified.

State Four"—that is, campus radicals Ric Erickson, Howie Emmer, Colin Neiburger, and Jeff Powell—who had been released from the Portage County jail on May 1.

FBI director Hoover forwarded the voluminous report to the Justice Department's Criminal Division. On June 19, Criminal Division deputy chief Robert Murphy drafted a six-page memo distilling the report. Titled "Kent State: Preliminary Conclusions and Recommendations," Murphy's memo concluded:

- "Guardsmen were undoubtedly angered by the actions of the students and were frustrated in their inability to either contain or disperse them."
- "The Guard was not surrounded and could have continued in the direction in which they were going."
- "Only a few students were within 30 yards of the Guard—none was closer than 20 yards."
- "Even if the Guard believed they were being charged by the students, other alternatives—specifically bayonets and a limited supply of tear gas—were available."
- "Some National Guardsmen intended to, and did, summarily punish members of the crowd by shooting at them."
- Brigadier General Canterbury's decisions reflected "foolhardiness and negligence"—but stupendously poor judgment was not a crime but a tragedy.

Murphy passed along his memo to the division chief, Jerris Leonard, who used it as the basis of a longer, thirty-five-page "general background summary" for Attorney General John Mitchell. Leonard's general background summary was leaked to the *Akron Beacon Journal*, which published the following excerpts on July 23:

- "The Guardsmen were not surrounded. They could have easily continued going in the direction which they had been going."
- "The lives of the members of the Guard were not in danger and it was not a shooting situation."

- Guardsmen "fired after they heard others fire or because after the shooting began, they assumed an order to fire in the air had been given."
- There was "some reason to believe that the claim by the National Guard that their lives were endangered by the students was fabricated subsequent to the event."

President Nixon phoned FBI director Hoover the next morning to complain about the leak. "The president was quite disturbed about the article," Hoover told aides later that day, "and directed me to take steps to have it 'knocked down.'" "I told him I would see that this was done."

The Ohio State Highway Patrol submitted its report on the Kent State shooting to Portage County prosecutor Ron Kane on July 23. The State Highway Patrol report put the shooting in the context of events beginning with the unrest in downtown Kent on the night of May 1, followed by the burning of the ROTC building the following night, then the sit-in and violent encounters on Sunday night, May 3. It included testimony from several Ohio National Guardsmen but few Kent State students. Unlike the U.S. Justice Department, the Ohio State Highway Patrol placed primary blame on the protestors rather than the National Guardsmen.

The Ohio Bureau of Criminal Identification and Investigation report contained background material on the 1969 disturbances at Kent State, a chronology of the events of May 1–4, 1970, and autopsy photographs of the slain students. The bureau concentrated, however, on the forensics of the shooting. Its investigators charted the location and numbers of guardsmen and students from the time protestors began gathering on the Commons to the moment the firing began. The report's most significant feature was a topographical analysis that integrated elevations and distances between the knoll from where the guardsmen fired and the impact points of the bullets. The topographical analysis revealed, for example, that Doug Wrentmore, shot in the parking lot about eighty-five yards away from the Pagoda, was twenty-three feet vertically below the level of the Pagoda when struck, and Scott MacKenzie, shot at the construction site adjacent to the parking lot, more than two hundred yards from the Pagoda, was twenty-five feet vertically below the level of the Pagoda when struck. This analysis raised two tragic possibilities: guardsmen who fired over the heads of approaching students may have killed or wounded those further back and lower down in the parking lot; and guardsmen who fired at the ground may have inadvertently struck students because some of the high-velocity bullets likely tunneled through the ground and sped onward.

The Ohio National Guard inspector general, Colonel Jean Peltier, wrote a report "For Official Use Only." It stated, wrongly, that fifty-one shots were fired and that it was "extremely doubtful" an order to fire was given but noted that multiple witnesses "heard one or two sounds" of "preliminary low caliber fire" before the volley. This, combined with the assertion that Scott MacKenzie was "definitely struck with a non-military bullet" (later disproven), strongly suggested that someone other than a guardsman had started the shooting. Peltier did not seek to determine who fired indiscriminately and discipline them because the Ohio National Guard's JAG office told General Del Corso to let civil authorities address the issue.

Colonel Peltier also criticized press coverage of the event, writing "media of all types has played down or ignored the injuries, threats, and abuse of the National Guard, while at the same time distorting the image of the rioters, e.g. printing high school pictures of the deceased students rather than how they appeared in college." Peltier concluded by effectively justifying the shooting: "Under the National Guard doctrine that in the absence of unit integrity and control, the individual soldier must determine by the exercise of reasonable judgment when his life is sufficiently in jeopardy to require the use of gunfire to protect himself, the guardsmen used proper means to defend themselves"—without addressing the core issue: the absence of unit integrity and fire-control discipline, which was the responsibility of his superior, General Robert Canterbury.

Finally, there was the Presidential Commission on Campus Unrest, popularly known as the Scranton Commission after its chairman, former Pennsylvania Republican governor William Scranton. Its staff interviewed hundreds of students, faculty, university administrators, law enforcement personnel, and townspeople. They also collected audio and visual evidence including photos, films, and audio recordings of the shooting. The commission did not seek to fix blame or legal culpability for the shooting but to explain why the shooting occurred and what lessons could be learned to prevent such a tragedy from ever happening again. The commission was granted subpoena power and could have used it to make public the four other investigative reports, but it chose not to do so. It also chose not to seek testimony from guardsmen to avoid prejudicing any possible future prosecutions.

The commission had at its disposal the findings of the 1968 National Advisory Commission on Civil Disorders, popularly known as the Kerner Commission, which had investigated urban riots in Newark, New Jersey, and Detroit, Michigan, during the long, hot summer of 1967. The Kerner Commission had faulted National Guardsmen for being jumpy and undisciplined and warned that a loaded rifle was a dangerously inappropriate tool for riot control. "It is a lethal weapon with ammunition designed to kill at great distances. Rifle bullets ricochet. They may kill or maim innocent people." The Kerner Commission had also warned that guardsmen with little military training and no combat experience might panic or misunderstand orders. A member of the Kerner Commission told the press, "Practically no National Guard force in the United States today is getting enough training to enable them to provide the quality of performance required in [such] tough situations." Ohio National Guard leadership failed to heed the Kerner Commission's warnings. If they had, the Kent State tragedy might have been averted.

General Canterbury testified publicly before the Scranton Commission on August 20 before a packed audience in Kent State's University Auditorium. Canterbury's lack of leadership, dismal judgment, and failure to control his men contributed centrally to the bloody tragedy, but he sought to deflect criticism by distorting the truth and arousing animosity toward student protestors. He asserted that the two students bayoneted on Sunday night, May 3, "tried to climb a fence, fell back off the fence, and into the soldiers with bayonets." He claimed Kent State's police chief, Donald Schwartzmiller, had been in charge on May 4, when in fact Canterbury ordered campus policeman Harold Rice to read the Riot Act to students, and the Ohio State Highway Patrol's Major Donald Manly had relieved Canterbury, not Schwartzmiller, of command on the scene after the shooting.

Canterbury also shifted responsibility for banning the noontime rally to university president Robert White. The general claimed to have no knowledge of guardsmen kneeling and pointing their rifles on the practice field—"I did not notice it at the time"—when in fact the order came from him. "Brigadier General Canterbury did not hesitate to throw his men under the bus to try to explain his action that day," Matt McManus later wrote in a letter to the author. "He referred to us as 'these people.' . . . He was like a Teflon pan burning everything to ashes while staying squeaky clean himself. He didn't hesitate to ricochet his own responsibility back onto the men under his command." It is hard to avoid the conclusion that Canterbury misled the Scranton Commission by creating a version of events that protected himself from legal liability.

The Scranton Commission issued its report five months after the shooting. The report opened by stressing the shooting's "roots in divisions of American society as deep as any since the Civil War." "Campus unrest reflects and increases a more profound crisis in the nation as a whole. . . . If this trend continues, if this crisis of understanding endures, the very survival of the nation will be threatened. A nation driven to use the weapons of war upon its youth is a nation on the edge of chaos. A nation that has lost the allegiance of part of its youth is a nation that has lost part of its future." And in a foreshadowing of the future, it warned that "we are in grave danger of losing what is common among us through growing intolerance of opposing views on issues and of diversity itself."

Regarding the shooting itself, the report noted that while "the actions of some students were violent and criminal and those of some others were dangerous, reckless, and irresponsible," "the indiscriminate firing of rifles into a crowd of students and the deaths that followed were unnecessary, unwarranted, and inexcusable." "Even if the guardsmen faced danger, it was not a danger that called for lethal force." "There was inadequate fire-control discipline on Blanket Hill. The Kent State tragedy must mark the last time that loaded rifles are issued as a matter of course to guardsmen confronting student demonstrators." The commission recommended that guardsmen be equipped with nonlethal tools—something between tear gas and live bullets—and that deadly force be used only as an "absolute last resort."

———

A month after the shooting, General Canterbury filed an after-action report with National Guard headquarters in Washington, D.C. The final two sections of the after-action report concerned "Problem Areas and Lessons Learned" and "Recommendations." Beside both, Canterbury wrote "None."

Chapter 8

THE CRIMINAL TRIAL

The Kent State shooting led to a decade-long, emotionally charged legal battle involving hundreds of witnesses, thousands of pages of depositions and court testimony, and numerous appeals all the way up to the U.S. Supreme Court. This legal battle became, in the words of one scholar, "one of the longest, costliest, and most complex set of courtroom struggles in American history." It culminated in three trials—one criminal and two civil. These trials helped to illuminate what happened on May 4, 1970, but they did not answer all the lingering questions. And in the end, no one was held accountable for the death of four students and the wounding of nine others.

On May 21, 1970, U.S. attorney general John Mitchell announced that the Justice Department would investigate the shooting. On June 25, Jerris Leonard, assistant attorney general for civil rights, traveled to Ravenna, Ohio, and met with Portage County prosecutor Ron Kane. At their meeting, Leonard stressed that it was the Justice Department's policy to defer to state authorities in lieu of federal prosecution. He pledged the Justice Department's support for a local grand jury investigation. Afterward, Attorney General Mitchell directed the FBI to turn over to Kane the information and evidence it had collected and to provide a copy of its report to Ohio attorney general Paul Brown.

Fortified by this support, on July 16 Kane asked Attorney General

Brown to fund the creation of a Portage County grand jury to investigate the shooting because the county lacked sufficient financial resources to do so. A close friend of Governor Jim Rhodes whom Rhodes later appointed to the Ohio Supreme Court, Brown declined Kane's request. Then, on August 3, Brown announced the creation of a special *state* grand jury to be led by former Allen County prosecutor Robert Balyeat and private attorney Seabury Ford. Rural Allen County was on the opposite side of the state and one of only five Ohio counties carried by right-wing presidential candidate Barry Goldwater in 1964. Ford chaired the Portage County Republican Party, had served in the Ohio National Guard's 107th Armored Cavalry Regiment, had a Confederate battle flag hanging on his office wall, and kept a Colt .45 pistol prominently displayed on his desk. When it became known that Ford was a former guardsman, Brown called it "irrelevant." Before the special state grand jury even convened, Brown publicly declared, "On the evidence we have available—and we have as much as anyone—I don't see any evidence upon which a grand jury would indict any guardsmen." Balyeat and Ford nonetheless touted the special state grand jury as "an effort at complete impartiality." Governor Rhodes, through Brown, fixed things so that the special state grand jury would exonerate him and the guard, which he controlled, while throwing blame on the protestors. Ohio National Guard officer Major Harry Jones candidly told a federal grand jury, "If you have one man controlling both"—the Ohio National Guard and the special state grand jury—"I don't know how the people shot get justice."

Like all grand juries, this one met in secret, and prosecutors selected the witnesses and presented evidence to secure indictments of those they considered culpable. The special state grand jury was granted access to the Ohio State Highway Patrol report (which blamed the students) but not the FBI report nor the Justice Department summary of it (which blamed the Ohio National Guard)—even though Balyeat and Ford had received both. The grand jury visited the Kent State campus and subpoenaed more than three hundred witnesses. Balyeat and Ford asked blatantly leading questions. Student Terri West remembered: "They ask[ed] questions like, 'Do you think it's right for people to destroy other people's property?' 'Do you think it's right for people to burn buildings?' 'Do you think it's right for people to throw rocks and bottles at people?' I mean really, who's going to say, 'Yes, I think it's right for people to hurt other people?' It was so absurd." "Half a dozen [grand jurors] stood up and told me what a scum I was," recalled protestor Michael Erwin. "I remember telling my dad as we were leaving, 'They're trying to pin this on the students.'"

National Guardsmen, on the other hand, were pitched softball questions. Leon Smith was asked, "Did you have reason to believe that some serious personal bodily injury could have come to you?" Two guardsmen whom Balyeat and Ford did not subpoena were Major John Simons and Captain Raymond Srp. Simons had been interviewed twice by the FBI, testified before the Scranton Commission, and publicly described the killing and wounding of students by the guardsmen as unnecessary. Srp had been at the Pagoda and told the FBI, "Our lives were not in danger. It was not a shooting situation." When it came time to discuss indicting guardsmen, the special state grand jury considered only whether to indict Joe Lewis's admitted shooter, Larry Shafer. The grand jury voted 15–0 to let Shafer go and, instead, indicted Lewis.

The special state grand jury released its eighteen-page report in the tension-filled courtroom of Judge Edwin Jones of the Court of Common Pleas in Ravenna on October 16. Contradicting the conclusions reached by the Justice Department and the Scranton Commission, the special state grand jury chastised the "laxity, over-indulgence, and permissiveness" of Kent State officials for allowing "a vocal minority" of radicals "to seize control of the university campus." It asserted that university administrators' failure to control a radical minority and its inability to rid the campus of troublemakers had set the stage for the violence of May 4. It devoted paragraphs to the vulgarities chanted by the protestors that day but made no mention of the fatalities. It found that guardsmen "fired their weapons in the honest and sincere belief and under circumstances which would have logically caused them to believe that they would suffer serious bodily injury had they not done so"—effectively blaming the victims rather than those who shot them—and stated that "if the order to disperse had been heeded, there would not have been the consequences of that fateful day."

The report did note, however, that "the order to disperse the crowd on the Commons put the guard in an untenable and dangerous position with weapons inappropriate in dealing with campus disorders" and that "words alone are never sufficient to justify the use of lethal force." After the report's release, Ford violated the legal ban on public comment about the case by telling the press that events leading up to the shooting had been "Communist inspired" and that university officials were "softies" who had "wilted" under pressure. He told a reporter that "National Guardsmen on campus last May should have shot all the troublemakers." "The whole damn country is not going to quiet down until police are ordered to shoot to kill. Why didn't the guard shoot more of them?"

The special state grand jury's exoneration of the guardsmen, castigation of university administrators, and condemnation of the protestors resonated with many—probably a majority of—Ohioans. The victims and their families, on the other hand, were incredulous. "You mean you can get away with murder in this country?," Martin Scheuer fumed. "They were throwing abuse—not bullets. It's ridiculous. They cannot exonerate the National Guard after students are maimed for life and killed." Art Krause called the report a "childishly prejudicial finding" and "an obscene travesty of justice." New Haven, Connecticut, police chief James Ahern, who had served on the Scranton Commission, said the special state grand jury's exoneration of the guard was "inconsistent with the facts." Another commission member, Joseph Rhodes, Jr., labeled the special state grand jury a "kangaroo court." NBC Evening News co-anchor David Brinkley termed the special state grand jury's report "utterly absurd." "The National Guard managed to kill four students," Brinkley said, "and the grand jury blamed everyone but the National Guard." Ohio's Democratic U.S. senator Stephen Young went even further, condemning the report for having been "conceived in fraud and fakery" and an effort "to whitewash Governor James Rhodes for his abominable blunder in calling out the National Guard to police the campus of Kent State University." Former Johnson administration U.S. attorney general Ramsey Clark said that the special state grand jury, "ignoring constitutional rights to a fair trial unprejudiced by pretrial publicity, issued a scathing denunciation of students and university administration that was full of anger and hatred."

The bravest response came from Glenn Frank, the Kent State professor who had helped avert even more bloodshed on May 4. Frank had testified before the special state grand jury and therefore was legally constrained from speaking publicly about it. To do so risked contempt of court and jail time. Despite this, Frank broke the court order on silence by holding a press conference in which he said:

> Someone must sacrifice himself. I speak now in contempt of court, in contempt of the naïve and stupid conclusions of the grand jury . . . and in personal contempt for lawyer Ford for his lack of understanding. . . . Ford is a troublemaker. . . . He has made his statement[s] in order to convince people who do not know the facts that he is a law-and-order man who will crack down on anyone who disagrees with the system he represents. However, that should not allow a prosecutor to make what I consider to be a farce out of justice. . . . I cannot live with a conscience that permits people to say "they should have shot all" the troublemakers.

"I was misquoted," Ford shot back. "I never said I wanted anybody shot—certainly not for publication."

Instead of indicting guardsmen for shooting unarmed students, Balyeat and Ford indicted twenty-four current or former students (including Alan Canfora, his sister Chic, and Joe Lewis) and one faculty member for inciting the downtown riot on May 1 and torching the ROTC building on May 2. "They blamed us," one of the indicted students said, "for getting in the way of the bullets." "The ones they missed with bullets they got with indictments," quipped another. Unbeknownst to them, "it appeared to Balyeat at the outset of the proceeding that the grand jury was inclined to indict literally hundreds of students on charges including failure to obey a lawful order to disperse. He told the grand jury that this was neither practical nor desirable." Many Kent residents complained bitterly nonetheless, saying "two hundred or three hundred brats" should have been "sent away for twenty years." A survey published in the *Akron Beacon Journal* on October 18 revealed that 58 percent of Ohio high schoolers faulted the students rather than the guardsmen for the tragedy at Kent State.

Once the trials of the "Kent 25" got under way, it quickly became clear that prosecutors lacked sufficient evidence to convict them. Only three defendants were convicted or pleaded guilty;* the rest of the cases were dismissed. Alan Canfora accepted a plea bargain, received probation, and was barred from Kent for two and a half years. On January 28, 1971, U.S. district judge William Thomas of Cleveland ruled the special state grand jury report prejudicial and inflammatory and ordered it to be expunged from the record and physically destroyed. In his ruling, Judge Thomas chastised Rhodes and Brown for creating the special state grand jury and prosecutors Balyeat and Ford for allowing it to operate, in effect, as a regular jury by ascribing guilt. He also criticized Balyeat and Ford for claiming the witnesses they called "fairly represented every aspect, attitude, and point of view concerning the events" of May 4.

―――――――

Although Nixon aide John Ehrlichman had promised Art Krause there would be no whitewash, on August 13, 1971, Attorney General John Mitchell announced that the Justice Department would not prosecute any Ohio National Guardsmen. Mitchell made clear in his announcement that he agreed with the Scranton Commission's conclusion that the shooting was "unnecessary, unwarranted, and inexcusable," but he also made clear that "there is no credible evidence of a conspiracy between National Guardsmen to shoot students on the campus and no likelihood of successful prosecutions of individual guardsmen." "I personally regret having to reach this conclusion," he wrote the slain students' parents afterward, "but it is a conclusion which is based on a realistic and impartial consideration of the prosecutive potential of the incident."

―――――――

* Jerry Rupe was convicted of interfering with a fireman. Thomas Fogelsong and Larry Shub pled guilty to first-degree riot.

Mitchell's decision was based on legal reasoning laid out by Justice Department Criminal Division head prosecutor Robert Murphy and Criminal Division chief William O'Connor. In a memo six weeks after the shooting, Murphy wrote:

> There is no indication that the shooting on the part of the Guardsmen was planned in advance. Although the essence of a conspiracy, the agreement or understanding, need not be expressed or stated, we would have to prove that the Guardsmen came to a mutual understanding . . . to injure or intimidate the students in the exercise of their Constitutional rights. The law is clear that mere similarity of conduct is not sufficient to establish a conspiracy. We must show a partnership in criminal purposes. Given the spontaneous nature of the shooting, I do not believe we could prove a conspiracy existed among the Guardsmen.
>
> I do not believe the National Guardsmen who did not fire at all or who fired in the air or into the ground should be considered as potential defendants. The requisite specific intent is lacking. Similarly, no superior officer or state official should be considered as a subject. Although their conduct showed foolhardiness and negligence, such is not the stuff of which specific intent is made.
>
> . . . A drawback to seeking the redressing of this tragedy through a criminal trial is that the rules of evidence probably will preclude telling the complete story of the incident. For example, testimony showing the incompetence and foolhardiness of the Guard superiors legally may be irrelevant to the case and hence to be excluded.

O'Connor also recommended against prosecution in a separate memo the following spring:

> Youthful, poorly trained, ill-equipped, and poorly led National Guardsmen were placed in a confrontation with student elements engaged in protest of a national policy. . . . Command responsibility of the National Guard units was in the hands of an incompetent who was

later discharged. Live ammo was issued to troops who had not been properly trained for fire control, despite the statutory responsibility of the leadership of the Guard to insure such training in conforming to Department of Defense standards. . . . Those persons who should be held responsible for the situation cannot be tried under any federal criminal statute, and proof, beyond a reasonable doubt, is absent as to those individuals who shot demonstrators.

Mitchell's successor as attorney general, Richard Kleindienst, reaffirmed his predecessor's decision in June 1972, as did White House legal counsel Leonard Garment in a letter to the slain students' parents a month later:

> Willfulness or specific criminal intent or planned or purposeful conspiracy must be proved in order to support a federal indictment; there is still no evidence available to prove such a violation of the Federal criminal statutes. . . . There is not an official in this entire Administration, from the President and the Attorney General on down, who is indifferent to your own personal grief at the death and injury which occurred on that day in May two years ago. As John Mitchell said, the President's commission was right in terming the rifle fire as "unnecessary, unwarranted, and inexcusable." But there is still no evidence known to the Attorney General of a *federally* punishable conspiracy. . . . We can hope, however, that the nation will pay attention to the lessons of this tragedy and that nothing like it will ever happen again.

Politics likely played a part too, however. Nixon sought reelection as president that year, Ohio was a critical component of his Electoral College strategy, and polling revealed that most Ohioans supported the National Guard. The opposite was true nationwide. A Harris poll the year before found that 55 percent of Americans viewed the shooting as unjustified and repressive.

The Justice Department's decision not to prosecute any guardsmen left victims' families feeling baffled and betrayed. It was not the wording of the law that mattered to them but the human casualties of May 4. "We have tried not to pre-judge the case," the families declared in a public statement. "We have struggled to not let our feelings indict those who appeared to be responsible, for we knew that the judicial system would make such a determination. We had faith in the action that would ulti-mately be taken by the Department of Justice, and we had faith in the system of justice for which it is responsible. Now we know the Department of Justice will not act. It is inconceivable to us that this is so, particularly because its own investigative reports indicate that such action would have been fully appropriate."

The families' frustration over the lack of accountability for the shoot-ing was fed by an atmosphere of paranoid suspicion and distrust that had developed in the country in the aftermath of Vietnam and Watergate. This atmosphere led many of the victims and their families to assume ill intent—perhaps even a cover-up. Radicalized by what he considered a perversion of justice, Tom Grace told an interviewer around this time that "the only way to get justice is to pick up a gun." Art Krause sought justice not by picking up a gun but by continuing his struggle to make the legal system work. "I don't believe in breaking windows or burning buildings," he said. "I was born in Europe and I always looked up to America as a place where there was more justice than any other country in the world. The system can be made to work. There is no better system in the world." He fervently believed once the facts came out in court, it would become clear that poorly trained and undisciplined guardsmen uncontrolled by officers had used inappropriate and excessive force to quell what began as a peaceful protest. He couldn't undo what had been done, but he wanted to make sure it would never be done again. His wife, Doris, agreed. Alli-son "was only with us for nineteen years. And when we go to her grave, what do we say? Do we say, 'There is no justice, Allison, that no one cares that you are dead, Allison, that you were executed.' Or do we say, 'There is justice, Allison.' How can I grieve for her and not work for justice? The

only thing I can do for her is . . . to work, *not to cry*," Doris said, her voice
rising then breaking.

The Krauses decided to push publicly and push they did—hard. They
wrote letters to newspaper editors. They pleaded on radio and television for
further investigation into the shooting. They followed up every lead from
every source that might have a bearing on their quest. Their efforts, perhaps
inevitably, generated backlash. The most surprising was a proffered bribe-
cum-threat made by a prominent New York free speech attorney affiliated
with the American Civil Liberties Union (ACLU). A native Alabamian,
Morris Ernst had been educated in the east and had grown increasingly
conservative over the years, becoming friends with FBI director J. Edgar
Hoover and Dominican Republic dictator Rafael Trujillo. When Art Krause
called on Ernst at his Park Avenue apartment, Ernst told him, "You're going
to lose, you know that. So why go through all this?" "Mr. Krause, What is
your price? You want a million dollars? I can get you a million. And if you
don't play it right, you may not have a job much longer." "Old man, you are
dirtying me," Art replied. After the meeting, Art wrote down what Ernst
had said and mailed it to a friend "because I thought we were going to get
killed the next day."

The Krauses would not be bribed or intimidated into silence. Instead,
they sought to get other victims' families involved. They began by inviting Martin and Sarah Scheuer to their home. Although both couples were
Jewish and both had lost a daughter, there was tension and resentment
between them at first. The Scheuers blamed demonstrators for the shooting. "If your daughter hadn't been out there protesting," Sarah told Doris,
"my daughter would be alive." "No meeting with the Krauses could make
us feel better," Martin later confessed. "This kind of thing happened in
Germany in the thirties," he bitterly added. "I am full of hate." But he and
Sarah eventually came around.

Most other victims' families got involved too—everyone except Elaine
Miller. She was simply in too much pain. She refused to discuss what had
happened with anyone but her immediate family. Her attitude was, "If it
can't bring Jeff back, what's the use?" She desperately wanted to forget,

but she "couldn't get away from it." Everywhere she went, she saw the iconic photo of Mary Vecchio kneeling over Jeff's body and then it would all come flooding back. "Looking at the photo, it was impossible to believe he was dead" because she had seen Jeff "so many times alive lying face down that way as he woke up in the morning." In the summer of 1973, Elaine and her second husband, Artie Holstein, visited Amsterdam. The hippies camped in Vondelpark reminded her of Jeff and this made her cry. Afterward, they toured the Anne Frank House. "As we walked through the house and I read about the people who kept quiet and let it happen, I was terribly shaken." "The pain wasn't going to go away no matter how long I hid" from it. When she got home, she reached out to the other victims' families and began working with them.

The other holdout was Barry Levine, who felt only cynicism. He poured out his bitterness in a letter to Art. "You have more patience than I and will probably continue hacking away to unveil the truth longer than I ever could. But with time you will be exposed to more lies, more red tape, more injustice. For this reason and this reason only, I hope this thing takes a God-awfully long time—not to kill your efforts, but to help you understand why kids today . . . are refusing to cooperate with people (governments) that lie, cheat, kill, distort truths to their own ends, and why some are resorting to violence. . . . I don't agree with what they're doing but I fully *understand* why."

The Justice Department had closed its Kent State investigation because it concluded that successful prosecution required overcoming two formidable legal obstacles. The first involved the doctrine of sovereign immunity (also known as governmental immunity). Sovereign immunity derived from English common-law tradition that exempted the monarch from any charges of wrongdoing. In the United States, sovereign immunity applied to the federal government and all fifty state governments and those acting on their behalf. Citizens could not hold criminally or civilly liable someone acting within the scope of their government duties—in this case, guardsmen serving the state of Ohio,* unless it could be demonstrated that they acted in bad faith.† The second obstacle required proving malicious intent—convincing a jury beyond a reasonable doubt that guardsmen deliberately sought to cause the death of students at Kent State.

There things stood until August 3, 1973, when Kleindienst's successor as U.S. attorney general, Elliot Richardson,‡ announced, without consulting the White House, that the Justice Department would reopen the case because of "the need to exhaust every potential for acquiring facts relating to this tragedy." Richardson's decision was largely due to lobbying by Stanley Pottinger, who had succeeded Jerris Leonard as assistant attorney general for civil rights. Receiving inquiries about Kent State at the time of the third anniversary of the shooting and knowing nothing about it, Pottinger began asking subordinates in the Civil Rights Division, "What's this all about?" The more Pottinger learned, the more moved he became by the slain families' "intense concern not to punish anyone or to be vindictive but to discover the truth." "That's got to impress anybody who works on an incident of this magnitude," he said. Pottinger ultimately decided there should be a federal grand jury investigation of the shooting and persuaded his boss Richardson to act.

Pottinger's efforts were reinforced by the relentless pushing and prodding of Reverend John Adams of the United Methodist Church and Peter Davies, a British-born insurance salesman in New York. Tall and thick-

---

* Section 2923.55 of the Ohio Revised Code stipulated that any law enforcement officer or member of the militia was "guiltless for killing, maiming, or injuring a rioter as a consequence of the use of such force as is necessary and proper to suppress the riot or disperse or apprehend rioters." Art Krause wanted to "get rid of [this] Divine Right of Kings." "I didn't realize that I couldn't sue the state until this particular incident. I don't want somebody who is an elected official abusing his power or forcing other people to abuse theirs." Quoted in Ron Henderson, "18 Months Later: Families of Kent Dead Speak Out," *American Report*, November 12, 1971.

† Two different federal judges had cited the doctrine of sovereign immunity as the basis for dismissing civil suits filed against the state of Ohio by Art Krause in June 1970 and Louis Schroeder in July 1971.

‡ Months later, President Nixon fired Richardson and his deputy for refusing to dismiss Watergate special prosecutor Archibald Cox. Richardson's successor as attorney general was Ohio Republican U.S. senator William Saxbe, a retired Ohio National Guard colonel and longtime friend of Governor Jim Rhodes.

waisted with receding grayish-brown hair and an unexpectedly high voice, Reverend Adams had been a B-24 bomber pilot in World War II who was shot down and spent eight and a half months in a German prison camp. It was there he decided to become a minister after the war. A crisis-intervention expert in the United Methodist Church's Washington office, Adams was always busy but never looked so. People found him immediately trustable. Initially he helped the victims' families work through their anger and grief during long phone calls and personal meetings. When Adams first reached out, he discovered they were not in contact with one another; all were pursuing their own legal efforts. Adams set up a phone network that enabled them to comfort and support each other and channel their sorrow in a positive direction. He became a liaison for the families with the media and federal agencies in Washington. A legal defense fund he organized raised more than $250,000 from more than twenty thousand contributors. "If it had not been for Adams," said Art Krause, "we would have been dead."

Peter Davies, a Staten Island insurance agent who had immigrated from Britain in the late 1950s, had never heard of Kent State before May 4, 1970. The shooting shocked Davies, and Kent State soon became his obsession. A soft-spoken, self-righteous idealist who needed the world as both audience and stage, the mutton-chopped Davies made a second career crusading against what he perceived as wrongdoing, particularly against young women.[*] "If I had kids that age and they happened to be on that campus that day, they could have been killed just like the four who were killed," he told an interviewer. "They were not the Weathermen. And yet these four became the sacrificial lambs to atone for that violence against society." "I couldn't forget about it." "I was afraid because if they could kill Allison and Jeffrey and Sandra and Bill—if they could get away with that—what could

---

[*] Davies had earlier championed a New York secretary convicted of carrying a concealed weapon after pulling a tear-gas pen from her purse to fight off a mugger. He would later rush to the defense of West Coast newspaper heiress Patty Hearst, kidnapped by the radical Symbionese Liberation Army (SLA) on February 4, 1974. Davies contended that Hearst had been forced to participate in the SLA robbery of a Hibernia, California, bank on April 15, 1974, and subsequently serve as a getaway driver during their robbery of the Crocker National Bank in Carmichael, California.

stop them from hurting me?" "To do nothing, I feel, is to approve the elevation of uniformed law enforcers above and beyond the law."

Davies spent evenings and weekends digging into the shooting, particularly the death of Allison Krause, which "deeply affected" him. He told friends that "he would never give up trying to get justice, that in some strange way he felt Allison's presence, and that Allison's death had somehow changed his life." "To die for dissent in a democracy is the ultimate tragedy," Davies declared. He would not let the Justice Department forget Kent State. He appeared on countless television shows and in newspaper op-ed pages pushing the theory that a cabal of guardsmen had conspired beforehand to shoot specific students. Davies elaborated his theory in a book, *The Truth About Kent State: A Challenge to the American Conscience*, which also assailed the Justice Department for failing to address the unanswered questions surrounding the events of May 4.

These pressures finally led the Justice Department to convene a federal grand jury, three and a half years after the shooting. On December 18, 1973, U.S. district judge Frank Battisti swore in twenty-three grand jurors in his cavernous third-floor courtroom, which was decorated with gold-leaf painting on the ceiling and the walls and located in the five-story granite Beaux-Arts Federal Building overlooking the Cuyahoga River in downtown Cleveland. A son of Italian immigrants, U.S. Army veteran, and Harvard Law School graduate who had thick, combed-back salt-and-pepper hair, dimpled chin, and black-framed glasses, Battisti had become the country's youngest federal judge in 1961 when appointed by President John F. Kennedy to the bench at the age of thirty-nine. "A classic 1960s liberal," in the words of one of his law clerks, Battisti "felt strongly that [the shooting] was a terrible thing that had happened and somebody ought to pay for it." But Battisti also had a reputation as an even-handed judge who did not shy from presiding at controversial trials.

The federal grand jury met in an eleventh-floor office in the nearby Williamson Building. To maintain secrecy, jurors and witnesses entered and exited the building through a back door to avoid reporters and television cameras gathered in the lobby. The federal grand jury held thirty-nine sessions over three and a half months and subpoenaed one hundred eighty witnesses, including many of the guardsmen who had been at or near the Pagoda during the shooting. Many guardsmen invoked their Fifth Amendment right against self-incrimination. Those who did testify denied any conspiracy to target specific students. The federal grand jury also subpoenaed Ohio National Guard commander "Tough Tony" Del Corso. They asked Del Corso sixteen times whether he thought the shootings were justified; each time Del Corso said no.

On March 29, 1974, the federal grand jury indicted eight guardsmen—Jim McGee, Matt McManus, Barry Morris, Bill Perkins, Jim Pierce, Larry Shafer, Leon Smith, and Ralph Zoller—publicly identifying them for the first time. All eight had fired in the direction of the students. They were charged with deliberately violating the demonstrators' civil rights.* The indictment alleged that the eight, "acting under color of the laws of the state of Ohio, aiding and abetting each other, did willfully assault and intimidate persons who were inhabitants of the State of Ohio . . . by willfully discharging loaded [weapons] at, over, into, and in the direction of [the victims], and did thereby willfully deprive said persons of the right secured and protected by the Constitution and laws of the United States not to be deprived of liberty without due process of law." The eight faced possible life imprisonment.

Ohio National Guard inspector general Colonel Jean Peltier had stressed in his report that "Guardsmen involved will need whatever legal assistance can be furnished by the State of Ohio." "This is based," wrote Peltier, "upon information that left-wing Communistic elements fronted by the ACLU will attempt to exploit this incident to the maximum by contrived distortion of the facts." Guard headquarters in Columbus promised guardsmen that "we have dozens of down-state lawyers working on your behalf." But none ever materialized.

Several indicted guardsmen approached Matt McManus and told him, "You're the senior NCO. We're worried. We were promised lawyers but see none. We need you to hire a lawyer to represent us all. We need someone to listen, to talk to." "Here I was, a young man of twenty-five who could barely spell lawyer—faced with hiring one," recalled McManus. "I made three calls.

---

* Section 242 of the U.S. Code guaranteed victims the right not to be summarily executed without receiving due process of law.

All were very cordial—but No, they could not help. On the fourth call, I hit paydirt. He agreed to listen and advise but pointed out that he could not be with us in the grand jury room. He met with each of us. What a relief it was to confer with him." When McManus informed his commanding officer that he had engaged an attorney, "you could feel the air being sucked out of the room." "The lawyer was not treated well." Ohio National Guard headquarters later (grudgingly) created a legal defense fund for the accused but insisted the fund's existence be kept secret. "It was a total hands-off deal," recalled McManus. "You give them their checks, but you don't do it in public." The state of Ohio eventually agreed to cover the defendants' legal expenses— but only after their attorneys agreed to a 40 percent reduction in their fees.

The federal prosecutor was Robert Murphy, who had led the Justice Department's investigation of the shooting. The defense attorneys were Gus Lambros representing McGee, Morris, Pierce, and Zoller; Bernard Stuplinsky representing McManus, Perkins, and Shafer; and Ed Wright representing Smith. Lambros, Stuplinsky, and Wright filed motion after motion for dismissal of the indictments, asserting the inadmissibility of their clients' statements to the Ohio National Guard, the FBI, and the Ohio State Highway Patrol. Judge Battisti rejected their motions, ruling that all the guardsmen's statements—except those made on the afternoon of the shooting*—were legally admissible as evidence. All eight of the indicted

* Captain Brent Robertson, who supervised the guardsmen's statements after the shooting, had been instructed by press officer Colonel William Spain *not* to remind the guardsmen of their constitutional right to remain silent. Robertson twice asked Spain, "Are you sure?," and twice Spain responded, "Yes." Spain and guard leadership wanted the guardsmen to be forthcoming and doubted they would be prosecuted. But failing to remind guardsmen of their Fifth Amendment right against self-incrimination made their May 4 postshooting statements inadmissible in court. Pretrial hearing, *United States v. Shafer et al.*, September 23, 1974. Guardsmen signed the statements after being told they "would never go beyond [guard] headquarters in Columbus." Bill Perkins trial testimony, June 10, 1975, vol. 9, p. 1931, KSC, SML, YU. Perkins testified that he did not read his entire statement before signing it and it did not accurately reflect everything he told the officer who took it down. He and other guardsmen were not told, as General Canterbury explained in a later deposition, that they did not have to sign their statements if they disagreed with what was contained in them. Deposition of Robert Canterbury, November 21, 1974, pp. 57–58, MS 1800, Box 11, KSC, SML, YU.

guardsmen had signed statements to the FBI that included the caution, "Anything you say may be held against you in a court of law."

———

The federal criminal trial of the eight Ohio National Guardsmen got under way with jury selection on October 21, 1974, in Judge Battisti's courtroom. Kent State had attracted enormous media attention in the four and a half years since the shooting. Battisti warned journalists to be careful about what they published to avoid creating a prejudicial atmosphere. That morning, Cleveland's *Plain Dealer* newspaper had run a front-page story quoting Jim Pierce saying that he had lost his job because he had to stand trial.

The emotion in the courtroom was palpable. Many of the eight guardsmen feared for their safety, particularly during breaks when they had no place to gather privately, and thus ended up on the streets of downtown Cleveland hounded by newsmen. After one break, as opposing counsels resumed their questioning of potential jurors, a man dressed in a black suit with a yellow flower in his lapel suddenly stood up and declared, "Your Honor, Your Honor!" Battisti responded, "Can I help you?" The man then reached in his pocket and screamed, "These men have killed innocent students and they too must die!" Battisti dove for the floor, shouting, "Marshals, Marshals!" Three U.S. Marshals burst into the courtroom, knocked the man down, and dragged him out kicking and screaming. When the trial resumed the next day, a metal detector had been installed at the building entrance, and U.S. Marshals escorted the guardsmen in and out of the courtroom.

Reporters phoned the indicted guardsmen at all hours of the day and night. Other guardsmen murmured within their earshot, "I wouldn't want to be called a killer." The accused felt tension and hostility wherever they went. "You could walk into a restaurant and feel it. People looking." "You get letters," said one. "One guy was going to blow me up. Another guy's family was threatened." A second guardsman moved away from Ohio because of constant harassment. A third quit his job, saying that seeing his name in the papers "was eating at him." The stress, pressure, and guilt that Matt McManus felt surfaced during a pretrial hearing. "I've been through four and a half years of this bullshit and I'm getting sick and tired of it," he shouted as he ran out of the courtroom crying. "It's hard on us no matter what everybody thinks," another said, "but it's harder on the people who lost someone that day. Just think how they feel."

An eight-man, four-woman jury was sworn in on October 29. The next morning, the prosecution and defense delivered their opening statements. It was the first opportunity for both sides to present their case to the jury. Prosecutor Murphy said that approximately seventy shots had been fired on May 4, a third of them by the defendants, and the defendants were the only guardsmen who fired into the crowd. He said he would introduce photographic evidence* documenting the guardsmen's movements from the time they crossed the access road onto the practice field to the time they marched back up Blanket Hill to the Pagoda. The photographs would show that "there was no massive rush of students toward the guardsmen. . . . No student was within sixty feet. . . . Thirteen people were shot from a distance of sixty to six hundred feet," and "only two of the thirteen were shot in the front." Murphy would introduce no ballistic evidence, however. The FBI had collected all the fired rifles shortly after the shooting, tagged each one with the name of the guardsman to whom it had been issued, and ran bullet identification tests in the FBI Laboratory in Washington—but the guardsmen had swapped rifles the morning of the shooting.

Defense attorneys then spoke to the jury. They portrayed the guardsmen as tired, inexperienced, and leaderless. Lambros stressed their lack of sleep in the days before the shooting and the frenzy of the protestors. "The mob was charging the Ohio National Guard at the top of the hill shouting 'Kill! Kill! Kill!'" he told the jury, and "the defendants had no specific intent to harm anyone." The guardsmen had no experience with campus disorders. Stuplinsky painted a picture not of students exercising their constitutional right to dissent but of riotous protestors throwing stones and chasing guardsmen. The guardsmen needed leadership that day, he said, and got none—with woeful consequences. Stuplinsky blamed senior

---

* During the trial, the prosecution would introduce one hundred thirty exhibits—mostly photos of the confrontation between students and guardsmen.

guard officers, particularly General Robert Canterbury. He concluded by saying the shooting was "a regrettable tragedy." Wright, a small-town lawyer rather than a big-city attorney like Lambros and Stuplinsky, made a similar but shorter and more understated argument on behalf of his client.

Later that morning, October 30, the jury, opposing counsels, and seven of the defendants traveled by bus to Kent to tour the scene of the shooting. They spent the early afternoon on campus. It was a damp, chilly day and many wore raincoats. They started at the site of the burned-out ROTC building, walked across the Commons to the Victory Bell, then up Blanket Hill. From the crest of Blanket Hill they followed the guardsmen's line of march down to the practice field then back up to the Pagoda. Finally, they made their way down to the Prentice Hall parking lot, where a U.S. Marshal using an aerial photograph taken the day after the shooting pointed out where the killed and wounded students had fallen.

Back in Cleveland the next day, jurors heard testimony from several pho-

Seven of the eight indicted Ohio National Guardsmen at Kent State, October 30, 1974. Left to right: Leon Smith, Barry Morris, Matt McManus, Jim McGee, Larry Shafer, Ralph Zoller, and Jim Pierce.

tographers who witnessed and took pictures during the shooting. No matter how many times the parents of the slain students saw the photos, they could never get used to them or the anguish the photos triggered in them. Nor could they become inured to the hate mail, the telephoned threats, the ostracization by relatives and neighbors, and—most painfully—the empty bedrooms and the letters found at the bottom of desk drawers.

On the morning of November 1, the first of the student victims to testify, Scott MacKenzie, took the stand. Scott said he had heckled the guardsmen at the Commons on the day of the shooting, then made his way down to the Prentice Hall parking lot. He saw no students rushing the guardsmen. When the guardsmen turned and fired, Scott said he watched at first, then ran. Asked what happened next, Scott's face contorted a bit and he answered very quietly. "I was shot in the back of the neck about an inch over from my spinal column." Jurors shifted in their seats as he spoke. Two looked horrified. Scott paused a couple of seconds and then pointed at his left cheek. The bullet "exited here, on my cheek." He stopped for a moment and then finished, "It knocked me off my feet." "Did you know the rally was illegal?" one of the defense attorneys asked. Judge Battisti interrupted and said the National Guardsmen, not the student protestors, were on trial. "You were not one of the more violent members of the crowd, were you?" defense counsel resumed. "In fact, you verbally tried to subdue some people, didn't you?" Scott said yes. "Do you remember anybody chanting, 'Kill! Kill! Kill!'?" asked Battisti. Scott said no.

That afternoon, Doug Wrentmore took the stand. He now sported long hair and a beard. He had been in "a negative rut, a negative kind of trap" since the shooting. The "twisted hate mail" he had received made him "shy away from talking" about what had happened to him and others. It was the first time Doug saw the faces of the guardsmen who fired into the crowd. He looked "right into their eyes to see who they were and how they were feeling." They could not avoid his eyes. "From most, I got a peculiarly good feeling," he later said. "Only three or four" seemed "really bad and twisted—as if a negative entity possessed them." The jury seemed alienated at first by Doug's appearance, but as he spoke his soft cadences made them visibly more sympathetic.

The next to testify was Robby Stamps. The four and a half years since the shooting had been tough for Robby. Like Doug Wrentmore, he felt uncomfortable talking about what had happened to him. Whenever a stranger asked "How'd you get hurt?," he'd tell them he'd been in an accident. Both of Robby's sisters criticized him for his involvement in the May 4 protest. The doctor who ran the East Side County Clinic where his mother Charlotte worked regularly disparaged her "hippie" son. His father, Floyd, a retired career U.S. Army officer, endured snarky comments from customers at his auto-leasing agency. Neighbors in their South Euclid neighborhood treated the family like pariahs and asked, "How involved was Robby?" Despite years of therapy, Robby couldn't shake the feeling that somehow he was to blame for being shot.

"I was scared to death as I took the witness stand," Robby later said. This was the first time he, too, saw the faces of the guardsmen who shot him and the others. Robby found them difficult to look at. Murphy led him through the day of the shooting beginning with his arrival at the Commons "partly to observe, partly to take part in the protest." Later, down in the Prentice Hall parking lot, Robby said he heard "one shot, then a couple, then all in a series in very short succession." As Robby spoke, his precise, carefully articulated speech became even more precise and the words even more carefully spoken until he described the moment when he was hit. At that point he began to stutter. He told the jury about being hit in the right buttock and the bullet lodging against his femur.

After adjourning for the weekend, the trial resumed on November 5, with testimony from photographers at Kent State that day. Donald Roese of the *Akron Beacon Journal*, near the guardsmen on their way up to the Pagoda, said he saw "small groups of students move closer to the guard" just before the shooting, but did not hear any order to fire. Another photographer, David Eads, said the protestors on the eastern slope of Taylor Hall were grouped like a handheld fan. Those at the bottom of the slope near the parking lot were the base of the fan, while those toward the top of the slope were more spread out and running toward the guard.

That afternoon, Alan Canfora took the stand. He felt "lucky to be alive" and also "very bitter." To him, the shooting had been "planned murder."

Under cross-examination, Alan was asked by Lambros, "Would you say that as many as five thousand [students and protestors] were there" that day? "I'd say that's an exaggeration," replied Alan. Lambros then quoted from a letter Alan wrote to Senator Young shortly after the shooting in which he said five thousand people had been at Kent State on May 4, 1970. "Do you remember a single shot before the volley?" asked Lambros. "No," answered Alan. Lambros again quoted from Alan's testimony before the federal grand jury saying that he heard a single shot. "Were you chanting?" asked Stuplinsky. "Yes." "What?" Alan wouldn't answer directly. "Did you shout any obscenities?" "Yes." "What?" Again, he gave no direct answer.

The following day, November 6, the wounded student closest to the guard when the shooting started, Joe Lewis, testified. He had never returned to school after the shooting. Instead, he left Ohio for Oregon. He was not intimidated; he looked the eight defendants in the eye. Defense counsel focused on the moments before the shooting. "Did the guard appear to be moving up the hill in an organized group?" he asked. "They seemed to be moving more in segments," answered Joe. "Isn't it a fact that this disorganized group was running up the hill and bumping into each other?" "Yes." "Were you able to determine that anyone was aiming at you?" "No." "Did you throw any rocks?" "No." "Shout any obscenities?" "No." "Did you not feel in any jeopardy?" "No." "You thought the demonstration was about over?" "Yes."

After Joe Lewis stepped down from the witness stand, the indicted guardsmen began their testimony. Sergeant Larry Shafer went first. A slender, medium-sized, doleful-looking man with a high forehead, thinning hair, and a drooping mustache, Shafer had nervously paced the hallway before entering the courtroom. Shafer had been on the right side of the line as it moved back up Blanket Hill. Shafer said he heard a single shot on his left at the top of the hill before the volley, "the man next to me" fired twice, then he fired three shots: one round over the protestors' heads, the second at Joe Lewis, and a third again over the protestors' heads. Shafer told the jury that Lewis "seemed to be about to inflict some harm on us or should not have been there in my opinion."

Corporal Jim Pierce followed Shafer. Well dressed, Pierce was the big, blond, former Kent High School track star who had attended the University of Hawaii for a year and told a friend the afternoon before the shooting that his nerves were frayed. Murphy read portions of Pierce's statement to the FBI into the record. In that statement, Pierce said that while on the practice field he had been struck on the leg by a brick that knocked him down. On the way back up Blanket Hill, he had been on the end of the line nearest the approaching protestors, whom he claimed came within ten feet of him. At the Pagoda, Pierce "heard a shot I thought came from the line" and he then fired four times. His first round went over the protestors' heads. His second shot targeted a demonstrator with a rock in his hand and his arm drawn back. He aimed his third shot toward the crowd. He fired his fourth and final shot at a nearby African American student who he said had a rock in his hand.* Pierce concluded his testimony by saying, "I truthfully thought I would not get out of the area alive. If I had not had on my gas mask and helmet, I would not have made it out of there alive."

John Cleary followed Pierce on the stand. Lambros read aloud portions of John's May 1974 statement to the FBI describing the guardsmen looking scared and panicked and some of the rocks thrown at them as big as softballs. Lambros then asked John, "Did the guard appear scary and panicky?" John said he couldn't recall; he had been under medication in May and his memory was better now, six months later. The day's final witness was Gregory Moore, another student photographer on May 4, who said the crowd noise increased just before the shooting.

The next day, after ten days of testimony from thirty-three witnesses, Battisti made an unexpected announcement. Battisti told Murphy to have his final arguments ready the following day in the event the defense made a motion for direct acquittal (which defense attorneys routinely do after the prosecution rests its case). Battisti added cryptically, "I may have something in writing." Judges customarily denied motions for direct acquittal. Would Battisti do the same?

---

* This was Brother Fargo, wearing a knitted tarboosh and cuffed blue jeans. Photographs show Fargo with his left hand to his mouth shouting at the guard but carrying no rock in his other hand.

At 10:15 a.m. the next morning, November 8, Murphy introduced the prosecution's final—and what he considered its strongest—evidence: Terry Strubbe's audio recording of the shooting. The courtroom hushed as the bailiff played Strubbe's recording of the terrible 12.53 seconds when guardsmen fired sixty-seven shots that killed four students and wounded nine others.

Battisti then ordered the bailiff to escort the jury from the courtroom. Once this had been done, defense attorneys made their expected motion for direct acquittal—asking that the charges against the eight guardsmen be dismissed because the prosecution had failed to prove its case.

Battisti looked toward the prosecution table below him about ten feet from the jury box and asked, "What specific intention have you proven?" (Before the trial began, Battisti had told the prosecution it was obliged to prove the guardsmen specifically intended to deprive students of their constitutional rights.) "We have shown that the shooting was unjustified, that there was no danger posed to the guardsmen's lives or danger of serious bodily injury," said Murphy. He continued, "The evidence reflects that no student was closer to the guardsmen than Joseph Lewis, who was approximately sixty feet away and standing still." "The evidence reflects that with the exception of Joseph Lewis, the nearest student was perhaps ninety feet away and greater distances." "We have proven that the National Guardsmen were not surrounded at the time of the shooting." All of this was true—but it did not answer Battisti's question.

"Tell me what the guardsmen did," pressed Battisti.

MURPHY: I think the only way you can prove intent in this case is through circumstantial evidence.

BATTISTI: Intent to do what?

MURPHY: Intent to deprive these students of their Constitutional rights. . . . These men acted in reckless disregard of these rights and that constituted specific intent under the law.

BATTISTI: There is no testimony indicating an expressed intention.

MURPHY: That's correct.

BATTISTI: Is not the evidence such that reasonable minds might also conclude that, at the moment of firing, the Guardsmen were not possessed
of specific intention to deprive one of civil rights?

MURPHY: The possibility exists. I would have to say yes to possibility.

BATTISTI: We are not dealing with a grossly negligent discharge of a
weapon which might result, in state court, in a conviction [for] man-
slaughter. We are not dealing with shooting with intent to wound or
to maim, which are offenses cognizable by the state criminal codes.
We are dealing only with, under [18 USC] 242, a specific intention to
deprive one of certain legal rights—for example, as I have said over and
over again, the right to a trial on the standards of due process. May this
jury or any reasonable jurors conclude on the [basis] of the evidence
that the defendants did not have that specific intention?

MURPHY: With all of the assumptions and caveats and qualifications—yes,
I would have to agree.

BATTISTI: Mr. Murphy, we really don't have to go much further.

Battisti summoned the jury back into the courtroom. He then issued a
verdict of acquittal because he ruled that the prosecution had failed to prove
specific intent beyond a reasonable doubt. Battisti explained his reasoning
by reading aloud a portion of his written opinion:

> The government has presented no evidence bearing directly on the
> intentions of those Guardsmen who fired their weapons.
>
> In a case so filled with emotional issues, and involving the behav-
> ior of so many persons, it seems important to note what this opinion
> does, and does not, hold.
>
> This opinion holds only that, based upon the evidence offered to
> the court, reasonable jurors must find that there is a reasonable doubt
> as to whether these eight defendants were possessed of a specific
> intention to deprive the students of Kent State University set forth in
> the indictment of their Constitutional and federal rights at the time
> they discharged their weapons.

This opinion does not hold that any of the defendants or other Guardsmen were justified in discharging their weapons on May 4, 1970, at Kent State University. Justification is irrelevant to a proceeding under 18 USC 242. That section is concerned with the intentions of the defendants and not with possible justification of their actions.

Very different considerations would obtain if this were a trial of these eight Guardsmen in state court on charges, for example, of shooting with intent to injure or maim. In that situation, the issues of justification, of the possible excessiveness of the force used, of provocation, of self-defense—might be relevant to the offense charged.[*]

In particular, it must be clearly understood that the conduct of the Guardsmen who fired, and of the Guard and state officials who placed their Guardsmen in the situation noted above, is neither approved nor vindicated by this opinion. . . .

The events at Kent State University were made up of a series of tragic blunders and mistakes of judgment. It is vital that state and National Guard officials not regard this decision as authorizing or approving the use of force against unarmed demonstrators, whatever the occasion or the issues involved. Such use of force is, and was, deplorable.

Issuing a verdict of direct acquittal was "a hard decision" for Battisti to make, his law clerk later explained, because, going into the trial, Battisti's "basic view was that this was a terrible thing and he was going to be the avenging angel." "It was a big emotional trip for him to get from there to saying, 'I'm going to throw this case out at the close of the prosecution's case.'"

Robert Murphy fought back tears as Battisti read his opinion, but Murphy was "not overwhelmed with surprise." He was deeply disappointed the case hadn't gone to the jury yet later confessed, "I wouldn't have put any money on it." Afterward, defense attorneys asked jurors how they would

---

[*] The State of Ohio's unwillingness to bring charges against the guardsmen had led to the federal criminal trial.

have voted. Their vote would have been 12 to 0 for acquittal. Four of the acquitted defendants—Matt McManus, Barry Morris, Bill Perkins, and Jim Pierce—insensitively autographed a trial exhibit photograph of the guardsmen at the Pagoda.

The plaintiffs reacted to Battisti's verdict with disbelief. At the start of the trial, Joe Lewis had told his mother, "I've got good vibes. I think we're gonna win." "When Battisti threw out the case," said Betty Lewis, "What could I say to him?" Art Krause was furious. He called Judge Battisti at home "and told him what I thought of him as an individual." Peter Davies accused prosecutors of a deliberate charade and the Justice Department of covering up something "big and horrible." Tom Grace felt "deeply angered" and "personally outraged." Asserting (incorrectly) that "the trial was terminated before the guardsmen were forced to testify," he argued in a letter to the editor of the *New York Times* that Battisti's ruling "merely continues the concealment of the murders at Kent State in a more disguised fashion" and that "justice serves . . . the class of financial rulers who first designed and assembled the legal apparatus." Robby Stamps reacted with less anger. "I'm glad they're not going to jail," Robby told the press. "The wrong people were on trial. The blame lies on the governor and the people who sent those poorly trained guardsmen with loaded rifles onto a college campus." Perhaps the most penetrating assessment came from David Hess of the *Akron Beacon Journal*, who wrote: "While the judge's interpretation of the law was a bit narrower than the law's language might have allowed, the fact remains the law is quite narrow. By fixing its sights on the intent of the alleged violator, the law largely misses the consequences of the violator's deed."

Assistant Attorney General Stanley Pottinger announced that Battisti's ruling ended the federal government's involvement in the case. "The decision to reopen the case was right. The grand jury's decision to indict was right. The trial of the case was thorough. The department has done everything in its power to air the causes of this tragedy and enforce the law," Pottinger concluded.

Chapter 9

THE CIVIL TRIALS

T he guardsmen's acquittal in federal criminal court did not end the legal battle over Kent State; it merely shifted the battle to federal civil court. The guardsmen "wanted it to end," Matt McManus later said, but the parents of those killed and wounded were upset, they were angry and disappointed, and they felt they had every right to be all three. They remained determined to bring the guardsmen to justice, called to account—and punished. Then, and only then, would the guardsmen suffer as they had suffered.

Art Krause recognized the challenge he and his fellow plaintiffs faced. "How do you keep fighting with a slingshot when the state is throwing all this money into it?" he despaired. "After all, the state only took my daughter away." He would not give up. He went back on radio and television talk shows. He wrote more letters to editors. He hired a fund-raiser to help him deal with mounting legal expenses. "I went out grubbing, begging, groveling. . . . I made a pain-in-the-ass of myself." And he filed suit, along with the other victims' families, in federal civil court.

The families' earlier suits had been dismissed on the basis of the principle of sovereign immunity. But on April 17, 1974, the U.S. Supreme Court reversed a lower-court decision exempting state officials from such suits. In an 8–0 decision, Nixon-appointed Chief Justice Warren Burger wrote that sovereign immunity provided "no shield for a state official confronted by the claim that he had deprived another of a federal right under the color of the law." The plaintiffs were not suing the state of Ohio "but seeking to impose individual and personal liability on the named defendants." Federal civil rights "would be drained of meaning were we to hold that the acts of a governor or other high executive officer has the quality of supreme and unchangeable edict, overriding all conflicting rights . . . and were unreviewable by the federal courts," Burger concluded. Sovereign immunity could be used as a defense, but not to block a trial for alleged gross abuse of official discretion. The Supreme Court remanded the Kent State case to the U.S. district court in Cleveland for civil trial. When Elaine Miller Holstein heard the news on her car radio, she thought it must be wrong, but it was not. "Now we go into wonderland," quipped Florence Schroeder.

The various civil suits by families of the slain and wounded students were consolidated into one: *Krause et al. v. Rhodes et al.* The suit alleged that Governor Rhodes and others "intentionally, recklessly, willfully and wantonly" deployed the Ohio National Guard to Kent State and ordered it to "perform illegal acts resulting in the students' deaths." By doing so, they violated due process through summary punishment—using the guardsmen as judges, jurors, and executioners. Agents of the state had no right to shoot people for shouting epithets and throwing stones. The plaintiffs sought $46 million in punitive damages. The defendants, who included Governor Rhodes, Ohio National Guard commander Del Corso (but not his number two, Robert Canterbury), former Kent State president Robert White, and twenty-seven former and current guardsmen faced charges similar to those the eight guardsmen had faced in criminal court. And their defense would be similar: guardsmen who fired had genuinely feared for their lives and safety. But in civil court the defendants would be judged by a different standard. Criminal cases required proving guilt beyond a reasonable doubt. Civil cases required proving guilt on the basis of a preponderance of the evidence—a lower bar. Many of the guardsmen resented being indicted nonetheless. "I was taught if you follow orders of officers above you and if you fire in self-defense," said Charles Fassinger, "you are covered under the Ohio Revised Code and sovereign immunity. It was a lie because we were indicted."

During the discovery phase prior to trial, plaintiffs' attorneys deposed new witnesses and gathered new evidence, including additional photos and exhibits. They also hired prominent fifty-four-year-old New York trial attorney Joe Kelner to lead their effort in court. Born in Iowa and reared in Detroit, Kelner had attended Detroit College,* worked his way through New York University Law School during the Depression, served in Army Intelligence during World War II, and after the war became a successful Manhattan litigator. Well educated and well spoken—he had served as president of both the New York City Trial Lawyers Association and the American Trial Lawyers Association—Kelner bore a resemblance to Teamster boss Jimmy Hoffa. And like Hoffa, he could be abrasive—an attribute that served him well in New York courtrooms but not necessarily in Ohio ones. "I haven't lost a case in three years," he boasted to his clients, "and I'm not going to lose this one."

Kelner had initially viewed the shooting victims as communists and troublemakers who had provoked the National Guard. And as a lawyer, he knew that provocation justified the guard in shooting in self-defense. But he received a phone call from Elaine Miller Holstein and agreed to meet and talk with her. He found her "numb, almost in tears, still in disbelief about what had happened to her son." She didn't want money—she wanted to find out why Jeff had been killed. Kelner's two college-age sons told him, "Dad, don't you refuse to take this case!" Kelner knew doing so would involve "years of struggle," but he agreed. In time he came to view it as the "most important case of my life."

Kelner led the plaintiffs' legal team, but it was plagued by internal division. The various attorneys who had heretofore represented the victims and their families did not get along, their egos often clashed, and—most significant—they disagreed over trial strategy. Each promoted his own approach, which often conflicted with others'. As a result, Cleveland's *Plain Dealer* newspaper later noted, the plaintiffs would fail "to present a clear and simple case focusing on only a few issues." Dean Kahler felt Kelner did not have enough gravitas to persuade a jury and presciently feared

---

* Today Wayne State University.

his New York style would alienate Ohioans. Art Krause had asked former U.S. attorney general Ramsey Clark to lead the plaintiffs' effort, but Clark had declined because he witnessed the internal bickering and considered it "highly destructive and damaging to the interests of the clients." "Poor Joe," remarked Art Krause, "trying to get nuts like us under control."

Kelner agreed to be chief counsel, but he joined the team late and failed to stop the internal bickering. Kelner's expertise, moreover, was in torts (negligence) cases, not civil rights violations—the heart of the plaintiffs' suit. The federal civil trial would last much longer than the federal criminal trial had and would introduce new evidence and testimony. It would be one of the most complex civil cases in the history of the American legal system and the most thorough airing of facts about the Kent State shooting. But the sheer weight of conflicting facts and testimony—more than a hundred witnesses and more than twelve thousand pages of trial transcript—would prove confusing and overwhelming for the jury.

Several victims insisted privately there was no way they could win. "You don't know the people" of Ohio, Robby Stamps told Kelner. "They hate us. They *wanted* us shot. To them, the minute we get into that courtroom, it will be *us* who are on trial, not the guardsmen." Kelner told Robby to trust in the legal system—trials were "instruments for achieving justice" and juries, when carefully chosen, were "composed of unprejudiced, unbiased individuals committed to truth" who could be "trusted to sift out lies and exaggerations." They would "rise to the occasion." He stressed the common-law tradition that "an adversary system in which each side is permitted to question witnesses," combined with "a fair judge," was the "best means of approaching and closely approximating truth."

"This isn't an accident case where someone has been run over by a car," responded Robby. "We've been run over by the governor and the whole state of Ohio. Any jury we get is going to think of themselves as protecting Ohio against a bunch of Communist hippies." Robby despised those he considered responsible such as Governor Rhodes and General Canterbury and those who lied such as Captain Snyder but "couldn't hate" those who pulled the trigger such as Bill Herschler. Kelner commissioned a private poll to gauge sentiment among Ohioans about the shooting. It revealed nearly 75 percent believed the shooting was justified. *Akron Beacon Journal* reporter John Dunphy, who had won a Pulitzer Prize for his reporting on the shooting, told Kelner that he didn't have a chance of winning. "Why not?" Kelner asked. "You'll never get an Ohio jury to vote against the guardsmen." "I have faith in the jury system," said Kelner. "You don't know Ohio," Dunphy replied.

On May 28, 1975, the federal civil trial got under way in downtown Cleveland. Art and Doris Krause had driven in from Pittsburgh the previous afternoon and checked into the Hollenden House Hotel near the Federal Building. The woman at the front desk looked at their names on the hotel register and snarked, "If I'd had a gun, I would have killed them all too."

U.S. district judge Don Young's courtroom lay at the west end of the second floor of the Federal Building. Oak wainscoting trimmed pale-yellow walls capped by a twelve-foot ceiling with recessed fluorescent lighting. A metal detector outside the door screened everyone who entered for firearms. Judge Young got the case after six other federal judges were ruled out because of conflicts of interest or heavy caseloads. Sixty-four years old, with a thin build, high forehead, brushed-back dark-gray hair, and rimless glasses, Young was the nephew of liberal Democratic U.S. senator Stephen Young, who had excoriated the Ohio National Guard's actions at Kent State on May 4. Judge Young had been on the federal bench for ten years. He could be sharply critical of both sides in cases and showed exasperation with trial tactics that strayed from efficient presentation of evidence. He was viewed in Ohio legal circles as "a pretty liberal guy." The *Plain Dealer* described him as "a civil libertarian with a strong sense of justice." Most informed observers thought if he had any bias, it would be in favor of the plaintiffs.

The courtroom was packed. Dean Kahler sat in his wheelchair at the far end of the front row reserved for the plaintiffs. He viewed the trial with mixed feelings. He wanted justice and to learn the truth, but he also knew that it would renew the hate mail he had received after the shooting. Tom Grace, radicalized by the events of May 4, felt "a great deal of bitterness toward the people who shot us. I would like to see them with rocks on the practice field and myself with an M-I." "At least in war," he added, "both sides are armed." Scott MacKenzie had found solace through yoga, Robby Stamps through psychological counseling. Joe Lewis and Jim Russell had coped with the stress by leaving Ohio and becoming wanderers. "All of us" seemed "paranoid and depressive," reflected Robby Stamps looking back.

The parents of the slain and wounded were there too. Among them, white-haired John Kahler sat next to his plump, red-headed wife, Elaine. John had fought in World War II. The bitter irony that the same type of rifle he had carried as a U.S. Army infantryman to liberate the Philippines had been used to paralyze his son twenty-five years later on an American campus constantly gnawed at him. Elaine was the only one of the victims' parents who could speak on amicable terms with guardsmen. Next to her sat Lou and Florence Schroeder. Shortly after the shooting, Lou had lost his job at the Fruehauf Trailer-Truck manufacturing plant in Lorain, where he had been a line supervisor for fifteen years, and suddenly found himself an unemployed fifty-five-year-old struggling to find work. Florence had closely followed developments in the case, attending every court hearing because "I don't have Bill to tell me." Bill's death had changed her politics. A patriotic Republican who had voted for Rhodes before the shooting, after the shooting she began to question the system and doubt that "authorities knew better." When a speaker at her church urged parishioners to support President Nixon, the military, and the boys in Vietnam "because everything America did was right," she had not joined in the applause. A congregation member afterward asked her why. She replied that it was people like the speaker who had killed her son. "For a lot of people in America, when the kids were shot at Kent State, it was the same as getting revenge," Florence told an interviewer. "They were shooting the Weathermen, they were shooting members of SDS. Our thirteen were symbolic. They think the shooting has stopped everything." Sitting in court that morning, Florence was nervous. She was on antianxiety medication, hadn't eaten anything, and couldn't sit still. She worried where jurors' sympathies lay but hoped they would base their verdict on what they heard under oath on the witness stand in the weeks to come. "There was nothing we could do except pray a little," she later said.

Nearby sat Al and Anna Canfora. Al had "lost everything" since the shooting—his vice presidency of the local United Auto Workers and his position on the Barberton city council. "The scandal of Kent State destroyed me politically in my union," he admitted. "I was at the peak of my career—and it all happened at once." "It was a nightmare." Fellow Goodyear Tire factory workers told him they thought it was okay to shoot the students. His local Veterans of Foreign Wars (VFW) post's weekly bingo games were held in Ravenna's National Guard Armory—managed by none other than First Sergeant "Pappy" Pryor. "You don't like me, do you?," Pryor would say when they encountered one another. "I never said I didn't like you," Al would reply. "My feelings were not going to upset our bingo games." Before the shooting, Al and Anna had argued frequently with Alan and Chic about long hair, the war in Vietnam, and the counterculture. But their arguments gradually subsided. Al and Anna began to see the wisdom in some of the things Alan and Chic were saying.

Tom Grace, Sr., and his wife, Collette, as well as Joe Sr. and Betty Lewis were also there for the opening of the trial. So, too, was pretty, petite Jan Wrentmore.* Before the shooting, Jan had been a conservative Republican who backed President Nixon. She and her husband, Don, had shared many friends with Charles and Janet Fassinger. Jan had initially opposed joining the civil lawsuit, preferring to "let it drop" because she "wanted Doug to heal." She told Doug, "You can wait until you're twenty-one and go ahead with the lawsuit then if you want." But Doug eventually persuaded her to join. The trial was "nasty from the beginning," she later said. "Every day was dramatic." Art Krause attended court infrequently. "If I went every day," he said, "I would have killed the judge." "Every time I looked at the Krauses," Betty Lewis said, "I saw Arthur's hate." Doris Krause attended court regularly, with and without her husband. "It was hard to sit there with those people who pulled the triggers," she later said. "I never thought I'd see them face to face." At the end of each day, "those killers would hold the [courtroom] door open for me and I would not walk through. I had very bad feelings for the officers more than the men."

---

* Doug's father, Don Wrentmore, had died of brain cancer on Christmas Eve 1970.

Elaine Miller Holstein and her second husband, Artie, attended regularly too. "Sitting in the Cleveland courtroom," she later wrote, "was an experience that defies description. There were elements of nightmare, anger, and disillusionment—but also some very positive and satisfying times in getting to know and become extremely close to the other young people who survived, their parents, and all the dedicated lawyers and assistants who worked so hard to try to find justice. I'll never get over [it]." "To see that the National Guardsmen"—the young men who had killed her youngest boy—"were only people in civilian clothes" "was not the impact that I expected." Some guardsmen struck Elaine as "icy cold, smug, and sarcastic." Those who wore dark glasses looked to her like "evil pimps." Sarah Scheuer stared at them as they walked the hallways during breaks. "If looks would kill," she said, "they would probably all be dead. Some of them couldn't look [me] in the eye." "They just looked away." Anna Canfora looked at them and prayed they would tell the truth. Everyone wanted to understand why some guardsmen had shot at their children.

The five years since the shooting had been an unending nightmare for all of them. Like Dean Kahler, they knew this latest trial would trigger a new wave of hate mail, telephone threats, and angry looks and stares from neighbors and relatives. Most had grown deeply cynical and skeptical about ever achieving justice. But they all desperately wanted to understand why guardsmen had fired on unarmed students. Each afternoon after court adjourned, they gathered in an adjacent room, licked their wounds, and comforted one another—all except Elaine Miller Holstein. Listening to testimony re-creating the shooting "over and over every day" left Elaine feeling "limp and extremely hurt." "I couldn't sit and rehash," she said. "It was too much—I couldn't stand it." All the other families "got real close," Al Canfora said, resolving to help one another "to the end."

The defendants sat in two rows of simple wooden chairs against the wall of the courtroom next to Judge Young's chambers. Halfway down the long line of guardsmen sat Governor Rhodes in a high-backed, padded leather chair. He had been returned to office the previous November. Every time Judge Young addressed Rhodes, he referred to him as "Your Excellency." The plaintiffs and their attorneys knew the presence of the sitting governor made it difficult to win. General Robert Canterbury was not among those indicted, but he attended the trial every day.

Over defense objections, Young decreed a twelve-person jury with a three-fourths majority (of nine) required for a verdict rather than a six-person jury whose verdict had to be unanimous. Jury selection followed. Dean Kahler studied the faces of potential jurors. They looked more like the guardsmen than like the students, he thought, and that worried him. There were many exclusions during jury selection. Attorneys for the defense disqualified a long-haired young man who lived in a commune, while attorneys for the plaintiffs disqualified a housewife who had lost two sons in Vietnam. The jury that emerged from the winnowing process comprised six men and six women, two of them African Americans, all middle aged. Unlike jurors in the federal criminal trial, they would be provided with a description of the events leading up to May 4 agreed to by both sides that would explain why the guard was in Kent and why antagonism already existed between guardsmen and students.

On the second day of the trial, the jury traveled by bus to Kent and toured the scene of the shooting and was guarded by a police escort and U.S. Marshals in plain clothes. The following morning, opening arguments—what Judge Young called "the picture on the cover of the jigsaw puzzle box"—got under way. As an experienced litigator, Joe Kelner was confident he could persuade jurors to do the right thing—"to well and truly try the case on the evidence." He knew from prior experience that some jurors wouldn't do this despite their oath, but any lawyer "worth his salt could get such jurors to excuse themselves." Kelner began by introducing himself as an attorney from New York City. To one of the defendants, he "looked like a duck out of water." Despite his talents, Kelner could be condescending—a serious error before a jury. (He later haughtily referred to the mood in the courtroom as a "hostile mid-American atmosphere.") Robby Stamps had warned him, "You've got a fast tongue. Watch yourself up there." Local reporters watching Kelner concluded that the plaintiffs would lose not because of the evidence but because of their attorney's demeanor.

Kelner condemned the shooting as a punitive violation of the constitutional right to dissent. He acknowledged the vandalism in downtown Kent on May 1 and the burning of the ROTC building on May 2, calling them "outrages." They "should be condemned by every right-thinking person in the community and in the campus and in the nation. Everyone doing it should be and probably was arrested." But "that is not our concern here," he stressed. The plaintiffs should not have been punished for what others had done earlier. He condemned the epithets and rock throwing on May 4, conceded that Alan Canfora, Tom Grace, Dean Kahler, Allison Krause, and Jeff Miller had taunted the guardsmen, but pointed out that they and other protestors did not know guardsmen carried loaded rifles and were never warned they might shoot. He then showed a map illustrating how far the slain and injured students stood from the guardsmen when they fired—sixty to seven hundred fifty feet—evidence, he argued, that the guardsmen had not shot in self-defense.

Burt Fulton and Charlie Brown were the principal defense attorneys. Fifty years old with crew-cut gray hair, snubby nose, and gaunt frame, Fulton had served in the U.S. Army in World War II, earning the Bronze Star and the Purple Heart for actions during the Battle of the Bulge. After the war, he made his career defending insurance companies in personal-injury cases. He was known in Ohio legal circles as "the silver fox." Although a partner in a large suburban Cleveland law firm, before juries he affected the image of a simple country lawyer. Fulton's every move was carefully choreographed. He stalked around the witness box and in front of the jury, scowling and muttering when he objected. He joked, smirked, and peered around the courtroom to see who was watching. Robby Stamps "wanted to bust his teeth in." Art Krause thought Fulton "absolutely slick." "The judge was not in control of the courtroom when it came to the defendants," Krause later said. "The silver fox was in control."

Sixty-year-old, gum-chewing, Clark Gable look-alike Charlie Brown of Columbus wore florid ties and white shoes paired with a white suit. Reputedly a heavy drinker, he had a loud, rasping voice and expressed himself with earthy gestures. He would draw the mucus from his nose down into his mouth, pull a handkerchief out of his pocket, spit into it, then clear his throat. Most observers saw him as the second string to Fulton. "Charlie

Brown was just a figurehead," concluded Art Krause. "The real reins of the operation were held by Fulton." Betty Lewis never smiled at either of them.

Fulton and Brown let the jury know they were "Ohio boys." They knew how to hold a jury's attention. Their voices would rise to a shout and fall to a whisper—depending on the circumstances. The first time Kelner raised an objection, Brown drawled, "Is that the way they do it in New York?" (He would repeat this tactic throughout the trial.) Whenever Kelner asked a question, both men loudly cleared their throats. Their opening statements resembled those delivered by defense attorneys at the earlier criminal trial. The issue was not constitutional rights—it was terror and safety. They characterized the students as a mob. "Burning, looting, rioting, and terrorism were the order of the day," Brown boomed—"This was not a May Day picnic, but an insurrection!" The guardsmen had been called out to protect life and property. Protestors had charged them, putting the guardsmen in fear of their lives.

Kelner opened the plaintiffs' case on May 30. One of the first witnesses he called was Dean Kahler, the most grievously injured surviving victim. Dean rolled his wheelchair up next to the witness stand to the left of Judge Young's bench and very near the jury box. Kelner had instructed the victims to cut their hair and look tidy, but Dean had refused. His appearance had changed dramatically in the five years since the shooting. Once clean-cut and outgoing, he now sported a Custer-like mustache, shoulder-length red wavy hair, and what an observer described as "an air of dark, brooding intensity."

Fulton sought to offset any jury sympathy for Dean in a wheelchair by asking him about his participation in the sit-down demonstration at the intersection of Main and Lincoln Streets on Sunday night, May 3. "Did you hear the one, two, three, four business?" "Yes, I did." "You heard the 'One, two, three, four, we don't want your fucking war!'?" "Yes, I did." And you, yourself, made some of those chants, didn't you?" "Yes, I did." John Kahler watched from the front row of the spectators' seats. "That's why my boy got shot," he thought to himself, "because he said 'f-u-c-k-i-n-g' to a bunch of weekend warriors."

After Dean Kahler came Larry Shafer, the guardsman who shot Joe

Lewis. Kelner decided to put Shafer and other guardsmen on the stand as hostile witnesses because their only defense was self-defense and he believed they couldn't show it. Instead, Kelner would show the jury the "stark nakedness of their brutality." The day of the shooting had been the first time Shafer had ever fired his rifle. Many others had also never fired their rifles and had little if any notion of the M-1's fearsome destructiveness. Hours after the shooting, several had examined bullet holes in the steel sculpture and surrounding trees. "God, those damn things are powerful," said one said as he traced his finger around a bullet hole that passed clean through an eight-inch-thick tree.

Kelner asked Shafer to pick up an M-1 rifle from the exhibit table and demonstrate how he had flicked off the safety before firing. Fulton fidgeted in his seat. Located at the front of the trigger guard, the safety had to be pushed forward before the rifle could be fired. Shafer released the safety and squeezed the trigger. A loud click echoed throughout the courtroom.

"Did you see anything in [Lewis's] hands?" asked Kelner.
"One hand was upraised giving the finger. The other hand was to his side and partially hidden behind him."
"Show us what he was doing with his finger."
"He was doing this," said Shafer, raising his right hand and sticking up the middle finger.
"Did it present a danger to your life?"
"Not that hand."
. . .
"It didn't upset you?"
"No, sir."
"Didn't make you angry?"
"No, sir."
"Had nothing to do with you firing at that individual?"
"No, sir."
"Why didn't you consider using your bayonet instead of firing, if you thought your life was in danger?"

"If my arm wasn't hurt, I might have considered using my bayonet."

"But you held your gun up with your arm?"

"Yes, I could do that."

Kelner called more guardsmen to the stand during the weeks that followed. They told similar stories: wearing gas masks that restricted their vision, they had endured rock barrages and shouted threats that made them fearful of being overrun by the approaching protestors—though Sergeant Lloyd Thomas testified that no rocks were falling when the shooting started and there had been no need to shoot; Privates James Farriss and Richard Snyder said they had seen no more than three or four students in front of them, none carrying rocks, and saw no need to shoot; and Captain [now Major] John Martin testified that he had seen no reason for any weapon to be fired, that he had felt no concern for his life, that he hadn't seen any guardsman hit with rocks after leaving the practice field, and that the guardsmen had not been assaulted.

Kelner also called to the stand several photographers who witnessed the shooting and submitted many of their photos as evidence. Most were taken at close range and showed only a part of the larger setting. Fulton asked them why so many photos focused on the guardsmen rather than on the protestors and noted that none had been taken from behind the guardsmen as they turned, showing their view down the eastern slope of Taylor Hall toward the parking lot. The jurors watched Kelner hand photos to witnesses, but Judge Young refused to let witnesses testify about what the photographs showed. He ruled that members of the jury could look at all the photos during their deliberations and determine then what they showed. Kelner then called witnesses who had seen guardsmen bayonet protestors the night before the shooting, thus suggesting the guard's predisposition to use excessive force.

One of Kelner's final witnesses was Tom Grace, who had become very outspoken politically. Kelner privately characterized him as "radical" and "brilliant." Kelner feared Fulton and Brown might bring up some of Tom's post–May 4 statements to inflame jurors. He was right.

"Have you ever made statements regarding the fact that everyone ought to
    be armed to defend themselves against the imperialistic government?
    Have you made statements like that, Mr. Grace?"

. . .

"I don't know what time you're referring to, Mr. Fulton."
"He is referring to any time prior to May 4," said Judge Young.
"No, I didn't."
"Have you made those statements since May 4?"

Kelner objected, Judge Young sustained the objection, and Tom did not
answer the question. But the jury had been made aware of his remark. Fulton finished his cross-examination by asking Tom what SDS stood for and
why he had refused to be interviewed by the FBI during its investigation.

Infuriated, afterward Tom urged Kelner to retaliate by asking the
National Guardsmen whether they believed protestors with long hair
should be shot and what their opinion was of the My Lai massacre. "He
can't do that," Robby Stamps interjected. Kelner was "showing them how
a trial ought to be conducted." "What does it matter if we lose?" fumed
Tom. "We won't lose," Robby now predicted. "If you listen to the evidence,
they haven't a leg to stand on." Tom would have none of it. "I'm glad I told
my father not to come and hear this garbage." He walked out of the court-
house and never returned.

On June 23, Kelner called Alan Canfora to the stand. Kelner privately
characterized him as "bright, strong-willed, and radical." "Of all the plaintiffs," Kelner later wrote, "Alan had been the most active demonstrator; he
was portrayed in at least a dozen photographs, taunting the guardsmen
with his black flag." Like Tom Grace, Alan had been radicalized and alienated by the shooting, and his volcanic anger lay just beneath the surface.
He had grown a ponytail since May 1970, but at Kelner's urging he agreed
to hide his long reddish-blond hair beneath a wig while testifying on the
stand. That way, the jurors would concentrate on his handsome face and
striking green eyes instead.

Alan nervously wiggled his toes as he sat in the witness chair. Kelner pitched him softball questions. Then Charlie Brown moved in. He asked Alan about his attendance at SDS meetings and why he had waved a black flag rather than an American flag on May 4.

"What were your philosophies in May of 1970?" "Were you a political activist?"

"Yes. In fact, I was even more active due to the fact that I had attended a funeral of a friend of mine who was killed in Vietnam the week before that."

"Have you ever thought it might be appropriate to make a protest at the ballot box?"

"I think it is a legitimate way to exercise your democratic rights in this country."

"Do you think it is as legitimate as throwing a stone?"

"I think it is more legitimate, yes."

"And you threw some stones, didn't you?"

"I threw a single stone, but it fell far short."

. . .

"Tell the court and jury why you threw it."

"Do you want me to explain?"

"Yes," Judge Young interjected. "When he asks why, the door is open, tell whatever you want to tell."

"I threw it as a gesture of frustration towards them and not intended to hit them."*

"Was it a pacifist gesture?"

"It was frustration and anger after being tear-gassed and chased by bayonets."

By the end of July, jurors had heard eight weeks of testimony from nearly seventy witnesses including all nine wounded students and three dozen

---

*   Guardsman Bill Perkins later testified that a person with a black flag hit him in the chest with a rock that knocked him backward. Deposition of William Perkins, pp. 51–52, MS 1800, Box 70, KSC, SML, YU.

National Guardsmen. On August 4, Kelner introduced a final, dramatic piece of evidence: film footage of the moments before, during, and after the shooting. Around 12:23 p.m., sophomore Chris Abell set his 8-mm home-movie camera on the windowsill of his fifth-floor dorm room in Wright Hall, part of the Tri-Towers complex half a mile east of Blanket Hill, and turned it on for a minute and a half. Taken with a zoom lens from a considerable distance, the film's resolution was very poor. Amid a tremendous amount of shouting, jeering, and bell-clanging, students appear as small fuzzy blobs moving between a walk and a run up the eastern slope of Taylor Hall toward the guardsmen who were nearing the top of Blanket Hill. When the shooting starts, the protestors suddenly reverse course, race down the eastern slope of Taylor Hall, fanning out toward the practice field and the parking lot. When the shooting stops, several seconds of eerie silence follow, then people start shouting and screaming. Judge Young again forbade testimony about what Abell's home movie showed, saying the jury would decide what the film showed during its deliberations.

Watching the fuzzy images in the film and hearing the cries at the end of it, Florence Schroeder wondered whether it wouldn't had been better to pretend that she had lost her Bill in an automobile accident. "She had thought the truth would prevent a future shooting, but what was the use when others did not care? Let them find out for themselves that trust was not enough. Let them lose their innocence as she had lost hers."

Kelner wrapped up the plaintiffs' case on August 6. Fulton and Brown took just five days to present their defense; they had already cross-examined many witnesses. "The brevity of the defense's case and the small number of witnesses it called did not at all mean that their case was less elaborate than ours," Kelner later wrote, "for most of the defendants had already testified, and the defense had been making its case as we were making ours."

Fulton and Brown in their opening statements emphasized events leading up to the shooting on May 4, including eyewitness descriptions of the rioting and vandalism downtown on Friday night, May 1; the torching of the ROTC building and interference with firemen on Saturday night, May 2; and the confrontations near the library and main gate on Sunday night, May 3. "Violence, burning, and terror were the order of the day," Brown told the jury. He and Fulton suggested an unknown gunman had fired at the guardsmen just before the shooting, even though no guardsman had testified to that effect. They called to the stand an eyewitness on the roof of Johnson Hall at the time of the shooting, Joy Bishop, a young woman who claimed to have seen a man in a "yellowish-gold" sport coat walk up behind guardsmen at the Pagoda, draw a pistol from a briefcase, and fire it in the air "two to five seconds" before the firing began. Bishop's account closely resembled the episode involving photographer Terry Norman, wearing a tan sport coat, who had been seen on Blanket Hill with a pistol being chased by others, including a man carrying a briefcase, *after* the shooting. The two students standing on either side of Bishop on the roof of Johnson Hall that day, her roommate Pat Rivera and Rivera's boyfriend, Bruce Phillips, disputed her story. Rivera later told reporters, "I don't think she's lying. I think she's just confused."

A few days later, Judge Young summoned the attorneys to his chamber. He informed them that alternate juror Richard Williams had been threatened.* As Williams waited for a bus outside the Federal Building one afternoon, a man in his thirties walked up and told him that "the day the trial ended" his house would be blown up and his family killed if he didn't vote for the plaintiffs. Three and a half hours later, the man approached Williams again near his home. He threw Williams against a wall and repeated his warning. Young informed the attorneys that he would sequester the jury and provide it with around-the-clock protection by federal marshals. "I have blood on my hands from ignoring previous threats in other cases," he explained. Young did not question Williams nor excuse him from the jury. He also failed to question other jurors about the impact of the threat on them.† (Williams later said that he found the Abell film compelling evidence against the plaintiffs. The alternate who would have replaced Williams, Blanche Layman, said that she would have voted

---

* Kelner himself received three separate threats to "lay off of the defendants, or we'll get you." *Akron Beacon Journal*, August 20, 1975, p. D6.

† An appellate court later ruled these fundamental procedural errors.

for the plaintiffs. If Layman had replaced Williams as an alternate and then become a regular juror, there would not have been nine votes required for a verdict of not guilty.)

Summations began the next morning. Kelner opened. "I felt I was in top form," he later boasted, "speaking in high, ringing tones, taking the jury into my confidence, lowering my voice as I read from a document as if imparting a secret, then shifting to a scolding note, 'You don't shoot!' (you warn, you threaten, you use butt strokes, you use bayonets). The Ohio National Guard, I told the jury, might be a wonderful institution. Governor Rhodes might be a splendid governor. But the National Guard was poorly run, and Governor Rhodes had goofed." Kelner took more than two hours to review his case to the jury. He quoted Rhodes's May 3 press conference statement that "the National Guard should use whatever force was necessary." "And what can 'whatever force was necessary,' what can that be but a green light to those who have loaded weapons?" "Irresponsible!" he told the jury. "Thoughtless and reckless!"

In the defense summation, Fulton and Brown emphasized that most of the plaintiffs had participated in one of the disturbances between Friday night, May 1, and Sunday night, May 3, and that the indicted guardsmen had cooperated with investigators after the shooting, hiding nothing. They characterized the May 4 protestors as a mob and cited Clarence Darrow's famous defense of an African American man who had fired into a mob attacking his home in a white neighborhood. Choked up with tears in his eyes, Fulton declared, "These guardsmen were in fear of their lives on that hill on May 4, 1970. What were they afraid of? That they were going to be overrun, their weapons taken from them. The crowd was coming in." Do "you have a First Amendment right to charge, yelling, 'Kill the pigs—Sieg heil!'?" "That's worse than saying you have got a right to go into a crowded theater and yell, 'Fire!'"

In rebuttal Kelner said, "This is not a criminal case, ladies and gentlemen. We only need to show their responsibility by a fair preponderance of the evidence." "We want responsibility fixed." "Students were running away from the very first shot and they kept shooting and shooting. Why?

Why? Why?" He then began a thirteen-second countdown. The courtroom grew silent. "Thirteen seconds, an eternity of time to stop shooting so that a boy like Dean Kahler won't be shot in the back or a girl like Allison Krause could have had her life saved."

"We had a great day," Kelner said to his clients afterward. "We had them nailed to the ground." Parents of the slain students congratulated him, confident they would win. Doug Wrentmore initially thought so too. But when he saw two female jurors crying, he suspected "something was going on." "I was no longer sure we would win." Robby Stamps had no doubt about the outcome. "I'm sorry we lost," he told Kelner. "I grew up in Cleveland and I know. I never want to see Ohio again." With that, he got up and walked out.

The next morning, August 21, Judge Young instructed the jury. His instructions ran to seventy-six pages. He explained that a preponderance of evidence had to show that the defendants had violated the statutory and constitutional rights of the plaintiffs, including the right to assemble peacefully, the right not to be deprived of life and liberty without due process of the law, the right not to suffer cruel and inhuman punishment, and the right to protection against excessive government force. When Judge Young finished, he told jurors, "From now until your verdict is returned, you people are in charge of the show."

Escorted by U.S. Marshals, the twelve jurors left the courtroom to begin their deliberations. For the next six days, they spent thirty-three hours together in the nearby jury room. People outside the jury room occasionally heard arguing and crying. The feelings were so tense that at one point it seemed like a bombshell was about to burst. The jurors did not ask for any evidence or request the reading of any testimony. They did ask to see some photographs, a map of campus, and the grainy 8-mm Abell film. On August 26, at 4:47 p.m., word went out that they had reached a verdict. Everyone returned to the courtroom the next morning. "Ladies and gentlemen," Judge Young addressed the jury and those sitting in the courtroom, "this has been a long and difficult trial, and it is the culmination of many years of effort. I know feelings are rising and rising very high. . . . I ask you please to make a final effort and keep your composure until the court is recessed." He then nodded at the clerk. "The clerk will read the verdicts."

The court clerk read aloud thirteen jury sheets listing each of the slain and injured students. After each one, the clerk announced, "We, the jury, on the issues joined, find in favor of the defendants." The vote in each instance was 9 to 3. The three dissenting jurors were Mary Blazina and Ellen Gaskalla of Bill Schroeder's hometown, Lorain, and Roberta Heckman of Avon, Ohio. Gaskalla told the *Plain Dealer* newspaper she felt they had to find in favor of or against all the defendants on the basis of Judge Young's instructions. She said she would have preferred judging the guardsmen "more on an individual basis." Another female juror said in the privacy of the jury room, "I know that all of you are probably right in the way you are voting, but I am just really confused, I can't sort it all out, and I have to vote against the defendants if I am not sure." The third female juror said that her religious beliefs would not allow her to vote any other way but against the defendants because they had hurt people and no matter what else happened, that was wrong.

Elaine Kahler couldn't believe the verdicts. Sarah Scheuer burst into tears and cried, "They're still murderers!" "Oh, my God!" bellowed Art Krause, denouncing the guard as "armed barbarians" and saying of the jury, "Thanks to them, murder by the state is correct." Lou and Florence Schroeder held each other's hands and wept. Tom Grace yelled, "They're still murderers!" then raised his left fist in a revolutionary salute. A federal marshal grabbed him. "Keep your hands off that boy!" shouted Art Krause. "This is an outrage!" screamed Alan Canfora, "There is no justice!" Judge Young said, "If you think that I am going to create more sympathy for you by citing you for contempt, you're wrong. But if you say anything again, I will have you removed." Alan's father thought, "What justifies killing in our justice system? Not anyone throwing a stone." Elaine Miller Holstein said the verdict gave the government "license to shoot anyone who doesn't agree with them." Joe Lewis said the trial made a mockery of justice. Joe's father told him, "Maybe you're right. There is no justice in Ohio." "I couldn't understand how the jury could vote against us," said Doug Wrentmore. "I felt pretty positive about all the jurors and hurt that they had misjudged" the

case. "I felt no animosity for them. They were manipulated." John Cleary
had been apprehensive about the trial from the beginning. Now he simply felt cynical—convinced "whoever has the best lawyer and the most
money can buy" justice. "You can't buck the system," he said. "So why try?"
Robby Stamps told everyone "I'm sorry we lost" and left for California. Dean
Kahler slumped in his wheelchair; Collette Grace thought he was going to
collapse. Dean's girlfriend, Valerie Manning, laid her head on his lap and
sobbed. After the trial, Dean spoke philosophically about the verdicts. "Justice is human," he reflected, "and what is human is that which may err."

"This is a sad day in American justice," Joe Kelner said. "The firing
on unarmed students by armed men will go down in history as a travesty
unless you set aside the verdict," he told Judge Young. Burt Fulton said
the trial had been "a tough business." "What people fail to realize is that
this trial has been a real tragedy in the hearts and minds of the guardsmen, too." Sarah Scheuer approached Fulton and told him this was not
the finish—she would see him in a higher court. Fulton coldly responded
that she was a poor sport.

The defendants expressed relief. Robert White placed his head in his
hands and sobbed. He never looked up as the clerk read the thirteen verdicts. "I'm pleased and relieved at the decision," he told reporters. "I didn't
say happy, because it is not possible to be happy about anything that happened on May 4, 1970." Matt McManus learned of his acquittal on his
car radio. He pulled over to the side of the road and cried like a baby. Bill
Herschler also wept when the verdicts flashed across his television screen.
"Maybe we will live a little freer and looser now," he told reporters.[*] Robert
Canterbury expressed sympathy for the plaintiffs. "I certainly feel a sense
of compassion for them," he said. "I've never felt so bad about winning
something," admitted Charles Fassinger. Governor Rhodes said that May
4, 1970, was "the most sorrowful day of my life."

---

[*] Herschler's brother later appeared at the Schroeders' door and begged them to cease
further litigation because Bill had suffered a mental breakdown after the shooting. James
Munves interview with Lou and Florence Schroeder, June 12, 1977, Laura Davis Papers,
Box 214, M4C, KSUL.

Former U.S. senator Stephen Young denounced the verdict as a miscar-
riage of justice and expressed regret for supporting his nephew's appoint-
ment to the federal bench. It was, he said, "the worst" recommendation
he ever made. But after the trial, every juror commended the judge for his
kindness, his intelligence, and his fairness in handling the case.

"You are entitled to the gratitude of all the people of this free land,"
Judge Young told the jurors before dismissing them. "What freedom?!"
shouted Tom Grace. "This trial has been a sham in every way!"

All the jurors except Ellen Gaskalla refused to publicly discuss how or
why they reached their verdicts. One male juror later agreed to a confidential interview with the National Jury Project, a polling organization of
Columbia University sociologists. In the interview he said, "I am still convinced we did the right thing, after really thinking about it for three weeks
after the trial. When you go over [the judge's] instructions very carefully
as we did, you can see there was no choice. If we were going to follow the
law as the judge gave it to us, then we had to vote the way we did." "We all
took our duty very seriously and did the best job we could in reaching our
decision. After we reached our decision, we broke into tears and we prayed.
We prayed that we had done the right thing." "It was a very hard thing to
do and we really felt the weight of our task."

Judge Young ordered the plaintiffs to pay the defendants' legal expenses.
His ruling led one commentator to observe, "The state, having licensed people to kill and having justified it, has now chosen to charge the survivors."

———

The plaintiffs appealed the verdict on the grounds that Judge Young had
denied them a fair trial. The Scheuers contacted the Ohio chapter of the
ACLU (the same organization, ironically, whose New York member Morris Ernst had threatened and attempted to bribe Art Krause). The ACLU
agreed to represent the plaintiffs pro bono and assigned Sanford Rosen,
a thirty-seven-year-old graduate of Yale Law School in the ACLU's San
Francisco office, to handle the case. Rosen had considerable appellate experience. He understood higher courts' reluctance to overrule lower-court
judges and second-guess juries. At his initial meeting with the plaintiffs,

Rosen told them the odds were 1,000 to 1 against them winning their appeal. The plaintiffs urged Rosen to proceed anyway. With help from the victims' previous lawyers, Rosen submitted a brief to the U.S. Court of Appeals for the Sixth Circuit in Cincinnati in May 1976. The brief included an eleven-volume appendix of documents, photographs, and excerpts from the civil trial transcript. Oral arguments did not come until more than a year later, on June 21, 1977. The mahogany-paneled courtroom was packed as Judges George Edwards, Jr., of Detroit, Michigan, Pierce Lively of Lexington, Kentucky, and Harry Phillips of Nashville, Tennessee, took their seats at the bench. In the audience sat the parents of the four slain students as well as the Graces, the Kahlers, Jan Wrentmore, and General Del Corso.

Rosen rested his oral argument on three points: (1) the events of May 1–3 did not justify a ban on the May 4 student rally; (2) there was insufficient evidence that the guardsmen's lives were in jeopardy when they opened fire; and (3) Judge Young had erred by failing to question the threatened alternate juror and remove him if he had been swayed by the threats. The appellate judges focused on the third point and asked many questions about it. Afterward, Rosen told the plaintiffs that the odds against them had shortened to 10 to 1—still a long shot.

On September 12, the Court of Appeals, citing the mishandling of the threatened alternate juror, ordered a new civil trial. The judges wrote in their unanimous opinion:

> Every litigant is entitled to a verdict which is free from improper influence. It was an error for the trial court to determine without any personal interrogation that a juror who had been threatened and assaulted and told that his home would be blown up could continue to serve unaffected by these incidents. . . . Unless the court was completely satisfied after questioning him that there was no possibility that the threatened juror would be affected in the performance of his duties, that juror should have been excused.

The judges, however, dismissed the plaintiffs' claim that the students' First Amendment rights to freedom of peaceful assembly had been violated. They ruled that the disturbances on May 1–3 justified authorities in banning the May 4 noon rally on campus.

The plaintiffs had won a new trial. But they resumed bickering—this time over who would lead their effort in court. Joe Kelner sought the role once more, as did Sanford Rosen. Each privately disparaged the other in letters to the plaintiffs. Rosen told the victims, "At the first trial, the case was not so much won by the defendants as lost by the plaintiffs." Kelner, in turn, said selecting Rosen to lead the effort courted disaster because he had never tried a case before a jury and "in the eyes of many prospective jurors, the ACLU itself is regarded as a radical organization."

In the end, the victims and their families selected Rosen. One of the first things Rosen did was to commission the National Jury Project to canvas potential jurors in northeastern Ohio about the chances of winning a new trial. Though nearly eight years had passed since the shooting, the poll revealed, as Rosen put it, that "there was a high degree of probability that we weren't going to win."

William Thomas, the U.S. district judge who had ordered the prejudicial special state grand jury report destroyed in February 1971, presided at the new trial. Appointed to the federal bench in 1966 by President Lyndon Johnson, the white-haired, long-faced, eagle-eyed, sixty-seven-year-old Thomas had an enviable reputation. "He is thorough, eminently fair, scholarly, respectful and courteous, lawyers say in on-the-record interviews," noted the *Plain Dealer*. Unlike many other judges, "lawyers never ask to go off the record regarding Thomas." He wrote lucid opinions and sympathized with the suffering of others because of the suffering he had experienced as a result of his involvement in the accidental death of his older brother in a hunting accident decades earlier.

Thomas's pretrial rulings differed significantly from Young's. He said plaintiffs' attorneys could ask witnesses their opinions about what photographs showed and prohibited defense attorneys from asking victims about their political beliefs. Despite these rulings, Rosen remained pessimistic about his clients' chances of success and frankly told them so.

The trial took place in Cleveland in the same downtown Federal Building as the 1975 civil trial, but in a different courtroom. Judge Thomas's courtroom had a high vaulted ceiling, handsome marble pilasters, and two enormous chandeliers. On the wall behind the bench hung an enormous painting of Lady Justice pointing to the Ten Commandments' prohibition, "Thou Shalt Not Kill." Thomas swore in the nine-man, three-woman jury on December 15, 1978.

A month before, Rosen had informed Thomas that the plaintiffs would settle in return for "a suitable letter of regret and sympathy" and $2 million in compensatory damages. Newspapers began publishing rumors about a settlement. Thomas, who strongly favored a settlement, recessed the trial on December 21 to give both sides more time to reach an agreement.

The plaintiffs had grown weary and discouraged after eight years of legal struggle. "I'm tired, sick and tired of fighting," Art Krause confessed. "Some of the families felt that we were passing up a chance to 'showcase' the event again," recalled Florence Schroeder. "On the other hand, some felt that there was nothing new to be learned and that we had little chance of any financial settlement, even with a favorable verdict. The lawyers were well prepared and we never lost confidence in their ability to present a winning case. *BUT*, there remained the physical condition of Dean Kahler and Joseph Lewis, and possibly others, who would need the financial settlement to help establish useful lives."

The defendants also wanted the legal battle to end and to put the long ordeal behind them. "A lot of us felt we'd had enough," said Matt McManus. "We just didn't want to face another trial. We gathered together—a group of us—and we decided we were going to settle. Our lawyers were very upset with us when we made the decision that we wanted to settle." The plaintiffs, in turn, accepted a settlement, Elaine Miller Holstein explained, "because we determined that it accomplished, to the greatest extent possible under present law, the objectives toward which we as families have struggled during the past eight years." The plaintiffs agreed to drop their lawsuit and relinquish all future claims against the defendants. In return, the defendants issued a Statement of Regret:

> In retrospect, the tragedy of May 4, 1970, should not have occurred.
> The students may have believed that they were right in continuing

their mass protest in response to the Cambodian invasion, even though this protest followed the posting and reading by the University of an order to ban rallies and an order to disperse. These orders have since been determined by the Sixth Circuit Court of Appeals to have been lawful.

Some of the Guardsmen on Blanket Hill, fearful and anxious from prior events, may have believed in their own minds that their lives were in danger. Hindsight suggests that another method would have resolved the confrontation. Better ways must be found to deal with such confrontations.

We devoutly wish that a means had been found to avoid the May 4 events culminating in the Guard shootings and the irreversible deaths and injuries. We deeply regret those events and are profoundly saddened by the deaths of four students and wounding of nine others which resulted. We hope that the agreement to end this litigation will help to assuage the tragic memories regarding that sad day.

The settlement awarded $675,000 (approximately $3 million in 2024 dollars) to the plaintiffs. It was a relatively small sum compared to damages awarded in most personal-injury and negligence suits. $350,000 went to Dean Kahler, permanently crippled, to meet his future medical expenses; $42,500 to Joe Lewis, missing several feet of intestine, suffering constant stomach trouble, and with a numb leg; $37,500 to Tom Grace, missing part of his left foot and in frequent discomfort; $27,500 to Scott MacKenzie, missing a piece of jawbone; $22,500 to John Cleary, missing three ribs and part of a lung; $15,000 each to Alan Canfora, shot through the wrist; Jim Russell, peppered with buckshot in the forehead and thigh; Robby Stamps, shot in the rear; and Doug Wrentmore, shot below the knee. The parents of the four dead students each received $15,000 in symbolic compensation for the loss of their loved ones. The remainder, $75,000, covered their lawyers' fees and legal expenses.

At the post-settlement news conference, Art Krause leaned against a wall, arms folded, his face blank. "We don't want the damn money, we want the truth. If we had wanted the money, I would have accepted the $1,500,000 bribe I was offered to drop the civil suit. We want the facts out about how the four died. We aren't afraid of the truth. We aren't the ones who have been saying 'no comment' for the past ten years." "Everyone in the world knows a monetary settlement is not made unless guilt and liability are involved." Elaine Kahler didn't want money; she wanted to "make sure this wouldn't happen to someone else's son." Martin Scheuer squeezed his wife Sarah's shoulder and sobbed. Doug Wrentmore "wouldn't have felt good about sending National Guardsmen to jail." "Prison rule was a jungle" and he "wouldn't want anything to do with sending anyone to prison." He simply wanted to "hold them responsible." Robby Stamps said, "It's good for all of us to put this chapter in our lives behind us and go on to other things." "I'm going to try to go about my life in a normal way. That's something I haven't been able to do for eight and a half years." Dean Kahler, in his wheelchair, held hands with his wife, Valerie. "I feel adequate with it," he said, "and coming from me, that's a compliment. They're saying they shot us when they shouldn't have shot us. I would not have minded being beaten over the head. I'd still be walking today." He nearly broke down. "I've struggled, since the moment I was shot, to stay alive [but] I hope I don't carry any feelings of hate, of mistrust. I hope someday I'll be able to go to sleep and spend eternity in peace." "The words in the settlement were not what I wanted," Elaine Miller Holstein said. "I wanted the impossible—I wanted Jeffrey back."

"There is symbolism in the closing agreement of Gov. James Rhodes and twenty-seven National Guardsmen—the defendants of the latest civil suit—to sign a statement of regret," the *New York Times* editorialized. "At long last, a note of decency supersedes the truculence with which Ohio officials responded time and again to the anger and anguish of the victims' families." The *Akron Beacon Journal* put it best: "It would be foolish to expect all disagreement over what happened on Kent State's Blanket Hill May 4, 1970, to be stilled; debate as to who was guilty of what will doubtless continue as long as memory of that tragic day persists. But [the] out-of-court settlement should at least put an end to painful judicial probing of the old wounds and help the long, slow process of healing. And the terms of the settlement perhaps come as close to 'justice' as any neutral observer could hope for."

Chapter 10

REMEMBRANCE

How Kent State is remembered has evolved a great deal over the years. During the 1970s and 1980s, May 4 was not officially commemorated—the day remained too controversial and contentious. Two decades passed before an official memorial to the slain students was erected on the Kent State campus in 1990. In the three decades since, official observances have become more common with less accompanying discord each passing year. By the fiftieth anniversary of the shooting in 2020, annual remembrances of May 4 had become elaborate fixed rituals. This shift in how the shooting has been commemorated parallels an evolution in popular thinking about the Vietnam War, protest movements, and government-sanctioned violence over the past fifty years.

For a decade after 1970, there were no official observances of May 4. Most Americans wanted to forget the shooting as much as they wanted to forget the disastrous and divisive Vietnam War that led to it. The first commemoration was a simple memorial service held on campus four months after the shooting, open only to students. The following spring, on the eve of the first anniversary of May 4, mourners gathered on the Commons for a candlelight march that ended where the four slain students had fallen. Participants then stood in silent vigil at these spots all through the night.

The next day, Dean Kahler spoke before an audience of several thousand people on campus. Parents of the four slain students had not been invited because Kent State president Robert White thought it would not be "beneficial" to them. "It's so damn senseless," Art Krause said. "They won't even invite us to their observance. They just want to forget. How can I forget?" He visited Allison's gravesite instead, where he noticed a flower that a stranger had left there. That night, he received a phone call from a man with a Southern drawl. It was a Vietnam veteran who told Art that he had left the flower at the base of Allison's granite headstone in honor of her memory. The next day, a plain white envelope decaled with an American flag arrived in the mail. "KRAUSE," the letter inside read, "YOUR DAUGHTER WAS A FOUL-MOUTHED WHORE, WHICH IS BAD ENOUGH, BUT YOU ARE A DIRTY PINK."

That same year, the campus Jewish organization, B'nai B'rith Hillel,[*] installed a cast aluminum plaque at the western edge of the Prentice Hall parking lot that read simply, "In Loving Memory" above the names of Allison Krause, Jeffrey Miller, Sandra Scheuer, and William Schroeder. Not long after the plaque was installed, vandals desecrated it with bullets. Three years later, the plaque was stolen. It was replaced with a marble marker the following year. That, too, was defaced and eventually replaced in 1979 by a third marker, a two-foot pink granite monument. The stonemason who installed the third marker had been a member of the Ohio National Guard on May 4. It remained the sole memorial of the shooting on the Kent State campus for nearly twenty years.

In 1974, the university took another step by creating a May 4 Resource Center on the ground floor of the new twelve-story Main Library. The walls were adorned with photos of Jeff Miller, Allison Krause, Sandy Scheuer, and Bill Schroeder. The center featured artwork and documentation about the events of May 1970, the Vietnam War, and campus unrest nationwide but with no interpretation—a testament to how sensitive and contentious these topics remained.

The events of May 1970 damaged Kent State's reputation throughout Ohio. The state legislature in Columbus reduced its budget. Enrollments

---

[*] Three of the four slain students—Allison Krause, Jeff Miller, and Sandy Scheuer—were Jewish.

and donations to the university dropped more than 25 percent. University leaders concluded the less attention devoted to May 4, the better. In 1975, Robert White's successor as president, Glenn Olds, decided to end support for campus commemorations of the shooting. May 4 survivors and victims' families reacted angrily. They considered themselves—and no one else— guardians of the memory of those killed at Kent State. They "owned" May 4 and they were determined to keep alive the memory of the shooting. In response to Olds's decision, Alan Canfora, Dean Kahler, and Robby Stamps created the May 4 Task Force to perpetuate awareness of the tragedy and ensure it would never be forgotten. Thereafter, the May 4 Task Force gathered periodically on campus to remember and to witness.

For years, Elaine Miller Holstein couldn't bring herself to visit the Kent State campus. Finally, in June 1975, she did, driving down from Cleveland during a break in the guardsmen's first federal civil trial. She took a guided tour of the campus because she wanted to see the spot where Jeff had fallen. Afterward, she visited the May 4 Resource Center in the lobby of the Main Library. She spent time there alone, carefully studying the photographs of her son and of Allison, Bill, and Sandy as they had been in life. Before her visit, she had imagined Kent State as "a sort of concentration camp," but she now realized it was "just a campus." And she was glad she went. She returned the following year for the candlelight march and vigil. Martin and Sarah Scheuer participated in the march and vigil for the first time in 1977. "I'm sorry we weren't here before," Sarah said. "We didn't know that this still mattered here."

That same year, the university decided to begin construction of an annex to Memorial Gymnasium* on the southern end of the practice field and the lower eastern slope of Blanket Hill. (The original decision to build the annex had been made before the shooting.) The gym annex would cover part of the area where students and guardsmen had confronted one another and where Jim Russell had been shot, but not the upper portion of Blanket Hill from where guardsmen had fired or any of the eastern slope of Taylor Hall or of the Prentice Hall parking lot where the slain and

---

* Today called the Memorial Athletic and Convocation Center (MACC).

other injured students had fallen. Protestors led by the May 4 Task Force vigorously opposed the gym annex. They viewed it as a deliberate insult to the victims, an attempt to "cover up the past," and a desecration of "sacred ground"—akin to putting a basketball court at Bunker Hill, a bowling alley at Valley Forge, or a tennis court at Gettysburg. May 4 Task Force activists rallied, picketed, and lobbied against the project, demanding that the gym annex be relocated or canceled. Polls showed that 70 percent of Kent State students agreed with them. Conservative townsfolk vehemently disagreed. "All that is at stake," said one Kent resident, "is a piece of ground where four anarchists were shot."

On the morning of May 12, 1977, activists shouting "Take the hill!" pitched tents on the planned construction site to block the project. Tent City, as the encampment came to be known, grew to sixty tents and two hundred inhabitants. The activists who camped there believed that drawing media attention would create image problems for the university, forcing a reversal of the decision. Townspeople, on the other hand, wrote letters to the local paper criticizing "rabble-rousers" and calling for the expulsion of the "squatters." They and other conservatives viewed opposition to the gym annex as a "fabrication" by "outside agitators."

The university went to court to have the squatters removed from Blanket Hill. A judge declared the encampment illegal and ordered it dismantled. On July 12, authorities began the clearance process. Tent City inhabitants and several hundred others including Alan Canfora and Martin and Sarah Scheuer sat on the ground and interlocked their arms and legs in an act of civil disobedience. Florence Schroeder read an emotional statement to television cameras. Dean Kahler was not there. "I wanted to be with you," he told the May 4 Task Force, "but I couldn't go up on that hill again. . . . All those things that happened seven years ago are still too much in my head." The media reported live as unarmed university police and county sheriffs disentangled and arrested 193 protestors without violence—evidence that law enforcement had learned some lessons from the tragedy of May 4. On September 19, construction began on the gym annex. It opened to students two years later.

In 1978, the Cleveland-based Mildred Andrews Fund commissioned a May 4 memorial on the Kent State campus by noted New York sculptor George Segal. Segal chose as his theme an Old Testament metaphor. Segal's sculpture, which he titled *Abraham's Sacrifice of Isaac*, depicted a knife-bearing father facing a kneeling youth with hands bound in front of him. "I found that sculpture interesting to do," Segal later said, "because I thought [May 4] was far more complicated than it appeared on the surface."

Like every previous effort to commemorate the shooting, Segal's sculpture provoked controversy and highlighted enduring divisions over the shooting. Proponents of the sculpture viewed it as a compelling depiction of the moral dilemma inherent in the treatment of student protestors by the state. Critics saw it as an explicit condemnation of the shooting. The new university president, Brage Golding, ultimately rejected the sculpture because he concluded it violated the school's steadfast neutrality on how—and even whether—to remember and interpret the events of May 4. Rejected by Kent State, Segal donated his sculpture to Princeton University instead—but not before a vandal broke off the blade of Abraham's knife. Princeton invited the victims' families to the dedication in the autumn of 1979. The repaired statue has stood ever since in Princeton's Modern Sculpture Garden.

The tenth anniversary of the shooting in 1980 marked an important moment because Larry Shafer used the occasion to break the long silence among the guardsmen who had fired on May 4. "It's time somebody gets the other side of the story," Shafer told the *Akron Beacon Journal*. He asserted that "the Kent State shooting could have been prevented with proper leadership" because "there was never any real need for the National Guard in May 1970." Mayor Satrom, he added, "pushed the panic button" when he requested the Ohio National Guard be sent to Kent. Shafer reserved his harshest criticism, however, for General Robert Canterbury. "If that general had had his head out of his ass," Shafer bluntly remarked, "he never would have put us in that situation." Shafer stressed there was no prior decision by the guardsmen to fire into the crowd of students. By breaking his silence, Shafer exposed the public to a new perspective on the shooting, affording an opportunity for a broadened and deepened understanding of the May 4 tragedy.

***

For years, the May 4 Task Force had viewed the absence of an official campus memorial to the victims of the shooting as evidence of the university's indifference, lack of vision, and reluctance to hallow the ground where the tragedy had occurred. Tom Grace argued to the university that an official campus memorial would "ensure that future generations will know and understand the bloody day. We owe that to the memory of those who died." "If Kent State wants to make peace with the past," he said, "they must make peace with the living. We will not rest until we are certain that our classmates are never forgotten."

University administrators finally embraced the idea of an official campus memorial in 1980. It had taken them a long time. President Golding explained why in a letter to alumni. "Had everyone who has expressed an opinion about the 'meaning of the Kent State tragedy' sent a check for $5," he observed, "we would have been able to erect a very imposing statue long ago. The trouble is, no group composed of more than one could have agreed on what it should look like."

Golding now concluded that the creation of an official memorial was important because "the one point that extremists at both ends of the spectrum seem to agree on is that there should be no memorial. Some say that to memorialize the slain students would be to glorify anarchy; others contend that to do so would be to cover up blame." He reasoned that enough years had passed and passions had cooled enough that an official memorial could be built—one that would begin to heal the wounds of May 4 rather than perpetuate or exacerbate them.

It took Kent State's board of trustees another five years to approve the construction of an official memorial on campus. The university did not, however, invite the May 4 Task Force or victims' families to participate in designing the memorial. "That shouldn't have been surprising considering the university's twenty-year record of total, blatant insensitiv-ity, . . . especially where the families are concerned," quipped one May 4 Task Force member.

In September 1985, a national design competition began for an official campus memorial that would promote healing and "avoid sources of fur-ther dissension." The National Endowment for the Arts financed the com-petition. It attracted nearly seven thousand submissions, more than any other American monument to date except the Vietnam Veterans Memorial in Washington, D.C.—evidence of how potent the meaning and memory of the Kent State shooting remained in the American mind. The jury chose Chicago architect Bruno Ast,* who proposed a 1,400-square-foot marble plaza containing a walkway embedded with four black granite disks leading to four black granite pylons and, at the opposite end, a black granite bench for contemplation, all set on a 2.5-acre wooded hill northwest of Taylor Hall overlooking the Commons. The plaza's threshold would be engraved with the words, "Inquire, Learn, Reflect." Kent State art professor Brinsley Tyrrell proposed adding 58,175 daffodils on the hillside to symbolize the number of Americans killed in Vietnam. (Daffodils are often in bloom in northeastern Ohio during the first week of May.)

Ast's design triggered controversy, which belied the reconciliation a memorial was intended to facilitate. The American Legion and the Frater-nal Order of Police denounced the proposed design as an "insult" and a "memorial to terrorists." The Ohio American Legion commander labeled it a monument to "John Dillinger types." "The only thing the guardsmen were guilty of," said another legionnaire, were being "poor shots"; incidents such as Kent State happened "when you have a bunch of terrorists leading [students]." Conservatives lobbied the legislature in Columbus to deny state funding for it and complained to Kent State's board of trustees "over the expenditure of any government funding for a memorial identifying the Anarchists that were killed on May 4."

"The American Legion ought to be ashamed of themselves," Art Krause

---

* The initial winner, Canadian Ian Taberner, was disqualified because contest rules required American citizenship.

declared. "It's so frustrating, after all these years, to hear people spouting the same old garbage, despite all available evidence to the contrary," Elaine Miller Holstein told the press, adding, "It's so much easier to allow oneself not to be confused by facts that don't match one's preconceived notions." She wanted Jeff and all the other victims' names etched into the memorial, as she had seen in a memorial at the Nazi death camp at Dachau. "I walked through the camp, unable to feel any emotion until I saw a plaque, alongside the ovens, on which the names of three young women were inscribed—young women who had been incinerated in those ovens—and *then* the impact hit me! It's only when you *name* the people—when you personalize—that the tragedy becomes meaningful." Kent State's board of trustees responded by ordering Ast to include a plaque bearing the thirteen students' names on the walkway leading up to the plaza.

Dedication of the official memorial took place on May 4, 1990. Hundreds of students—many not yet been born in May 1970—stood in pouring rain as a small group of conservative Vietnam veterans looked on in silent protest. Ohio Democratic governor Dick Celeste recalled the tragic day and expressed "disbelief that we had turned our weapons on our own children." He offered official contrition—something that had never been done in twenty years. "To Allison Krause, your family and your friends, I am sorry," Celeste said in an emotion-filled voice. "To Jeff Miller, your family and your friends, I am sorry. To Sandy Scheuer, your family and your friends, I am sorry. To Bill Schroeder, your family and your friends, I am sorry. To Dean Kahler, all of those who were wounded, and all of those who suffered twenty years ago today on this campus, I am sorry."

Former South Dakota U.S. senator and 1972 Democratic presidential candidate George McGovern followed Celeste at the podium. McGovern acknowledged the continuing controversy over May 4. "This was brought home to me after I accepted the invitation to be a speaker here today," he said. "Several groups and individuals wrote to me objecting to this memorial service for a variety of reasons. Some of the correspondents begged me not to come. Others suggested that it would be hazardous for me to write my own remarks today without their guidance." "Sometimes I think a memorial can help us come to terms with these divisions and the larger tragedy we recall today," McGovern continued. He cited the Vietnam Veterans Memorial in Washington, D.C. It had aroused enormous controversy when first proposed but, in time, became the most visited monument in the nation's capital. "We pray that here at Kent State the memorial we now dedicate will serve to deepen our appreciation and our understanding of one of the most tragic episodes of the [Vietnam] War." "Let us do these things while recalling the ancient biblical promise, 'When a man's ways please the Lord, he maketh even his enemies to be at peace with him.'"

A tearful Florence Schroeder, speaking on behalf of her husband and Martin and Sarah Scheuer, said, "We feel this is a fine memorial. But memorials thrive on the events of the past and do not affect the future unless we strive for a better way to prevent similar events." Dean Kahler told the crowd, "The injustices committed here should never be forgotten, but as a wounded student, I feel no bitterness. Only forgiveness is in my heart." Listening in the audience was Charles Fassinger—back for the first time since May 4, 1970. Fassinger faulted the university for not inviting guardsmen to the dedication, but he praised the memorial as "a place to learn and reflect." Robby Stamps spoke for many when he said, "The May 4 Memorial . . . helped many who were involved get some finality and peace of mind after all these years of turmoil and contention."

———

The university's reaction to the shooting over the years mirrored that of the nation itself—awkward sensitivity at first, followed by studied indifference, gradually giving way to acceptance, and eventually full recognition. Coming to terms with the tragedy of May 4 had been no easy task. For years, university administrators felt embarrassed by the shooting. "Many wanted to just forget about it, pretend it didn't happen or turn our back on it," said one professor. They recognized the historical importance of May 4, but they rued the negative publicity it brought the school. They particularly fretted about how parents felt about sending their children (and tuition money) to "Chaos U." May 4 was the reason Kent State was known throughout the country and around the world.

The administration desperately sought to distance the university from the tragedy. "The history of Kent State University is made up of more than one day," President Golding defensively argued. To that end, in 1986 his successor, Michael Schwartz, hired a public-relations firm to improve the university's image. The firm's recommendations included rebranding the university as "Kent." "Kent University" would be less identified with the shooting and therefore attract less adverse publicity. "We wanted to get people to think of the university in other terms," Schwartz later admitted.

In 1991, Carol Cartwright succeeded Michael Schwartz as president. Cartwright felt she had a responsibility "to deal differently" with May 4. The first thing she did was put "State" back into the university's name. Cartwright wanted to lead "a university that remembers its past, its history, and has learned from the event." "We should more positively embrace May 4 and use it in a more positive way and help people look forward," she said. "We have no choice but to remember May 4 because society demands it."

Until 1998, the spaces in the Prentice Hall parking lot where Allison Krause, Bill Schroeder, and Sandy Scheuer had fallen were still in daily use. That year, students petitioned Cartwright to install commemorative markers to block off the three parking spaces and the spot on Midway Drive where Jeff Miller had died. Cartwright quickly agreed. Illuminated black concrete bollards were installed around each space, in the center of which was placed a small granite marker bearing the student's name and the date May 4, 1970. The project was paid for by funds from private donors, including Cartwright. At the dedication ceremony in September 1999, she told the victims' families, "It is our hope that each of you finds solace in knowing that your precious sons, daughters, brothers, and sisters have never, and will never, be forgotten." In the years since, the spaces have become focal points during the annual candlelight vigil. Small stones are placed atop the bollards in the Jewish tradition of leaving stones at gravesites. "For 364 days a year, it's a parking lot," noted the *Record-Courier*. "For one day, it's a shrine."

The same is true of Donald Drumm's steel sculpture *Solar Totem #1* located just off the eastern terrace of Taylor Hall. Every May 4, the bullet-scarred sculpture is adorned with daffodils from the memorial hillside, embellished with candle wax from prayer vigils, and marked in chalk with notes calling for remembrance and peace. Drumm requested that the bullet hole, which he labeled "a fingerprint in time," be preserved untouched.

In 2007, an Ohio Historical Marker was installed between Taylor Hall and the Prentice Hall parking lot. The state historical marker presented the basic facts of May 4 and ended by quoting the Scranton Commission's conclusion that the shooting was "unnecessary, unwarranted, and inexcusable." In 2009, the university petitioned the U.S. Department of the Interior (DOI) to have a seventeen-acre portion of campus including the Commons, Blanket Hill, the Prentice Hall parking lot, and the sports practice field listed on the National Register of Historic Places. The DOI approved the application the following year—despite the fact that sites are normally added to the National Register of Historic Places only after fifty years—because of "the exceptional importance of the events that took place at Kent State." At a campus ceremony on May 4, 2010, celebrating the DOI's decision, ninety-year-old Florence Schroder said, "For me, it is a day of closure. . . . It still hurts after all these years, but you have to go on living." In 2016, the DOI designated the Kent State shooting site as a National Historic Landmark, an even rarer distinction.

The university also inaugurated a walking tour that linked the various commemorative spaces on campus and was tied to an audio tour. The walking tour featured trail markers with photos, maps, and narratives tracing the events of May 4. Shortly thereafter, the May 4 Task Force proposed and Cartwright's successor as president, Lester Lefton, endorsed the creation of a visitors' center devoted to the shooting and even helped raise money to build it. The visitors center opened in October 2012 on the ground floor of Taylor Hall just a few steps from where the tragedy unfolded. It featured displays in three spacious galleries that presented information about the civil rights movement, the Vietnam War, student antiwar protests, and the shooting through artifacts, photos, and statements by individuals across the political spectrum. Visitors were invited to record their reactions in writing or by video. Cleveland's *Plain Dealer* praised the center as "an important step on the journey" of healing "for the community, the university, and the nation." It had taken four decades for such a center to be created, but its opening suggested at least the possibility of an emerging consensus about the tragedy.

———

The attitude of May 4 survivors also suggested a mellowing of sorts. At a news conference at the end of the 2012 anniversary commemoration, Alan Canfora acknowledged that for years after the shooting he had been "an angry young man," but "the time for antagonism" against the guardsmen was "over." "Many of us now believe that those guardsmen who were ordered to fire had the burden on their shoulders all these years forced upon them by their commanding officers. In a way, they've been victimized just as we have." It was a compassionate insight coming from a once embittered victim. Canfora still yearned, however, to understand why the shooting happened. "There are people who know things who have yet to tell their stories," he perceptively surmised. "That's why we're asking them to join with us for the sake of truth and for the sake of healing." Dean Kahler also implored guardsmen still living to resolve the unanswered questions. "It's important to get the truth out before it's too late," he stressed.

As an illustration of how much tempers had cooled with the passage of years, Ohio Republican governor Mike DeWine ordered flags at state facilities flown at half-staff on the fiftieth anniversary of the shooting. Later in 2020, the university placed circular stone markers where each of the nine wounded students had been hit by gunfire, noting the distance of each from the guardsmen. "Annual commemorations on May 4 have served as a path to healing," Chic Canfora, Alan's sister and an eyewitness to the shooting, said at the dedication of the markers. Such commemorations "enable us to manage the heartbreak we will carry for a lifetime."

"The dust of history is settling," her brother observed that same year. But Tom Grace correctly noted that the divide created by the shooting endures. He cited a passage from novelist John Steinbeck's *Cannery Row*: "It's all fine to say that 'Time will heal everything,' but when you are [involved], there is no passage of time, people do not forget and are in the middle of something that does not change." Those caught up in the tragedy of May

4 continue to work through a past that has never passed away for them and never fully will.

More than half a century later, Americans still argue about how to remember and interpret the tragedy of May 4, 1970. These arguments reflect the present as much as they do the past. The passions generated by today's cultural and political divide often take the form of arguments about events long ago. This is what makes May 4 a source of continuing controversy. Kent State's place in our national memory haunts us still. The politics of memory remain part of everyday life.

Chapter 11

LEGACY

Those touched by the events of May 4, 1970, coped with its consequences in different ways. But the tragic day remained lodged in their minds, buried deep in their hearts. "A day doesn't go by that I don't think about it," said one former student. "It's still with me and always will be with me." Several guardsmen spoke similar words. The trauma and the memories are still alive.

The four slain students' families struggled to come to terms with their personal losses. Many of them never found closure or healed their wounded hearts. "The bullet that ended Jeff's life," Elaine Miller Holstein wrote years later, "is the one experience I will never recover from." Every time she received a letter or a postcard about Jeff or saw the photo of Mary Ann Vecchio kneeling over his lifeless body, her insides clenched. She dreamed often about that fateful day. In those dreams, she saw "nightmarish National Guardsmen in gas masks" who "picked out victims to shoot." Images floated across her mind, including grisly ones of Jeff's head "shot off." Then she would wake up crying.

Elaine thought Jeff's death would kill her mother. Instead, her mother was a big comfort because she was very open in talking about their shared grief. On the other hand, Jeff's death became the one subject she and her older son, Russ, never discussed. "Neither of us dared to talk about what happened at Kent State for fear that we'd open floodgates of emotion that we couldn't deal with." Russ couldn't talk about what happened to his brother. Then one day, his wall of silence crumbled. Nine months after the shooting, while honeymooning with his new wife, Marlene, he broke down and sobbed over Jeff's death. Marlene had never seen him cry before. Six years after the shooting, Russ, Marlene, and their three-year-old son named Jeff moved from New Jersey to California and stopped in Kent along the way. "I had never been there before," Russ said. "Kent was just an abstract place for me." The three of them found the spot where his brother had fallen and stared up at the sky. "Marlene and I were in tears." Russ then snapped a photo of young Jeff beside the marble marker memorializing the slain students.

As the years passed, Russ and his mother learned to grieve together. "Whenever there was a death in the family," Elaine said, "we mourned not only the elderly parent or grandparent or aunt who passed away; we also experienced again the loss of Jeff." "It's as if somebody stole something from you," Russ told a reporter in 2021. "You wonder what could have been. Who would Jeff [have] become? All those things are just big question marks."

Hard though it was, Elaine got on with her life. She quit her job as a high school secretary, earned a master's degree, and became a psychiatric social worker at the age of sixty-two. But she never recovered from her personal loss. "There is buried inside me the knowledge that I've been cheated," she confessed late in life. "It doesn't go away—I don't want it to go away." When she was diagnosed with terminal cancer on May 4, 2018, she told a friend, "I had a good life. The only horrible thing that ever happened to me was Jeff's death." She died two weeks later at the age of ninety-six, the last surviving parent of the slain students.

Art and Doris Krause never recovered from the loss of Allison, either; their wounds ran too deep. Their pain was inflamed by the years of investigation and litigation that Art spearheaded on behalf of the victims' families and by the lingering unanswered questions about why the guardsmen fired on the unarmed students. "May 4, 1970, is frozen in time for us," Doris said. "It altered our lives. They were never the same from that day on." She didn't like to discuss what happened—but she thought about it often.

"When I sit in a restaurant, I see people with their families around them." It reminded her that "I will never have any grandchildren from [Allison]." For years, she and Art kept Allison's room just as her daughter left it, her big-eyed teddy bear still perched atop a bookcase, her blouses and skirts still hanging in the closet. "Every time I go to take them out," Doris said, "I just don't know what to do with them." Art put the bloodied clothes Allison wore the day she was killed in a box and sealed them behind a wall in her room—a metaphor for his heart. He visited her room often, where he paused pensively over mementos of his daughter. His heartache and bitterness never went away. Art "never really fully recuperated from her death," said Dean Kahler. A sensitive, emotional man beneath his fierce, prickly, and stubborn exterior, Art drank himself to death at the age of sixty-four in 1988. Doris carried a great deal of pain for the rest of her life, too. "After Allison was killed," she said in 2007, "friends compiled a reel of home movies of Allison. I still haven't been able to look at it because Allison is partly alive in those films. It's just too hard. The anniversaries don't get any easier with time. They just point out what I have missed in my life." Doris passed away in 2016 at the age of ninety.

Their younger daughter, Laurel, who had been very close to her older sister, lives with the pain of her personal loss to this day. On April 23, 2021—what would have been Allison's seventieth birthday—Laurel declared in a public letter, "Your little sister still looks up to you. I still want to tag along with you and follow your lead." "I've healed a little each day," she said. But she was still "searching for truth and accountability related to your killing."

Barry Levine visited the Krauses for a few years after 1970 but found the meetings uncomfortable and upsetting, particularly talking with Doris. "I'd see Allison in her face" and it "was devastating to me." He moved to Southern California, made a career as a realtor, got married, and had a son. But life was never the same for him. "You miss somebody. You can't let go. You don't *want* to let go." The emotional pain gradually eased with time, but it never entirely went away. "Not a day goes by that I don't think about her," he said nearly forty years after the shooting. He learned to move on with his life by creating two "boxes" concerning Allison. "One is physical, which I keep with letters, books, notes, and little trinkets. I take it out every once in a while, I look at it, and I reminisce. It hurts and it's sad, but at the same time it feels good. I also have a little 'box' in my chest, so to speak. Every once in a while, I take it out and live with it. If it were just sadness, I'd lock it away, but I've got some great life-enriching memories that I want to hold on to."

It took Barry many years, but he eventually returned to Kent State. "People said to me, 'How can you go back there? Wasn't it horrible?' Well, part of it [was] horrible, but I spent nine months there and while that one day was the worst day of my life, I also had some of the best days of my life at Kent, because of Allison. So, I visit the places where we played, or where we walked, or where we flew a kite." He went back for the twenty-fifth and thirtieth anniversary commemorations—but not to hear speeches. He went back to see "a young girl walking around the campus with a smile on her face, enjoying life." After many years, he also reconnected with Doris Krause, and he would visit her twice a year until her death. "It [was] a healing time for me, and for her too," he said, "because it [was] something that we shared. Since she lost her husband, who else [was] she going to share the memories of Allison with?"

"I said that I would never cry in public again," Florence Schroeder wrote a friend after Bill's death, but "I am crying now, in private." Shedding tears was cathartic for her, helping her to feel "that I have done my best to confront the circumstances that were thrust upon me on May 4, 1970." The coming of spring each year, on the other hand, was an ordeal. It "used to mean pruning the roses and planting bulbs and cleaning house. Now it means trying to fortify myself for the increase in the communication regarding Kent—and that means a great swell of love and longing for Bill."

"In spite of the heart-breaking death of our son, whom we loved and still love dearly," she wrote that her and Lou's lives were "enriched by [Bill] having existed. His life is reflected in the rainbows, in the morning and evening stars, in the butterflies and the flowers, and all the beauty of the earth. I know that heaven has meant an access to all Truth for him. He was always so eager to learn, and he pressed more into his short lifetime than many others do in a four-score life. He would have contributed so much to the quality of life in this great country." Looking back, she felt proud that

Bill had decided "to be a part of the activity that day, and that he did not hide his true feelings about [the] war in Vietnam." "As the general public has become aware that our involvement in Vietnam was not in the best interest of this country, or even in the best interest of Vietnam," she went on, "there has been a corresponding realization that the students were right in the first place." "If we, as adults and as citizens of the USA, had *listened* instead of reacting with [a] 'military mentality,' many lives would have been saved, in Vietnam as well as at Kent State University."

Along with such reflections came occasional outbursts of anger and bitterness at the guard. "The individuals who actually did the killing will have to live with their consciences for the rest of their lives," Florence acidly remarked. But then her humble, compassionate nature reasserted itself. "I don't want any National Guardsman to go to prison," she said, because they had been "pushed into a situation." "Maybe it's as much my fault because I voted for Rhodes."

May 4 cast a shadow over the entire Schroeder family. Their younger son, Rudy, never got over his older brother's death. Unlike Bill, who excelled at everything, Rudy struggled to cope with what happened to the older brother whom he idolized and adored. Rudy carried this burden inside himself for many years. When he was forty-nine, he shot himself to death. "I think one bullet took both my uncles," their nephew David Tuttle later said. Lou Schroeder passed away at eighty-five in 2000. Florence died in 2017 at the age of ninety-seven.

Martin Scheuer did not blame National Guard general Robert Canterbury for his daughter Sandy's death, as many did. He blamed Kent State president Robert White. White "was supposed to take my place, represent me, and take care of my daughter—protect her," Martin told an interviewer shortly after her death. Instead, "he allowed the National Guard to enter the university with loaded rifles." It was an unfair statement but an understandable one. Sandy's killing left him utterly bereft. "She was the most precious jewel in our life—she was everything we lived for—and now our lives are an empty shell," Martin admitted with devastating candor. He and his wife couldn't bear to discuss Sandy's death, even with other family members. "We never talk about it," Sarah told an interviewer. It was simply too raw and too painful.

Their home was haunted by Sandy's memory. "I could not stand that house" after her death, Sarah said, because "I always saw Sandy taking a sunbath in the backyard." They sold the house and moved away. May 4 was their wedding anniversary. Sandy's anniversary card in 1970 arrived the day they made her funeral arrangements. They never celebrated their wedding anniversary again. And then there were lilac blossoms. When Sarah and her mother had visited Sandy the last time on Saturday, May 2, they saw lilacs blooming in the backyard of her rented house in Kent. Sarah remembered that Sandy "loved them so and said that she wished that she could bring them all inside the house." "Those were the last words I heard Sandy speak," she said, her voice breaking. "I cannot look at lilacs without feeling a pain in my heart." Shortly after Sandy's death, Martin encountered a little boy in a grocery store, who noticed him wearing something on his shirt. "What is that?" the boy asked. "A mourning badge," Martin said. "What is mourning?" Martin explained that his daughter had been killed. "Where is she now?" the boy asked. Martin teared up and couldn't speak for a moment. "She's in heaven," he finally told the boy. Martin died at the age of eighty-eight in 1999. Sarah passed away at eighty-six in 2010.

———

The nine students wounded on May 4 bore visible and invisible scars for the rest of their lives. The most seriously injured, Dean Kahler, expressed surprisingly little animosity in the months after the shooting. "I'm not a victim of anything," he told an interviewer in January 1971. "It's just that I was at the wrong place at the wrong time." Another reporter who spent time with him during this period wrote that "his friendliness, serenity, and optimism seem almost unimpaired." Some fellow protestors were secretly annoyed that he didn't excoriate the Ohio National Guard for what they did that day. "He was too nice. Too gentle. Too forgiving, in my opinion," said one. Dean's reply? "I was just so glad to be alive after the shooting that I couldn't be depressed."

He felt angry and bitter, to be sure, but he kept his anger and bitterness to himself and refused to give in to them. Instead, he later explained, "I tried to turn that energy around and use it constructively" by making the best of his situation and becoming as independent as possible. He learned how to load his wheelchair in and out of a car by himself. He took and passed the special state test required of drivers using hand controls. And he became adept at moving his chair well enough and fast enough that he could pop wheelies, hot-rod down ramps, and play wheelchair basketball. In these games, he whizzed himself down the court and laid up shot after shot before reversing his chair to avoid hitting the wall behind the hoop.

Dean dealt with the reality of being a paraplegic without the least hint of self-consciousness or self-pity, approaching the day-to-day challenges of living in a wheelchair with quiet resolution. Every day, he checked his body from the chest down with a hand mirror to make sure he wasn't bleeding; he wouldn't feel the warmth or wetness if he was. In 1973, he and Kent State activist Paul Keane drove to Washington to deliver a petition signed by fifty thousand college students demanding a federal grand jury investigation of the Ohio National Guardsmen. While in DC, they visited the Tomb of the Unknown Soldier in nearby Arlington National Cemetery. As the U.S. Army sentry clicked his metal heels in front of the tomb before a whispering crowd of sightseers, Dean grasped the arms of his wheelchair and lifted his hips from the seat—not to get a better view but to encourage the flow of urine through a plastic tube into a rubber discharge bladder strapped to his stick-like leg with adhesive tape. He performed this ritual without thought throughout each day, not knowing if there was anything to void because he couldn't feel anything below his chest. Afterward, at their hotel (this was long before the Americans with Disabilities Act), Dean's wheelchair got stuck between the bathroom sink and the toilet. While helping him get unstuck, Keane saw the scar that the post-shooting surgery had left on his torso. "The sight of that scar filled my body with terror," Keane later wrote.

Deep down, Dean's anger remained—anger that impeded his emotional healing. The resilience he had displayed after the shooting slowly eroded as the 1970s went on. He returned to Kent State but changed his major often and struggled to finish school. (He eventually graduated in 1977 with a degree in secondary education.) He preoccupied himself with trying to make sense of what had happened to him, why, and—perhaps most difficult—come to terms with its irreversible consequences. He stopped cutting his hair, grew a beard, and sported a beret. The long legal battle he and other victims waged against the guard took its toll, too. During the trials, Dean was one of the few victims willing to talk with the defendants, even as he tried to console his fellow plaintiffs. But the failure to win any convictions—and thus any legal accountability—was a bitter disappointment that fed his disillusionment, cynicism, and alienation. "I had grown up believing that whatever went wrong with the system, the government would do something to correct it," he told a journalist after the guardsmen's acquittal in federal criminal court. "But all these naïve beliefs—in democracy, the Constitution, all the traditions this country was built on—have collapsed under me, along with my legs." He moved into a secluded house in the rolling hills of southeastern Ohio with his second wife, Elizabeth, and struggled to put "hatred outside my life," focusing instead on finding inner peace.

As the years went by, he was able to put May 4 in greater perspective and view it with greater detachment. The passage of time also enabled him to continue the psychic healing process. "There are days when it's easy to lapse into feeling sorry for myself," he said, "but I just go to church and ask God to help me get over the tough times. Springtime is always a real tough time—[especially] May 4. There's all this renewal that's happening every year, and this [near] death thing happened to me at that point in time. So, it's sometimes hard to deal with. But I think I've come to peace with the shooting and with the person who shot me." "It wouldn't be hard for me to destroy myself," he admitted. "But I have no reason to because I know that the sun's going to come up tomorrow and that I'll want to get up to see it. As long as I know that, I'll live each day as it comes."

He learned, in time, how to let go of his anger and to forgive the unknown guardsman who crippled him because, as he said, "I can't live hating." "The National Guard should be forgiven," he told an interviewer. "I have a lot of sympathy for them; they've had to live with this nightmare" too. At the dedication of the official Kent State memorial in 1990, he met with Charles Fassinger and talked at length with him. Dean still blamed the guard for shooting unarmed protestors, but he admitted to Fassinger that he had been swept up by the heated antiwar rhetoric of 1970.

Forgiveness allowed Dean to heal his emotional wounds, accept his physical ones, and get on with his life. He cut his hair, put on a suit and tie, and—overcoming his earlier political cynicism—went to work for the state of Ohio, serving two years with the Ohio Industrial Commission on occupational safety and accessibility issues, then six years as a field representative for the Ohio secretary of state and later the Ohio attorney general. In 1984, he won election as an Athens County commissioner and served two four-year terms. "Our job as citizens," he told his constituents, "is to participate in our democratic process and vote. Our founding fathers would be appalled at our lack of participation in our political system." Later he taught history and government to high school seniors at a vocational school outside Athens. "What happened at Kent is just a piece of who I am," he explained to an interviewer. "Sure, I think about it every morning when I wake up and see the chair, but I soon move on with whatever I'm doing that day."

As the decades went by, his carrot-red hair and beard turned white, but he continued to compete in wheelchair races and marathons, with a wheelchair odometer to mark his progress. But the long-term consequences of his paralysis slowly began to manifest themselves—the muscles in his paralyzed legs inexorably atrophied, necessitating surgery, and circulation problems led to the amputation of both his lower legs in 2009. Because he couldn't feel anything below his waist, he couldn't feel the pressure on his hip bone caused by thrusting himself out of bed into the wheelchair each morning. This led to a serious infection that put him in a nursing home for a spell.

While on his daily four-mile wheelchair "run" in the summer of 2021, he hit a pothole and tumbled onto the sidewalk, breaking his right femur (though he didn't know it). Unable to get back in his wheelchair, he lay there until a truck with two young men stopped. They lifted him under his arms and helped him back into the chair. He thanked them, rolled his way home, closed up the house, then caught a bus to the local hospital. Physically if not emotionally, May 4, 1970, continued to haunt Dean Kahler for the remainder of his days.

After recovering from his wounds, Joe Lewis returned to Kent State but had trouble focusing on his studies. He left the university after two years and began an aimless hitchhiking odyssey that ended at a hilltop commune in Oregon. "I was dealing with what we now call PTSD [post-traumatic stress disorder], but then there was no care or counseling for that," he later said. He felt survivor's guilt because he had been standing much closer to the guard than the others who were killed. He later worked as a housepainter but couldn't use a ladder because one of the two bullets that struck him had left him with no feeling in his left ankle and foot. In 1980 he went to work for a municipal water-treatment plant, where he spent twenty years as the union president and shop steward, eventually rising to supervisor before retiring in 2013.

May 4 destroyed Joe's idealism and made him enduringly suspicious of authority and abidingly cynical about the media. "The lessons I take away from my experience with the Kent State University shooting is I don't believe hardly anything that the media says and I don't believe hardly any-thing the government says because they both lied, in my case, too many times that mattered a lot," he said. Still, Kent State remained an important part of his life; he missed only one commemoration between 1995 and 2020. "For me, it's a very bittersweet time because it brings back horrible memories of pain and suffering for not just me, but everyone who was there," he told an interviewer on the fiftieth anniversary. "But it's also a wonderful reunion for [those] I see during those commemorations. It's the extreme of both feelings of sadness and joy like a lot of things in life. It's very complicated."

A photo of unconscious, open-mouthed John Cleary laying death-like on the grass off the Taylor Hall terrace appeared on the cover of *Life* magazine the week after the shooting and became one of the most famous images of May 4. In the years that followed, his punctured lung occasionally caused John shortness of breath, he wore out more easily, and a large area beneath his right armpit remained numb.

In the aftermath of the shooting, his conservative family and neighbors in upstate New York pressured him to say nothing critical about the guardsmen who had shot him and twelve others. Many people expressed sorrow about what happened to him—but then told him that "I was a stupid fool to be in that area, they had rifles. It was my ignorance and if I did die, it was my stupidity." The one friend who *was* upset served in the New York National Guard.

John did not want to make waves. "I have a tendency to accept," he admitted, "to put [things] in the past and go about living today." And because Kent State was such a polarizing issue—people were either "very sympathetic or very unsympathetic" toward him—he did not want to go through "the big ordeal of explaining" his involvement in the shooting. So, he began not just hiding his involvement but denying it.

The long and unsuccessful legal battle he and other victims waged against the Ohio National Guard during the 1970s left John feeling "very cynical" about America's judicial system. "I think it is whoever has the best lawyer and has the most money and can buy the best services," he concluded. "You can't buck the system. Why try?" He felt especially bitter about the lack of accountability. "Some people just can't admit that *everybody* makes mistakes, even National Guardsmen," he observed. He thought those responsible "should not cover it up but see that it doesn't happen again." For many years, he did not attend annual commemorations at Kent State, but he started doing so when his son started school there. Today he is a retired architect living outside Pittsburgh. He considers it important to keep alive the memory of Kent State, "to not let people forget what happened and to understand its significance." May 4 "made me look at life a little more day-to-day. Life is precious, and we need to realize we're not going to be here forever on earth."

Because a bullet blew off his left heel and the inside of his left foot, Tom Grace always had to buy two pairs of shoes: a size 8 for his left foot and a size 10 for his right foot. He had limited motion and could walk only short distances; when he exercised, he'd have a noticeable limp for several days afterward. The discomfort was particularly acute in wintertime when the bullet fragments in his foot would react to the cold and dampness. More than fifty years later, he still feels some pain in his foot. "I'm glad just to be able to get out of bed and put my socks on," he says. Such physical limitations served as a daily reminder of May 4.

The trauma he experienced that day radicalized him politically. At the second anniversary commemoration at Kent State, Tom declared that the American system was in "total bankruptcy" and called for "revolt and revolution" to overturn the "bourgeois state . . . based on violence." May 4 also left him seething with anger at the guardsmen. He fantasized about turning the tables—"I would like to see them with rocks on the practice field and myself with an M-1," he coldly told an interviewer several years later. "I would have liked them to have been in the position I was—to be unarmed. One does not have to be a radical to have the instinct to survive when one is being fired at. At least in a war both sides are armed."

Articulate and charismatic, Tom became a favorite of journalists and historians seeking interviews about May 4. "Once fate had me in front of a bullet and fortunate enough to survive it, that conferred a certain amount of authority, irrespective of whether it was deserved or not," he said. He returned to Kent State often to give speeches and moderate panels.

"My intention in going to Kent State," Tom later said, "was to study history, not to become part of it." The shooting reordered his priorities. He set aside his aspiration to become a history professor, earned a master's degree in psychiatric social work, and assisted the developmentally disabled for thirty years. Late in life, he returned to his original goal, earned a doctorate in history, and became an adjunct professor at Erie Community College in Buffalo. In 2016, he published a memoir of May 4, *Kent State: Death and Dissent in the Long Sixties.*

For a long time, Tom resented Kent State for what he perceived as its apathy toward the shooting victims, but he and the university eventually made peace. On the fiftieth anniversary of the shooting, he said, "Kent State has come to terms with its past and I've been a direct witness to that. It has contributed significantly to my coming to terms with the lethal actions committed by the Ohio National Guard in May 1970, and I salute [the university] for that." Both had learned how to move on without forgetting.

Alan Canfora's physical injuries had been minor—soft tissue damage

to his right wrist—but the shooting had a major effect on him emotionally. He became the most outspoken of the nine wounded students. Some
thought he suffered from PTSD, which expressed itself in drug use (which
he conquered after a few years) and outbursts in court during the long
legal battle following the shooting. It even led him to believe "the system"
allowed unseen forces "to pull the wool over [the public's] eyes and deceive
the people." After the passage of twenty-five years, he still believed that
"we don't have the truth—there's been no healing." Alongside his anger,
however, existed a streak of compassionate humanitarianism. In 1974, he
set up a nonprofit food co-op in his hometown of Barberton because he
believed local growers were gouging the poor and the elderly. Before dawn
each morning, he drove out to surrounding farms to purchase fruit, veg-
etables, cheeses, and eggs from local growers and then sold them at cost,
keeping just enough money to pay the rent.

Although Alan later worked as a legal librarian and served for many
years as a Democratic Party organizer and fund-raiser in Barberton and
as a county elections commissioner, pursuing the truth about May 4 and
ensuring it would never be forgotten became his lifelong crusade. He
became the most vocal keeper of the flame and the implacable bête noire
of Kent State administrators who, he believed, wanted to bury the tragedy.
He gave countless newspaper interviews, appeared on radio and television,
conducted campus tours, delivered lectures at hundreds of colleges around
the country, and directed the May 4 Center in Kent, an unaffiliated educational institution where he spent much of his time answering queries
from schoolchildren curious about the history of that day.

"Pugnacious and partisan throughout his life," in the words of his lifelong friend Tom Grace, Alan's sharp elbows and self-promotional zeal
rubbed many people the wrong way. In 2007, he gained national attention when he "discovered" a copy of Terry Strubbe's audiotape in the Ohio
ACLU May 4 archive at Yale University and persuaded Cleveland's *Plain
Dealer* to fund a forensic analysis of the recording, which he asserted proved
there had been an order to fire on the students.* "His passion resulted in a

---

* See the second footnote on page 146.

backlash from guard apologists and callous dismissals from many in local media who advised him to 'get a life,'" an acquaintance noted, but he would not "'move on' until the truth was known."

Alan never ceased blaming the guard for what happened on May 4, but later in life his attitude softened and became more nuanced. After one of his May 4 lectures, the daughter of one of the guardsmen came up to him and tearfully said her father had suffered too. Speechless at first, he rethought his approach and embarked on a mission of healing and rapprochement. "Unfortunately, I was an angry young man, very frustrated by the lack of justice," he admitted in 2010. "As I've gotten older, quite honestly I think I've mellowed considerably." But he never stopped seeking answers to the lingering questions: Who gave the order to fire? Why? And why was no one held accountable? He died of complications from kidney disease at the age of seventy-one in December 2020. After his death, Kent State University established the Alan Canfora Activism Scholarship on behalf of students who demonstrate a commitment to social justice and advocacy.

The shooting affected Doug Wrentmore too. He felt occasional pain and instability in his right knee, but the emotional wounds ran much deeper. "I realized how transitory life is," he later said, and "could no longer take ordinary patterns of life seriously." "If there's a chance that you may be shot dead tomorrow while walking to class, why bother with nonessentials?" He fell into a "deep depression," in his own words, and retreated to a quiet cabin in the woods. Like Henry David Thoreau at Walden Pond, solitude and introspection helped him. "I was driven to identify what I truly believed, and the more I thought the more I saw that I was committed to nonviolence," he recalled. "I came to the conclusion that even though my draft board [had] given me a conscientious objector status, I could not in conscience cooperate with the draft in any degree. I concluded that I would have to return my draft card," even though this meant risking a prison sentence. "I thought about this carefully. I walked in the woods, with my mending knee, and decided that I never again wanted to be associated with violence in any form, and that if my government was going to use violence as an act of national policy, I could not conform. So, I went to the post office and mailed [back] my card." "I haven't regretted it for a minute," he said looking back. "I've been more spiritually content than ever before in my life." In time, Doug became a vegetarian, finished his studies at Hiram College outside Cleveland, and became a social worker, first in New Jersey and later in Iowa.

By the late 1970s, Doug was living a simple life in an old house with little furniture, sleeping on a mattress on the floor, conversing with guests seated in the lotus position. He dabbled in mysticism, numerology, and the occult, and came to believe a "karmatic link" existed between those shot on May 4 and those who did the shooting. He spoke at length with James Michener during the author's research for his 1971 book on the shooting—at greater length than any of the other wounded students—but as the years went by, he grew increasingly reclusive and granted fewer and fewer interviews. "I have a great deal of feeling about what happened," he acknowledged in a rare interview, "but I'm not very good at sharing it." Today he lives a quiet life in retirement in a small town in Ohio.

Robby Stamps suffered few lasting effects from his gunshot wound, except on cold, damp mornings when his buttocks ached, making it difficult to walk. "I don't blame any [guardsman] for what happened," he said shortly after the shooting. "I blame the people who put the guard there. They were scared, they had not had adequate riot training." "Put me in the same position and maybe I would have done the same thing," he empathized. "If I could find the guardsman who shot me, I would say, 'If you feel bad because you shot me, please don't because it wasn't your fault.'" Robby directed his anger, instead, at "the system," which he came to deeply distrust. "What I thought then is that we had a military-industrial complex in charge of things, profiting handsomely from making war," he said in 2000. "And I think the same thing today. I think something like this could happen again easily, especially if students decide they have a bellyful of a government put up for sale to the highest bidder."

Robby's alienation made him restless. He moved around often—first to Hawaii, then to Florida—changing jobs and careers often along the way. (He once even applied to become an FBI special agent.) He eventually returned to Kent State for graduate study but felt ostracized by town residents and unsupported by the university administration. "Ohio's been blind to May 4 since day one," he complained bitterly. "I want to forget." So he left his home state once more, this time for California. He eventually moved back to Florida, still haunted by the ghosts of May 4. He died of pneumonia in 2008 at the age of 57.

The bullet that entered the back of Scott MacKenzie's neck passed within an inch of his spinal cord before exiting his left cheek. He was very lucky to survive. Surgeons wired shut his jaw for ten weeks. He could only drink finely ground mush through a straw and lost thirty pounds. Thereafter the lower left side of his face, lips, chin, and some teeth remained numb. As a result, he drooled occasionally without knowing it. He also experienced pain while chewing on the left side of his mouth and a sharp, stinging sensation when eating certain foods. But the most lasting effect of the shooting was to make him doubt that justice existed in America. "We just don't really get to the truth [and] the responsible parties weren't held as accountable as they should be," he said. He came to believe there had been a cover-up of some kind by either the university or the government.

Scott resolved not to relive May 4 every day but to get on with his life. He returned to Kent State and graduated, taught high school shop classes for a few years, then ran a custom furniture business before eventually becoming a professor of applied design in Montana and later South Dakota before retiring to Colorado in 2018. One of the most reserved of the nine wounded students, he kept his May 4 involvement under wraps and remained hesitant to talk about the shooting but would do so if asked. "Of course, it does change you," he said, but "it is bad to hate. It doesn't accomplish anything."

Jim Russell had a difficult time after the shooting. His family completely disowned him, and the birdshot wound to his upper right temple caused him frequent headaches. He had nightmares about guardsmen turning and firing, and he became convinced that a guardsman had deliberately aimed at him. That guardsman "was on a turkey shoot," he surmised. "I was just a target. He saw me running away and he just wanted to bag a student."

During the 1975 civil trial, he developed a warm friendship with Joe Lewis, who had moved to Oregon to escape Ohio's conservative hostility toward student protestors. Joe invited Jim to visit, and Jim moved to Oregon himself in 1975. He settled in St. Helens and later Deer Island about fifty miles north of Portland, where he felt accepted immediately. "This Oregon country is a place of healing," he said with relief.

For many years, though, Jim was unable to talk about May 4 with anyone outside his inner circle. "He didn't want anyone to know he'd been a part of it, he was still so traumatized," his daughter Becka later explained. "And he had his conspiracy theories: he still thought 'they' might come after him." He believed the university would "never come to grips with the cruelty that went on that day" and called the 1990 memorial dedication "a sham." "The campus can burn down for all I care," he said in 2000.

Gradually, Jim learned to bury his bitterness as he and Joe Lewis "helped each other heal through [their] friendship," in Jim's words. The two delivered talks to high school and college students around Oregon about campus unrest during the Vietnam era and the tragedy of May 4. The words they spoke and the questions they answered helped them to continue mending their lingering emotional wounds. Jim began returning to Kent State for anniversaries and to speak on panels about the shooting. Now he would say, "I had five great years at Kent State and one really bad day." "Spiritually, he had completely healed," Becka proudly said. The oldest of the nine wounded students, Jim Russell was the first of them to die, passing away from a heart attack at the age of sixty in 2007.

———

M ary Ann Vecchio was the fourteen-year-old South Florida runaway who had been hitchhiking for months when happenstance led her to the Kent State campus on May 4, 1970. The Pulitzer Prize–winning photograph of her screaming in horror as she knelt over the body of Jeff Miller became the iconic image of the shooting. Her face appeared in newspapers and on magazine covers, posters, and handbills around the world. "That picture hijacked my life," she sighed years later. People on the right vilified her as one of the counterculture "bums" Nixon had blasted just days before the shooting. Her family received phone calls and letters disparaging her as a drug addict, a tramp, and a Communist: "It's too bad it wasn't you who was shot." "What you need is a good beating until you bleed red." "I hope you enjoyed sleep-

ing with all those Negroes and dope fiends." Florida's Republican governor,
Claude Kirk, labeled her "part of a nationally organized conspiracy of pro-
fessional agitators" "responsible for the students' deaths." Her former high
school principal publicly praised schoolmates who ostracized her.

"Everyone had a piece of me," she later said. "And when everyone in the
world thinks they know who you are, *you* don't want to be who you are." "It
really destroyed my life." Mary Ann became severely withdrawn but didn't
get counseling. "I was too afraid. I was just a runaway. I felt less than. And
I felt like I did something dirty because that's the way I was treated." She
ran away again, got caught again, and this time ended up in juvenile deten-
tion. She was later arrested for prostitution in Miami. In 1977, the television
newsmagazine *60 Minutes* profiled her as a "maladjusted kid." Eventually
she moved to Las Vegas, where she married, got a job as a cashier at a
casino, and built a new life far removed from the shooting. Years later she
returned to South Florida, where she earned a high school diploma at age
thirty-nine and became a health therapist. The fourteen-year-old girl who
became a prominent symbol of protest against the Vietnam War eventually worked at the Miami Veterans Administration Hospital caring for
Vietnam veterans. She never told them she was the girl in the Kent State
photo, but she saw ways in which their trauma echoed her own, and she
learned about resilience. Today she lives a quiet life in retirement growing
avocadoes and oranges at the edge of the Florida Everglades, occasionally
delivering home-cooked meals to older neighbors. "It's been fifty years,"
she said in 2020. "Why can't I move on?"

Professor Glenn Frank, who had helped avert a second tragedy on May 4,
struggled to let go of that day as well. His courageous action that afternoon
landed him on two assassination lists—one radical, the other right-wing.
One night a few years later, a van pulled up in front of his house with its
lights off. The driver shined a flashlight on the mailbox. Frank thought,
"This is it." It took Frank years to share his thoughts and feelings about
that day. He did so in 1980 in response to an Ohio eighth-grader who wrote
him for information about the events of May 4. "I have trouble describing

them," he responded. Although many considered him an unsung hero of that day, Frank confessed, "I am sad that I was even remotely involved in this tragedy since my mental and physical well-being has certainly been affected." Frank died of kidney cancer in 1983 at the age of sixty-five.

———

Former governor Jim Rhodes never spoke publicly about Kent State after the shooting. He repeatedly declined interview requests about it. Thirty-five years would pass before a ninety-year-old Rhodes finally told a reporter, "Certainly, I felt bad about it. But I couldn't help it. They elected me governor to keep law and order, and I did my best." "It was a terrible thing, but no one plans a train wreck. It just happened." A former guardsman saw it differently. "I think that the stupid officials [who] let that happen hold way more responsibility than the guys who shot into a crowd." "I don't know how to forgive them. I bet they never forgave themselves."

———

"To have gone through May 4 one way or the other," a campus radical later said, "I think you carry this with you forever." And indeed, many of the guardsmen found it difficult to move on as well. They suffered and struggled too, in less obvious but real ways. "Those men weren't put on [campus] to kill people. They weren't brought in to wound and maim, to take life away," said a fellow guardsman and Kent State alumnus. "No one came and said, 'Let's go kill some of those damn college students.' If anything, we had to keep some of the townspeople from doing that." "I talked to a lot of those guys. We still talk. Many of those men are as torn up about what happened as the families of those who were killed." "I'm sorry it happened," he finished. "I think we're all sorry it happened."

The reaction of most guardsmen in the aftermath of May 4 was silence. General Canterbury ordered them to talk with federal and state investigators but not to the press. Most of them were quite content to obey. They didn't want to discuss the shooting with each other or anyone else for that matter—especially those who had fired. "No one in the guard wanted to talk about it," remembered Charles Fassinger, the lieutenant colonel of the 107th Armored Cavalry. For some, it was because they feared putting themselves in legal jeopardy. For others, it was for the same reason that combat veterans often don't like to discuss their experiences: the trauma caused by violence inflicted by human beings on other human beings.

Guardsmen at Kent State afflicted with PTSD had no access to counseling; they had to cope with their trauma alone. Some had recurrent nightmares. Others were upset by what happened but struggled not to show it—men of their generation did not exhibit such emotions. Still others lived with grief and guilt. Moving on was impossible; flashbacks sapped their energy and concentration, their self-worth plummeted, and they withdrew, preferring isolation. Sergeant Larry Shafer became a recluse. Captain John Martin, commander of Company A, 145th Infantry, was on Blanket Hill but didn't fire his weapon. "I don't think I did anything wrong," he said twenty-five years later, his voice trailing off before adding quietly, "But then why do I remember the faces of the dead students, their names and where they fell, the faces of their parents at the trial?"

Others suffered even more. First Sergeant "Pappy" Pryor "took it really hard," said Charles Fassinger. "His wife divorced him over that, and all kind of stuff." Corporal Robert James remained "nervous, depressed, and on medication to control his physical and emotional problems" more than eight years after the shooting, according to his physician. "I knew a couple of guys who had mental breakdowns later on because they fired and they couldn't remember if their bullet killed anybody or not," Keith Crilow said. "One got a medical discharge before his time was up because he had a mental fricking breakdown over the whole thing. He was so depressed over the fact that he might have shot somebody, but he didn't know whether he did or not." "It was very painful," admitted Jerry Damerow looking back. "I really couldn't talk about it for a while—for a long while. It was just traumatic. And the students who lost their lives and those who were injured and crippled—my heart goes out to them." "It was something I wanted to erase," confessed Terry Lucas. It took Lucas fifteen years before he could talk about May 4.

Some guardsmen still don't. The wall of silence among most of those who fired into the crowd—intangible as smoke—remains solid to this day.

Partly, it's because they fear anything they say may be misconstrued or used against them. And partly it's because "the ones who don't talk about it are those who had it the roughest," explained former guardsman B. J. Long. "It affected their lives forever, knowing that you might have been the person who killed that gal or that guy," Ron Gammell said about other guardsmen he knew. "You think about that the rest of your life. 'I wish it hadn't happened. I wish I could turn back the clock.'"

Many guardsmen preferred that people simply forget May 4. But they could not. The sense of rebirth that comes each spring with the buds and blossoms of early May in northeastern Ohio triggers difficult memories for the former guardsmen. "I think about the shooting every May for every day of the month," confessed B. J. Long. "I close my eyes. I see everything. It's something you never erase from your memory."

Charles Fassinger had been the senior uniformed officer at Kent State on May 4; the largest number of guardsmen who fired that day fell under his command. Fassinger held himself responsible for their actions, yet he could never find a "simple, clear answer" to explain the sudden outburst of violence. He always wondered, "Is there anything that I could have done differently?" The self-searching and self-recrimination never ended. Fassinger was still looking for that answer when he died in 2008 at the age of seventy-eight.

In 1971, the Ohio National Guard recommended that General Robert Canterbury be awarded the Legion of Merit. When the recommendation reached Washington, the secretary of the army rejected it, noting that Canterbury bore substantial responsibility for the deficiencies and excesses of the guard at Kent State. He declared it "unthinkable" to present Canterbury with the award. Many critics believed that Canterbury should have been court-martialed instead. But he was not. Former guardsman Arthur Krummel wondered—as many others have ever since May 4—"What kind of leader would stick a bunch of kids in the middle of a bunch of other kids and the other kids were mad at these other kids who happened to be in the National Guard and then give the one side real bullets?" Such a leader, he said, was "crazy to issue live ammunition in that volatile situation to relatively untrained kids and expect a different outcome."

Matt McManus spoke about himself as much as any other guardsman when he told a television interviewer years later, "We're deeply regretful about what took place." He could never undo what happened because of his order to fire in the air. By finally revealing the truth, he hoped to be understood; he did not expect to be exonerated.

After the shooting, McManus received letters written in animal blood threatening revenge. Once, when he deposited his paycheck at the local bank, a young teller looked at the name on the check and blurted, "Oh my God, you're one of the Kent State murderers!" One of his sisters wrote him to say that she considered him a killer and vowed never to speak to him again. One of his brothers who was later adopted after they were orphaned did the same. "I respected their decisions," he said. He later learned that his nephew had been a prominent student protestor on May 4 who did not know his uncle was one of the guardsmen on Blanket Hill that day. "Can you imagine how I would have felt if I'd gone into a group of students with a bayonet and found him on the end of it? It's just a horrible thought."

At the time of the shooting, McManus was a design engineer at International Paper Company in Wooster, Ohio. He still worked there when his name appeared in the papers in March 1974 as one of eight guardsmen indicted on federal criminal charges. When the trial ended, he promptly lost his job, despite being acquitted. Each time he started a new job, his new employer would receive an anonymous letter that warned, "You have a murderer in your employ." So he decided to become a truck driver. "It worked perfectly," he later explained, "because I wanted to be alone. I didn't want people asking questions. I didn't want to be asked."

During the years that followed, he logged more than four million miles on the open road—countless solitary hours to contemplate the tragedy he had inadvertently helped trigger. "Every now and then, traveling the highways at two or three o'clock in the morning, somebody would come on the CB radio[*] and say, 'Well, I was at Kent State. We should've shot every son-of-a-bitch there!' I would listen to their BS. They couldn't describe a blade

---

[*] Citizens band radio—a primary means of communication between truckers before the appearance of cell phones.

of grass at Kent State, let alone have been there. I would come on the radio and say, 'You know, you should be very careful because there might just be somebody out there who was at Kent State and knows what you're saying is a bunch of BS.' Then I'd hear silence. Total silence."

"I wish I could get rid of the pain," he said after more than fifty years.

———

Kent State's repercussions extended far beyond those directly involved in the events of May 4. "I made a commitment that day," said a female student who saw Dean Kahler and Jeff Miller on the ground bleeding. "I [became] a pacifist. Nobody can come out of that thinking that guns were the answer to anything." It was a powerful demonstration of the consequences of confrontation and how fragile human life can be. The shooting also compelled a generation of people who thought they could change the world to reevaluate their political engagement. Many now felt hopeless about effecting change. "If you try to change things," the saying went, "you can get killed." "It put 'Paid' to the idea of student activism all over the country," one of them recalled. "I remember that afternoon kids saying stuff like: 'That does it.' 'I'm not going to stay interested in politics.'" "On the spot, all those raging disputes became less and less important. People started talking about going to Vermont, living in an ashram, moving to California, getting away from it all, not talking about it." "If you want to know when the Sixties died, they died on May 4, 1970, right there and then, at 12:24 in the afternoon."

Acknowledgments

Conceiving a book is simple, making it a reality is not. That requires the help of many people, to each of whom I am deeply grateful.

Special thanks go to hard-working archivists at four institutions holding most primary sources related to the shooting. At Kent State University Library's Special Collections and Archives, Liz Campion and Kate Medicus generously shared their time and expertise with me from the project's beginning to its end. At Yale University, the Sterling Memorial Library's Manuscripts and Archives division staff made their extensive collection of Kent State records readily accessible. At the Ohio History Center Archives and Library in Columbus, Connie Conners, Amy Czubak, and their colleagues helped me navigate numerous state files related to the shooting and expedited the files' review by the Ohio Attorney General's office. The FBI Records office in Washington, D.C., facilitated access to the agency's declassified files concerning its investigation of the shooting.

Eminent Vietnam-era historian George Herring generously and movingly set aside time shortly before his death from cancer to read and critique a full draft of the manuscript. At the United States Naval Academy, Annapolis, where I have taught history since 1990, my colleague Professor Tom McCarthy, a fellow historian of twentieth-century America, also gave the manuscript a close and constructive reading. A Naval Academy School of Humanities and Social Sciences' Volgenau Fellowship funded much of my research travel.

My literary agent and longtime friend, Michael Carlisle of Inkwell Management, helped me conceptualize the book and served as its constant and capable advocate, ably assisted by Mike Mungiello. Another longtime friend, freelance editor Geoff Shandler, offered early and crucial encouragement. A third valued friend and editor, Paul Golob, thoughtfully critiqued an intermediate draft of the manuscript. Researcher Julie Tesser capably assisted in locating photos.

Fellow scholar and Pulitzer Prize–winning author Bill Taubman kindly assisted my search for the right publisher—W. W. Norton. The talented team at Norton helped me make the book the best it could be. Among those who assisted along the way were copyeditor Christopher Curioli, Lauren Abbate, Rebecca Homiski, Susan Sanfrey, Helen Thomaides, Chris Welch, and, above all, executive editor John Glusman, who demonstrated an exceptional blend of insight, candor, and grace. A great editor is a writer's best friend, and John fits the description perfectly.

Finally, I thank my wife, Donna, whose extraordinary patience and steadfast support were indispensable. I am indebted to her for these and so many other things.

Notes

Chapter 1: The Divided America of 1970

3 **Protestors carried a forest**: *Time*, October 27, 1967.

3 **One participant lauded**: Joseph Loftus, "Guards Repulse War Protesters at the Pentagon," *New York Times*, October 22, 1967, pp. 1 and 58; and William Chapman, "152 Arrested as Violence Takes Over," *Washington Post*, October 22, 1967, pp. A1 and A10.

4 **Back at the line**: Quoted in Jimmy Breslin, "Quiet Rally Turns Vicious," *Washington Post*, October 22, 1967, pp. A1 and A10.

4 **"It is difficult"**: James Reston in *New York Times*, October 23, 1967.

5 **"Something happened to many"**: Quoted in Bruce Jackson, "The Battle of the Pentagon," *The Atlantic*, January 1968, p. 41.

5 **Nevertheless, nearly 60 percent**: *Washington Post*, December 18, 1967.

6 **University faculty asked**: Quoted in Dan Berger, *Outlaws of America: The Weather Underground and the Politics of Solidarity* (AK Press, 2006), p. 52.

9 **"They've got guns"**: Berger, *Outlaws of America*, p. 126.

9 **"What was in my mind"**: Craig McNamara, quoted in Tom Wells, *The War Within; America's Battle Over Vietnam* (University of California Press, 1994), p. 110.

10 **"We are tired"**: Bill Ayers, quoted in Thomas Powers, *Diana: The Making of a Terrorist* (Houghton Mifflin, 1971), p. 88.

10 **"The ruling class uses"**: Quoted in Kirkpatrick Sale, *SDS* (Random House, 1973), p. 504.

10 **a "bourgeois hang-up"**: *New Left Notes*, August 29, 1969.

10 **"I acquiesced to"**: Mark Rudd, quoted in Sam Green and Bill Siegel, *The Weather Underground: The Explosive Story of America's Most Notorious Revolutionaries* [documentary], KQED Public Television/San Francisco and ITVS, 2000.

10 **They could not see**: Kenneth Keniston, "The Agony of the Counterculture," in *The Eloquence of Protest: Voices of the 70's*, ed. Harrison E. Salisbury (Houghton Mifflin, 1972), p. 225.

11 **"We actually believed"**: Quoted in Bryan Burrough, *Days of Rage: America's Radical Underground, the FBI, and the Forgotten Age of Revolutionary Violence* (Penguin Press, 2015), p. 63.

11 **"They wanted a revolution"**: Powers, *Diana*, p. 122.

11 **Anyone who did not share**: Weatherman pamphlet, October 1969; and Jonathan Lerner, "I Was a Terrorist," *Washington Post*, February 24, 2002.

12 **"We turned against"**: Bernardine Dohrn and Scott Braley, quoted in Berger, *Outlaws of America*, pp. 113–14.

12 **"The dialectic is not"**: John Jacobs, quoted in Peter Collier and David Horowitz, "Doing It: The Inside Story of the Rise and Fall of the Weather Underground," *Rolling Stone*, September 30, 1982, p. 26.

12 **The only way to**: Bill Ayers, *Fugitive Days: A Memoir* (Beacon Press, 2001), p. 145.

12 **They hijacked**: Lerner, "I Was a Terrorist."

13 **"America is in its death throes"**: Quoted in Susan Stern, *With the Weathermen: The Journey of a Revolutionary Woman* (Doubleday, 1975), p. 84.

13 **They prowled**: *New Left Notes*, September 12, 1969.

13 **"The Man can't fight"**: Quoted in Powers, *Diana*, p. 134.

13 **They assumed working-class kids**: *New Left Notes*, September 12, 1969.

13 **"We put our phone number"**: Quoted in Berger, *Outlaws of America*, p. 104.

13 **"We were telling them"**: Quoted in Sale, *SDS*, pp. 582–83.

13 **The Weathermen convinced**: Ayers, *Fugitive Days*, p. 165.

13 **They had spent**: Mark Rudd, *Underground: My Life with SDS and the Weathermen* (William Morrow, 2009), p. 159; and Mark Rudd, "The Death of SDS," Markrudd.com, accessed August 7, 2023, https://www.markrudd.com/index70bc.html?sds-and-weather/the-death-of-sds.html.

14 **That autumn of 1969, Weathermen**: *Fire!*, October 21, 1969. *Fire!* was the Weathermen's propaganda sheet that replaced SDS's newspaper *New Left Notes*.

14 **"During the 1960's"**: *Fire!*, December 6, 1969.

14 **One Weatherman looked**: Sale, *SDS*, pp. 603–4; and Ayers, quoted in Green and Siegel, *The Weather Underground*.

14 **A third thought**: Bernardine Dohrn, quoted in Jeremy Varon, *Bringing the War Home: The Weather Underground, the Red Army Faction, and Revolutionary Violence in the Sixties and Seventies* (University of California Press, 2004) p. 81.

15 **"I don't know"**: Quoted in Wells, *War Within*, p. 367.

15 **On they went**: Varon, *Bringing the War Home*, p. 74.

15 **The next morning**: Varon, *Bringing the War Home*, p. 81.

15 **Chicago Black Panther**: Quoted in Thai Jones, *A Radical Line: From the Labor Movement to the Weather Underground, One Family's Century of Conscience* (Free Press, 2004), p. 204.

16 **A young Puerto Rican**: Quoted in *Ann Arbor Argus*, November 18–December 11, 1969, pp. 8–9.

16 **A New Leftist who**: Bettina Aptheker, quoted in Wells, *War Within*, p. 297.

16 **Another New Leftist**: "Greg Calvert, SDS, and the New Left" [video], Alternative Views #22, Alternative Information Network, 1979, https://archive.org/details/AV_022-GREG_CALVERT_SDS_AND_THE_NEW_LEFT.

16 **Still another looked**: David McReynolds, quoted in Wells, *War Within*, p. 298.

16 **"A lot of things that happened"**: Bill Ayers, quoted in Wells, *War Within*, p. 336; and Ayers, *Fugitive Days*, pp. 63, 127.

17 **"the heartland folks"**: Quoted in Stanley Karnow, *Vietnam: A History*, rev. ed. (Viking, 1991), p. 613.

17 **But one moratorium organizer**: Quoted in David Paul Kuhn, *The Hardhat Riot: Nixon, New York City, and the Dawn of the White Working-Class Revolution* (Oxford University Press, 2020), p. 36.

18 **A poll taken**: David Farber, *The Age of Great Dreams: America in the 1960s* (Hill & Wang, 1994), p. 167.

19 **"tapeworm[s] in the belly"**: Stern, *With the Weathermen*, p. 204.

20 **"Our strategy has to be"**: Harold Jacobs, ed., *Weatherman* (Ramparts Press, 1970), p. 444.

20 **"deadly serious"**: Stern, *With the Weathermen*, p. 204.

20 **To raise revolutionary**: Jacobs, *Weatherman*, p. 353.

20 **Then came speeches**: Quoted in Sale, *SDS*, pp. 626–29.

21 **"Anything was applauded"**: Stern, *With the Weathermen*, p. 205.

21 **"We psyched ourselves"**: David Gilbert, *Love and Struggle: My Life in SDS, the Weather Underground, and Beyond* (PM Press, 2012), p. 123.

21 **"Paranoia plus egotism"**: Lerner, "I Was a Terrorist."

21 **The day before**: U.S. Senate, Committee on the Judiciary, 94th Congress, 1st Session, *The Weather Underground* (U.S. Government Printing Office, 1975), pp. 21–22.

21 **"I remember talking"**: Quoted in Burrough, *Days of Rage*, pp. 93–95.

22 **"We wanted to do it"**: Burrough, *Days of Rage*, pp. 95–96.

22 **"I'll be dead"**: Quoted in Ayers, *Fugitive Days*, p. 177.

23 **Two fifty-pound cartons**: U.S. Senate, Committee on the Judiciary, *Weather Underground*, pp. 133–34.

24 **"Son, I believe"**: Albert Jones, father of Jeff Jones, quoted in Jones, *A Radical Line*, p. 12.

24 **The Fork had planned**: Burrough, *Days of Rage*, p. 104.

24 **The cold and grisly logic**: Burrough, *Days of Rage*, p. 98; Larry Grathwohl as told to Frank Reagan, *Bringing Down America: An FBI Informer with the Weathermen* (Arlington House, 1976), p. 143; Lerner, "I Was a Terrorist"; Stern, *With the Weathermen*, p. 91; and Green and Siegel, *The Weather Underground*.

25 **"Everything I got"**: Quoted in Kuhn, *Hardhat Riot*, p. 18.

26 **"A working-class father"**: "The Fear Campaign," *Time*, October 4, 1968.

26 **"All I can see"**: Quoted in Phillip Caputo, *13 Seconds: A Look Back at the Kent State Shootings* (Penguin, 2005), p. 35.

Chapter 2: The Sixties Come to Kent State

28 **A professor asked**: Jerry M. Lewis, "The Kent Story," *New Politics*, Fall 1970, p. 44.

29 **"I remember one of us"**: Richard Carl Watkins Oral History, 1990, Kent State Shooting Oral History Program (hereafter cited as KSSOHP).

29 **"This is a campus"**: I. F. Stone, "Strange Lessons for the Young," *New York Review of Books*, November 2, 1970. Reprinted in I. F. Stone, *The Killings at Kent State: How Murder Went Unpunished* (New York Review Books, 1971), p. 34.

29 **"a puny little committee"**: Quoted in James A. Michener, *Kent State: What Happened and Why* (Random House, Reader's Digest Books, 1971), p. 142.

30   **"The campus looked at us"**: Quoted in Michener, *Kent State*, p. 516.

30   **"When I came"**: Carole Barbato and Laura Davis, "Ordinary Lives: Kent State, May 4, 1970," in *Time It Was: American Stories from the Sixties*, ed. Karen Manners Smith and Tim Koster (Pearson, 2008), p. 363.

30   **"there weren't enough"**: Quoted in Thomas M. Grace, *Kent State: Death and Dissent in the Long Sixties* (University of Massachusetts Press, 2016), p. 86.

30   **A campus poll**: Grace, *Kent State*, p. 85.

31   **By the end of 1968**: Joe Eszterhas and Michael D. Roberts, *Thirteen Seconds: Confrontation at Kent State* (Dodd, Mead, 1970), p. 13.

31   **Their outlook had been shaped**: Quoted in Grace, *Kent State*, p. 6.

31   **A campus informer**: C.A.T. Research in FBI Conintelpro Files, December 6, 1977, Charles A. Thomas Papers (hereafter cited as CTP), Box 64B, Folder 10, May 4 Collection, Kent State University Library (hereafter cited as M4C, KSUL).

32   **Another member**: Quoted in Grace, *Kent State*, p. 134.

32   **Rudd shrugged his shoulders**: Background Notes, James A. Michener Papers (hereafter cited as JAMP), Container No. II: 29, Manuscript Division, Library of Congress, Washington, D.C. (hereafter cited as MD, LOC).

32   **no more than twenty students**: Eszterhas and Roberts, *Thirteen Seconds*, p. 48.

33   **"The invasion of classrooms"**: Quoted in Michener, *Kent State*, p. 145.

33   **"They used guns"**: C.A.T. Research, December 2, 1977, Previously Unrestricted (Open Stack Area) Scranton Commission Records, "Records of the Kent State Investigative Team," CTP, Box 64B, Folder 10, M4C, KSUL.

34   **"Time of the Furnace"**: Terry Robbins, Howie Emmer, Bill Whittaker, Rick Skirvin, Enid Zuckerman, Lisa Meisel, Mark Real, Ric Erickson, Corky Benedict, and Arnie Schwartz, "Time of the Furnace: An Organizers' Manual for the Spring Offensive," n.d.; and Terry Robbins and Lisa Meisel, "The War at Kent State," Spring 1969.

35   **"Ames easily sustained"**: Barclay D. McMillen, "Kent State, May 4, 1970: Who Really Was Responsible for the Shootings?," 1999.

35   **To this reasoned appeal**: Quoted in Michener, *Kent State*, p. 104.

35   **University police**: McMillen, "Kent State, May 4, 1970."

35   **"open and collective hearings"**: Quoted in Michener, *Kent State*, pp. 169–70.

36   **"The revolution is on"**: Transcript of April 16, 1969, Rally, Box 80, M4C, KSUL.

36   **"open up bullshit hearings"**: Kent State SDS, "Kent Thugs," April 17, 1969, Series 2062, Box 2821, Ohio Historical Society, State Archives, Columbus, Ohio (hereafter cited as OHSSA).

37   **"Let's raise the dues"**: Quoted in Kirkpatrick Sale, *SDS* (Random House, 1973), pp. 522–23.

37   **"good looks, glib speech"**: Jonathan Lerner, "I Was a Terrorist," *Washington Post*, February 24, 2002.

37   **During a speech**: Quoted in Michener, *Kent State*, p. 91.

37   **"I could murder "**: Quoted in Eszterhas and Roberts, *Thirteen Seconds*, pp. 49–50.

38   **"We'll start blowing up"**: Eszterhas and Roberts, *Thirteen Seconds*, p. 68.

38   **"We must attack"**: Eszterhas and Roberts, *Thirteen Seconds*, p. 47.

38   **"I really believed"**: Helene Cooley interview with Timothy DeFrange, April 30, 1990, KSSOHP.

38   **Another student observed**: Robert Stamps interview with Scranton Commis-

sion, August 19, 1970, MS 1800, Box 75, Kent State Collection, Manuscripts and Archives, Sterling Memorial Library, Yale University (hereafter cited as KSC, SML, YU).

39 **"I was somewhat"**: Quoted in Milton Viorst, *Fire in the Streets: America in the 1960s* (Simon & Schuster, 1979), p. 519.

39 **Antiwar demonstrations**: See Sale, *SDS*, p. 632.

39 **A poll conducted**: Grace, *Kent State*, p. 193.

39 **Our "feeling of powerlessness"**: Craig Simpson interview with Catherine DeLattre, November 13, 2008, KSSOHP.

40 **"By the following autumn"**: Connie Sickels interview with Bruce Dzeda, May 2, 1995, KSSOHP.

40 **"This is a different place"**: Quoted in Eszterhas and Roberts, *Thirteen Seconds*, p. 17.

40 **Rhodes was an up-by-the-bootstraps**: Quoted in Eszterhas and Roberts, *Thirteen Seconds*, p. 132.

41 **"If Rhodes's toilet"**: Author's interview with Gabe Brachna, October 3, 2020.

41 **The 145th Infantry Regiment**: Laura Davis and Carole Barbato interview with Charles Fassinger, 1 of 5, April 1, 2007, Laura Davis Papers, Box 214A, M4C, KSUL.

41 **"part of the international Communist"**: Quoted in *Citizen-Journal* (Columbus, OH), March 31, 1970.

42 **Even normally apathetic**: Lae'l Hughes-Watkins interview with Paul Tople, April 25, 2017, KSSOHP.

42 **"My birthday was April 23"**: Kathleen Siebert Medicus interview with John Wilsterman, January 24, 2020, KSSOHP.

42 **"What does it matter"**: Quoted in Michener, *Kent State*, p. 171.

42 **"When two young men"**: Craig Simpson interview with Chuck Ayers, August 16, 2007, KSSOHP.

42 **"My major was staying"**: Sandra Halem interview with Steve Sharp, May 3, 2000, KSSOHP.

43 **"an American GI posing"**: Helene Cooley interview with Timothy DeFrange, April 30, 1990, KSSOHP.

43 **"The first part"**: Quoted in Alan Stang, "Kent State: Proof to Save the Guardsmen," *American Opinion*, June 1974, pp. 3–4.

44 **"most of the kids"**: Quoted in "Notes of Kent State Shooting Story," JAMP, Container No. II: 29, MD, LOC.

44 **"The antiwar feelings"**: Craig Simpson interview with Chuck Ayers, August 16, 2007, KSSOHP.

44 **About ten days after**: Thomas Gallagher, "The Kent State Tragedy," p. 15, MSS 954, Scheuer Family Papers, Box 2, OHSSA.

45 **"I didn't go for the war"**: Thomas Gallagher, "Tragedy at Kent State," *Good Housekeeping*, October 1970.

45 **Kent State president**: Quoted in Scranton Commission Report.

45 **"Oh no, this is going"**: Lae'l Hughes-Watkins interview with Paul Tople, April 25, 2017, KSSOHP.

45 **"Everyone knew something"**: Interview with Doug Wrentmore, June 25, 1977, MS 804, James Munves Papers, 1970–1981, Series IV, Box 1, KSC, SML, YU.

Chapter 3: Thirteen Students

46 **"Not many kids"**: Quoted in Milton Viorst, *Fire in the Streets: America in the 1960s* (Simon & Schuster, 1979), p. 510.

47 **"These people weren't willing"**: Viorst, *Fire in the Streets*, pp. 512–14.

47 **By 1970, Tom**: Interview with Tom Grace, MS 804, James Munves Papers, Box 1, Kent State Collection, Manuscripts and Archives, Sterling Memorial Library, Yale University (hereafter cited as KSC, SML, YU).

47 **"a process of radicalization"**: Quoted in Erin Kosnac and Melissa Hostetler, "Then I Was Shot," *The Burr*, May 4, 2000, p. 20.

48 **"Tom and I had heard"**: Quoted in Viorst, *Fire in the Streets*, pp. 511–12.

48 **"Counter Inaugural"**: Viorst, *Fire in the Streets*, pp. 513–14.

48 **"When Nixon came by"**: Viorst, *Fire in the Streets*, p. 514.

49 **"The first thing"**: Viorst, *Fire in the Streets*, pp. 515–16.

49 **"I had known him"**: Quoted in Viorst, *Fire in the Streets*, pp. 524–25; interview with Alan Canfora, June 14, 1977, James Munves Papers, 1970–1981, Box 1, KSC, SML, YU; and *Fire in the Heartland: May 4 and Student Protest in America* [documentary], Oregon Public Broadcasting, 2021.

50 **A conservative student**: Robert Stamps interview with Scranton Commission, August 19, 1970, MS 1800, Box 75, KSC, SML, YU.

50 **"a group of concerned citizens"**: "Crowd Rallies to Stop Napalming of Dog," *Daily Kent Stater*, April 23, 1970.

50 **"I am getting really pissed"**: Undated letter to Nancy, in Ohio Bureau of Criminal Identification and Investigation, Memorandum for KSU Riot Investigation File, RE: Robert Stamps (Injured), May 21, 1970, 5 p.m., Series 2062, Box 2821, Ohio Historical Society, State Archives, Columbus, Ohio (hereafter cited as OHSSA).

51 **"Allison and Barry"**: Quoted in Erich Segal, "Death Story," *Ladies Home Journal*, October 1970.

52 **"They couldn't answer any"**: Quoted in James A. Michener, *Kent State: What Happened and Why* (Random House, Reader's Digest Books, 1971), p. 316.

52 **Other students liked Allison**: Michener, *Kent State*, p. 319.

52 **"She was very headstrong"**: Quoted in Jeff Kisseloff, *Generation on Fire: Voices of Protest from the 1960s* (University Press of Kentucky, 2007), p. 244.

52 **"When he was little"**: Clevelandjewishnews.com, May 28, 2018.

52 **"He was very upset"**: Interview with Elaine Miller Holstein, April 18, 1977, MS 804, James Munves Papers, Box 1, KSC, SML, YU.

53 **"The strife and fighting"**: Elaine Miller Holstein to Jim Munves, April 25, 1977, MS 804, James Munves Papers, Box 1, KSC, SML, YU.

54 **"Russ would have gone"**: Interview with Elaine Miller Holstein, April 18, 1977, James Munves Papers, Box 1, KSC, SML, YU.

55 **"I'm more into the peace thing"**: Quoted in Draft Manuscript, V-A-9, James A. Michener Papers, Manuscript Division, Library of Congress, Washington, D.C.

55 **"By the spring of 1970"**: May 4 Visitor Center, Kent State University.

55 **"What are we supposed to do?"**: Quoted in Joe Eszterhas and Michael D. Roberts, *Thirteen Seconds: Confrontation at Kent State* (Dodd, Mead, 1970), p. 268.

55 **"hippie radical"**: Elaine [Miller] Holstein, "Anniversary," *The Progressive*, May 1988, p. 34.

55 **"Who Is To Say?"**: The drawing today is in Special Collections and Archives, Kent State University Library.

56 **"everybody's pal"**: Thomas Gallagher, "The Kent State Tragedy," p. 2, MSS 954, Scheuer Family Papers (hereafter cited as SFP), Box 2, OHSSA.

56 **"She bubbled over"**: Interview with Mr. and Mrs. Martin Scheuer, MS 804, Accession 1983-M-017, Box 1, KSC, SML, YU.

56 **"I have never known"**: Marilyn Broodus to Mr. and Mrs. Scheuer, May 5, 1970, SFP, Box 1, OHSSA.

57 **"She had a quiet grace"**: Marty Levick, quoted in J. Gregory Payne, *MAYDAY: Kent State* (Kendall/Hunt, 1981), p. 85.

57 **"She had a laugh"**: Quoted in Michener, *Kent State*, p. 299.

57 **"In a crowd"**: Quoted in Michener, *Kent State*, p. 300.

57 **"She was beautiful"**: Steve Drucker, quoted in Jeff Sallot, "Reunion at Kent State," *Globe and Mail*, May 5, 1995.

57 **"Maybe I'm not going to"**: Quoted in Michener, *Kent State*, p. 300.

57 **"her empathy and sensitivity"**: Quoted in Eszterhas and Roberts, *Thirteen Seconds*, pp. 223–24.

57 **"Some of the guys"**: Quoted in Michener, *Kent State*, pp. 302–3.

57 **"Sandy lived for what"**: Quoted in *Time*, May 18, 1970, p. 14.

57 **"I'm getting worried"**: Quoted in Michener, *Kent State*, p. 36.

58 **"I am really scared"**: Sandy Scheuer, "Society's Effect on Man," February 10, 1969, SFP, Box 1, OHSSA.

58 **"As a C.O. I can"**: Quoted in Howard E. Royer, "Non-Violence Is the Only Way," *Messenger*, January 1, 1971.

59 **"He looked like the poster boy"**: Kelly Riley and Kathleen Siebert Medicus interview with Greg Long, January 23, 2020, Kent State Shooting Oral History Program (hereafter cited as KSSOHP).

59 He **"could walk and talk"**: Quoted in Payne, *MAYDAY*, p. 77.

59 **"I found him to be"**: Quoted in Payne, *MAYDAY*, p. 80.

60 **"but he'd always"**: Quoted in John Pekkanen, "A Boy Who Was Just 'There Watching It and Making Up His Mind,'" *Life*, May 15, 1970, p. 37.

60 **"he lives as he wants to"**: Quoted in Michener, *Kent State*, p. 311.

60 **"the coolest motherfucker"**: Quoted in Eszterhas and Roberts, *Thirteen Seconds*, p. 245.

60 **"The Stones symbolized"**: Quoted in Eszterhas and Roberts, *Thirteen Seconds*, p. 245.

60 **"He would have fondled"**: Quoted in Eszterhas and Roberts, *Thirteen Seconds*, p. 233.

60 **"he decided that the presence"**: Quoted in "William Knox Schroeder," *Kent State Magazine*, Spring/Summer 2020, p. 23.

60 **"He could argue"**: Quoted in Ron Henderson, "18 Months Later: Families of Kent Dead Speak Out," *American Report*, November 12, 1971.

61 **"go in there"**: Quoted in *Life*, May 15, 1970, p. 36.

61 **"We disagree a lot"**: Quoted in Eszterhas and Roberts, *Thirteen Seconds*, p. 243.

61 **"He wanted to understand"**: Quoted in Eszterhas and Roberts, *Thirteen Seconds*, pp. 242–43.

61 **"When I first got"**: Quoted in Michener, *Kent State*, pp. 312–13.

61 **"It bothered him that"**: Quoted in Eszterhas and Roberts, *Thirteen Seconds*, pp. 242–244.

61 **"Being an ROTC student"**: Quoted in Henderson, "18 Months Later."

61 **"I just don't know"**: Quoted in *Plain Dealer* (Cleveland, OH), May 1, 2000, p. 1.

62 **He "pelted"**: Louis P. Cusella, "Real-Fiction Versus Historical Reality: Rhetorical Purification in 'Kent State'—The Docudrama," *Communication Quarterly* 30, no. 3 (Summer 1982): p. 161.

62 **"He hoped that"**: Quoted in Henderson, "18 Months Later."

62 **He had recently expressed**: FBI Memo, May 21, 1970, Field Office File No. 98-2140, FBI Records: The Vault (online), Kent State, File No. 98-46479. Most of these documents concern the May 2 burning of the ROTC building rather than the May 4 shooting.

62 **He went out of curiosity**: Testimony of Joe Lewis, 1975 Civil Trial, p. 1657, MS 1800, Box 67, KSC, SML, YU.

62 **"I was in my own"**: Interview with John Cleary, MS 804, James Munves Papers, Box 1, KSC, SML, YU.

62 **"I had no strong views"**: Testimony of John Cleary, June 1975 Civil Trial, p. 4125, MS 1800, Box 62, KSC, SML, YU; and Craig Simpson interview with John Cleary, May 3, 2010, KSSOHP.

63 **"I was personally opposed"**: Quoted in *The Burr*, May 4, 2000, p. 18.

63 **"I didn't think"**: Quoted in Lisa Abraham, "May 4: Where the Nine Wounded Are Now," *Kent State Magazine*, Spring/Summer 2020, p. 20.

63 **"ridiculous" things**: Testimony of Scott MacKenzie, 1975 Civil Trial, p. 2168, MS 1800, Box 68, KSC, SML, YU.

63 **"commies"**: Testimony of James Russell, 1975 Civil Trial, p. 3590, MS 1800, Box 73, KSC, SML, YU.

Chapter 4: May 1–3, 1970

66 **"evil incarnate"**: Tom Grace in *Fire in the Heartland: May 4 and Student Protest in America* [documentary], Oregon Public Broadcasting, 2021.

66 **"If a nation"**: Quoted in James A. Michener, *Kent State: What Happened and Why* (Random House, Reader's Digest Books, 1971), p. 13.

67 **student in the crowd**: FBI Memo, Cleveland Office, May 21, 1970, Field Office File No. 98-2140, FBI Records: The Vault (online), Kent State, File No. 98-46479 (hereafter cited as FBIRTV, KS).

67 **"I'm so disgusted"**: Quoted in Michener, *Kent State*, p. 15; and Joe Eszterhas and Michael D. Roberts, *Thirteen Seconds: Confrontation at Kent State* (Dodd, Mead, 1970), p. 30.

67 **On a nearby tree**: FBI Memo, Cleveland Office, May 21, 1970, FBIRTV, KS.

67 **"Wow, that was a little"**: "Chronology of Students' Activities, Friday, May 1," James A. Michener Papers (hereafter cited as JAMP), Container No. II: 34, Manuscript Division, Library of Congress, Washington, D.C. (hereafter cited as MD, LOC).

68 **"Sieg heil! Sieg heil!"**: Quoted in Eszterhas and Roberts, *Thirteen Seconds*, p. 41.

68 **"the musical sound"**: Quoted in *Plain Dealer* (Cleveland, OH), May 1, 2000, p. 6-A.

68 **"I think it's important"**: Quoted in Milton Viorst, *Fire in the Streets: America in the 1960s* (Simon & Schuster, 1979), pp. 529–30.

68 **Jeff Miller didn't**: "Chronology of Students' Activities, Saturday, May 2," JAMP, Container No. 2: 34, MD, LOC.

68 **she "didn't see"**: Sandra Halem interview with Carol Mirman, April 1, 2000, Kent State Shooting Oral History Program (hereafter cited as KSSOHP).

68 **"was totally unfounded"**: Testimony of Tom Grace to Federal Grand Jury, p. 1206, MS 1800, Box 65, Kent State Collection, Manuscripts and Archives, Sterling Memorial Library, Yale University (hereafter cited as KSC, SML, YU).

68 **"I think it's crazy"**: Quoted in Michener, *Kent State*, pp. 216–17.

68 **Jim Russell**: Testimony of James Russell to Federal Grand Jury, p. 1078, MS 1800, Box 73, KSC, SML, YU.

69 **"The university had grown"**: Quoted in Howard Means, *67 Shots: Kent State and the End of American Innocence* (Da Capo Press, 2016), p. 15.

69 **But "beneath that surface"**: Quoted in Thomas M. Grace, *Kent State: Death and Dissent in the Long Sixties* (University of Massachusetts Press, 2016), p. 66.

69 **"You might as well"**: Quoted in Richard Oliver, "In Kent, a Wide Town-Gown Gap," *The News*, May 7, 1970.

69 **"I wish that Kent"**: Quoted in Michener, *Kent State*, p. 519.

70 **"They scared hell"**: Quoted in Eszterhas and Roberts, *Thirteen Seconds*, p. 46.

70 **"They got a lot of people"**: Quoted in Eszterhas and Roberts, *Thirteen Seconds*, p. 34.

70 **"As far as us"**: Quoted in "Tragedy in Our Midst—A Special Report," *Akron Beacon Journal*, May 24, 1970.

71 **"anger at the students"**: Quoted in *Kent State: The Day the War Came Home* [documentary], Learning Channel, 2000. First shown on the Learning Channel in May 2000, this film won an Emmy in 2001 for best documentary.

71 **"guys with red headbands"**: Quoted in Eszterhas and Roberts, *Thirteen Seconds*, p. 74.

71 **"Feelings were strong"**: Donald Frantz to *Akron Beacon Journal*, April 3, 1990, Box 74, May 4 Collection, Kent State University Library (hereafter cited as M4C, KSUL).

72 **"MIND F.U.C.K."**: Kent sds, SFP, Box 2, Ohio Historical Society, State Archives, Columbus, Ohio (hereafter cited as OHSSA).

73 **"The point of discussion"**: Quoted in Michener, *Kent State*, p. 192.

73 **"a moving mob"**: Les Stegh interview with Carl Moore, September 10, 1973, KSSOHP.

73 **"Get it!," Burn it!"**: George Skoch Personal Narrative, Narratives and Commentaries Related to the Kent State Shootings (hereafter cited as NCRKSS), M4C, KSUL.

73 a **"sheep pen"**: Harris Dante Oral History, November 19, 1991, Kent Historical Society and Museum, Kent, Ohio.

73 **"It's symbolic"**: Quoted in "Tragedy in Our Midst—A Special Report," *Akron Beacon Journal*.

73 **"Everyone knew ROTC"**: Quoted in Michener, *Kent State*, p. 210.

74 **"Down with ROTC!"**: Quoted in Michener, *Kent State*, p. 203.

74 **"There's no need"**: Quoted in Draft Manuscript, III-M-2, JAMP, Container No. II: 29, MD, LOC.

74 **"I have never"**: Public testimony before the Scranton Commission, August 19, 1970.

74 **"chuck it"**: William Gardner interview with Robert Stamps, November 26, 1973, MS 1800, Box 75, KSC, SML, YU.

75 **Freshman Peter Bliek**: Memorandum for KSU Riot Investigation File Re. Bliek, Peter C., Ohio Bureau of Criminal Identification and Investigation, SAS 6524, OHSSA.

75 **"You fuckers"**: Quoted in "Tragedy in Our Midst—A Special Report," *Akron Beacon Journal*.

75 **Joe Lewis wanted**: Interview with Joe Lewis and his mother, Betty Lewis, MS 804, James Munves Papers, Box 1, KSC, SML, YU.

75 **"It seemed futile"**: Quoted in Daniel St. Albin Greene, "When a World Collapsed," *National Observer* (Washington, DC), May 3, 1975.

75 **He saw people**: Testimony of John Cleary, June 1975 Civil Trial, p. 4129, MS 1800, Box 62, KSC, SML, YU.

75 **He understood the frustration**: Interview with John Cleary, MS 804, James Munves Papers, Box 1, KSC, SML, YU.

75 **"stay away from trouble"**: Quoted in Eszterhas and Roberts, *Thirteen Seconds*, p. 201; and Thomas Gallagher, "Tragedy at Kent State," *Good Housekeeping*, October 1970.

76 **"understood the danger"**: "Chronology of Students' Activities, Saturday, May 2," JAMP, Container No. 2: 34, MD, LOC.

76 **Allison and her friend**: Barry Levine to Charles Thomas, June 22, 1978, Charles A. Thomas Papers (hereafter cited as CTP), Box 64B, M4C, KSUL.

76 **"We both wanted"**: Quoted in Michener, *Kent State*, p. 217.

76 **"grabbing the hose"**: Kathleen Siebert Medicus interview with Terry Strubbe, January 31, 2020, KSSOHP.

76 **"Gee, that's crazy"**: B. Payne interview with Dean Kahler, November 12, 1979, MS 804, Series Accession 1983-M-017, Box 1, KSC, SML, YU.

76 **"I'd heard rumors"**: Quoted in Michener, *Kent State*, p. 218.

77 **"violence for the sake of violence"**: Quoted in Eszterhas and Roberts, *Thirteen Seconds*, p. 249.

77 **"We watched the building burn"**: Quoted in Michener, *Kent State*, p. 209.

77 **"I'm surprised it wasn't"**: Quoted in Michener, *Kent State*, p. 261.

77 **"this rather crazed student"**: Quoted in *Sunday Plain Dealer* (Cleveland, OH), May 3, 2020, p. A10.

78 **Pentagon surveys confirmed**: Alfred B. Fitt, "The National Guard and Civil Disturbance," *City: The Magazine of Urban Life and Environment*, August/September 1970.

78 **"I joined the guard instead"**: Testimony of James Pierce, June 25, 1975, MS 1800, Box 71, KSC, SML, YU.

78 **"If we were unsat"**: Sandra Halem interview with anonymous National Guardsman, May 2, 2000, KSSOHP.

78 **"When you're in the military"**: Author's telephone interview with B. J. Long, May 5, 2022.

78 **They were taught**: Annex F (Pre-Employment Briefing) to Oplan 2 (Aid to Civil Authorities), Adjutant General of Ohio, May 16, 1969, M4C, KSUL. See also "Pre-Deployment Briefing" Notes, MS 1800, Box 61, KSC, SML, YU.

79 **"Good judgment"**: Annex F (Pre-Employment Briefing) to Oplan 2 (Aid to Civil Authorities), Adjutant General of Ohio; and Robert Canterbury, Distribution of Lesson Plan and Transparencies, "Legal Consequences of State Active Duty in Aid to Civil Authorities," October 1, 1969, M4C, KSUL.

79 **"in any instance where"**: Quoted in U.S. Justice Department Summary of FBI Reports, July 1970.

79 **"if they had sixteen hours"**: Federal Grand Jury Testimony of Harry Jones, p. 4625, MS 804, Accession 1989-M-048, Box 36, KSC, SML, YU.

79   **Efforts were made**: U.S. Army Inspection 25175, USCONARC Message 52788, February 21, 1968, KSC, SML, YU.

79   **They received no instruction**: Deposition of Lieutenant Dwight Cline, April 2, 1975, MS 1800, Box 62, KSC, SML, YU.

79   **One sergeant later noted**: Testimony of Richard Love, Federal Civil Trial, June 16, 1975, p. 2835, MS 804, Accession 1989-M-048, Box 36, Folder 470, KSC, SML, YU.

79   **"I don't remember"**: Deposition of Rodney Biddle, p. 44, Box 35, KSC, SML, YU.

79   **In simulated riots**: CTP, Box 64D, Folder 1, M4C, KSUL.

80   **"they got totally out of hand"**: Trial Testimony of Bill Herschler, July 17, 1975, p. 7542, KSC, SML, YU.

80   **"When you're trying"**: Lae'l Hughes-Watkins interview with James Stroh, November 16, 2016, KSSHOP.

80   **"There was [tear] gas"**: John Simons, quoted in "Tragedy in Our Midst—A Special Report," *Akron Beacon Journal*.

80   **"We were only equipped"**: Lieutenant Colonel Charles Fassinger, quoted in Rachel Dissell, "The Right to Be Afraid," *Daily Burr*, March 22, 2007.

80   **In the spring of 1970**: Author's interview with Mathew McManus, October 24, 2020.

80   **"We [were] virtually untrained"**: Anonymous guardsman (later identified as Michael Delaney), Letter to *Akron Beacon Journal*, August 18, 1971.

80   **"It was miserable"**: Author's interview with Mathew McManus, October 24, 2020.

81   **"Had we had"**: Ed Grant and Mike Hill, *I Was There: What Really Went on at Kent State* (C. S. S. Publishing, 1974), p. 37.

81   **"It was just one building"**: Author's interview with Mathew McManus, October 24, 2020.

81   **"My God, the whole town"**: Sandra Halem interview with anonymous guardsman, May 2, 2000, KSSOHP.

81   **"It was like something"**: Quoted in William Barry Furlong, "The Guardsmen's View of the Tragedy at Kent State," *New York Times Magazine*, June 21, 1970.

81   **"I was driving"**: James Pierce Statement to Ohio State Highway Patrol, in Ohio State Highway Patrol Report of Investigation, June 9, 1970, p. 2, Case 400-67A-132, Series 2062, Box 2823, OHSSA.

81   **"We can't control them"**: Author's interview with Mathew McManus, October 24, 2020.

81   **"I was shocked"**: Author's interview with Mathew McManus, October 24, 2020.

81   **Del Corso also ordered**: Interview with John Backlawski, radio station WKSU, Laura Davis Papers (hereafter cited as LDP), Box 177, Tape 2, M4C, KSUL.

82   **"That night I saw"**: Terry Lucas, quoted in Sarah Crump, "May 4 Journal," *Cleveland Magazine*, May 1995, p. 61.

82   **"If these little bastards"**: Quoted in Joe Eszterhas and Michael Roberts, "James Michener's Kent State: A Study in Distortion," *The Progressive*, September 1971, p. 38.

82   **He reached down**: *Cleveland Press*, June 18, 1975, p. G-8.

82   **"Go back to your dormitories"**: Ottavio M. Casale and Louis Paskoff, eds., *The Kent Affair: Documents and Interpretations* (Houghton Mifflin, 1971), p. 5.

83   **"She was slapping"**: Murvin Perry Oral History, April 18, 2008, KSSOHP.

83   **"I said to one of them"**: Deposition of Alan Canfora, p. 86, MS 804, Accession 1989-M-048, Box 35, KSC, SML, YU.

83   **"a terrible way"**: Quoted in *New York Times*, May 5, 1970, p. 17.

83 **"I got about five and a half"**: Quoted in Furlong, "The Guardsmen's View of the Tragedy at Kent State," p. 69.

83 **"Sergeant McManus,"**: Dale Antram interview, February 27, 2020, Kent State Guardsmen Oral History Project, Ohio Northern University (hereafter cited as KSGOHP, ONU).

84 **"It was a nice day"**: Matt McManus interview, April 8, 2020, KSGOHP, ONU.

84 **"was a more powerful weapon"**: Deposition of Robert Canterbury, November 21, 1974, MS 804, Accession 1989-M-048, Box 35, KSC, SML, YU.

84 **"What are we doing here?"**: Matt McManus to author, September 19, 2020; and author's interview with Mathew McManus, October 24, 2020.

85 **"I'd been told when"**: Quoted in Furlong, "The Guardsmen's View of the Tragedy at Kent State," p. 12.

85 **"We looked upon them"**: Quoted in Joan Morrison and Robert K. Morrison, *From Camelot to Kent State: The Sixties Experience in the Words of Those Who Lived It* (Times Books, 1987; reprint ed., Oxford University Press, 2001), p. 330.

85 **"God—He had had long hair"**: Quoted in Furlong, "The Guardsmen's View of the Tragedy at Kent State," p. 64; and Charles Fassinger interview with M. Uryccki, LDP, Box 214, M4C, KSUL.

85 **"They brought with them"**: Gordon W. Keller, "Kent State a Year Later," *Dissent*, April 1971, p. 172.

85 **"These kids just don't understand"**: Quoted in "Tragedy in Our Midst—A Special Report," *Akron Beacon Journal*.

85 **"I'd like to sit down"**: Quoted in Furlong, "The Guardsmen's View of the Tragedy at Kent State," p. 64.

85 **Many guardsmen felt**: Interview with Lynn Stovall, MS 804, Accession 1983-M-017, Box 1, KSC, SML, YU.

85 **Robby Stamps recognized**: Robert Stamps Testimony to Federal Grand Jury, p. 1111, MS 1800, Box 75, KSC, SML, YU.

86 **When a male student**: Quoted in Michener, *Kent State*, p. 257; Means, *67 Shots*, p. 50; and Eszterhas and Roberts, *Thirteen Seconds*, p. 115.

86 **"The majority of them"**: Kathleen Siebert Medicus interview with Terri West, April 29, 2020, KSSOHP.

86 **"They probably preferred"**: Richard Carl Watkins Oral History, 1990, KSSOHP.

86 **"it seemed as if"**: Quoted in Eszterhas and Roberts, *Thirteen Seconds*, p. 113.

86 **"no fear, no anxiety"**: Quoted in Michener, *Kent State*, p. 255.

86 **Joe Lewis remembered**: Interview with Joe Lewis and his mother, Betty Lewis, MS 804, James Munves Papers, Box 1, KSC, SML, YU.

86 **"People [said] 'Hey' "**: Robert Bossar in *Kent State: The Day the War Came Home*, Learning Channel.

87 **"that things had calmed down"**: Interview with John Cleary, MS 804, James Munves Papers, Box 1, KSC, SML, YU.

87 **"Who is fucking"**: Student statement to Ohio State Highway Patrol, June 15, 1970, Case No. 400-67A-132, Series 2062, Box 2823, OHSSA.

88 **"If there's trouble"**: Interview with Joe Lewis and his mother, Betty Lewis, MS 804, James Munves Papers, Box 1, KSC, SML, YU.

88 **"Why are you guarding"**: Author's telephone interview with B. J. Long, May 4, 2022.

88 **"He stood quietly alone"**: Quoted in J. Gregory Payne, *MAYDAY: Kent State* (Kendall/

Hunt, 1981), pp. 95–96; *Kent State: The Day the War Came Home*, Learning Channel; and "Allison Krause," May 4 Archive, https://www.may4archive.org/allison_krause.html.

88   **The officer turned**: Allison Center for Peace, facebook.com, August 22, 2022.

89   **"You have live ammunition"**: Quoted in Eszterhas and Roberts, *Thirteen Seconds*, pp. 115–16.

89   **"He was definitely not happy"**: Author's interview with Matt McManus, October 24, 2020.

90   **"You university people"**: Quoted in Michener, *Kent State*, p. 250.

90   **"whatever force necessary"**: "Rhodes Okayed Force, Kent Grand Jury Told," *Cleveland Press*, January 7, 1974.

90   **"There was no discussion"**: Quoted in *Newsweek*, May 18, 1970, p. 31.

91   **"As the Ohio law says"**: Quoted in Joe Eszterhas, "Ohio Honors Its Dead: One Nation, Under God, Indivisible, with Liberty and Justice for All," *Rolling Stone*, June 10, 1971, p. 17.

91   **"What conclusions"**: Professor Myron Lunine quoted in Michener, *Kent State*, p. 254.

92   **"The situation can come"**: Interview with Ron Kane, MS 804, Accession 1983-M-017, Box 1, KSC, SML, YU.

92   **"I told the governor"**: Quoted in Eszterhas and Roberts, *Thirteen Seconds*, p. 112.

92   **"Get everybody the fuck out"**: Interview with Ron Kane, MS 804, Accession 1983-M-017, Box 1, KSC, SML, YU.

92   **"No—we mustn't do that!"**: Quoted in Michener, *Kent State*, pp. 252–53.

92   **"really, really inflamed"**: Robert Stamps interview with Scranton Commission, August 19, 1970, MS 1800, Box 75, KSC, SML, YU.

92   **"If the president thinks"**: Quoted in Michener, *Kent State*, pp. 253–54.

93   **"It was sort of spooky"**: Quoted in Furlong, "The Guardsmen's View of the Tragedy at Kent State," p. 68.

93   **"What are we gonna do"**: Sandra Halem interview with anonymous guardsman, May 2, 2000, KSSOHP.

93   **"Present arms!"**: Mathew McManus interview, April 8, 2020, KSGOHP, ONU.

93   **"This is an illegal assembly"**: Author's interview with Mathew McManus, October 24, 2020.

93   **"people were loading"**: Quoted in Gallagher, "Tragedy at Kent State."

94   **"Kill those SOBs"**: Grant and Hill, *I Was There*, p. 53; and author's interview with Gabe Brachna, October 3, 2020.

94   **"A demonstrator crept"**: Grant and Hill, *I Was There*, p. 55.

94   **One student spit**: Testimony of Lieutenant Alexander Stevenson, 1975 Federal Civil Trial, pp. 6351–63, MS 1800, Box 75, KSC, SML, YU; and Deposition of Lloyd Thomas, p. 54, Box 76, KSC, SML, YU.

94   **"I know your face"**: Sandra Halem interview with anonymous guardsman, May 2, 2000, KSSOHP.

94   **"Cut off their fucking balls!"**: Statement of Specialist Richard Lutey to FBI, May 11, 1970, CV 44-703, MS 804, Accession 1989-M-048, Box 28, KSC, SML, YU.

95   **"Maybe we can calm"**: Sandra Halem interview with anonymous guardsman, May 2, 2000, KSSOHP.

95   **"They threw rocks"**: Second Lieutenant Bill Clossey, quoted in *Ohio Bell/Perspective* (Ohio Bell Telephone Company, 1970).

95 **"I was sitting"**: B. Payne interview with Dean Kahler, November 12, 1979, MS 804, Series Accession 1983—M-017, Box 1, KSC, SML, YU.

95 **"about staying out of trouble"**: Quoted in *Echoes* (Ohio Historical Society), 38, no. 5 (October/November 1999): pp. 2–3.

95 **"Dean, mind your business"**: Interview with Elaine and John Kahler, July 15, 1977, MS 804, James Munves Papers, Box 1, KSC, SML, YU.

95 **"Keep away from stuff"**: Quoted in *Plain Dealer* (Cleveland, OH), May 1, 2000, p. 6-A.

95 **"I'd seen demonstrations"**: Interview with Dean Kahler, 2015, "Dean Kahler Shot at Kent State, May 4, 1970" [video], Youtube.com.

95 **"Just as my father"**: Interview with Elaine and John Kahler, July 15, 1977, MS 804, James Munves Papers, Box 1, KSC, SML, YU.

96 **"If you get off the street"**: Interview with Scott MacKenzie, MS 804, James Munves Papers, Box 1, KSC, SML, YU; and B. Payne interview with Dean Kahler, November 12, 1979, MS 804, Accession 1983-M-017, Box 1, KSC, SML, YU.

96 **"The next thing I heard"**: B. Payne interview with Dean Kahler, November 12, 1979, MS 804, Accession 1983-M-017, Box 1, KSC, SML, YU.

96 **"I remember hearing"**: Arthur Koushel Oral History, May 1995, KSSOHP.

96 **"charged right into the crowd"**: Sandra Halem interview with Jim Vacarella, April 3, 2000, KSSOHP.

96 **"I was walking"**: Quoted in Eszterhas and Roberts, *Thirteen Seconds*, p. 148.

96 **A different guardsman ordered**: *Cleveland Press*, July 15, 1975.

96 **"We don't have to take this stuff"**: Grant and Hill, *I Was There*, p. 57.

97 **"We have a right"**: Quoted in Michener, *Kent State*, pp. 286–87.

97 **"came up over the hills"**: John Burnell interview with William Derry Heasley, May 4, 1990, KSSOHP.

97 **"It was a night"**: Quoted in Michener, *Kent State*, p. 278.

97 **Joe Lewis watched guardsmen**: Testimony of Joe Lewis, 1975 Civil Trial, p. 1607, MS 1800, Box 67, KSC, SML, YU.

97 **"We had to leave"**: Craig Simpson interview with John Cleary, May 3, 2010, KSSOHP.

97 **Dean Kahler ran back**: Gregory Wilson interview with Dean Kahler, May 14, 2012, KSSOHP.

97 **"I want to go"**: Larry Raines Personal Narrative, March 24, 1997, NCRKSS, M4C, KSUL.

98 **"all upset"**: Interview with Elaine and John Kahler, July 15, 1977, MS 804, James Munves Papers, Box 1, KSC, SML, YU.

98 **Scott MacKenzie made his way**: Testimony of Scott MacKenzie, 1975 Civil Trial, p. 2133, MS 1800, Box 68, KSC, SML, YU.

98 **He felt scared**: Interview with Scott MacKenzie, MS 804, James Munves Papers, Box 1, KSC, SML, YU.

98 **"When we heard"**: Michener, *Kent State*, pp. 287–88.

98 **Allison screamed obscenities**: Robert A. Murphy and Robert Hocutt to Jerris Leonard, "Summary of the Kent State Incident," June 18, 1970, U.S. Department of Justice 144-57-338.

98 **"Her face was ashen"**: C.A.T. Research: Papers of James A. Michener, Library of Congress Reading Room, January 4–6, 1978, CTP, Box 64B, M4C, KSUL.

98 **Allison phoned her parents**: Jeff Kisseloff, *Generation on Fire: Voices of Protest from the 1960s* (University Press of Kentucky, 2007), pp. 252–53.

99 **"The problem is over"**: Deposition of John Cleary, June 12, 1975, p. 87, MS 1800, Box 62, KSC, SML, YU.

99 **"That asshole"**: Quoted in Eszterhas and Roberts, *Thirteen Seconds*, p. 250.

99 **"Will you stand by me"**: Quoted in Ron Henderson, "18 Months Later: Families of Kent Dead Speak Out," *American Report*, November 12, 1971.

99 **"Christ, Louie"**: Quoted in Eszterhas and Roberts, *Thirteen Seconds*, pp. 234–35.

99 **"I'm afraid of what's going"**: Quoted in Michener, *Kent State*, pp. 277–78, 284.

Chapter 5: May 4, 1970—The Tragic Day, Part I

102 **"I was not in the chain of command"**: Deposition of Robert Canterbury, November 21, 1974, p. 144, MS 804, Accession 1989-M-048, Box 35, Kent State Collection, Manuscripts and Archives, Sterling Memorial Library, Yale University (hereafter cited as KSC, SML, YU); Deposition of Charles Fassinger, September 3, 1974, p. 113, MS 1800, Box 64, KSC, SML, YU; and Deposition of Harry Jones, September 19, 1974, Accession 1989-M-048, Box 35, KSC, SML, YU. See also Testimony of Charles Fassinger to Special State Grand Jury, September 22, 1970, pp. 5–6, MS 1800, Box 64, KSC, SML, YU.

102 **"desk officer"**: Mathew McManus interview, April 7, 2020, Kent State Guardsmen Oral History Project, Ohio Northern University (hereafter cited as KSGOHP, ONU).

103 **"clearly illogical"**: Deposition of Robert Canterbury, November 22, 1974, Box 64D, Folder 19, May 4 Collection, Kent State University Library (hereafter cited as M4C, KSUL).

103 **"The general led us"**: Mathew McManus quoted in *Cleveland Press*, April 3, 1974, p. 1.

104 **"It's almost over with"**: Quoted in Scott L. Bills, ed., *Kent State/May 4: Echoes Through a Decade* (Kent State University Press, 1982), p. 125.

104 **Another thought**: Statement of Myron Pryor to FBI, May 9, 1970, MS 804, Accession 1988-M-048, Box 37, Folder 483, KSC, SML, YU.

104 **"there was an air"**: Henry Halem interview with Jim Sprance, May 4, 2000, Kent State Shooting Oral History Program (hereafter cited as KSSOHP).

104 **"I had an uneasy feeling"**: Bill Rubenstein, "Tragedy at Kent," MS 804, Accession 1983-M-017, Box 1, KSC, SML, YU.

104 **"both felt they had"**: James J. Best, "Kent State: Answers and Questions," in *Kent State and May 4th: A Social Science Perspective*, 3rd ed., ed. Thomas R. Hensley and Jerry M. Lewis (Kent State University Press, 2010), p. 28.

104 **"stay in the dorm"**: Interview with Joe Lewis and his mother, Betty Lewis, MS 804, James Munves Papers, Box 1, KSC, SML, YU.

104 **"Hey Stamps!"**: Quoted in James A. Michener, *Kent State: What Happened and Why* (Random House, Reader's Digest Books, 1971), p. 350; and Taped interview with Robby Stamps, October 9, 1970, James A. Michener Papers (hereafter cited as JAMP), Manuscript Division, Library of Congress, Washington, D.C. (hereafter cited as MD, LOC).

104 **"We said, 'Oh, not' "**: Sandra Halem interview with anonymous guardsman, May 2, 2000, KSSOHP.

105 **"Captain Martin slammed down"**: Author's interview with Mathew McManus, October 24, 2020.

105 **Rifles were then handed out**: Author's telephone interview with B. J. Long, May 5, 2022.

105 **"They weren't too happy"**: Mathew McManus interview, April 7, 2020, KSGOHP, ONU.

105 **They received no briefing**: Deposition of Lieutenant Dwight Cline, April 2, 1975, p. 52, MS 1800, Box 62, KSC, SML, YU.

105 **"Sergeant McManus, those men"**: Author's interview with Mathew McManus, October 24, 2020.

105 **"Fuck Weekend Warrior Pigs!"**: Testimony of Leon Smith, 1975 Federal Civil Trial, p. 5908, Laura Davis Papers (hereafter cited as LDP), Box 214, M4C, KSUL.

105 **Students standing in the windows**: James Crater to author, November 2, 2020.

105 **At that hour**: "The Innocent Bystander," *Cleveland Press*, October 19, 1974.

105 **"You want this assembly"**: Deposition of Robert Canterbury, November 21, 1974, pp. 133–43, MS 804, Accession 1989-M-048, Box 35, KSC, SML, YU.

105 **"I took that to mean"**: See William Scranton, Chairman, Scranton Commission, *Report of the President's Commission on Campus Unrest.*

106 **other guard officers**: Robert A. Murphy and Robert Hocutt to Jerris Leonard, "Summary of the Kent State Incident," June 18, 1970, U.S. Department of Justice 144-57-338.

106 **"John, Del [Corso] and I"**: John Simons Personal Narrative, Narratives and Commentaries Related to the Kent State Shootings (hereafter cited as NCRKSS), M4C, KSUL.

106 **"Otherwise, he wouldn't"**: National Geographic, *Kent State 2* [documentary].

106 **"Hey boy, what's that"**: Quoted in Joe Eszterhas and Michael D. Roberts, *Thirteen Seconds: Confrontation at Kent State* (Dodd, Mead, 1970), p. 148.

106 **"We're going to make you"**: Quoted in Milton Viorst, *Fire in the Streets: America in the 1960s* (Simon & Schuster, 1979), p. 507.

107 **"Vietnam had receded"**: Joe Lewis in *Kent State: The Day the War Came Home* [documentary], Learning Channel, 2000.

107 **"It wasn't an antiwar rally"**: Barbara Hipsman-Springer interview with Patrick G. Smith, May 1, 2020, KSSOHP.

107 **"Excitement was in the air"**: Lae'l Hughes-Watkins interview with Glen Schultz, November 1, 2017, KSSOHP.

107 **A student noticed**: Terry Strubbe Statement to FBI, May 11, 1970, MS 804, Accession 1989-M-048, Box 34, Folder 438, KSC, SML, YU.

107 **"My main reason"**: Quoted on WKSU, May 4, 2020.

108 **"Be careful, Tommy"**: Interview with Tom Sr. and Collette Grace, MS 804, James Munves Papers, Box 1, KSC, SML, YU.

108 **"experiencing a deep feeling"**: Thomas M. Grace, *Kent State: Death and Dissent in the Long Sixties* (University of Massachusetts Press, 2016), p. 218.

109 **"I'd been hunting"**: Quoted in Howard Means, *67 Shots: Kent State and the End of American Innocence* (Da Capo Press, 2016), p. 210.

109 **Angered by what had happened**: Quoted in Joseph Kelner and James Munves, *The Kent State Coverup* (Harper & Row, 1980), p. 50.

109 **"I went primarily"**: Quoted in Sarah Crump, "May 4 Journal," *Cleveland Magazine*, May 1995, p. 60; and Means, *67 Shots*, p. 65.

109 **mocked "the Establishment"**: Larry Raines Personal Narrative, March 24, 1997, NCRKSS, M4C, KSUL.

109 **"everything is all right"**: Quoted in *Record-Courier* (Ravenna, OH), May 5, 1970.

109 **Her boyfriend**: Quoted in James Munves interview with Art and Doris Krause, June 12, 1977, LDP, Box 214, M4C, KSUL.

111 **"Out of curiosity"**: Testimony of John Cleary, June 1975 Civil Trial, pp. 4138–41, MS 1800, Box 62, KSC, SML, YU.

111 **"because he was curious"**: Quoted in *Life*, May 15, 1970, p. 37.

111 **"It feels like we're walking"**: Quoted in Draft Manuscript, V-L-3, JAMP, MD, LOC.

111 **"I just want to see"**: Quoted in Michener, *Kent State*, p. 394.

111 **"I hope there aren't any"**: Quoted in *Lorain Journal* (Lorain, OH), May 6, 1970.

112 **"If there's trouble"**: James Munves interview with Martin and Sarah Scheuer, June 12, 1977, LDP, Box 214, M4C, KSUL; and Eszterhas and Roberts, *Thirteen Seconds*, p. 225.

112 **"I told [Sandy]"**: Note Fragment, "Monday," JAMP, Container No. II: 34, MD, LOC.

112 **"I was interested in"**: "Jim Russell – Student," Interview, MS 1800, Box 73, KSC, SML, YU.

112 **"the building tops"**: Lorrie J. Accettola Personal Narrative, November 13, 1999, NCRKSS, M4C, KSUL.

112 **"I wanted to see"**: Gregory Wilson interview with Rick Byrum, March 30, 2013, KSSOHP.

112 **"It struck me"**: Ken Schaub Personal Narrative, May 16, 2000, NCRKSS, M4C, KSUL.

112 **"running around telling"**: Sue Mishoff Oral History, May 3, 1990, KSSOHP.

112 **"There were people"**: Sandra Halem interview with Michael Erwin, April 4, 2000, KSSOHP.

112 **"You had super-straight"**: Quoted in Eszterhas and Roberts, *Thirteen Seconds*, p. 151.

112 **"a couple thousand"**: Ken Hammond, quoted in Means, *67 Shots*, p. 195.

112 **"You never knew who"**: Paul Naujoks, quoted in "Tragedy in Our Midst—A Special Report," *Akron Beacon Journal*, May 24, 1970.

113 **"Sure, we wanted"**: Quoted in Michener, *Kent State*, p. 34.

113 **"You better get out of here"**: Quoted in *Plain Dealer* (Cleveland, OH), June 18, 1975, sec. B; and Grace, *Kent State*, p. 213.

113 **"Professor"**: Quoted in Michener, *Kent State*, p. 346.

114 **"I'll never forget"**: Statement of Dennis Breckinridge to FBI, May 11, 1970, MS 804, Accession 1989-M-048, Box 34, KSC, SML, YU.

114 **"There was a lot going on"**: Author's interview with Mathew McManus, October 24, 2020.

114 **"Did you have any understanding"**: Deposition of Dennis Breckenridge, February 6, 1975, p. 56, MS 1800, Box 12, KSC, SML, YU.

115 **"I didn't even know"**: Testimony of Robert James, 1975 Civilian Trial, pp. 5991–92, MS 1800, Box 66, KSC, SML, YU.

115 **"What are you gonna do now"**: Author's interview with Mathew McManus, October 24, 2020.

115 **"seemed much more hostile"**: Statement of Robert Canterbury to FBI, May 7, 1970, MS 1800, Box 61, KSC, SML, YU.

115 **"It was a crowd"**: Laura Davis and Carole Barbato interview with Charles Fassinger, 2 of 5, April 1, 2007, LDP, Box 214A, M4C, KSUL; and Testimony of Charles Fassinger to Special State Grand Jury, September 22, 1970, p. 22, MS 1800, Box 64, KSC, SML, YU.

115 **"a kind of picnic"**: Trial transcript 7714, vol. 3310, lines 4–15, KSC, SML, YU.

115 **"The students who were assembled"**: Proffer of Testimony, MS 804, Accession 1989-M-048, Box 29, KSC, SML, YU.

115 **"a totally peaceful assembly"**: Deposition of Mike Delaney quoted in "Engdahl Memo-

randum I, Kent State Civil Cases—January 16, 1975," MS 804, Series I, Box 1, Folder 38, KSC, SML, YU.

115 **"didn't see any physically"**: Testimony of Lloyd Thomas, 1975 Federal Civil Trial, p. 2069; and Deposition of Lloyd Thomas, MS 1800, Box 76, KSC, SML, YU.

115 **"All I saw"**: Testimony of Rodney Biddle, 1975 Federal Civil Trial, p. 5560, MS 804, Accession 1989-M-048, Box 35, KSC, SML, YU.

115 **"There was just noise"**: Testimony of Larry Mowrer, Federal Civil Trial, June 16, 1975, Box 36, KSC, SML, YU.

115 **"prior to the attempt"**: Affidavit of Donald Schwartzmiller, March 13, 1975, MS 1800, Box 50, KSC, SML, YU.

116 **"We're going to clear"**: Mathew McManus interview, April 7, 2020, KSGOHP, ONU.

116 **"I was a staff officer"**: Deposition of Harry Jones, MS 804, Accession 1989-M-048, Box 36, KSC, SML, YU.

116 **"I asked him if he wanted"**: Statement of Harold E. Rice, May 11, 1970, Charles Thomas Papers (hereafter cited as CTP), Box 64D, Folder 1, M4C, KSUL.

117 **"Please leave the area!"**: Quoted in Mike York and Fred Kirsch, "Eyewitness Report of Kent Massacre," *The Militant*, May 15, 1970, p. 1.

117 **"Forget it!"**: Testimony of Scott MacKenzie, Criminal Trial, p. 291, MS 1800, Box 68, KSC, SML, YU.

117 **A stone hit**: Statement of Harold E. Rice, May 11, 1970, CTP, Box 64D, Folder 1, M4C, KSUL.

117 **"He had the best of intentions"**: Quoted in Joan Morrison and Robert K. Morrison, *From Camelot to Kent State: The Sixties Experience in the Words of Those Who Lived It* (Times Books, 1987), p. 331.

117 It was **"so loud and so clear"**: Lorrie J. Accettola Personal Narrative, November 13, 1999, NCRKSS, M4C, KSUL; and Dave Rogers Statement to FBI, May 11, 1970, MS 1800, Box 72, KSC, SML, YU.

117 **"We just couldn't believe"**: "Kent State: Martyrdom That Shook the Country," *Time*, May 18, 1970, pp. 12–16.

117 **"If anyone ought to leave"**: Quoted in Morrison and Morrison, *From Camelot to Kent State*, p. 331.

117 It **"was like waving a cape"**: Quoted in Means, *67 Shots*, p. 69.

117 **"My dorm is right here"**: Quoted in Steve Duin, "Kent State: Not Forgiven, Not Forgotten," *The Oregonian*, May 4, 1995.

117 **Robby Stamps gave the guardsmen**: William L. Gardner (Department of Justice) interview with Robert Stamps, November 21, 1973, MS 1800, Box 75, KSC, SML, YU.

117 **"Off the pigs! Sieg heil!"**: Quoted in "Tragedy in Our Midst—A Special Report," *Akron Beacon Journal*.

117 **"How stupid is this?"**: Author's telephone interview with B. J. Long, May 5, 2022.

117 **"Pigs off campus"**: Quoted in Michener, *Kent State*, p. 392.

117 **He had called his mother**: J. Gregory Payne, *MAYDAY: Kent State* (Kendall/Hunt, 1981), p. 89; Eszterhas and Roberts, *Thirteen Seconds*, p. 270; "4 Dead in Ohio" [video], Al Jazeera English, 2010, Youtube.com; Thomas Gallagher, "Tragedy at Kent State," *Good Housekeeping*, October 1970; and Interview with Elaine Miller Holstein, April 18, 1977, MS 804, James Munves Papers, Box 1, KSC, SML, YU.

118 **"the guardsmen were taking it"**: Barry Levine in *Kent State: The Day the War Came Home*, Learning Channel.

118 **"Generally speaking,"**: E-mail from anonymous guardsman, September 2, 2020.

118 **"She had this bandana"**: Quoted in Means, *67 Shots*, p. 67.
118 **"We were definitely"**: Telephone interview with Keith Crilow, February 28, 2020, KSGOHP, ONU.
119 **"look[ed] into the faces"**: Statement of Harold Rice, May 11, 1970, CTP, Box 64D, Folder 1, M4C, KSUL.
119 **"I see your name"**: Sandra Halem interview with anonymous guardsman, May 2, 2000, KSSOHP.
119 **"It was so unorganized"**: Author's interview with Ron Gammell, October 24, 2020.
119 **"[We] had no understanding"**: Deposition of Lloyd Thomas, p. 28, MS 804, Accession 1989-M-048, Box 37, KSC, SML, YU.
119 **"We had never been"**: Telephone interview with Keith Crilow, February 28, 2020, KSGOHP, ONU.
119 **"Loaded rifles"**: Jerry Damerow interview, March 11, 2020, KSGOHP, ONU.
119 **"Why would you put"**: Author's telephone interview with Gabe Brachna, January 25, 2023.
119 **"Someone had put you"**: Robert Hatfield interview, March 6, 2021, KSGOHP, ONU.
119 **" 'I wish I could go' "**: Sandra Halem interview with anonymous National Guardsman, May 2, 2000, KSSOHP.
119 **"You take the military uniform off"**: Author's interview with Gabe Brachna, October 3, 2020.
119 **"This looks bad"**: Quoted in Ed Grant and Mike Hill, *I Was There: What Really Went on at Kent State* (C. S. S. Publishing, 1974), p. 67.
119 **"We were beat"**: Author's interview with Ron Gammell, October 24, 2020.
120 **"The only thing I saw"**: Quoted in Eszterhas and Roberts, *Thirteen Seconds*, p. 146.
120 **"I personally didn't think"**: Author's interview with Ron Gammell, October 24, 2020.
120 **"nervous as a hawk"**: Charles Madonio Notes, November 18, 1970, JAMP, Container II: 30, Folder 6, MD, LOC.
120 **"Somebody is going"**: Statement of Harold Rice, May 11, 1970, CTP, Box 64D, Folder 1, M4C, KSUL.
120 **"rifles will be carried"**: Quoted in Stanley Rosenblatt, *Justice Denied* (Nash Publishing, 1971), p. 243.
121 **"Some in my platoon"**: Quoted in *Time*, May 18, 1970.
121 **One private had never**: Testimony of Rodney Biddle to Federal Grand Jury, p. 4125, MS 804, Accession 1989-M-048, Box 35, KSC, SML, YU.
121 **Another was so unfamiliar**: James McGee, "Tuesday, October 30, 1974, Fifth Day of the Trial," Box 64D, Folder 9, M4C, KSUL.
121 **"I was confronted with"**: Fitt, "The National Guard and Civil Disturbance," *City: Magazine of Urban Life and Environment*, August/September 1970.
121 **"saw no weapons—none"**: Author's interview with Mathew McManus, October 24, 2020.
121 **"These weapons weren't play toys"**: Author's interview with Gabe Brachna, October 3, 2020.
121 **"it didn't make sense"**: Testimony of Joe Lewis, 1975 Civil Trial, p. 1624, MS 1800, Box 67, KSC, SML, YU.
122 **"If that general had"**: Quoted in Means, *67 Shots*, p. 200.
122 **Those in Company A**: Alexander Stevenson Statement to FBI, May 13, 1970, MS 1800, Box 75, KSC, SML, YU.

122 **"Half of [my] company"**: Testimony of Larry Mowrer, Federal Civil Trial, June 16, 1975, MS 804, Accession 1989-M-048, Box 36, KSC, SML, YU.

122 **"The gas mask wouldn't seal"**: Testimony of Robert James, Federal Civil Trial, July 8, 1975, MS 804, Accession 1989-M-048, Box 36, KSC, SML, YU.

122 **A corporal broke off**: Deposition of Larry Mowrer, MS 804, Accession 1989-M-048, Box 36, KSC, SML, YU.

122 **"a blur"**: Testimony of Larry Mowrer, Federal Civil Trial, June 30, 1975, p. 2671, MS 1800, Box 70, KSC, SML, YU; and Statement of Larry Mowrer to Ohio State Highway Patrol, June 13, 1970, Series 2062, Box 2842, Ohio Historical Society, State Archives, Columbus, Ohio (hereafter cited as OHSSA).

123 **Ohio National Guard headquarters**: *Plain Dealer* (Cleveland, OH), July 8, 1975, p. 2-A.

123 **It was difficult for officers**: Testimony of Charles Fassinger to Special State Grand Jury, October 24, 1970, p. 23, MS 1800, Box 64, KSC, SML, YU.

123 **"the gas masks were heavy"**: Quoted in Michener, *Kent State*, p. 335.

123 **"It's impossible"**: Transcript of Federal Civil Trial Testimony, June 5, 1975, vol. 7, p. 1355, KSC, SML, YU.

123 **"For crying out loud"**: Author's interview with Mathew McManus, October 24, 2020.

123 **"to get out of there"**: Testimony of Robert Canterbury before the Scranton Commission, August 8, 1970.

123 **"that actual dispersal"**: Deposition of Robert Canterbury, November 22, 1974, CTP, Box 64D, Folder 19, M4C, KSUL.

123 **"Move 'em out"**: Laura Davis and Carole Barbato interview with Charles Fassinger, 3 of 5, April 1, 2007, LDP, Box 214A, M4C, KSUL.

123 **"I stood there"**: Quoted in *Cleveland Press*, April 3, 1974, p. A3.

124 **"A tear-gas canister"**: Quoted in Erin Kosnac and Melissa Hostetler, "Then I Was Shot," *The Burr*, May 4, 2000, p. 19.

124 **"We're not going to move them"**: Author's interview with Mathew McManus, October 24, 2020.

124 **"The tear gas didn't have much"**: National Geographic, *Kent State 2*.

124 **"It was like a game"**: Quoted in "Tragedy in Our Midst—A Special Report," *Akron Beacon Journal*.

124 **"They were having fun"**: Quoted in Michener, *Kent State*, p. 365.

125 **"Why are they doing that?"**: Sandra Halem interview with Robert Pescatore, May 4, 2000, KSSOHP.

125 **Doug Wrentmore**: Michener, *Kent State*, p. 353; and photograph nos. 18–20 in Peter Davies, *The Truth About Kent State: A Challenge to the American Conscience* (Farrar, Straus and Giroux, 1973).

125 **"Why are they doing this to us?"**: Quoted in Payne, *MAYDAY*, p. 98.

125 **"You motherfuckers"**: Cited in Peter Davies to Charles Thomas, July 15, 1978, CTP, M4C, KSUL.

126 **"I can't convey"**: Quoted in Charles Thomas, *Blood of Isaac* [ebook], chap. 6, LDP, M4C, KSUL.

126 **"I remember breathing"**: Quoted in "Tragedy in Our Midst—A Special Report," *Akron Beacon Journal*.

126 **"We halted momentarily"**: Quoted in Thomas, *Blood of Isaac*.

126 **"Sergeant—"**: Author's interview with Mathew McManus, October 24, 2020.

126 **At this point**: Laura Davis and Carole Barbato interview with Charles Fassinger, 2 of 5, April 1, 2007, LDP, Box 214A, M4C, KSUL.

127 **"I asked him why"**: Quoted in Eszterhas and Roberts, *Thirteen Seconds*, pp. 178–79.

127 **"That silly Canterbury"**: Quoted in Eszterhas and Roberts, *Thirteen Seconds*, p. 157. Lieutenant Colonel Charles Fassinger also later testified, "I would consider the crowd dispersed if they broke into smaller groups." Deposition of Charles Fassinger, p. 150, MS 1800, Box 64, KSC, SML, YU.

127 **Simons would later say**: Quoted in Kelner and Munves, *Kent State Coverup*, p. 135.

127 **"Kent State is not Iwo Jima"**: *CBS Evening News*, November 3, 1970.

127 **"Canterbury is a general"**: Quoted in Eszterhas and Roberts, *Thirteen Seconds*, p. 178.

127 **"paper soldier"**: Quoted in interview with Joseph Kelner, April 25, 1977, MS 804, James Munves Papers, Box 1, KSC, SML, YU.

128 **"groups of five"**: Testimony of Tom Grace, December 19, 1978, Heidloff-Reichard Papers, Box 22, Folder 21, M4C, KSUL; John Burnell interview with William Derry Heasley, May 4, 1990, KSSOHP; and student statement to Ohio State Highway Patrol, July 2, 1970, Case No. 400-67A-132, Series 2062, Box 2823, OHSSA.

128 **Company C was nowhere**: Author's interview with Mathew McManus, October 24, 2020.

129 **"they were caught"**: John Simons quoted in *Akron Beacon Journal*, November 4, 1970.

129 **"The students began to realize"**: Statement of student Cathy Pfefferle, CTP, Box 64D, Folder 1, M4C, KSUL.

130 **"The students started gaining"**: Quoted in Eszterhas and Roberts, *Thirteen Seconds*, p. 157.

130 **"people laughing and going"**: Larry Shank Oral History, March 14 and April 12, 2019, KSSOHP.

130 **"It was terribly loud"**: Testimony of Lloyd Thomas, 1975 Federal Civil Trial, p. 2089, MS 1800, Box 76, KSC, SML, YU.

130 **One protestor in the parking lot**: Craig Simpson interview with anonymous student, May 4, 2010, KSSOHP.

132 **"large enough that it took"**: Testimony of Paul Locher, 1975 Federal Civil Trial, MS 804, Accession 1989-M-048, Box 36, Folder 469, KSC, SML, YU.

132 **"Two of my men"**: Author's interview with Mathew McManus, October 24, 2020.

132 **An observer on the Taylor Hall terrace**: Kurt Eberly interview with Gusztav Asboth, February 8, 2020, KSSOHP.

132 **Others saw a stone**: Eszterhas and Roberts, *Thirteen Seconds*, p. 159; and Sandra Halem interview with Carol Mirman, April 1, 2000, KSSOHP.

132 **Another brick struck**: *Akron Beacon Journal*, June 6, 1975, p. B3.

132 **Acting Sergeant Bill Herschler**: Testimony of Bill Herschler, Federal Civil Trial, July 17, 1975, pp. 7550–51, KSC, SML, YU.

132 **A brick hit**: Statement of James Pierce to FBI, May 7, 1970, MS 804, Accession 1989-M-048, Box 34, KSC, SML, YU.

132 **"The guard was rattled"**: Quoted in "Tragedy in Our Midst—A Special Report," *Akron Beacon Journal*.

132 **"It started all closing in"**: Quoted in Krista Ramsey, "13 Deadly Seconds," *Cincinnati Enquirer*, May 1, 1995.

132 **About two dozen students**: Abstract of a deposition given by Harry Jones, April 14, 1975, CTP, Box 64B, M4C, KSUL; and Ohio State Highway Patrol, Report of Investi-

gation, "Riot at Kent State University," June 22, 1970, Case No. 400-67A-132, Series 2062, Box 2823, OHSSA.

132 **"I was very upset"**: Testimony of Dean Kahler, Federal Civil Trial, June 4, 1975, vol. 6, pp. 1177–78, KSC, SML, YU.

133 **"because a lot of the guardsmen"**: Testimony of Tom Grace to Federal Grand Jury, p. 1206, MS 1800, Box 65, KSC, SML, YU.

133 **"Don't be an idiot!"**: Quoted in Kelner and Munves, *Kent State Coverup*, p. 94.

133 **"If I was in the position"**: Federal Grand Jury Testimony of Douglas Wrentmore, MS 804, Accession 1989-M-048, Box 37, KSC, SML, YU.

133 **"Somebody would come running up"**: Craig R. Simpson interview with Chuck Ayers, August 16, 2007, KSSOHP.

133 **"Kill the pigs! The pigggs!!"**: Quoted in John Lombardi, "Kent State Shootings: A Lot of People Were Crying, and the Guard Walked Away," *Rolling Stone*, June 11, 1970.

133 **"We know you can't shoot!"**: Testimony of James Pierce to Special Grand Jury, p. 10, MS 804, Accession 1989-M-048, Box 37, Folder 482, KSC, SML, YU.

133 **Thirty-nine-year-old First Sergeant**: Author's interview with Gabe Brachna, October 3, 2020.

134 **"a 'scare tactic' "**: Statement of Sergeant Lloyd Thomas, CTP, Box 64D, Folder 1, M4C, KSUL.

134 **"Don't fire, just aim"**: Statement of Captain Raymond Srp, CTP, Box 64D, Folder 1, M4C, KSUL.

134 **"you don't point"**: Testimony of Charles Fassinger, June 1975 Civil Trial, p. 7257, MS 1800, Box 61, KSC, SML, YU.

134 **"Keep your cool"**: James Pierce statement to Ohio State Highway Patrol, MS 804, Box 37, KSC, SML, YU. Pryor testified in a 1974 deposition that he did not give this order. "That order came from behind me," he said. Deposition of Myron Pryor, September 18, 1974, p. 112, MS 1800, Box 9, KSC, SML, YU.

134 **"a bluff to push"**: Quoted in *Akron Beacon Journal*, June 10, 1975, p. 10.

134 **"The games are over"**: Larry Shafer in *Kent State: The Day the War Came Home*, Learning Channel.

135 **"that was not a good move"**: Rudy Morris in *Kent State: The Day the War Came Home*, Learning Channel.

135 **"Here was this symbol"**: Craig Simpson interview with Chuck Ayers, August 16, 2007, KSSOHP.

135 **"Shoot! Shoot! Shoot!"**: Quoted in Eszterhas and Roberts, *Thirteen Seconds*, p. 159.

135 **"People were saying"**: Henry Halem interview with Rob Fox, May 4, 2000, KSSOHP.

135 **"They can't possibly"**: Quoted in Draft Manuscript, V-L-7, JAMP, MD, LOC.

135 **"They were talking to"**: Author's interview with Mathew McManus, October 24, 2020.

135 **"Now what do we do?"**: Quoted in Jeff Kisseloff, *Generation on Fire: Voices of Protest from the 1960s* (University Press of Kentucky, 2007), p. 254.

136 **"How in the hell?"**: Rudy Morris quoted in *Kent State: The Day the War Came Home*, Learning Channel.

136 **"That's a good idea"**: Excerpts of Harry Jones Deposition, LDP, Box 214, M4C, KSUL.

136 **"line up, form a wedge"**: Testimony of General Robert Canterbury before the Scranton Commission, August 8, 1970; and Harry Jones legal deposition, 1975, MS 804, Boxes 9 and 36, KSC, SML, YU.

136 **"My purpose"**: Testimony of General Robert Canterbury before the Scranton Commission, August 8, 1970.

136 **"a confused mixture"**: Author's interview with Gabe Brachna, October 3, 2020.

136 **"I thought it was humorous"**: Quoted in *Cleveland Press*, June 24, 1975, p. A15.

136 **"I was aware of the officers"**: Author's interview with Gabe Brachna, October 3, 2020.

136 **"No one knew who was in charge"**: Quoted in *Kent State: The Day the War Came Home*, Learning Channel.

136 **"They ran out of [tear] gas!"**: Quoted in Draft Manuscript, V-L-7, JAMP, MD, LOC.

136 **"The crowd sensed a turn"**: Statement of Captain Raymond Srp, CTP, Box 64D, Folder 1, M4C, KSUL.

136 **"The guard had failed"**: Quoted in "Tragedy in Our Midst—A Special Report," *Akron Beacon Journal*; and *Kent State: The Day the War Came Home*, Learning Channel.

136 **"That's when a great number"**: Interview with anonymous witness, MS 804, James Munves Papers, Box 2, KSC, SML, YU.

136 **"We sort of closed in"**: Barry Levine quoted in "Tragedy in Our Midst—A Special Report," *Akron Beacon Journal*.

137 **"Let's surround them!"**: Statement of Cathy Pfefferle, Report of the Ohio National Guard Inspector General, Kent State University Riot, 4 May 1970, May 22, 1970, MS 804, Accession 1989-M-048, Box 30, Folder 373, KSC, SML, YU.

137 **Some walked**: Testimony of Tom Grace, December 19, 1978, Heidloff-Reichard Papers, Box 22, Folder 21, M4C, KSUL.

137 **"like children"**: Robert Ray quoted in Thomas Gallagher, "The Kent State Tragedy," p. 8, Scheuer Family Papers (hereafter cited as SFP), Box 2, OHSSA.

137 **"as if you had just cut"**: Deposition of William Perkins, p. 80, MS 1800, Box 70, KSC, SML, YU.

137 **"As they were walking off"**: Transcript of interview with James Dawson, p. 3, SFP, Box 2, OHSSA.

137 **"we started to move out"**: Author's interview with Mathew McManus, October 24, 2020. Sergeant Barry Morris and Corporal Leon Smith also recalled hearing the words, "Kill! Kill! Kill!" Deposition of Barry Morris, MS 804, Accession 1989-M-048, Box 3, Folder 34, KSC, SM L, YU; and Testimony of Leon Smith, 1975 Federal Civil Trial, p. 5911, LDP, Box 214, M4C, KSUL.

137 **"Get the weapons!"**: Testimony of Harry Jones, 1975 Federal Civil Trial, p. 5175, MS 804, Accession 1989-M-048, Box 36, KSC, SML, YU.

137 **As the guardsmen neared**: James Russell interview with Scranton Commission, August 5, 1970, MS 1800, Box 73, KSC, SML, YU.

137 **Alan Canfora, Jeff Miller**: Photograph nos. 39–40 (by John P. Filo) in Davies, *The Truth About Kent State*.

137 **"It was hard to see"**: Quoted in Eszterhas and Roberts, *Thirteen Seconds*, p. 160.

137 **More guardsmen turned**: Photograph nos. 41–43 (by John P. Filo) in Davies, *The Truth About Kent State*.

137 **Tom Grace started up**: Interview with Scott MacKenzie, MS 804, James Munves Papers, Box 1, KSC, SML, YU.

137 **"Get out of here!"**: *New York Times*, June 8, 1975; Kelner, *Kent State Coverup*, p. 51; and Morrison and Morrison, *From Camelot to Kent State*, p. 332.

137 **Scott MacKenzie**: Interview with Scott MacKenzie, MS 804, James Munves Papers, Box 1, KSC, SML, YU.

137   **"The intensity continued to increase"**: Transcript of Harry Jones Testimony, July 1, 1975, vol. 20, p. 5176, LDP, Box 214, M4C, KSUL.

137   **As the guardsmen proceeded**: Statement of Captain Raymond Srp, CTP, Box 64D, Folder 1, M4C, KSUL.

138   **John Cleary**: Statement of John Cleary to FBI, May 14, 1970, CV 44-703, MS 804, Accession 1989-M-048, Box 30, Folder 366, KSC, SML, YU.

138   **"As the rock-throwing group"**: Statement of John Cleary to FBI, May 10, 1970, KSC, SML, YU.

138   **Another photographer saw**: Testimony of Howard Ruffner, December 19, 1978, Heidloff-Reichard Papers, Box 22, Folder 21, M4C, KSUL.

138   **"I can remember"**: Quoted in *Plain Dealer* (Cleveland, OH), September 12, 1971, pp. 1, 4; and Laura Davis interview with John Backlawski, WKSU, LDP, Box 214, M4C, KSUL.

138   **"Most of the men"**: Statement of Staff Sergeant Barry Morris, CTP, Box 64D, Folder 1, M4C, KSUL.

138   **"We were thinking behind us"**: Quoted in "Tragedy in Our Midst—A Special Report," *Akron Beacon Journal*.

138   **"I could see a kid"**: Quoted in Eszterhas and Roberts, *Thirteen Seconds*, p. 161.

138   **A chunk of concrete**: Testimony of John Filo, October 31, 1974, CTP, Box 64D, Folder 9, M4C, KSUL.

138   **A piece of brick**: Deposition of Robert James, MS 804, Accession 1989-M-048, Box 36, KSC, SML, YU.

138   **Half a brick**: Author's telephone interview with B. J. Long, May 5, 2022. Long was next to Hinton.

138   **"It hit me"**: Statement of Major Harry Jones, CTP, Box 64D, Folder 1, M4C, KSUL; Abstract of a Deposition Given by Harry Jones, April 14, 1975, CTP, Box 64B, M4C, KSUL; and Testimony of Major Harry Jones, July 1, 1975, transcript p. 5176, LDP, Box 214, M4C, KSUL.

138   **"I said, 'Hey, buddy'"**: FBI interview of Mathew McManus, May 9, 1970, CTP, Box 64 D, Folder 9, M4C, KSUL.

138   **"I was hit"**: Statement of Lieutenant Colonel Charles Fassinger, MS 1800, Box 64, KSC, SML, YU.

139   **"Look out!" "I turned around"**: Author's interview with Mathew McManus, October 24, 2020. Student Bruno Spreco witnessed this incident. See Eszterhas and Roberts, *Thirteen Seconds*, p. 161.

139   **Students quickened their pace**: Interview of Paul Locher, MS 804, Accession 1989-M-048, Box 29, Folder 350, KSC, SML, YU.

139   **"Some students were running"**: Testimony of Tom Grace to Federal Grand Jury, p. 1202, MS 1800, Box 65, KSC, SML, YU.

139   **"The crowd grew increasingly hostile"**: Testimony of Paul Locher, 1975 Federal Civil Trial, Accession 19890-M-048, Box 36, Folder 469, KSC, SML, YU.

139   **"Almost all of us"**: Quoted in "Tragedy in Our Midst—A Special Report," *Akron Beacon Journal*; Testimony of Tom Grace to Federal Grand Jury, pp. 1201–1202, MS 804, Accession 1989-M-048, Box 35, KSC, SML, YU; and photograph no. 45 (by Mike Glaser) and no. 49 (by John P. Filo) in Davies, *The Truth About Kent State*.

139   **"about ten people broke away"**: Student interview with Ohio Bureau of Criminal Identification and Investigation, May 20, 1970, 1:10–2:15 p.m., p. 2, Series 2062, Box 2821, OHSSA.

139 **"I was pretty close"**: Gregory Wilson interview with Joe Cullum, May 11, 2012, KSSOHP; and transcript of Joe Cullum interview, SFP, Box 2, OHSSA. Jim Russell, standing nearby, said that "the crowd that had been [in front of] Prentice Hall moved to twenty to thirty yards from the guard as the guard approached the crest." Statement of James Russell to FBI, May 8, 1970, MS 1800, Box 73, KSC, SML, YU.

139 **"about fifteen feet away"**: Transcript of interview with James J. Minard, p. 3, SFP, Box 2, OHSSA.

139 **"At first, they were just walking"**: 1975 Civil Trial Transcript, vol. 11, p. 2605, KSC, SML, YU.

139 **Major Jones waved**: *Plain Dealer* (Cleveland, OH), July 2, 1975, p. 4-A.

139 **"I was hollering"**: Transcript of Harry Jones Testimony, July 1, 1975, p. 5077, LDP, Box 214, M4C, KSUL.

139 **People screamed, "Get them!"**: Author's interview with Matt McManus, October 24, 2020.

139 **"Charge! Charge!"**: *Cleveland Press*, August 29, 1975, p. A16.

139 **"Those students were controlled"**: Richard Lutey statement to Ohio State Highway Patrol, June 22, 1970, in Ohio State Highway Patrol, Report of Investigation, June 30, 1970, Case No. 400-67A-132, Series 2062, Box 2823, OHSSA.

139 **"It didn't exactly"**: Author's interview with Matt McManus, October 24, 2020.

140 **"a lot of yelling"**: Testimony of Rodney Biddle, 1975 Federal Civil Trial, p. 5578, MS 804, Accession 1989-M-048, Box 35, KSC, SML, YU.

140 **"You couldn't hardly hear anything"**: Testimony of Leon Smith, 1975 Federal Civil Trial, p. 5911, LDP, Box 214, M4C, KSUL.

140 **"yelling at the top of my lungs"**: Testimony of James McGee to Federal Grand Jury, February 1974, p. 4982, KSC, SML, YU.

140 **"chanting, cheering"**: Testimony of James Pierce, 1975 Federal Civil Trial, p. 4428, MS 804, Accession 1989-M-048, Box 37, Folder 482, KSC, SML, YU.

140 **"closing in"**: Transcript of Harry Jones Testimony, July 1, 1975, p. 5184, LDP, Box 214, M4C, KSUL.

140 **"We were tensed up"**: Statement of Ronnie Myers to Ohio State Highway Patrol, June 13, 1970, MS 1800, Box 70, KSC, SML, YU.

140 **"I was nervous"**: Testimony of William Herschler, 1975 Civil Trial, pp. 7550–51, Box 66, KSC, SML, YU; and Statement of William Herschler to Ohio State Highway Patrol, June 25, 1970, KSC, SML, YU.

140 **A third guardsman was so frightened**: Deposition of William Perkins, p. 82, Box 70, KSC, SML, YU.

140 **"Fear"**: Transcript of Civil Trial Testimony, June 10, 1975, vol. 9, p. 1883, KSC, SML, YU.

140 **"kept getting closer"**: Telephone interview with Jeffrey Jones, March 20, 2020, KSGOHP, ONU.

140 **Many felt vulnerable**: Quoted in Eszterhas and Roberts, *Thirteen Seconds*, p. 161; and author's interview with Mathew McManus, October 24, 2020.

140 **"I figured we were going"**: Quoted in *Akron Beacon Journal*, June 19, 1975.

140 **"They had hate in them"**: Statement of Sergeant James Case, CTP, Box 64D, Folder 1, M4C, KSUL.

140 **"The mob was in a frenzied state"**: Deposition of Barry Morris, February 25, 1975, pp. 195 and 192, MS 1800, Box 14, KSC, SML, YU.

140 **"It would be all"**: Student statements, May 4 and 22, 1970, in Ohio State Highway

Patrol, Reports of Investigation, May 22 and 23, 1970, Case No. 400-67A-132, Series 2062, Box 2823, OHSSA.

140   "it was volatile": Laura Davis and Carole Barbato interview with Charles Fassinger, 4 of 5, April 1, 2007, LDP, Box 214A, M4C, KSUL.

140   "scared little boys": Gerald "Jerry" Casale, Speech at Fortieth Anniversary Commemoration of the Shootings, Kent State University, May 4, 2010.

140   "At first . . . to death.": Trial Transcript, Krause et al. v. Rhodes et al., vol. 11, p. 2605.

141   "would not have made it": Kent State: The Day the War Came Home, Learning Channel.

141   "You didn't have protestors": Author's interview with Gabe Brachna, October 3, 2020.

141   "I was very frightened": Statement of Corporal James McGee, CTP, Box 64D, Folder 1, M4C, KSUL.

141   "Man, how are we going": Quoted in "Tragedy in Our Midst—A Special Report," Akron Beacon Journal.

141   "In a crisis": Author's interview with Gabe Brachna, October 3, 2020.

141   "was literally praying": Deposition of William Perkins, p. 57A, MS 1800, Box 70, KSC, SML, YU.

141   "the shock": Deposition of James Case, March 6, 1975, p. 53, Box 15, KSC, SML, YU.

141   "I was shaking like a leaf": Guardsman statement to Ohio State Highway Patrol, June 21, 1970, in Ohio State Highway Patrol, Report of Investigation, June 29, 1970, Case No. 400-67A-132, Series 2062, Box 2823, OHHSA.

141   Matt McManus: FBI interview with Mathew McManus, July 20, 1970, CTP, Box 64D, Folder 26, M4C, KSUL.

141   "I felt out there": Author's interview with Mathew McManus, October 24, 2020.

141   An eyewitness "estimate[d]": Statement of John Filo to FBI, May 7, 1970, CTP, Box 64B, M4C, KSUL.

142   To their upper right: Transcript of interview with anonymous student, Tape No. 1, Side 2, SFP, Box 2, OHSSA.

142   "All I saw": Deposition of James Pierce, February 19, 1975, p. 131, MS 1800, Box 13, KSC, SML, YU.

142   "It seemed to me": Barry Morris statement to Ohio State Highway Patrol, May 27, 1970, in Ohio State Highway Patrol, Report of Investigation, June 4, 1970, Case No. 400-67A-132, Series 2062, Box 2823, OHSSA.

142   Joe Lewis: Daniel St. Albin Greene, "When a World Collapsed," National Observer (Washington, DC), May 3, 1975; and Testimony of Joe Lewis, 1975 Civil Trial, p. 1528, MS 1800, Box 67, KSC, SML, YU.

142   "I wanted to get": Craig Simpson interview with John Cleary, May 3, 2010, KSSOHP.

142   Jeff Miller was a short distance: Craig Simpson interview with Eldon Fender, November 28, 2007, KSSOHP.

142   "I'll be a lot safer": Draft Manuscript, V-L-9, JAMP, MD, LOC.

143   "They seemed to be very scared": Statement of John Cleary to FBI, May 10, 1970, MS 804, Accession 1989-M-048, Box 30, Folder 366, KSC, SML, YU.

143   "the National Guardsmen had to do something": Transcript of interview with James Dawson, p. 3, SFP, Box 2, OHSSA.

143   "As we got to the top of the hill": Testimony of Rodney Biddle to Federal Grand Jury, p. 4098; and Deposition of Rodney Biddle, p. 57, MS 804, Accession 1989-M-048, Box 35, KSC, SML, YU.

143   "Halt, turn, stand your ground": Quoted in Cleveland Press, June 17, 1975; and Akron Beacon Journal, June 18, 1975, p. D5. See also Statement of Sergeant Lloyd Thomas,

M4C, KSUL. Pryor later denied ordering guardsmen to turn, asserting instead that another guardsman turned first and he immediately followed suit. Deposition of Myron Pryor, September 18, 1974, MS 1800, Box 9, KSC, SML, YU.

143 **About a dozen guardsmen**: *Plain Dealer* (Cleveland, OH), June 29, 1975; *Plain Dealer* (Cleveland, OH), June 11, 1975, p. 9-A; and *Akron Beacon Journal*, June 11, 1975, p. F11.

144 **"When we were down"**: Statement of James Pierce to Ohio State Highway Patrol, cited in Robert J. Murphy to J. Stanley Pottinger, March 8, 1974, DOJ 60-76-262, Box 122, M4C, KSUL.

144 **"We tried to stop them"**: Statement of Sergeant Dale Sholl, CTP, Box 64D, Folder 1, M4C, KSUL; and "Kent State: Scranton Commission Files: Wrap-up," CTP, Box 64D, Folder 38, M4C, KSUL.

144 **"All of a sudden "**: FBI "Reports of Witnesses and Participants," p. 557.

144 **"They just turned"**: Quoted in "Tragedy in Our Midst—A Special Report," *Akron Beacon Journal.*

145 **"saw them turn"**: "Dean Kahler Shot at Kent State, May 4, 1970" [video], Youtube.com.

145 a **"threatening gesture"**: *Kent State: The Day the War Came Home*, Learning Channel.

145 **"This is from me to you"**: Quoted in Kelner and Munves, *Kent State Coverup*, p. 94.

145 **"When the line suddenly turned"**: Author's interview with Mathew McManus, October 24, 2020.

145 **"Out of the corner"**: Matt McManus interview, April 8, 2020, KSGOHP, ONU.

145 **"Troops on the right flank"**: Statement of Major Harry Jones, CTP, Box 64D, Folder 1, M4C, KSUL.

145 **"I had the feeling"**: Deposition of Harry Jones, p. 116; and Federal Grand Jury Testimony of Harry Jones, p. 4560, MS 804, Accession 1989-M-048, Box 36, Folder 465, KSC, SML, YU.

146 **"I could see Major Jones"**: Author's interview with Mathew McManus, October 24, 2020.

146 **McManus's voice thickened**: Author's interview with Mathew McManus, October 24, 2020.

146 **"I had no training"**: Deposition of Lloyd Thomas, pp. 29–30, MS 1800, Box 76, KSC, SML, YU.

147 **"In order to avoid"**: Appendix 5 (Special Instructions) to Annex C (Concept of Operations) to USCONARC Civil Disturbance Plan (Garden Plot), May 1, 1969, Series 2062, Box 2824, OHSSA.

147 **"I heard firing"**: Statement of Staff Sergeant Mathew McManus, CTP, Box 64D, Folder 1, M4C, KSUL. This statement to the FBI was the same one submitted to the Ohio National Guard Inspector General.

147 **"I naturally assumed"**: Statement of Mathew J. McManus, June 13, 1970, Ohio State Highway Patrol Report of Investigation, Case No. 400-67A-132, M4C, KSUL.

147 **"I saw three National Guardsmen"**: Testimony of Mathew McManus to Special State Grand Jury, MS 804, Accession 1989-M-048, Box 36, Folder 473, KSC, SML, YU.

147 **"the sound of the first shots"**: Deposition of Mathew McManus, February 19, 1975, pp. 119 and 122, MS 1800, Box 13, KSC, SML, YU.

147 **"initially heard a burst"**: Testimony of Mathew McManus, 1975 Civil Trial, pp. 5349–52, 5366, Box 69, KSC, SML, YU.

148 **"The truth about Kent State"**: Quoted in *Cleveland Free Press*, April 3, 1974.

148 **"I believe that eventually"**: Statement of Mathew J. McManus, June 13, 1970, Ohio

State Highway Patrol, Report of Investigation, Case No. 400-67A-132, Box 28, M4C, KSUL.

148   **"the shots did not immediately follow"**: Testimony of Richard Love, 1975 Civil Trial, p. 2858, MS 1800, Box 68, KSC, SML, YU.

148   **"noticed one guardsman turn"**: Charles Thomas Research Notes: Scranton Commission Administration Files (Screened): September 28, 1977, CTP, Box 64B, Folder 8, M4C, KSUL.

148   **"the order was given"**: Statement of Sergeant Lloyd Thomas, CTP, Box 64D, Folder 1, M4C, KSUL.

148   **"The order to fire seemed"**: Deposition of Lloyd Thomas, pp. 10–12, MS 804, Accession 1989-M-048, Box 37, KSC, SML, YU.

148   **"heard someone yell, 'Fire' "**: Statement of Sergeant Dale Sholl, Ohio State Highway Patrol, Report of Investigation, Box 28, M4C, KSUL; and *Akron Beacon Journal*, June 11, 1975, p. F11.

148   **"I did not hear the order"**: Statement of Sergeant James Case, Ohio State Highway Patrol, Report of Investigation, Box 28, M4C, KSUL. See also Deposition of James Case, March 6, 1975, pp. 55–56, MS 1800, Box 15, KSC, SML, YU.

148   **"heard somebody yell"**: Statement of Corporal Richard Lutey, June 22, 1970, Ohio State Highway Patrol, Report of Investigation, June 30, 1970, M4C, KSUL.

148   **Lieutenant Dwight Cline**: Deposition of Dwight Cline, April 2, 1975, p. 72, MS 1800, Box 62, KSC, SML, YU.

148   **saw "troops on the right flank"**: Deposition of Harry Jones, pp. 234 and 237, Box 36, Folder 465, KSC, SML, YU; Federal Grand Jury Testimony of Harry Jones, p. 4559, Box 36, KSC, SML, YU; and Statement of MAJ Harry B. Jones, S-3, 1/145 INF, Report of the Ohio National Guard Inspector General, Kent State University Riot, 4 May 1970, May 22, 1970, MS 804, Accession 1989-M-048, Box 30, Folder 373, KSC, SML, YU.

149   **"I distinctly remember"**: Sandra Halem interview with Carol Mirman, April 1, 2000, KSSOHP.

149   **"It came from behind me"**: Statement of Richard Shade to Ohio State Highway Patrol, June 15, 1970, MS 1800, Box 73, KSC, SML, YU.

149   **Nearly two dozen**: They were, in alphabetical order: *Student Michael Anderson*: "While observing I heard a shot. The shot sounded like a small-caliber weapon. About three to five seconds later, I saw and heard the National Guard troops fire." Statement of Michael Curtis Anderson, Report of the Ohio National Guard Inspector General, Kent State University Riot, 4 May 1970, May 22, 1970, MS 804, Accession 1989-M-048, Box 30, Folder 373, KSC, SML, YU. *Guardsman Dale Antram*: "I heard one shot and then I heard more shots. I turned to my right and saw some of my compatriots in the guard firing their weapons." Dale Antram interview, February 27, 2020, KSGOHP, ONU. *Guardsman John Backlawski*: "I heard a shot fired and it seemed like right after that that everything opened up." Interview with John Backlawski, WKSU, LDP, Box 214, M4C, KSUL. *University policeman Francis Bertholdi*: "A single shot was fired . . . this shot was of a lesser caliber than an M1 rifle . . . a volley of shots followed." Statement of Joseph Francis Bertholdi, May 13, 1970, Report of the Ohio National Guard Inspector General, Kent State University Riot, 4 May 1970, May 22, 1970, MS 804, Accession 1989-M-048, Box 30, Folder 373, KSC, SML, YU. *National Guard officer James Booth*: "I heard one single shot, followed by a volley that lasted several seconds." Statement of Captain James Booth, KSGOHP, ONU. *Guardsman Dennis Breckenridge*:

"I heard one single shot fired from behind." "Then I heard a volley." Deposition of
Dennis Breckenridge, MS 804, Accession 1989-M-048, Box 3, Folder 32, KSC, SML,
YU. *Protestor Alan Canfora*: "I heard the firing start . . . one shot at first, which was
followed by a whole barrage of shots." Testimony of Alan Canfora to Federal Grand
Jury, p. 1126, cited in Federal Criminal Trial Testimony, p. 512, KSC, SML, YU. *General Robert Canterbury*: "I heard a single shot precede the volley. It was a split second
before the volley." "In my opinion, this was fired from a non-military weapon based
on the sound." Robert Canterbury Statement to Scranton Commission, August 25,
1970, Closed Scranton Commission Administrative Files, Box 91 (Witness File), CTP,
Box 64B, Folder 8, M4C, KSUL. *Lieutenant Colonel Charles Fassinger*: "As we reached
the top of the hill by Taylor Hall, there was what sounded like a shot"—"a different
sound"—"there was a few seconds of silence, a few of the troops dropped to their
knees, and then some troops fired their weapons." Statement of Lieutenant Colonel
Charles Fassinger, M4C, KSUL; and Engdahl Memorandum I, Kent State Civil Cases
- January 16, 1975, Charles Thomas Papers, Box 64C, MSC, KSUL *Protestor Tom Grace*:
"There was definitely one shot prior to the volley." Deposition of Tom Grace, p. 84, MS
804, Accession 1989-M-048, Box 35, Folder 460, KSC, SML, YU. *Guardsman Robert
James*: "I thought I just heard 'Fire!'" Deposition of Robert James, MS 804, Accession
1989-M-048, Box 36, KSC, SML, YU. *Guardsman Richard Love*: "I did not hear an
order to 'fire' but I did hear a volley of shots. I felt that probably an order had been
given to 'fire over their heads' and so I fired my M-1 rifle in a relatively high arc over
the heads of the demonstrators in front of me and to the right." Statement of Sergeant
Richard Love to FBI, May 10, 1970, MS 804, Accession 1989-M-048, Box 34, KSC,
SML, YU. *Guardsman Richard Lutey*: He heard someone yell, "Warning shots." Deposition of Richard Lutey, March 12, 1975, MS 1800, Box 68, KSC, SML, YU. *Guardsman
Barry Morris*: He believed a shot "came from my rear. It didn't sound like a military
weapon." "It sounded like it was muffled from being low. . . . It wasn't a clear, loud
crack." MS 804, Accession 1989-M-048, Box 34, KSC, SML, YU; and Deposition of
Barry Morris, February 25, 1975, p. 117, MS 1800, Box 14, KSC, SML, YU. *Guardsman
Rudy Morris*: He heard the word, "Fire" before any shots were fired. Statement to FBI
excerpted in MS 1800, Box 61, KSC, SML, YU. *Student photographer Terry Norman*:
"the guardsmen leveled their weapons toward the crowd. A short time after that, I
heard what seemed to be a small-caliber weapon or a firecracker. Right afterwards,
the guard opened up." Terrence Norman statement to Ohio State Highway Patrol,
June 1, 1970, in Ohio State Highway Patrol, Report of Investigation, June 2, 1970,
Case No. 400-67A-132, Series 2062, Box 2823, OHSSA. *Guardsman Bill Perkins*: He
heard a shot "to my right [down the hill]. It was a different sound." MS 804, Accession
1989-M-048, Box 34, Folder 460, KSC, SML, YU. *Construction worker Lowell Powers*:
"I heard a noise that sounded like a small-caliber round. Knowing the sound of a
30-caliber rifle, I knew that this was definitely smaller caliber. Several seconds later,
there was a volley of larger-caliber fire from the guard weapons." Affidavit of Lowell
Powers, May 13, 1970, Report of the Ohio National Guard Inspector General, Kent
State University Riot, 4 May 1970, May 22, 1970, MS 804, Accession 1989-M-048,
Box 30, Folder 373, KSC, SML, YU. *Guardsman Leon Smith*: "I heard what sounded
like a single shot from my immediate right." "Seconds after I heard that, there was
a complete volley, several shots." Testimony of Leon Smith, 1975 Federal Civil Trial,
pp. 5877–78, LDP, Box 214, M4C, KSUL. *Protestor Robby Stamps*: He "heard one shot
then a whole bunch" of shots." Testimony of Robert Stamps, Federal Grand Jury, p.

1088, MS 804, Accession 1989-M-048, Box 37, KSC, SML, YU. *National Guard officer Ralph Tucker:* "A shot was fired followed very closely by a volley-type series of shots." Statement of First Lieutenant Ralph Tucker, CTP, Box 64D, Folder 1, M4C, KSUL. *Guardsman Ralph Zoller:* "I heard a single shot come from behind me—further down the hill." It did not sound like an M-1 rifle. "Several seconds elapsed between this shot and a barrage of shots the guard fired." Quoted in *Cleveland Press,* July 10, 1975, p. B2. *Guardsmen James Farriss* and *Roger Maas* said they, too, heard some kind of order to fire. Statements of Corporal James Farriss and Sergeant Roger Maas, CTP, Box 64D, Folder 1, M4C, KSUL. Still more eyewitnesses said "the first shot sounded to them similar to that made by a shotgun." Justice Department Summary of FBI investigation, quoted in *New York Times,* October 31, 1970.

149 **Major Harry Jones later testified:** Transcript of Harry Jones Testimony, 1975 Federal Civil Trial, vol. 20, p. 4936, LDP, Box 214, M4C, KSUL. Charles Fassinger made a similar point. See Laura Davis and Carole Barbato interview with Charles Fassinger, 4 of 5, April 1, 2007, LDP, Box 214A, M4C, KSUL.

149 **"if they recognized his voice":** Quoted in William A. Gordon, *The Fourth of May: Killings and Coverups at Kent State* (Prometheus Books, 1990), p. 171.

149 **"Who was the senior officer":** Deposition of Robert Canterbury, November 22, 1974, CTP, Box 64D, Folder 19, M4C, KSUL; and *Time,* May 18, 1970.

149 **Canterbury's devastating admission:** Charles Fassinger stressed this point in court. Testimony of Charles Fassinger, June 1975 Civil Trial, p. 7360, MS 1800, Box 61, KSC, SML, YU.

150 **"It is necessary":** Robert H. Canterbury, "Distribution of Lesson Plan and Transparencies, 'Legal Consequences of State Active Duty in Aid to Civil Authorities,'" October 1, 1969, CTP, Box 64D, Folder 19, M4C, KSUL; and *Time,* May 18, 1970.

Chapter 6: May 4, 1970—The Tragic Day, Part II

151 **"I yelled as loud as I could":** Author's interview with Matt McManus, October 24, 2020.

151 **"One shot was all it took":** Author's telephone interview with B. J. Long, May 5, 2022.

151 **"Under the pressure":** Howard Means, *67 Shots: Kent State and the End of American Innocence* (Da Capo Press, 2016), p. 82.

151 **"were shoulder to shoulder":** Author's interview with Matt McManus, October 24, 2020.

151 **"you learn to do":** Deposition of James Pierce, p. 56, MS 804, Accession 1989-M-048, Box 37, Folder 482, Kent State Collection, Manuscripts and Archives, Sterling Memorial Library, Yale University (hereafter cited as KSC, SML, YU).

151 **"The military trains you":** Telephone interview with William Herthneck, February 17, 2020, Kent State Guardsmen Oral History Project, Ohio Northern University (hereafter cited as KSGOHP, ONU).

151 **"'God, someone else is shooting'":** Sandra Halem interview with anonymous guardsman, May 2, 2000, Kent State Shooting Oral History Program (hereafter cited as KSSOHP).

152 **"Everyone—students and guardsmen"**: Deposition of Harry Jones, p. 244, MS 804, Accession 1989-M-048, Box 36, Folder 465, KSC, SML, YU.

152 **"Someone just snapped"**: Telephone interview with Keith Crilow, February 28, 2020, KSGOHP, ONU.

152 **"They were in a position"**: *CBS Evening News*, November 3, 1970.

152 **"A bunch of scared"**: George Warren (Scranton Commission) interview with Robby Stamps, August 19, 1970, MS 1800, Box 75, KSC, SML, YU.

152 **"In the end"**: National Geographic, *Kent State 2* [documentary].

152 **"Anger and fear"**: Jim Banks quoted in *Sunday Plain Dealer* (Cleveland, OH), May 3, 2020, p. A10.

152 **"It was indiscriminate shooting"**: Quoted in *Plain Dealer* (Cleveland, OH), July 2, 1975, p. 4A.

152 **"I thought that any rounds"**: Statement of Sergeant Lloyd Thomas, May 4 Collection, Kent State University Library (hereafter cited as M4C, KSUL).

152 **Private Lonnie Hinton**: Author's telephone interview with B. J. Long, May 5, 2022. Long was next to Hinton but did not fire.

152 **"I felt firing a shot in the air"**: Deposition of Robert James, MS 804, Accession 1989-M-048, Box 36, KSC, SML, YU.

152 **"The pagoda on Blanket Hill"**: James J. Best, "The Tragic Weekend of May 1–4, 1970," in *Kent State and May 4th: A Social Science Perspective*, 3rd ed., ed. Thomas R. Hensley and Jerry M. Lewis (Kent State University Press, 2010), p. 23.

153 **"Everything happened so fast"**: "Tragedy in Our Midst—A Special Report," *Akron Beacon Journal*, May 24, 1970.

153 **"Your sergeant's shooting"**: Author's interview with Gabe Brachna, October 3, 2020.

153 **because of hearing**: Statement of Private Robert Hatfield, M4C, KSUL.

153 **"Why did you fire?"**: Specialist Robert James Statement to Ohio State Highway Patrol, June 9, 1970, M4C, KSUL.

153 **"I thought we were under order"**: Statement of Specialist Richard Lutey to Ohio State Highway Patrol, June 22, 1970, Ohio State Highway Patrol, Report of Investigation, June 30, 1970, 400-67A-132, MS 804, Accession 1989-M-048, Box 28, KSC, SML, YU.

153 **"never thought about"**: Quoted in William A. Gordon, *The Fourth of May: Killings and Coverups at Kent State* (Prometheus Books, 1990), p. 209, n. 2; see also Statement of James McGee to Ohio State Highway Patrol, MS 804, Accession 1989-M-048, Box 36, Folder 472, KSC, SML, YU; and *Plain Dealer* (Cleveland, OH), July 8, 1975, p. 2-A.

153 **"A lieutenant to my left"**: Statement of Staff Sergeant Barry Morris to Ohio State Highway Patrol, cited in Robert A. Murphy to J. Stanley Pottinger, March 8, 1974, DOJ 60-76-262, M4C, KSUL.

154 **"a chain reaction"**: Deposition of Larry Mowrer, MS 804, Accession 1989-M-048, Box 36, Folder 479, KSC, SML, YU.

154 **"I fired instinctively"**: Larry Mowrer Statement to Ohio State Highway Patrol, June 8, 1970, and 1975 Deposition, Box 36, M4C, KSUL; and *Akron Beacon Journal*, June 17, 1975, p. B10.

154 **"realize[d] that [other guardsmen]"**: Statement of Specialist William Perkins, M4C, KSUL.

154 **"When the men around me"**: Statement of Specialist James Pierce, M4C, KSUL.

154 **"there was sweat"**: Deposition of James Pierce, February 19, 1975, p. 104, MS 1800, Box 13, KSC, SML, YU; and James Pierce statement to Ohio State Highway Patrol, in Ohio State Highway Patrol, Report of Investigation, "Riot at Kent State University," June 9, 1970, p. 5, Case No. 400-67A-132, Series 2062, Box 2823, Ohio Historical Society, State Archives, Columbus, Ohio (hereafter cited as OHSSA). "I feared for my life," Pierce later said. "When the firing happened, I felt I did not panic. [I] held my ground and obeyed my orders. After the firing, I felt no remorse because it seemed to me the only way to defend myself. I feel that if we wouldn't have shot *at* them, we would have been overrun and killed. I don't feel they were people but 'savage animals.' I am sorry it came to this, but I don't feel there was any alternat[ive]." Statement of Specialist James Pierce to the FBI, Charles A. Thomas Papers (hereafter cited as CTP), Box 64D, Folder 1, M4C, KSUL.

154 **"The man beside me"**: Statement of Sergeant Lawrence Shafer, CTP, Box 64D, Folder 1, M4C, KSUL.

154 **"I heard shots"**: Statement of Specialist Ralph Zoller, CTP, Box 64D, Folder 1, M4C, KSUL.

154 **"I heard the first shot"**: "Tragedy in Our Midst—A Special Report," *Akron Beacon Journal.*

154 **"A great deal of them"**: Telephone interview with Keith Crilow, February 28, 2020, KSGOHP, ONU.

155 **"I and the boy standing"**: Recollection of Judy Cox, James A. Michener Papers (hereafter cited as JAMP), Manuscript Division, Library of Congress, Washington, D.C. (hereafter cited as MD, LOC).

155 **"They are using blanks"**: Quoted in James A. Michener, *Kent State: What Happened and Why* (Random House, Reader's Digest Books, 1971), p. 374.

155 **"until I saw bullets"**: Quoted in "Tragedy in Our Midst—A Special Report," *Akron Beacon Journal.*

155 **So, too, did photographer John Filo**: John Filo Statement to FBI, June 7, 1970, CTP, Box 64B, M4C, KSUL.

155 **"Everyone was running"**: David Wolfson Personal Narrative, 2020, Narratives and Commentaries Related to the Kent State Shootings (hereafter cited as NCRKSS), M4C, KSUL.

155 **"There were people"**: John Filo in "How It Was: Death at Kent State."

155 **"one kid standing"**: Quoted in "Tragedy in Our Midst—A Special Report," *Akron Beacon Journal.*

155 **"They're shooting their guns!"**: *Kent State: The Day the War Came Home* [documentary], Learning Channel, 2000.

155 **"the sound of bullets"**: Lorrie J. Accettola Personal Narrative, November 13, 1999, NCRKSS, M4C, KSUL.

155 **Jim Minard lying**: Transcript of interview with James J. Minard, p. 5, Scheuer Family Papers (hereafter cited as SFP), Box 2, OHSSA.

155 **"Where am I?"**: Quoted in Joe Eszterhas and Michael D. Roberts, *Thirteen Seconds: Confrontation at Kent State* (Dodd, Mead, 1970), p. 166.

155 **Photographer Dan Smith**: Craig Simpson interview with Chuck Ayers, August 16, 2007, KSSOHP.

155 **"Who would discharge"**: Testimony of Harry Jones, 1975 Federal Civil Trial, p. 5185, MS 804, Accession 1989-M-048, Box 36, KSC, SML, YU; and Deposition of Harry

Jones quoted in "Engdahl Memorandum I, Kent State Civil Cases–January 16, 1975," MS 804, Series I, Box 1, Folder 38, KSC, SML, YU.

155 **"indiscriminate firing"**: Deposition of Harry Jones, p. 117, MS 804, Accession 1989-M-048, Box 36, KSC, SML, YU.

156 **"I had my stick"**: Quoted in "Tragedy in Our Midst—A Special Report," *Akron Beacon Journal.*

156 **"Put that damn thing"**: Statement of Myron Pryor to FBI, May 13, 1970, MS 804, Accession 1989-M-048, Box 34, KSC, SML, YU; see also Legal Deposition of Myron Pryor, April 14, 1975, Box 28, KSC, SML, YU.

156 **"High port—"**: Statement of Myron Pryor to FBI, May 13, 1970, MS 804, Accession 1989-M-048, Box 34, KSC, SML, YU.

156 **"What the hell"**: Quoted in telephone interview with Keith Crilow, February 28, 2020, KSGOHP, ONU.

156 **"The major really risked"**: Quoted in "Tragedy in Our Midst—A Special Report," *Akron Beacon Journal.*

156 **"If I wouldn't have"**: Quoted in *Plain Dealer* (Cleveland, OH), July 2, 1975, p. 4-A.

156 **Another officer hit a guardsman**: Author's telephone interview with B. J. Long, May 5, 2022.

156 **First Lieutenant Ralph Tucker**: Statement of First Lieutenant Ralph Tucker, CTP, Box 64D, Folder 1, M4C, KSUL.

156 **Many guardsmen had to be shaken**: Statement of Captain Raymond Srp, MSC, KSUL.

156 **"Who gave you men"**: Statement of Specialist Richard Lutey to FBI, May 11, 1970, CV 44-703, Accession 1989-M-048, Box 28, KSC, SML, YU.

156 **"Major Jones was shaking"**: Private Paul Naujoks quoted in "Tragedy in Our Midst—A Special Report," *Akron Beacon Journal.*

157 **"was shocked"**: Quoted in *Akron Beacon Journal*, June 27, 1975.

157 **"What the hell"**: Quoted in *Plain Dealer* (Cleveland, OH), July 17, 1975, p. A16.

157 **"For Christ's sake"**: Quoted in "Tragedy in Our Midst—A Special Report," *Akron Beacon Journal.*

157 **Canterbury**: Deposition of Robert Canterbury, November 21, 1974, p. 60, MS 804, Accession 1989-M-048, Box 35, KSC, SML, YU.

157 **"horrified"**: Quoted in *New York Times*, July 29, 1975.

157 **"Put the weapons down!"**: Deposition of Robert Canterbury, November 22, 1974, Box 64D, Folder 19, M4C, KSUL.

157 **a "deathly silence"**: Sandra Halem interview with Michael Erwin, April 4, 2000, KSSOHP.

157 **"Everything slowed down"**: Chrissie Hynde, *Reckless* (Ebury Press, 2015), pp. 80–81.

157 **"It was almost like time"**: Kathleen Siebert Medicus interview with Terry Strubbe, January 31, 2020, KSSOHP.

157 **"Oh, my God!," "Murderers!"**: Rudy Morris in *Kent State: The Day the War Came Home*, Learning Channel; and author's interview with Ron Gammell, October 24, 2020.

158 **"I thought they were firing blanks"**: Quoted in Daniel St. Albin Greene, "When a World Collapsed," *National Observer* (Washington, DC), May 3, 1975.

158 **"My God"**: Quoted in Joseph Kelner and James Munves, *The Kent State Coverup* (Harper & Row, 1980), p. 94.

158 **Then Sergeant Larry Shafer's rifle**: *Cleveland Press*, July 10, 1975, p. B2.

158 **Joe screamed:** Stephanie Tulley interview with Ellen Mann, May 3, 2010, KSSOHP; and Statement of First Lieutenant Ralph Tucker to FBI, CTP, Box 64D, Folder 1, M4C, KSUL.

158 **"I didn't lose consciousness":** *NBC News*, May 3, 2020.

158 **He thought the bullets:** Quoted in *Akron Beacon Journal*, May 5, 1970.

158 **"Well, this could be it":** *Kent State: The Day the War Came Home*, Learning Channel.

158 **"I was facing directly":** Statement of John Cleary to FBI, May 10, 1970, CV 44-703, MS 804, Accession 1989-M-048, Box 30, Folder 366, KSC, SML, YU; and Testimony of John Cleary, Federal Criminal Trial, p. 625, MS 1800, Box 62, KSC, SML, YU.

160 **"Look what you did!":** Quoted in "Tragedy in Our Midst—A Special Report," *Akron Beacon Journal*.

160 **Jeff's "intent":** Craig Simpson interview with Eldon Fender, November 28, 2007, KSSOHP.

160 **"saw Miller's mouth":** Quoted in Charles Thomas, *Blood of Isaac* [ebook], Laura Davis Papers (hereafter cited as LDP), M4C, KSUL.

160 **"I saw what happened":** Author's interview with Matt McManus, October 24, 2020.

160 **Jeff "jerk[ed] like a puppet":** Quoted in Eszterhas and Roberts, *Thirteen Seconds*, pp. 165, 164.

160 **"stumble a good fifty feet":** Craig Simpson interview with Eldon Fender, November 28, 2007, KSSOHP.

160 **"I looked over to him":** Quoted in "Tragedy in Our Midst—A Special Report," *Akron Beacon Journal*.

160 **"His face was a sickening mess":** Transcript of James Dawson interview, SFP, Box 2, OHSSA.

161 **"I'd never seen blood":** Sandra Halem interview with Carol Mirman, April 1, 2000, KSSOHP.

162 **"I'll never forget how":** *Kent State: The Day the War Came Home*, Leaning Channel.

162 **"I was scared. . . . I knew":** Quoted in Sarah Crump, "May 4 Journal," *Cleveland Magazine*, May 1995, p. 62.

162 **"They shot him!":** Quoted in "Tragedy in Our Midst—A Special Report," *Akron Beacon Journal*.

162 **"She felt like a block of ice":** Sandra Halem interview with Carol Mirman, April 1, 2000, KSSOHP.

162 **Another student stood:** "Tragedy in Our Midst—A Special Report," *Akron Beacon Journal*.

162 **Tom Grace:** "Tragedy in Our Midst—A Special Report," *Akron Beacon Journal*.

162 **Jeff "being shot":** Testimony of Tom Grace, December 19, 1978, Heidloff-Reichard Papers, Box 22, Folder 2, M4C, KSUL.

162 **"All of a sudden":** Quoted in Joan Morrison and Robert K. Morrison, *From Camelot to Kent State: The Sixties Experience in the Words of Those Who Lived It* (Times Books, 1987), p. 332.

163 **"It was the loneliest and sickest":** Tom Grace in *Fire in the Heartland: May 4 and Student Protest in America* [documentary], Oregon Public Broadcasting, 2021; and Interview with Tom Grace, MS 804, James Munves Papers, Box 1, KSC, SML, YU.

163 **"I had my flag":** Quoted in Eszterhas and Roberts, *Thirteen Seconds*, p. 161.

163 **"I heard bullets":** Phillip Caputo, *13 Seconds: A Look Back at the Kent State Shootings* (Penguin, 2005), p. 72; Krista Ramsey, "13 Deadly Seconds," *Cincinnati Enquirer*, May

1, 1995; Milton Viorst, *Fire in the Streets: America in the 1960s* (Simon & Schuster, 1979), pp. 538–39; Testimony of Alan Canfora to Federal Grand Jury, p. 1146, MS 804, Accession 1989-M-048, Box 35, KSC, SML, YU; and Alan Canfora interview with FBI, May 8, 1970, p. 5, KSC, SML, YU.

163 **"I remember looking"**: Quoted in Crump, "May 4 Journal," p. 60.

164 **"I knew I had gotten shot"**: "Dean Kahler Shot at Kent State, May 4, 1970" [video], Youtube.com; Dean Kahler in *Kent State: The Day the War Came Home*, Learning Channel; B. Payne interview with Dean Kahler, November 12, 1979, MS 804, Accession 1983-M-017, Box 1, KSC, SML, YU; and Dean Kahler in "How It Was: Death at Kent State."

164 **He could feel nothing**: Kelner and Munves, *Kent State Coverup*, p. 51.

164 **"I knew I had"**: Quoted in Crump, "May 4 Journal," p. 60; and "4 Dead in Ohio" [video], Al Jazeera English, 2010, Youtube.com.

164 **The bullet disintegrated**: Interview with Elaine and John Kahler, July 15, 1977, MS 804, James Munves Papers, Box 1, KSC, SML, YU; and Testimony of Dean Kahler to Federal Grand Jury, p. 1282, MS 1800, Box 67, KSC, SML, YU.

164 **"The only thought"**: "Dean Kahler Shot at Kent State, May 4, 1970," Youtube.com.

164 **"Someone roll me over"**: Transcript of Federal Civil Trial Testimony, June 4, 1975, vol. 6, p. 1195, KSC, SML, YU.

164 **"The one thing"**: *Kent State: The Day the War Came Home*, Learning Channel.

165 **"I was walking away"**: Doug Wrentmore in "Kent State Shooting Anniversary," April 30, 2010.

165 **"I took a couple of steps"**: Quoted in "Tragedy in Our Midst—A Special Report," *Akron Beacon Journal*.

165 **"Get down!"**: Quoted in Michener, *Kent State*, p. 397; and Kelner and Munves, *Kent State Coverup*, p. 113.

165 **"They're shooting at *me*!"**: Interview with Doug Wrentmore, June 25, 1977, MS 804, James Munves Papers, Box 1, KSC, SML, YU.

165 **"I had my back"**: Quoted in "Tragedy in Our Midst—A Special Report," *Akron Beacon Journal*; *Kent State: The Day the War Came Home*, Learning Channel; and Jeff Kisseloff, *Generation on Fire: Voices of Protest from the 1960s* (University Press of Kentucky, 2007), p. 255.

166 **"We tried to put"**: Marion Stroud letter to editor, *Akron Beacon Journal*, May 6, 1970, p. A6.

166 **"The impact of the bullet"**: Craig Simpson interview with Henry Mankowski, May 18, 2010, KSSOHP.

166 **"His eyes were open"**: Quoted in Thomas M. Grace, *Kent State: Death and Dissent in the Long Sixties* (University of Massachusetts Press, 2016), p. 227.

166 **"It was all very messy"**: Quoted in "Tragedy in Our Midst—A Special Report," *Akron Beacon Journal*.

167 **"I happened to see Sandy Scheuer"**: Ellis Berns to James Michener, Kent, August 17, 1970, JAMP, Container No. II: 34, MD, LOC.

167 **"I grabbed her and tried"**: Transcript of James Minard Interview Tape, SFP, Box 2, OHSSA.

168 **"The bleeding was bad"**: Quoted in *Plain Dealer* (Cleveland, OH), May 5, 1970.

168 **"I had a yellow towel"**: Ellis Berns to James Michener, Kent, August 17, 1970, JAMP, Container No. II: 34, MD, LOC.

168 **"She wasn't talking"**: Quoted in *The Burr*, May 4, 2000, p. 31.

168 **"We couldn't carry her"**: Quoted in "Tragedy in Our Midst—A Special Report," *Akron Beacon Journal*; Craig Simpson interview with Ellis Burns, May 4, 2010, KSSOHP; and Eszterhas and Roberts, *Thirteen Seconds*, p. 165.

168 **"She was so blue"**: *Kent State: The Day the War Came Home*, Learning Channel.

168 **"Why Sandy!?"**: Larry Raines Personal Narrative, March 24, 1997, NCRKSS, M4C, KSUL.

168 **"I thought the rally"**: Quoted in "Tragedy in Our Midst—A Special Report," *Akron Beacon Journal*; Interview with Robby Stamps, MS 804, James Munves Papers, Box 1, KSC, SML, YU; Taped interview with Robby Stamps, October 9, 1970, JAMP, MD, LOC; and Ramsey, "13 Deadly Seconds," May 1, 1995.

169 **"When I heard the volley"**: Quoted in Erin Kosnac and Melissa Hostetler, "Then I Was Shot," *The Burr*, May 4, 2000, p. 17; and Deposition of Scott MacKenzie, November 1, 1974, p. 23, MS 1800, Box 68, KSC, SML, YU.

169 **"Help, help"**: Interview with Scott MacKenzie, MS 804, James Munves Papers, Box 1, KSC, SML, YU; and Kelner and Munves, *Kent State Coverup*, p. 103.

169 **Jim Russell**: Statement of Mathew McManus to Ohio State Highway Patrol, June 13, 1970, CTP, Box 64D, Folder 4, M4C, KSUL.

170 **"I didn't know what had hit me"**: "Jim Russell – Student," Interview, MS 1800, Box 73, KSC, SML, YU; Testimony of James Russell, 1975 Federal Civil Trial, p. 3585, MS 804, Accession 1989-M-048, Box 37, KSC, SML, YU; Testimony of James Russell to Federal Grand Jury, p. 1062, MS 1800, Box 73, KSC, SML, YU; "Tragedy in Our Midst—A Special Report," *Akron Beacon Journal*; and "Kent State Shootings," May 4, 2020, tribdem.com.

170 **"You nearly took a person's life"**: Author's interview with Matt McManus, October 24, 2020.

170 **"I could not believe it"**: Lae'l Hughes-Watkins interview with Glen Schultz, November 1, 2017, KSSOHP.

170 **"a distinctive wailing and screaming"**: Quoted in Means, *67 Shots*, p. 105.

170 **"Hell, I was in Nam"**: JAMP, Container No, II: 29, MD, LOC.

171 **"Some [rifles] were pointed"**: Deposition of Dale Antram, March 12, 1975, p. 43, MS 1800, Box 15, KSC, SML, YU.

171 **"was sick"**: *Akron Beacon Journal*, June 17, 1976, p. B10; and Statement of Larry Mowrer to Ohio State Highway Patrol, MS 1800, Box 70, KSC, SML, YU.

171 **"could not believe"**: Robert A. Murphy and Robert Hocutt to Jerris Leonard, "Summary of Kent State Incident," June 18, 1970, U.S. Department of Justice 144-57-338.

171 **"about knee level"**: Barry Morris statement to Ohio State Highway Patrol, May 27, 1970, in Ohio State Highway Patrol, Report of Investigation, June 4, 1970, Case No. 400-67A-132, Series 2062, Box 2823, OHSSA.

172 **"firmly believed"**: Craig Simpson interview with Eldon Fender, November 28, 2007, KSSOHP.

172 **Platoon sergeant Matt McManus**: Statement of William Herschler to FBI, May 8, 1970, MS 804, Accession 1989-M-048, Box 34, KSC, SML, YU; FBI interview with Mathew McManus, July 20, 1970, CTP, Box 64D, Folder 26, M4C, KSUL; and Federal Civil Trial Testimony of William Herschler, July 17, 1975, pp. 7507–8. Herschler was unequivocal in his statement to the FBI: "At no time did I fire my weapon!" Private Larry Mowrer supported Herschler's account. Deposition of Larry Mowrer, pp. 52–53, MS 1800, Box 70, KSC, SML, YU. Private Paul Naujoks corroborated McManus's

account. See Testimony of Paul Naujoks to Federal Grand Jury, pp. 2518–2616, MS 1800, Box 70, KSC, SML, YU; and Deposition of Paul Naujoks, p. 66, MS 1800, Box 70, KSC, SML, YU.

172 **"I don't know if I hit anyone"**: Testimony of William Perkins to Special State Grand Jury, pp. 11-12, MS 1800, Box 70, KSC, SML, YU.

172 **"Most of the guardsmen"**: Student statements, May 4 and 22, 1970, in Ohio State Highway Patrol, Reports of Investigation, May 22 and 23, 1970, Case No. 400-67A-132, Series 2062, Box 2823, OHSSA.

172 **"were as shocked as I was"**: Sandra Halem interview with Carol Mirman, April 1, 2000, KSSOHP.

172 **"As I bent down"**: Quoted in Michener, *Kent State*, p. 383. See also Snyder interview with the Ohio State Highway Patrol, September 9, 1970, Series 2062, Box 2823, OHSSA.

173 **"Pigs! Murderers!"**: Statement of Captain Ron Snyder, CTP, Box 64D, Folder 1, M4C, KSUL.

173 **"As the [guardsmen] were backing up"**: John Filo Statement to FBI, May 7, 1970, Box 64B, M4C, KSUL.

173 **"we were pretty much in shock"**: Statement of Mathew McManus to Ohio State Highway Patrol, June 13, 1970, Box 64D, Folder 4, M4C, KSUL.

173 **"I couldn't believe it"**: Author's interview with Ron Gammell, October 24, 2020.

173 **"I was stunned"**: Author's telephone interview with Gabe Brachna, May 22, 2022.

173 **"My mind was racing"**: *Kent State: The Day the War Came Home*, Learning Channel.

173 **"shook their heads in disbelief"**: Author's telephone interview with B. J. Long, May 5, 2022.

173 **"I couldn't believe"**: Deposition of Robert James, MS 804, Accession 1989-M-048, Box 36, KSC, SML, YU.

173 **"I saw tears"**: Alexander Stevenson Statement to Ohio State Highway Patrol, June 9, 1970, MS 1800, Box 75, KSC, SML, YU.

173 **Another officer tried to talk**: Interview with Ralph Tucker, MS 804, Accession 1983-M-017, Box 1, KSC, SML, YU.

173 **"Now they'll know"**: Quoted in Michener, *Kent State*, p. 389.

173 **"It's about time"**: Quoted in *Newsweek*, May 18, 1970.

173 **"We had no idea"**: *Kent State: The Day the War Came Home*, Learning Channel.

173 **"Coming back down the hill"**: Statement of Specialist James Case, CTP, Box 64D, Folder 1, M4C, KSUL; and Deposition of James Case, March 6, 1975, p. 59, MS 1800, Box 15, KSC, SML, YU.

173 **"The closest guardsman"**: Henry Halem interview with Bill Barrett, May 4, 2000, KSSOHP.

174 **"noticed that one guardsman"**: John Filo Statement to FBI, May 7, 1970, CTP, Box 64B, M4C, KSUL.

174 **"looked stunned"**: Hynde, *Reckless*, pp. 80–81.

174 **"I told him I didn't know"**: Deposition of Harry Jones, pp. 266–67, MS 804, Accession 1989-M-048, Box 36, Folder 465, KSC, SML, YU.

174 **"I fired right down the gulley"**: Quoted in Eszterhas and Roberts, *Thirteen Seconds*, p. 167.

174 **"I think this guy was tired"**: "Kent State: Scranton Commission Files: Wrap-up," CTP, Box 64D, Folder 38, M4C, KSUL.

174 **"He had put it"**: *CBS Evening News*, November 3, 1970.

174 **"I don't think anybody"**: Quoted in "Tragedy in Our Midst—A Special Report," *Akron Beacon Journal.*

174 **"Only that person"**: Quoted in Crump, "May 4 Journal."

174 **"The next time I saw Jim"**: Charles Madonio Notes, November 18, 1970, JAMP, Container II: 30, Folder 6, MD, LOC.

175 **"sorry it happened"**: Statement of James Pierce to Ohio State Highway Patrol, quoted in Robert J. Murphy to J. Stanley Pottinger, March 8, 1974, DOJ 60-76-262, M4C, KSUL; and Summary of James Pierce Statement to Ohio State Highway Patrol, MS 804, Accession 1989-M-049, Box 37, Folder 482, KSC, SML, YU.

175 **"weren't talking"**: National Geographic, *Kent State 2.*

175 **"Everybody was in a daze"**: Testimony of Larry Mowrer, Federal Civil Trial, June 16, 1975, p. 2710, MS 804, Accession 1989-M-048, Box 36, KSC, SML, YU.

175 **Many of those who fired**: Interview with Ralph Tucker, MS 804, Accession 1983-M-017, Box 1, KSC, SML, YU.

175 **"After it happened"**: Quoted in *New York Post*, May 5, 1970.

175 **"Don't worry about it"**: Deposition of Barry Morris, February 25, 1975, p. 200, MS 1800, Box 14, KSC, SML, YU.

175 **"The fact that someone"**: Statement to Ohio State Highway Patrol, June 12, 1970, 11:42 p.m., in Ohio State Highway Patrol, Report of Investigation, June 15, 1970, p. 4, Case No. 44-67A-132, Series 2062, Box 2823, OHSSA.

175 **"pretty shook up"**: Testimony of Rodney Biddle to Federal Grand Jury, p. 4108, MS 804, Accession 1989-M-048, Box 35, KSC, SML, YU.

175 **"took off his helmet"**: Statement of Howard Fallon to Ohio State Highway Patrol, June 15, 1970, MS 1800, Box 64, KSC, SML, YU.

175 **"I got a terrible headache"**: William Herschler statement to Ohio State Highway Patrol, June 19, 1970, 12:10 p.m., in Ohio State Highway Patrol, Report of Investigation, June 25, 1970, p. 3, Case No. 400-67A-132, Series 2062, Box 2823, OHSSA.

175 **"I shot two teenagers!"**: Testimony of Rodney Biddle to Federal Grand Jury, p. 4126, Accession 1989-M-048, Box 35, KSC, SML, YU; Michener, *Kent State*, p. 343; FBI interview with Mathew McManus, July 20, 1970, CTP, Box 64D, Folder 26, M4C, KSUL; and Deposition of Rodney Biddle, Box 12, KSC, SML, YU.

175 **"was in a state of shock"**: Testimony of Raymond Srp, p. 3635, Box 29, KSC, SML, YU.

175 **"ashamed"**: Testimony of Larry Mowrer, Federal Civil Trial, June 16, 1975, pp. 2699 and 2711, Box 36, KSC, SML, YU.

175 **"I was praying"**: Deposition of James Case, March 6, 1975, p. 72, MS 1800, Box 15, KSC, SML, YU.

175 **"Until we came off the hill"**: Quoted in *Plain Dealer* (Cleveland, OH), September 12, 1971, p. 4.

175 **"I just wanted"**: Quoted in *Cleveland Press*, June 13, 1975.

176 **"all messed up inside"**: Statement of Specialist Ralph Zoller to FBI, quoted in Robert J. Murphy to J. Stanley Pottinger, March 8, 1974, U.S. Department of Justice 60-76-262, M4C, KSUL.

176 **"really [didn't] want to know"**: Special State Grand Jury Testimony of Specialist William Perkins, quoted in Robert J. Murphy to J. Stanley Pottinger, Marc 8, 1974, U.S. Department of Justice 60-76-262, M4C, KSUL.

176 **Staff Sergeant Rudy Morris**: "IV. Afterwards," MS 1800, Box 61, KSC, SML, YU.

176   **"The only thing"**: Laura Davis interview with John Backlawski, WKSU, LDP, Box 214, M4C, KSUL.

176   **"I couldn't believe it"**: Quoted in Michener, *Kent State*, p. 391.

176   **Two guardsmen laid down**: Testimony of Raymond Srp, p. 3645, MS 804, Accession 1989-M-048, Box 29, KSC, SML, YU.

176   **"They were already withdrawing"**: Quoted in "Tragedy in Our Midst—A Special Report," *Akron Beacon Journal*.

176   **"throw down their weapons"**: Quoted in Eszterhas and Roberts, *Thirteen Seconds*, p. 171.

176   **"a time to weep"**: Quoted in Eszterhas and Roberts, *Thirteen Seconds*, pp. 182, 187.

176   **Private Richard Shade**: "Tragedy in Our Midst—A Special Report," *Akron Beacon Journal*.

176   **"I talked to one guard"**: Quoted in John Lombardi, "Kent State Shootings: A Lot of People Were Crying, and the Guard Walked Away," *Rolling Stone*, June 11, 1970.

176   **"Only God can take lives"**: Statement of Specialist James Case, CTP, Box 64D, Folder 1, M4C, KSUL.

176   **Afterward he was so shaken**: "Kent State: Scranton Commission Files: Wrap-up," CTP, Box 64D, Folder 38, M4C, KSUL.

176   **"taking another person's life"**: Quoted in William Barry Furlong, "The Guardsmen's View of the Tragedy at Kent State," *New York Times Magazine*, June 21, 1970, p. 70.

176   **"wanted to throw their weapons"**: "Kent State: Scranton Commission Files: Wrap-up," CTP, Box 64D, Folder 38, M4C, KSUL.

176   **"People don't realize"**: Author's interview with Ron Gammell, October 24, 2020.

176   **Around this time**: Terrence Norman statement to Ohio State Highway Patrol, June 1, in Ohio State Highway Patrol, Report of Investigation, June 2, 1970, Case No. 400-67A-132, Series 2062, Box 2823, OHSSA; and David Engdahl and Galen Keller, "Deegan, Jack – Interview Summary," May 27, 1975, MS 1800, Box 62, KSC, SML, YU.

177   **"I took the gun"**: Statement of Patrolman Harold Rice, May 11, 1970, M4C, KSUL. See corroborating eyewitness testimony of Bill Barrett in Henry Halem interview with Bill Barrett, May 4, 2000, KSSOHP; Ohio State Highway Patrol Major Donald Manly in Major General Dana Stewart to Governor John Gilligan, August 13, 1973, CTP, Box 64D, Folder 1, M4C, KSUL; and Statements of Detective Thomas E. Kelley, Patrolman Thomas B. Williams, and Terrence Norman [to Sergeant D. C. Wells, Ohio State Highway Patrol, June 1, 1970], CTP, Box 64D, Folder 1, M4C, KSUL.

177   **"hands-on"**: Laura Davis and Carole Barbato interview with Charles Fassinger, 4 of 5, April 1, 2007, LDP, Box 214A, M4C, KSUL.

177   **"Look, no one is going"**: Deposition of Lieutenant Dwight Cline, April 2, 1975, p. 2858, MS 1800, Box 62, KSC, SML, YU.

177   **Each guardsman unloaded his rifle**: Statement of Lieutenant Colonel Charles Fassinger, CTP, Box 64D, Folder 1, M4C, KSUL.

177   **"I took out my notebook"**: "Kent State: Scranton Commission Files: Wrap-up," CTP, Box 64D, Folder 38, M4C, KSUL.

178   **First Lieutenant Ralph Tucker**: Interview with Ralph Tucker, MS 804, Accession 1983-M-017, Box 1, KSC, SML, YU.

178   **Later that afternoon**: These Firing Incident Reports and subsequent statements to the Ohio National Guard Adjutant General, the FBI, and the Ohio State Highway Patrol

became central to later investigations and legal proceedings. Copies are archived in KSC, SML, YU; M4C, KSUL; and OHSSA.

178 **"No one briefed us"**: Testimony of James Pierce, 1975 Federal Civil Trial, p. 4430, MS 804, Accession 1989-M-048, Box 37, Folder 482, KSC, SML, YU.

178 **"Sit down and write"**: Laura Davis and Carole Barbato interview with Charles Fassinger, 4 of 5, April 1, 2007, LDP, Box 214A, M4C, KSUL.

178 **"Murderers! Killers!"**: Author's interview with Matt McManus, October 24, 2020.

178 **"the scene was grotesque"**: Larry Raines Personal Narrative, March 24, 1997, NCRKSS, M4C, KSUL.

179 **"When I saw fellow students"**: David Wolfson Personal Narrative, 2020, NCRKSS, M4C, KSUL.

179 **"We need a doctor!"**: Ellis Berns to James Michener, Kent, August 17, 1970, JAMP, Container No. II: 34, MD, LOC.

179 **Doug Wrentmore**: Interview with Jan Wrentmore, June 17, 1977, MS 804, James Munves Papers, Box 1, KSC, SML, YU.

179 **"You won't be taking part"**: Quoted in Kelner and Munves, *Kent State Coverup*, p. 113.

179 **"I watched the [other shooting victims]"**: Quoted in "Tragedy in Our Midst—A Special Report," *Akron Beacon Journal*.

179 **"profound effect"**: Interview with Doug Wrentmore, June 25, 1977, MS 804, James Munves Papers, Box 1, KSC, SML, YU.

179 **A friend phoned . . . were vicious**: Interview with Jan Wrentmore, June 17, 1977, MS 804, James Munves Papers, Box 1, KSC, SML, YU; and Michener, *Kent State*, pp. 476–78.

180 **Joe Lewis opened . . . expect him to live**: Interview with Joe Lewis and his mother, Betty Lewis, James Munves Papers, Box 1, KSC, SML, YU.

181 **"What did you do?!"**: Quoted in Kelner and Munves, *Kent State Coverup*, p. 93.

181 **Joe's steady improvement . . . she countered**: Interview with Joe Lewis and his mother, Betty Lewis, James Munves Papers, Box 1, KSC, SML, YU.

181 **"put me into a numbing shock"**: Testimony of John Cleary, 1975 Federal Civil Trial, p. 4154, MS 1800, Box 62, KSC, SML, YU.

181 **"I can't believe they"**: Deposition of John Cleary, June 12, 1975, pp. 14–15, MS 1800, Box 62, KSC, SML, YU.

181 **"I remember being afraid"**: Craig Simpson interview with John Cleary, May 3, 2010, KSSOHP; Ramsey, "13 Deadly Seconds," May 1, 1995; and Interview with John Cleary, MS 804, James Munves Papers, Box 1, KSC, SML, YU.

181 **"I promised [my parents]"**: Quoted in Kosnac and Hostetler, "Then I Was Shot," p. 19.

181 **Tom Grace writhed . . . Tom screamed**: Interview with Tom Sr. and Collette Grace, MS 804, James Munves Papers, Box 1, KSC, SML, YU.

182 **"I remember my foot" . . . "the whole day"**: Quoted in *Akron Beacon Journal*, May 3, 2020.

182 **"The full impact"**: Interview with Tom Grace, MS 804, James Munves Papers, Box 1, KSC, SML, YU.

182 **"Please give me something"**: Quoted in Morrison and Morrison, *From Camelot to Kent State*, pp. 333–34; *Fire in the Heartland: May 4 and Student Protest in America*, Oregon Public Broadcasting; and Taped interview with Robby Stamps, October 9, 1970, JAMP, MD, LOC.

183 **"shaken up"**: Christina Bucciere, "Caring for May 4," *The Burr*, April 2014.

183   **"If not for my mother"**: Quoted in Lisa Abraham, "Where the Nine Wounded Are
      Now," *Kent State Magazine*, Spring/Summer 2020, p. 19.
183   **Nurses gave him . . . rest of his life**: Interview with Tom Grace, MS 804, James
      Munves Papers, Box 1, KSC, SML, YU.
183   **"It was kind of" . . . "wounded more severely"**: Quoted in Bud Schultz and Ruth
      Schultz, *The Price of Dissent: Testimonies to Political Repression in America* (University
      of California Press, 2001), pp. 363–65.
183   **Al Canfora was . . . "get out of town"**: Interview with Albert Canfora, MS 804, James
      Munves Papers, Box 1, KSC, SML, YU.
184   **Dean Kahler tried . . . "the operating room"**: Quoted in Crump, "May 4 Journal," May
      1995.
184   **"We talked about life"**: Helene Cooley interview with Timothy DeFrange, April 30,
      1990, KSSOHP.
184   **Elaine Kahler got . . . "with no color"**: Interview with Elaine and John Kahler, July 15,
      1977, MS 804, James Munves Papers, Box 1, KSC, SML, YU.
185   **"I woke up"**: Quoted in Howard E. Royer, "Nonviolence Is the Only Way," *Messenger*,
      January 1, 1971, p. 4.
185   **The pain was so huge . . . "ready to cry"**: B. Payne interview with Dean Kahler, Novem-
      ber 12, 1979, MS 804, Accession 1983-M-017, Box 1, KSC, SML, YU; and Testimony
      of Dean Kahler to Federal Grand Jury, MS 1800, Box 67, KSC, SML, YU.
185   **"Man, I'll be" . . . " 'you are dead.' "**: Crump, "May 4 Journal," May 1995; *Echoes* (Ohio
      Historical Society), 38, no. 5 (October/November 1999): pp. 2–3; "4 Dead in Ohio"
      [video], Al Jazeera English; and Interview with Elaine and John Kahler, July 15, 1977,
      MS 804, James Munves Papers, Box 1, KSC, SML, YU.
185   **"He's no radical"**: Interview with Elaine and John Kahler, July 15, 1977, MS 804,
      James Munves Papers, Box 1, KSC, SML, YU.
185   **"Ambulance! Ambulance!"**: Quoted in Michener, *Kent State*, p. 396.
185   **"After the shooting" . . . "would be all right"**: Quoted in Michener, *Kent State*, p. 465.
186   **"Don't worry"**: Quoted in Eszterhas and Roberts, *Thirteen Seconds*, p. 207.
187   **"She'll be okay"**: Quoted in Kisseloff, *Generation on Fire*, p. 255.
187   **"The door to the morgue"**: Quoted in Scott L. Bills, ed., *Kent State/May 4: Echoes
      Through a Decade* (Kent State University Press, 1982), p. 114.
187   **"Where the hell is the ambulance?"**: Transcript of interview with James J. Minard,
      p. 5, SFP, Box 2, OHSSA.
187   **"William Schneider"**: Quoted in Kelner and Munves, *Kent State Coverup*, p. 195.
187   **Robby Stamps heard . . . "you're all right"**: Taped interview with Robby Stamps, Octo-
      ber 9, 1970, JAMP, MD, LOC; George Warren (Scranton Commission) interview with
      Robby Stamps, August 19, 1970, MS 1800, Box 75, KSC, SML, YU; William Gardner
      (Department of Justice) interview with Robby Stamps, DJ 144-57-338, November 26,
      1973, MS 1800, Box 75, KSC, SML, YU; Robert Stamps Testimony to Federal Grand
      Jury, p. 1091, MS 1800, Box 75, KSC, SML, YU; Greene, "When a World Collapsed";
      Kosnac and Hostetler, "Then I Was Shot," p. 19; and Interview with Charlotte and
      Floyd Stamps, MS 804, James Munves Papers, Box 1, KSC, SML, YU.
189   **"We're going to hold you"**: Quoted in Steve Duin, "The Long Road Back from Kent
      State," *The Oregonian*, July 1, 2007.
189   **Fearful that he**: Statement of James Russell to FBI, May 8, 1970, MS 804, Accession
      1989-M-048, Box 37, KSC, SML, YU.

189 **"Lord, Nick has had"**: Helene Cooley interview with Timothy DeFrange, April 30, 1990, KSSOHP.

189 **"Get the guard!"**: Charles Fassinger interview with M. Uryccki, LDP, Box 214, M4C, KSUL.

189 **"We didn't know what we"**: Stephanie Tulley interview with Denny Benedict, April 8, 2020, KSSOHP.

189 **"Anything could have happened"**: Charles Fassinger interview with M. Uryccki, LDP, Box 214, M4C, KSUL.

190 **"There was horror"**: National Geographic, *Kent State 2*.

190 **"Some came right up"**: Telephone interview with Keith Crilow, February 28, 2020, KSGOHP, ONU.

190 **"If you don't watch it"**: Guardsman statement, June 22, 1970, in Ohio State Highway Patrol, Report of Investigation, June 30, 1970, Case No. 400-67A-132, Series 2062, Box 2823, OHSSA.

190 **"could feel the grief"**: Larry Raines Personal Narrative, March 24, 1997, NCRKSS, M4C, KSUL.

190 **"felt like tearing up"**: Quoted in *New York Times*, May 11, 1970, p. 11.

190 **"Let's go get them!"**: Testimony of Robert Canterbury, Federal Civil Trial, p. 8597, MS 1800, Box 61, KSC, SML, YU.

190 **"If you move any closer"**: Author's telephone interview with Gabe Brachna, May 22, 2022.

190 **"I certainly wasn't"**: Testimony of Robert Canterbury, Federal Civil Trial, p. 8598, MS 1800, Box 61, KSC, SML, YU.

190 **"There was tremendous"**: Quoted in "Tragedy in Our Midst—A Special Report," *Akron Beacon Journal*.

190 **"There wasn't any rational"**: Sandra Halem interview with Jim Vacarella, April 3, 2000, KSSOHP.

190 **"The crowd became one"**: David Wolfson Personal Narrative, 2020, NCRKSS, M4C, KSUL.

191 **"Pig! Pig! Pig!"**: Arthur Koushel Oral History, May 1995, KSSOHP; Sandra Hallem interview with Jim Vacarella, April 3, 2000, KSSOHP; and Michener, *Kent State*, p. 400.

191 **"You felt like"**: Rob Fox Oral History, KSSOHP.

191 **"Everybody was in shock"**: Craig Simpson interview with anonymous student, May 4, 2010, KSSOHP.

191 **"God, again?"**: Quoted in Eszterhas and Roberts, *Thirteen Seconds*, p. 172.

191 **Ellis Burns . . . "completely shocked"**: Craig Simpson interview with Ellis Burns, May 4, 2010, KSSOHP.

191 **"Move them out"**: Larry Raines Personal Narrative, March 24, 1997, NCRKSS, M4C, KSUL.

191 **"General Canterbury wants"**: Matt McManus interview, April 8, 2020, KSGOHP, ONU.

191 **Canterbury told Sharoff . . . "have to move"**: "Kent State: Scranton Commission Files: Wrap-up," CTP, Box 64D, File 38, M4C, KSUL; and Means, *67 Shots*, pp. 99–100.

191 **Sy Baron . . . "have his conscience"**: Quoted in Michener, *Kent State*, p. 402.

192 **Baron approached . . . "this killing stuff"**: "How It Was: Death at Kent State."

192 **"Tell your men" . . . "this man away"**: Quoted in Eszterhas and Roberts, *Thirteen Seconds*, p. 173; Michener, *Kent State*, pp. 331, 402; Stanley Rosenblatt, *Justice Denied* (Nash Publishing, 1971), p. 247; and National Geographic, *Kent State 2*.

193 **"How many bullets"**: Author's telephone interview with B. J. Long, May 5, 2022.

193 **Baron went back . . . "if you stay!"**: Quoted in Michener, *Kent State*, p. 404; Eszterhas and Roberts, *Thirteen Seconds*, p. 175; "Tragedy in Our Midst—A Special Report," *Akron Beacon Journal*; and transcript of audio recording, JAMP, MD, LOC.

193 **"I felt the anger"**: Glenn Frank's May 1980 letter to an Ohio eighth grader who solicited his thoughts on the Kent State shooting. The full text of Frank's letter is available at www.may4archive.org/survivors.html#8.

194 **"like a chicken"**: Quoted in Ed Grant and Mike Hill, *I Was There: What Really Went on at Kent State* (C. S. S. Publishing, 1974), p. 99.

194 **"For God's sake" . . . "using their head"**: Grant and Hill, *I Was There*, p. 106.

194 **"Give me some"**: Quoted in *New York Times*, July 29, 1975.

194 **"You'll what?!"**: Author's interview with Matt McManus, October 24, 2020.

194 **"How could he"**: Matt McManus interview, April 8, 2020, KSGOHP, ONU.

194 **"I didn't want to go"**: Statement of Mathew J. McManus, June 13, 1970, Ohio State Highway Patrol Report of Investigation, Case No. 400-67A-132, M4C, KSUL.

195 **"We were in no condition" . . . "their weapons down"**: Quoted in Michener, *Kent State*, p. 406; and author's interview with Matt McManus, October 24, 2020.

195 **"Please listen to me!" . . . "Oh, all right"**: Quoted in Eszterhas and Roberts, *Thirteen Seconds*, p. 173.

195 **Another guard officer**: Testimony of Captain Ron Snyder, 1975 Federal Civil Trial, vol. 20, p. 4908, LDP, Box 214, M4C, KSUL.

195 **"Break it up"**: Interview with Ralph Tucker, MS 804, Accession 1983-M-017, Box 1, KSC, SML, YU.

195 **"I was so glad"**: Author's interview with Matt McManus, October 24, 2020.

196 **"The difference between"**: Ken Schaub Personal Narrative and Commentary, May 16, 2000, Special Collections and Archives, KSUL.

196 **"When the state police" . . . "kept him surrounded"**: Kathleen Siebert Medicus interview with Howard Ruffner, September 20, 2019, KSSOHP.

196 **"You're no longer"**: Author's interview with Matt McManus, October 24, 2020.

197 **"Glenn Frank made us"**: National Geographic, *Kent State 2*.

197 **"Finally, the sense"**: *Kent State: The Day the War Came Home*, Learning Channel.

197 **"I could barely walk"**: Quoted in Eszterhas and Roberts, *Thirteen Seconds*, p. 173.

197 **"My God"**: Quoted in Eszterhas and Roberts, *Thirteen Seconds*, p. 176.

197 **"I better call Jeff" . . . "He's dead"**: *Kent State: The Day the War Came Home*, Learning Channel; and interview with Joseph Kelner, March 30, 1977, MS 804, James Munves Papers, Box 1, KSC, SML, YU.

198 **"Then I knew"**: Clevelandjewishnews.com, May 28, 2018.

198 **"The rifle bullet" . . . "anyone I loved"**: Quoted in J. Gregory Payne, *MAYDAY: Kent State* (Kendall/Hunt, 1981), p. 87.

198 **"People of your ilk"**: Quoted in *New York Times*, April 23, 1990, p. A19.

198 **"It was like darts"**: "4 Dead in Ohio," Al Jazeera English, 2010.

198 **"shutting it out"**: Interview with Elaine Miller Holstein, April 18, 1977, James Munves Papers, Box 1, KSC, SML, YU.

198 **"My life is worthless"**: Quoted in *Akron Beacon Journal*, October 17, 1970.

198 **"Jeff was killed" . . . "all carrying flowers"**: Elaine Miller Holstein to Ms. Blume, August 17, 1986, MS 804, Accession 1991-M-004, Box 1, KSC, SML, YU.

199 **"Hushed and solemn"**: *New Yorker*, May 16, 1970, p. 34.

199 **"Jeff was no radical"** . . . **"in their chambers"**: Quoted in Eszterhas and Roberts, *Thirteen Seconds*, pp. 273, 275; and Thomas Gallagher, "The Kent State Tragedy," p. 14, MSS 954, SFP, Box 2, OHSSA.

200 **"My younger daughter"** . . . **"does it?"**: James Munves interview with Art and Doris Krause, June 12, 1977, LDP, Box 214, M4C, KSUL; and Kisseloff, *Generation on Fire*, pp. 256–57.

200 **"just a couple of kids"**: Quoted in Eszterhas and Roberts, *Thirteen Seconds*, p. 209.

201 **"We went in"**: Quoted in Gallagher, "The Kent State Tragedy," p. 13.

201 **"Any comments"** . . . **"job to do"**: Quoted in Eszterhas and Roberts, *Thirteen Seconds*, pp. 210–11.

201 **"resented being called"** . . . **"of her government?!"**: Arthur Krause in "The Day the 60s Died."

201 **"Some people said"** . . . **"You butchers!"**: Quoted in *Washington Post*, May 19, 1971.

201 **"My daughter would"** . . . **"shut her off"**: Quoted in Ron Henderson, "18 Months Later," *American Report*, November 12, 1971.

201 **"that if her father beat her"**: Student interview with Ohio Bureau of Criminal Identification and Investigation, June 18, 1970, 1:40–3:15 p.m., in Ohio Bureau of Criminal Identification and Investigation, Memorandum for Kent State University Riot Investigation File, Series 2062, Box 2821, OHSSA.

201 **"loved, cherished, and understood"**: Quoted in Michener, *Kent State*, p. 481.

202 **"I told him"**: Quoted in Joe Eszterhas, "Ohio Honors Its Dead: One Nation, Under God, Indivisible, with Liberty and Justice for All," *Rolling Stone*, June 10, 1971, p. 16.

202 **"body was so filthy"**: James Munves interview with Art and Doris Krause, June 12, 1977, LDP, Box 214, M4C, KSUL.

202 **"Everybody's out mourning"**: Quoted in Michener, *Kent State*, p. 479.

202 **"I do not think"**: Quoted in *National Observer* (Washington, DC), August 18, 1973.

202 **"FLOWERS ARE BETTER"** . . . **"she was"**: Quoted in Payne, *MAYDAY*, p. 95.

203 **"Why do you want it?"**: Quoted in Kelner and Munves, *Kent State Coverup*, p. 195.

203 **"It won't be"** . . . **"it's him!"**: Quoted in Eszterhas and Roberts, *Thirteen Seconds*, pp. 254–55.

204 **"extra-special son"**: Quoted in *Lorain Journal* (Lorain, OH), May 8, 1970.

204 **"I had paint"** . . . **"Sandy's been hurt"**: James Munves interview with Martin and Sarah Scheuer, June 12, 1977, LDP, Box 214, M4C, KSUL.

204 **"Where is she"** . . . **"had better come"**: Quoted in Kelner and Munves, *Kent State Coverup*, p. 60.

204 **"I expected the worst"**: Interview with Martin and Sarah Scheuer, MS 804, James Munves Papers, Box 1, KSC, SML, YU.

204 **"Is she wearing"**: Quoted in Eszterhas and Roberts, *Thirteen Seconds*, p. 229.

204 **"Dear God"**: Quoted in Means, *67 Shots*, p. 89.

204 **"there was a rainbow"**: James Munves interview with Martin and Sarah Scheuer, June 12, 1977, LDP, Box 214, M4C, KSUL.

204 **"We drove right towards"**: Interview with Mr. and Mrs. Martin Scheuer, MS 804, Accession 1983-M-017, Box 1, KSC, SML, YU.

205 **"What greater anguish"**: "Our Beloved Sandy is Gone Forever," SFP, Box 1, OHSSA.

205 **"We are heartbroken"** . . . **"when it happened"**: Martin Scheuer to Mrs. Schneider, June 21, 1970, SFP, Box 1, OHSSA.

205 **"I just don't understand"**: Quoted in "Bitter Memories Over Kent Killing," *Free Press*, SFP, Box 2, OHSSA.

205 **"We were so embittered"**: Interview with Martin and Sarah Scheuer, June 1977, MS 804, James Munves Papers, Box 1, KSC, SML, YU.

205 **"Maybe 1 percent"**: "Our Beloved Sandy is Gone Forever," in *The Eloquence of Protest: Voices of the 70's*, ed. Harrison E. Salisbury (Houghton Mifflin, 1972), p. 199.

205 **"Now you know"** . . . **"to deny it"**: Anonymous letters to Martin and Sarah Scheuer, SFP, Box 1, OHSSA.

205 **"Heard the Scheuer girl"** . . . **"always be there"**: Quoted in Payne, *MAYDAY*, p. 83.

205 **"The grief in my chest"**: Quoted in Eszterhas and Roberts, *Thirteen Seconds*, pp. 213–14, 216.

Chapter 7: Aftermath and Investigations

206 **News of the Kent State shooting**: Charles Chandler Oral History, April 30, 1996, Kent Historical Society and Museum, Kent, Ohio.

206 **"grim-faced"** . . . **"stunned silence"**: Charles W. Colson, *Born Again* (Chosen Books, 1976), pp. 39–40.

206 **"shell-shocked"**: Henry Kissinger, *White House Years* (Little, Brown, 1979), pp. 513, 511.

207 **"sickened and saddened"**: Quoted in Joe Eszterhas and Michael D. Roberts, *Thirteen Seconds: Confrontation at Kent State* (Dodd, Mead, 1970), p. 289.

207 **"very disturbed"** . . . **"more facts"**: H. R. Haldeman, *The Haldeman Diaries* (G.P. Putnam's Sons, 1994), p. 159.

207 **"had never seen him"**: Quoted in David Paul Kuhn, *The Hardhat Riot: Nixon, New York City, and the Dawn of the White Working-Class Revolution* (Oxford University Press, 2020), p. 118.

207 **"I could not"** . . . **"campus demonstration"**: Richard Nixon, *RN: The Memoirs of Richard Nixon* (Grosset & Dunlap, 1978), p. 457.

207 **"I thought"** . . . **"all gone"**: Quoted in Kuhn, *Hardhat Riot*, p. 117.

207 **"Those few days"**: Nixon, *RN*, p. 457.

207 **"take comfort from"**: Quoted in Arthur S. Krause, "A Memo to Mr. Nixon," *New York Times*, May 7, 1978.

207 **"as parents of"**: James Munves interview with Martin and Sarah Scheuer, June 12, 1977, Laura Davis Papers, Box 214, May 4 Collection, Kent State University Library (hereafter cited as M4C, KSUL).

207 **"certainly nothing can lessen"**: Quoted in *Lorain Journal* (Lorain, OH), May 18, 1970.

207 **"Nixon acts as if"**: Quoted in "Kent State: Four Deaths at Noon," *Life*, May 15, 1970, p. 34.

208 **"there will be a complete investigation"**: Quoted in *Akron Beacon Journal*, May 5, 1978.

208 **"foolish rhetorical self-indulgence"**: *The Economist*, May 16, 1970, p. 41.

208 **"obviously realize[d]"**: Haldeman, *Haldeman Diaries*, p. 161.

208 **"They are trying"** . . . **"through my mind"**: Nixon, *RN*, p. 459.

208 **"They were not unfriendly"**: Nixon, *RN*, p. 461.

208   **"I could well"** . . . **"the football team":** *Washington Post,* May 10, 1970.

208   **"avoid any remarks":** Haldeman, *Haldeman Diaries,* p. 162.

209   **"one or two"** . . . **"heat of anger":** Quoted in I. F. Stone, *The Killings at Kent State: How Murder Went Unpunished* (New York Review Books, 1971), pp. 139–40.

209   **"Four American students":** "The Day the 60s Died."

209   **"Who of us"** . . . **"murder[ing]":** Quoted in "Tragedy in Our Midst—A Special Report," *Akron Beacon Journal,* May 24, 1970.

209   **"a senile old liar"** . . . **"'with a skunk'":** Quoted in Ottavio M. Casale and Louis Paskoff, eds., *The Kent Affair: Documents and Interpretations* (Houghton Mifflin, 1971), p. 24.

209   **Ohio National Guard headquarters:** "Public Supports National Guard 20 to 1," *On Guard,* June 1970, p. 2.

209   **"the campus whore":** Quotes are in James A. Michener, *Kent State: What Happened and Why* (Random House, Reader's Digest Books, 1971), p. 465.

210   **"had a neighbor":** Lisa Whalen interview with Arthur Koushel, May 1995, Kent State Shooting Oral History Program (hereafter cited as KSSOHP).

210   **"Mom, . . . that's me":** "Aftermath" Notes, James A. Michener Papers, Container No. II: 29, Manuscript Division, Library of Congress, Washington, D.C.

210   **"You can't believe"** . . . **"have moved out":** "How It Was: Death at Kent State."

210   **"At least we got":** Byron G. Lander, "Functions of Letters to the Editor: A Re-Examination," *Journalism Quarterly* 49, no. 2 (1972): pp. 142–43.

210   **"We feel that"** . . . **"what they need":** Quoted in "Tragedy in Our Midst—A Special Report," *Akron Beacon Journal.*

210   **"How are things"** . . . **"the little bastards":** Quoted in William Barry Furlong, "The Guardsmen's View of the Tragedy at Kent State," *New York Times Magazine,* June 21, 1970, p. 70.

210   **"a lot of callers"** . . . **"the country needs":** Quoted in Eszterhas and Roberts, *Thirteen Seconds,* p. 180.

211   **"I am sure . . . lives were irretrievable":** Quoted in Eszterhas and Roberts, *Thirteen Seconds,* pp. 181–82.

211   **"shut up":** Quoted in Joseph Kelner and James Munves, *Kent State Coverup* (Harper & Row, 1980), p. 16.

211   **"There's nothing better":** Quoted in J. Gregory Payne, *MAYDAY: Kent State* (Kendall/ Hunt, 1981), pp. 76–77.

212   **"Uncle Sam taught"** . . . **"guy's head in":** Quoted in Thomas M. Grace, *Kent State: Death and Dissent in the Long Sixties* (University of Massachusetts Press, 2016), p. 231.

212   **"even the score"** . . . **"Guardsmen shot":** Barbara Hipsman-Springer interview with Patrick G. Smith, May 1, 2020, KSSOHP.

212   **"I carried a pistol"** . . . **"You're fired":** Author's telephone interview with B. J. Long, May 5, 2022.

212   **Barry Morris:** Deposition of Barry Morris, February 25, 1975, p. 205, MS 1800, Box 14, Kent State Collection, Manuscripts and Archives, Sterling Memorial Library, Yale University (hereafter cited as KSC, SML, YU).

212   **Another guardsman who fired:** Deposition of James Pierce, February 19, 1975, p. 134, Box 13, KSC, SML, YU.

213   **"I went down"** . . . **"war with itself":** *Nixon: A Presidency Revealed,* History Channel, February 15, 2007.

214   **"the absolute minimum"** . . . **"should be nonlethal":** Quoted in Tom Wells, *The War Within: America's Battle over Vietnam* (University of California Press, 1994), p. 436.

214 **"Fucking pig!"** . . . **"us to do?"**: Quoted in Kuhn, *Hardhat Riot*, p. 112.
214 **"The general effect"**: Quoted in Wells, *War Within*, p. 425.
215 **"I'M A BUM"** . . . **"us next week!"**: Quoted in Kuhn, *Hardhat Riot*, p. 127.
215 **"one could disapprove** . . . **to give everything"**: Quoted in Kuhn, *Hardhat Riot*, p. 76.
216 **"U-S-A"** . . . **"long-haired dissenter"**: Frances X. Clines, "Workers Find Protest a 2-Way Street, *New York Times*, May 13, 1970, p. 18.
217 **Polls revealed that**: Louis Harris, *The Anguish of Change* (Norton, 1973).
217 **"awfully hot"**: Hoover to Tolson, DeLoach, Rosen, Sullivan, and Bishop, 10:27 a.m., May 11, 1970, Re Phone Call from Egil Krough, FBI Report, Raw Inputs, FOIA January 1979, Charles A. Thomas Papers (hereafter cited as CTP), Box 64D, Folder 32, M4C, KSUL.
217 **"the students invited"**: Hoover to Tolson, DeLoach, Rosen, Sullivan, and Bishop, 10:27 a.m., May 11, 1970, Re Phone Call from Egil Krough.
217 **"same-day copies"** . . . **"or condensed"**: John D. Ehrlichman to Jerris Leonard, May 8, 1970, Box 122, DOJ, M4C, KSUL.
217 **General Canterbury ordered**: Deposition of James Pierce, February 19, 1975, pp. 107–8, MS 1800, Box 13, KSC, SML, YU.
217 **The agents did not**: Motions Hearing: Kent State Criminal Trial, received by ACLU of Ohio October 23, 1974, Box 64D, Folder 9, M4C, KSUL.
217 **they told the guardsmen**: Deposition of James Pierce, February 19, 1975, p. 110, MS 1800, Box 13, KSC, SML, YU.
218 **"was a young guy"** . . . **"'be nervous too.'"**: Author's interview with Matt McManus, October 24, 2020.
218 **After six weeks**: The FBI report also included six supplements divided into twelve categories: (1) proclamations and injunctions, (2) charts, (3) additional background information, (4) more hospital and medical records, (5) additional statements by law enforcement officers, (6) further eyewitness reports, (7) inquiries into radical campus groups at Kent State and elsewhere, (8) allegations concerning sniper activities, (9) photographic identification of participants, (10) physical evidence such as rocks collected at the scene after the shooting, (11) an index, and (12) an appendix consisting of photographs documenting the events of May 4. David E. Engdahl Memorandum to Kent State Plaintiffs' Lawyers Concerning FBI Report, February 12, 1975, MS 804, Accession 1989-M-048, Box 8, KSC, SML, YU.
219 **"Guardsmen were undoubtedly"** . . . **"foolhardiness and negligence"**: Quoted in William A. Gordon, *The Fourth of May: Killings and Coverups at Kent State* (Prometheus Books, 1990), p. 62.
219 **"The Guardsmen were not"** . . . **"subsequent to the event"**: Quoted in *Akron Beacon Journal*, July 23, 1970, p. 1. The *New York Times* published additional portions of the summary on October 31, 1970.
220 **"The president was quite disturbed"**: Hoover to Tolson, Sullivan, Brennan, etc., 8:47 a.m., July 24, 1970, FBI Report, Raw Inputs, FOIA January 1979, CTP, Box 64D, Folder 32, M4C, KSUL.
220 **The Ohio State Highway Patrol**: The Ohio State Highway Patrol's investigative files are located in Series 2062, Box 2823, Ohio Historical Society, State Archives, Columbus, Ohio (hereafter cited as OHSSA).
220 **The Ohio Bureau of Criminal Identification and Investigation**: Ohio Bureau of Criminal Identification and Investigation, Charts of Movements and Shooting Incident,

May 4, 1970, 400-67A-132, MS 804, Accession 1989-M-048, Box 30, Folder 363, KSC, SML, YU; see also the Ohio Bureau of Criminal Identification and Investigation files in Series 2062, Box 2821, OHSSA.

221 **"For Official Use Only" . . . "to defend themselves"**: Report of the Ohio National Guard Inspector General, Kent State University Riot, 4 May 1970, May 22, 1970, MS 804, Accession 1989-M-048, Box 30, Folder 373, KSC, SML, YU.

221 **Finally, there was the Presidential Commission**: Its other members included a college president, James Cheek of Howard University; a police chief, James Ahern of New Haven, Connecticut, home of Yale University; a retired Air Force general, Benjamin Davis, public safety director of Cleveland; the editor of a national newspaper, Erwin Canham of the *Christian Science Monitor*; three academics, Martha Derthick of Boston College, Bayless Manning of Stanford University Law School, and Joseph Rhodes, Jr., former student president at the California Institute of Technology and Harvard Junior Fellow; and an attorney, Revius Ortique, Jr., of New Orleans, past president of the National Bar Association.

222 **"It is a lethal weapon" . . . "[such] tough situations"**: Quoted in *U.S. News & World Report*, May 18, 1970, p. 32.

223 **"I did not notice"**: Scranton Commission Hearings: General Robert Canterbury Testimony, Audio Recording, Kent State University Library.

223 **"Brigadier General Canterbury" . . . "under his command"**: Mathew McManus to author, September 19, 2020.

223 **"roots in divisions" . . . "of diversity itself"**: Scranton Commission Report, October 4, 1970.

224 **"Problem Areas"**: Robert Canterbury After-Action Report, Kent State University, June 2–8, 1970, Box 64D, M4C, KSUL.

Chapter 8: The Criminal Trial

225 **"one of the longest"**: Thomas R. Hensley, "The May 4th Trials," in *Kent State and May 4th: A Social Science Perspective*, ed. Thomas R. Hensley and Jerry M. Lewis (Kent State University Press, 2010), p. 64.

225 **At their meeting**: Department of Justice Memo, July 6, 1970, Field Office File No. 98-2140, FBI Records: The Vault (online), Kent State, File No. 98-46479.

225 **He pledged**: Jerris Leonard to Will P. Wilson, Assistant Attorney General, Criminal Division, and J. Walter Yeagley, Assistant Attorney General, Internal Security Division, July 7, 1970; and Handwritten Notes, Charles Thomas Papers, Box 64D, May 4 Collection, Kent State University Library (hereafter cited as M4C, KSUL).

225 **Fortified by this support**: See Ronald Kane to James Michener, December 31, 1970, James A. Michener Papers, Container No. II: 33, Manuscript Division, Library of Congress, Washington, D.C.

226 **"irrelevant" . . . "complete impartiality"**: Quoted in James A. Michener, *Kent State: What Happened and Why* (Random House, Reader's Digest Books, 1971), p. 528n.

226 **"If you have one man"**: Federal Grand Jury Testimony of Harry Jones, p. 4661, MS 804, Accession 1989-M-048, Box 36, Kent State Collection, Manuscripts and Archives, Sterling Memorial Library, Yale University (hereafter cited as KSC, SML, YU).

226 **"They ask[ed] questions"** . . . **"was so absurd"**: Kathleen Siebert Medicus interview with Terri West, April 29, 2020, Kent State Shooting Oral History Program (hereafter cited as KSSOHP).

227 **"Half a dozen"** . . . **"on the students"**: Quoted in *The Burr*, May 4, 2000, p. 38.

227 **"laxity, over-indulgence"** . . . **"use of lethal force"**: Special State Grand Jury Report, published in the *Akron Beacon Journal*, October 17, 1970.

228 **"Communist inspired"** . . . **"more of them?"**: *Akron Beacon Journal*, October 24, 1970.

228 **"You mean you"** . . . **"life and killed"**: *Akron Beacon Journal*, October 17, 1970.

228 **"childishly prejudicial"** . . . **"travesty of justice"**: Arthur S. Krause, "May 4, 1970," *New York Times*, May 4, 1972.

228 **"inconsistent with"** . . . **"but the National Guard"**: David Brinkley comments at Johns Hopkins University Eisenhower Symposium on Perspectives on Violence, November 17, 1970.

228 **"conceived in fraud"** . . . **"Kent State University"**: *Congressional Record*, vol. 116, no. 203, December 17, 1970.

228 **"ignoring constitutional rights"**: Quoted in *Cleveland State Law Review* 22, no. 1 (Winter 1973): p. 1.

229 **"Someone must sacrifice . . . the troublemakers"**: Quoted in *Akron Beacon Journal*, October 25, 1970.

229 **"I was misquoted"**: Quoted in Michener, *Kent State*, pp. 536–37.

229 **"They blamed us"**: Quoted in Kirkpatrick Sale, *SDS* (Random House, 1973), pp. 641–42.

229 **"The ones they missed"**: Interview with Bill Arthrell, MS 804, Accession 1983-M-017, Box 1, KSC, SML, YU.

229 **"it appeared to Balyeat"**: Robert Murphy to Jerris Leonard, November 4, 1970, MS 804, Accession 1989-M-048, Box 32, KSC, SML, YU.

230 **"two hundred or three hundred brats"** . . . **"for twenty years"**: Quoted in Michener, *Kent State*, p. 530.

230 **Alan Canfora accepted**: Interview with Alan Canfora, June 14, 1977, MS 804, James Munves Papers, 1970–1981, Box 1, KSC, SML, YU.

230 **"fairly represented every"**: "Legal Chronology, May 5, 1970 - January 4, 1979," Special Collections and Archives (hereafter cited as SC&A), KSUL.

230 **"there is no credible"** . . . **"of the incident"**: Attorney General John Mitchell to Mr. and Mrs. Martin Scheuer, August 11, 1971, Box 122A, M4C, KSUL.

231 **"There is no indication . . . to be excluded"**: Jerris Leonard to Robert Murphy, "Kent State: Preliminary Conclusions and Recommendations," U.S. Department of Justice 144-57-338, June 19, 1970, Box 122, M4C, KSUL.

231 **"Youthful, poorly trained . . . who shot demonstrators"**: William O'Connor to Attorney General Mitchell, March 9, 1971, M4C, KSUL

232 **"Willfulness or specific . . . ever happen again"**: Leonard Garment to Mr. and Mrs. Schroeder, July 6, 1972, MS 804, Accession 1983-M-017, Box 1, KSC, SML, YU.

232 **Politics likely played**: *Akron Beacon Journal*, October 16, 1974.

232 **The opposite was true**: *New York Post*, October 3, 1973.

233 **"We have tried . . . fully appropriate"**: Mrs. and Mrs. Arthur Krause, Mrs. Elaine Miller, Mr. and Mrs. Martin Scheuer, and Mrs. and Mrs. Louis Schroeder, MS 804, James Munves Papers, Box 1, KSC, SML, YU.

233 **"the only way"**: Quoted in William A. Gordon, *The Fourth of May: Killings and Cover-ups at Kent State* (Prometheus Books, 1990), p. 82n.

233   **"I don't believe . . . in the world"**: Quoted in Ron Henderson, "18 Months Later: Families of Kent Dead Speak Out," *American Report*, November 12, 1971.

233   **"was only with us . . . *not to cry*"**: Quoted in J. Gregory Payne, *MAYDAY: Kent State* (Kendall/Hunt, 1981), p. 57; and Joe Eszterhas, "Ohio Honors Its Dead: One Nation, Under God, Indivisible, with Liberty and Justice for All," *Rolling Stone*, June 10, 1971, p. 16.

234   **"You're going to lose" . . . "the next day"**: James Munves interview with Art and Doris Krause, June 12, 1977, Laura Davis Papers (hereafter cited as LDP), M4C, KSUL.

234   **"If your daughter"**: Quoted in *Santa Fe New Mexican*, April 8, 2020.

234   **"No meeting with" . . . "full of hate"**: Interview with Martin and Sarah Scheuer, June 1977, MS 804, James Munves Papers, 1970–1981, Box 1, KSC, SML, YU.

234   **"If it can't" . . . "in the morning"**: Interview with Elaine Miller Holstein, April 18, 1977, MS 804, James Munves Papers, 1970–1981, Box 1, KSC, SML, YU.

235   **"As we walked" . . . "long I hid"**: Quoted in Payne, *MAYDAY*, p. 91.

235   **"You have more patience"**: Barry Levine to Art Krause, May 12, 1971, excerpted in John Adams, "Kent State—Justice and Morality," p. 38.

236   **"the need to exhaust"**: "Legal Chronology, May 4, 1970 - January 4, 1979," SC&A, KSUL.

236   **"What's this all about?"**: Quoted in *Akron Beacon Journal*, May 20, 1975.

236   **"intense concern"**: "Kent State: Struggle for Justice," *Bill Moyers' Journal*, PBS-TV, January 16, 1974.

237   **"If it had not been for Adams"**: Interview with Art and Doris Krause, MS 804, James Munves Papers, Box 1, KSC, SML, YU.

237   **"If I had kids" . . . "forget about it"**: "Kent State: Struggle for Justice," *Bill Moyers' Journal*, PBS-TV.

237   **"I was afraid"**: Interview Notes, MS 804, James Munves Papers, Box 1, KSC, SML, YU.

238   **"To do nothing"**: Peter Davies to Mrs. Sarah Scheuer, September 10, 1970, Scheuer Family Papers, Box 1, Ohio Historical Society, State Archives, Columbus, Ohio.

238   **"deeply affected"**: "Kent State: Struggle for Justice," *Bill Moyers' Journal*, PBS-TV.

238   **"he would never"**: Quoted in Gordon, *Fourth of May*, p. 93.

238   *The Truth About Kent State*: Farrar, Straus and Giroux, 1973.

238   **"A classic 1960s liberal" . . . "to pay for it"**: Kathleen Siebert Medicus interview with Mark Wallach, July 16, 2020, KSSOHP.

239   **"Guardsmen involved" . . . "of the facts"**: Report of the Ohio National Guard Inspector General, Kent State University Riot, 4 May 1970, May 22, 1970, MS 804, Accession 1989-M-048, Box 30, Folder 373, KSC, SML, YU.

239   **"we have dozens" . . . "not treated well"**: Matt McManus to author, September 19, 2020.

240   **"You give them"**: Author's interview with Matt McManus, October 24, 2020.

241   **"Your Honor" . . . "Marshals!"**: Matt McManus to author, September 19, 2020.

241   **"I wouldn't want" . . . "tired of it"**: Quoted in Anne Taylor Memo to Joe Kelner, May 22, 1975, MS 1800, Box 69, KSC, SML, YU.

242   **"It's hard on us"**: Quoted in *Plain Dealer* (Cleveland, OH), September 12, 1971, p. 4-A.

242   **An eight-man . . . of his client**: "Tuesday, October 30, 1974, Fifth Day of the Trial," Box 64D, Folder 9, M4C, KSUL.

244 "a negative rut" . . . "entity possessed them": Interview with Doug Wrentmore, June 25, 1977, MS 804, James Munves Papers, Box 1, KSC, SML, YU.
245 "How'd you get hurt" . . . "involved was Robby?": Interview with Charlotte and Floyd Stamps, MS 804, James Munves Papers, Box 1, KSC, SML, YU.
245 "I was scared to death": Interview with Robby Stamps, MS 804, James Munves Papers, Box 1, KSC, SML, YU.
245 This was the first time . . . against his femur: "Friday, November 1, 1974, Eighth Day of the Trial," Box 64D, Folder 9, M4C, KSUL.
245 "lucky to be alive" . . . "planned murder": Alan Canfora to Senator Stephen Young, May/June 1970; and Alan Canfora interview with FBI, May 8, 1970, p. 5, MS 804, Accession 1989-M-048, Box 35, KSC, SML, YU.
246 "Would you say" . . . no direct answer: "Tuesday, November 5, 1974, Ninth Day of the Trial," Box 64D, Folder 9, M4C, KSUL.
246 The following day . . . just before the shooting: "Wednesday, November 6, 1974, Tenth Day of the Trial," Box 64D, M4C, KSUL.
247 "I may have something": Quoted in *Akron Beacon Journal*, November 8, 1974.
248 At 10:15 a.m. . . . "and was, deplorable": "Friday, November 8, 1974, Twelfth Day of the Trial," Box 64D, Folder 9, M4C, KSUL; and Memorandum of Opinion and Order of Federal Judge Frank J. Battisti, United States v. Lawrence Shafer et al., November 8, 1974.
250 "a hard decision" . . . "'the prosecution's case.'": Kathleen Siebert Medicus interview with Mark Wallach, July 16, 2020, KSSOHP.
250 "not overwhelmed": Quoted in *Youngstown Vindicator*, November 9, 1974.
250 "I wouldn't have put": Quoted in *Akron Beacon Journal*, May 20, 1975.
250 Afterward, defense attorneys: Dick Feagler, "How to Pick a Packed Jury," *The Sun* (Baltimore, MD), November 11, 1974.
251 "I've got good vibes" . . . "say to him?": Interview with Joe Lewis and his mother, Betty Lewis, MS 804, James Munves Papers, Box 1, KSC, SML, YU.
251 "and told him": James Munves interview with Art and Doris Krause, June 12, 1977, LDP, Box 214, M4C, KSUL.
251 "big and horrible": Quoted in Gordon, *Fourth of May*, p. 122.
251 "deeply angered" . . . "legal apparatus": Tom Grace, Letter to the Editor, *New York Times*, November 17, 1974, p. 18.
251 "I'm glad they're not": Quoted in *Youngstown Vindicator*, November 9, 1974.
251 "While the judge's . . . the violator's deed": David Hess, "Laws on Civil Rights Need to Be Revised," *Akron Beacon Journal*, November 17, 1974.

Chapter 9: The Civil Trials

252 "wanted it to end": Matt McManus to author, September 19, 2020.
252 "How do you" . . . "my daughter away": Quoted in Ricci, "Tormented Crusader," *Akron Beacon Journal*, June 25, 1972.
252 "I went out grubbing": James Munves interview with Art and Doris Krause, June 12, 1977, Laura Davis Papers (hereafter cited as LDP), Box 214, May 4 Collection, Kent State University Library (hereafter cited as M4C, KSUL).

253   **"Now we go"**: Interview with Elaine Miller Holstein, April 18, 1977, MS 804, James
      Munves Papers, Box 1, Kent State Collection, Manuscripts and Archives, Sterling
      Memorial Library, Yale University (hereafter cited as KSC, SML, YU).

253   **"I was taught"** . . . **"we were indicted"**: Charles Fassinger interview with M. Uryccki,
      LDP, Box 214, M4C, KSUL.

254   **"I haven't lost"**: Quoted in Joseph Kelner and James Munves, *The Kent State Coverup*
      (Harper & Row, 1980), p. 141.

254   **"numb"** . . . **"case of my life"**: Interview with Joseph Kelner, March 30, 1977, MS 804,
      James Munves Papers, Box 1, KSC, SML, YU.

254   **"to present a clear"**: "Law Favored the State in Kent Trial: Plaintiffs' Lawyers Muddied
      the Case," *Plain Dealer* (Cleveland, OH), August 31, 1975.

254   **Dean Kahler**: Interview with Elaine and John Kahler, July 15, 1977, MS 804, James
      Munves Papers, Box 1, KSC, SML, YU.

255   **"highly destructive"**: Quoted in William A. Gordon, *The Fourth of May: Killings and
      Coverups at Kent State* (Prometheus Books, 1990), p. 135.

255   **"Poor Joe"**: Interview with Art and Doris Krause, MS 804, James Munves Papers,
      Box 1, KSC, SML, YU.

255   **"You don't know"** . . . **"approximating truth"**: Interview with Joseph Kelner, March
      30, 1977, MS 804, James Munves Papers, Box 1, KSC, SML, YU.

255   **"This isn't"** . . . **"couldn't hate"**: Interview with Robby Stamps, MS 804, James Munves
      Papers, Box 1, KSC, SML, YU.

256   **"Why not?"** . . . **"You don't know Ohio"**: Quoted in Kelner and Munves, *Kent State
      Coverup*, pp. 26, 37.

256   **"If I'd had a gun"**: James Munves interview with Art and Doris Krause, June 12, 1977,
      LDP, Box 214, M4C, KSUL.

256   **"a pretty liberal guy"**: Quoted in Gordon, *Fourth of May*, p. 143.

256   **"a great deal"** . . . **"are armed"**: Interview with Tom Grace, MS 804, James Munves
      Papers, Box 1, KSC, SML, YU.

257   **"All of us"**: Interview with Robby Stamps, MS 804, James Munves Papers, Box 1,
      KSC, SML, YU.

257   **The parents of the slain**: Interview with Joseph Kelner, April 8, 1977, MS 804, James
      Munves Papers, Box 1, KSC, SML, YU.

257   **"I don't have Bill"**: "Notes on Plaintiffs and Defendants," MS 804, James Munves
      Papers, Box 2, KSC, SML, YU.

257   **"authorities knew better"** . . . **"has stopped everything"**: Interview with Lou and Flor-
      ence Schroeder, MS 804, James Munves Papers, Box 1, KSC, SML, YU.

257   **"There was nothing"**: James Munves interview with Lou and Florence Schroeder,
      June 12, 1977, LDP, Box 214, M4C, KSUL.

258   **"lost everything"** . . . **"bingo games"**: Interview with Albert Canfora, MS 804, James
      Munves Papers, Box 1, KSC, SML, YU.

258   **"let it drop"** . . . **"was dramatic"**: Interview with Jan Wrentmore, June 17, 1977, MS
      804, James Munves Papers, Box 1, KSC, SML, YU.

258   **"If I went"**: James Munves interview with Art and Doris Krause, LDP, Box 214, M4C,
      KSUL.

258   **"Every time"** . . . **"Arthur's hate"**: Interview with Joe Lewis and his mother, Betty
      Lewis, MS 804, James Munves Papers, Box 1, KSC, SML, YU.

258   **"It was hard"** . . . **"the men"**: James Munves interview with Art and Doris Krause,
      LDP, Box 214, M4C, KSUL.

259   **"Sitting in"** . . . **"get over [it]"**; Elaine Miller Holstein to James Michener, September 21, 1975, MS 804, Accession 1991-M-048, Box 1, KSC SML, YU.

259   **"To see"** . . . **"evil pimps"**: Interview with Elaine Miller Holstein, April 18, 1977, MS 804, James Munves Papers, 1970–1981, Box 1, KSC, SML, YU.

259   **"If looks"** . . . **"looked away"**: Interview with Mr. and Mrs. Scheuer, MS 804, Accession 1983-M-017, Box 1, MS 804, James Munves Papers, 1970–1981, Box 1, KSC, SML, YU.

259   **"over and over"** . . . **"couldn't stand it"**: Interview with Elaine Miller Holstein, April 18, 1977, MS 804, James Munves Papers, 1970–1981, Box 1, KSC, SML, YU.

259   **"got real close"** . . . **"to the end"**: Interview with Albert Canfora, MS 804, James Munves Papers, 1970–1981, Box 1, KSC, SML, YU.

260   **"the picture"** . . . **"excuse themselves"**: Interview with Joseph Kelner, March 30, 1977, MS 804, James Munves Papers, 1970–1981, Box 1, KSC, SML, YU.

260   **"looked like a duck"**: Author's interview with Matt McManus, October 24, 2020.

260   **"hostile mid-American"**: Quoted in Kelner and Munves, *Kent State Coverup*, p. 237.

260   **"You've got** . . . **up there"**: Interview with Robby Stamps, MS 804, James Munves Papers, Box 1, KSC, SML, YU.

261   **"outrages"** . . . **"his teeth in"**: "Notes on Plaintiffs and Defendants," MS 804, James Munves Papers, Box 2, KSC, SML, YU.

261   **"The judge"** . . . **"held by Fulton"**: Interview with Art and Doris Krause, MS 804, James Munves Papers, Box 1, KSC, SML, YU

262   **"Ohio boys"** . . . **"weekend warriors"**: Quoted in Kelner and Munves, *Kent State Coverup*, p. 85.

263   **"stark nakedness"**: Interview with Joseph Kelner, April 8, 1977, MS 804, James Munves Papers, Box 1, KSC, SML, YU.

263   **"God, those damn things"**: Quoted in "Tragedy in Our Midst—A Special Report," *Akron Beacon Journal*, May 24, 1970.

263   **"Did you see"** . . . **"brilliant"**: Interview with Joseph Kelner, April 8, 1977, MS 804, James Munves Papers, Box 1, KSC, SML, YU.

265   **"Have you ever"** . . . **"this garbage"**: Quoted in Kelner and Munves, *Kent State Coverup*, pp. 117–18.

265   **"bright, strong-willed"**: Interview with Joseph Kelner, April 8, 1977, MS 804, James Munves Papers, Box 1, KSC, SML, YU.

265   **"Of all"** . . . **"black flag"**: Quoted in Kelner and Munves, *Kent State Coverup*, p. 118.

266   **"What were your"** . . . **"lost hers"**: Quoted in Kelner and Munves, *Kent State Coverup*, p. 171.

267   **"The brevity"** . . . **"making ours"**: Quoted in Kelner and Munves, *Kent State Coverup*, p. 201.

267   **"Violence, burning"**: Handwritten Notes, "Def's Opening Statement," MS 804, Accession 1989-M-048, Box 15, KSC, SML, YU.

268   **"yellowish-gold"** . . . **"just confused"**: "KSU Civilian Shot Story Disputed," *Akron Beacon Journal*, August 20, 1975.

268   **"the day the trial"** . . . **"her life saved"**: Quoted in Kelner and Munves, *Kent State Coverup*, p. 238.

270   **"We had them nailed to the ground"**: Interview with John Cleary, MS 804, James Munves Papers, Box 1, KSC, SML, YU.

270   **"I was no longer"**: Interview with Doug Wrentmore, June 25, 1977, MS 804, James Munves Papers, Box 1, KSC, SML, YU.

270 **"I'm sorry"** . . . **"Ohio again"**: Interview with Robby Stamps, MS 804, James Munves Papers, Box 1, KSC, SML, YU.

270 **Escorted by U.S. Marshals** . . . **about to burst**: Confidential Report on Interview of Kent State Jurors, MS 804, Accession 1989-M-048, Box 29, KSC, SML, YU.

271 **"more on an individual"**: *Plain Dealer* (Cleveland, OH), August 30, 1975, p. 13A.

271 **"I know that"** . . . **that was wrong**: Confidential Report on Interview of Kent State Jurors, MS 804, Accession 1989-M-048, Box 29, KSC, SML, YU.

271 **"They're still"** . . . **"have you removed"**: Confidential Report on Interview of Kent State Jurors.

271 **"What justifies** . . . **a stone"**: Interview with Albert Canfora, MS 804, James Munves Papers, 1970–1981, Box 1, KSC, SML, YU.

271 **"Maybe you're right"**: Interview with Joe Lewis and his mother, Betty Lewis, MS 804, James Munves Papers, 1970–1981, Box 1, KSC, SML, YU.

271 **"I couldn't understand"** . . . **"were manipulated"**: Interview with Doug Wrentmore, June 25, 1977, MS 804, James Munves Papers, 1970–1981, Box 1, KSC, SML, YU.

272 **"whoever has"** . . . **"why try?"**: Interview with John Cleary, MS 804, James Munves Papers, 1970–1981, Box 1, KSC, SML, YU.

272 **Collette Grace**: Interview with Tom Sr. and Collette Grace, MS 804, James Munves Papers, 1970–1981, Box 1, KSC, SML, YU.

272 **"Justice is human"** . . . **"may err"**: Quoted in *Akron Beacon Journal*, August 28, 1975, p. 1; and *Time*, September 8, 1975, p. 11.

272 **"This is a sad day"** . . . **"set aside the verdict"**: Quoted in *New York Times*, August 28, 1975, p. 15.

272 **"a tough business** . . . **the guardsmen, too"**: Quoted in *Cleveland Press*, August 28, 1975, p. 1.

272 **Sarah Scheuer**: Interview with Martin and Sarah Scheuer, MS 804, James Munves Papers, Box 1, KSC, SML, YU.

272 **"I'm pleased"** . . . **"May 4, 1970"**: Quoted in *Cleveland Press*, August 28, 1975, p. 1.

273 **"I am still convinced"** . . . **"our task"**: Confidential Report on Interview of Kent State Jurors, MS 804, Accession 1989-M-048, Box 29, KSC, SML, YU.

273 **"The state, having licensed"**: *Akron Beacon Journal*, October 24, 1975.

275 **"At the first trial"** . . . **"radical organization"**: Quoted in Gordon, *Fourth of May*, p. 152.

275 **"there was a high degree"**: Quoted in Gordon, *Fourth of May*, p. 153.

275 **"He is thorough"** . . . **"regarding Thomas"**: "Fair Praise," *Plain Dealer* (Cleveland, OH), March 13, 1994.

276 **"a suitable letter"**: Sanford Rosen to Hon. William K. Thomas, November 13, 1978, Heidloff-Reichard Papers, Box 82, Folder 11, M4C, KSUL.

276 **"I'm tired"**: Quoted in Kelner and Munves, *Kent State Coverup*, p. 265.

276 **"Some of the families"** . . . **"useful lives"**: Quoted in J. Gregory Payne, *MAYDAY: Kent State* (Kendall/Hunt, 1981), p. 75.

276 **"A lot of us"** . . . **"wanted to settle"**: Matt McManus interview, April 8, 2020, Kent State Guardsmen Oral History Project, Ohio Northern University.

276 **"because we determined"**: Quoted in *New York Times*, April 23, 1990, p. A19.

277 **"We don't want"** . . . **"are involved"**: Quoted in Payne, *MAYDAY*, p. 93.

278 **"make sure this"**: Interview with Elaine and John Kahler, July 15, 1977, MS 804, James Munves Papers, Box 1, KSC, SML, YU.

278 **"wouldn't have felt"** . . . **"them responsible"**: Interview with Doug Wrentmore, June 25, 1977, MS 804, James Munves Papers, Box 1, KSC, SML, YU.
278 **"It's good for all"**: Quoted in *Cleveland Press*, January 4, 1979.
278 **"I'm going to try"** . . . **"eternity in peace"**: Quoted in *New York Times*, April 23, 1990, p. A19.
278 **"The words"** . . . **"Jeffrey back"**: Quoted in *Record-Courier* (Ravenna, OH), January 5, 1979, p. 11.
278 **"There is symbolism"** . . . **"victims' families"**: *New York Times*, January 8, 1979, p. A-20.
278 **"It would be"** . . . **"could hope for"**: *Akron Beacon Journal*, January 5, 1979, p. A6.

Chapter 10: Remembrance

280 **"It's so damn** . . . **"I forget?"**: Quoted in Joe Eszterhas, "Ohio Honors Its Dead: One Nation, Under God, Indivisible, with Liberty and Justice for All," *Rolling Stone*, June 10, 1971, p. 16.
280 **"KRAUSE"**: Quoted in Eszterhas, "Ohio Honors Its Dead," p. 18.
281 **"a sort of concentration camp"**: Interview with Elaine Miller Holstein, April 18, 1977, MS 804, James Munves Papers, Box 1, Kent State Collection, Manuscripts and Archives, Sterling Memorial Library, Yale University (hereafter cited as KSC, SML, YU).
281 **"I'm sorry"** . . . **"mattered here"**: Quoted in *Akron Beacon Journal*, May 4, 1977, p. A1.
281 **That same year**: Brage Golding to Kent State University Board of Trustees, September 5, 1977, MS 804, Accession 1989-M-048, Box 32, KSC, SML, YU.
282 **"All that is at stake"**: Quoted in *Record-Courier* (Ravenna, OH), August 19, 1977.
282 **"I wanted to be with you"**: Quoted in Ted Joy, "The Cost of Freedom," *Rolling Stone*, August 25, 1977.
283 **"I found that sculpture"**: Quoted in *Saturday Review*, May 1981, p. 30.
283 **"It's time"** . . . **"that situation"**: Quoted in *Akron Beacon Journal*, May 4, 1980.
284 **"ensure that"** . . . **"never forgotten"**: Quoted in Alan Canfora to Michael Schwartz, August 21, 1984, Box 85A, May 4 Collection, Kent State University Library (hereafter cited as M4C, KSUL).
284 **"Had everyone"** . . . **"look like"**: Brage Golding to Gregory P. Torre, October 27, 1978, Box 85B, Folder 12, M4C, KSUL.
284 **"That shouldn't have"**: Lisa Lynott Recorded Remembrance, May 4, 1990, Kent State Shooting Oral History Program.
285 **"avoid sources"**: "Competition Announcement: Kent State May 4 Memorial National Open Design Competition," National Endowment for the Arts, October 1985.
285 **"insult"** . . . **"leading [students]"**: Quoted in *Plain Dealer* (Cleveland, OH), July 13, 1986.
285 **"over the expenditure"**: Major General Nan Wong, USAF (Ret.), to Kent State Board of Trustees, December 12, 1988, Box 85B, Folder 1, M4C, KSUL.
285 **"The American Legion"**: Quoted in *Plain Dealer* (Cleveland, OH), July 13, 1986.
286 **"It's so frustrating"** . . . **"preconceived notions"**: Elaine Miller Holstein to Alan Canfora, August 21, 1986, MS 804, Accession 1991-M-004, Box 1, KSC, SML, YU.

---

286 "I walked through": Miller Holstein to Canfora, August 21, 1986.

287 "a place to learn": Interview with Mark Uryccki, Laura Davis Papers, Box 214, M4C, KSUL.

287 "The May 4 Memorial": Quoted in *Akron Beacon Journal*, March 6, 1996.

287 "Many wanted": Thomas Hensley, quoted in *The Burr*, May 4, 2000.

288 "The history": Brage Golding to Kent State University Board of Trustees, September 5, 1977, MS 804, Accession 1989-M-048, Box 32, KSC, SML, YU.

288 "to deal differently": Craig Simpson interview with Carol Cartwright, June 30, 2008, MS 804, Accession 1989-M-048, Box 32, KSC, SML, YU.

288 "a university": Quoted in *Record-Courier* (Ravenna, OH), February 10, 1995.

288 "We should" . . . "demands it": Quoted in *Cincinnati Enquirer*, January 30, 2000; and *The Burr*, May 4, 2000.

288 "For 364 days . . . a shrine": *Sunday Plain Dealer* (Cleveland, OH), May 3, 2020, p. A10.

289 "a fingerprint": "Memorials of May 4," *Kent State Magazine*, Spring/Summer 2020, p. 15

289 "the exceptional importance": Quoted in *Plain Dealer* (Cleveland, OH), February 24, 2010.

289 "For me, it is a day": Quoted in *Plain Dealer* (Cleveland, OH), May 4, 2010.

289 "an important step" . . . "the nation": *Plain Dealer* (Cleveland, OH), May 4, 2013.

290 "an angry young man" . . . "too late": Quoted in *Plain Dealer* (Cleveland, OH), May 4, 2012.

290 "The dust of history": Quoted in *New York Times*, January 16, 2021.

Chapter 11: Legacy

292 "A day doesn't": Kathleen Siebert Medicus interview with Claudia Franks Yates, May 18, 2020, Kent State Shooting Oral History Program (hereafter cited as KSSOHP).

292 "The bullet . . . recover from": Elaine Holstein, "Anniversary," *The Progressive*, May 1988, p. 34.

292 Every time she received: Elaine Miller Holstein letter, November 17, 1982, Accession 1991-M-004, Box 1, Kent State Collection, Manuscripts and Archives, Sterling Memorial Library, Yale University (hereafter cited as KSC, SML, YU).

292 "nightmarish" . . . "shot off": Interview with Elaine Miller Holstein, April 18, 1977, James Munves Papers, Box 1, KSC, SML, YU.

292 "Neither of us": Holstein, "Anniversary," p. 34.

293 Russ couldn't talk: Interview with Elaine Miller Holstein, April 18, 1977, James Munves Papers, Box 1, KSC, SML, YU.

293 "I had never" . . . "in tears": Quoted in Abigail Miller, "Our Brother Jeff," November 20, 2019, kentwired.com.

293 "Whenever" . . . "of Jeff": Holstein, "Anniversary," p. 34.

293 "It's as if" . . . "question marks": Quoted in *The Burr*, May 19, 2021.

293 "There is buried" . . . "go away": "4 Dead in Ohio" [video], Al Jazeera English, 2010, Youtube.com; and Elaine Miller Holstein letter, November 17, 1982, Accession 1991-M-004, Box 1, KSC, SML, YU.

293 **"I had a good life"**: Clevelandjewishnews.com, May 28, 2018.

293 **"May 4"** . . . **"from [Allison]"**: Quoted in *Atlanta Constitution*, May 3, 1980.

294 **"Every time"** . . . **"with them"**: Quoted in *Akron Beacon Journal*, June 25, 1972, p. 11.

294 **"never really fully"**: Quoted in Kendra Lee Hicks, "A Tribute to Arthur Krause: Delivered at Kent State University, May 4, 1989," *Vietnam Generation* 2, no. 2, Article 7.

294 **"After Allison"** . . . **"my life"**: Quoted in Jeff Kisseloff, *Generation on Fire: Voices of Protest from the 1960s* (University Press of Kentucky, 2007), p. 264.

294 **"Your little sister"** . . . **"your killing"**: Laurel Krause, "Letter to Allison," April 23, 2021, Kent State Truth Tribunal, www.truthtribunal.org/letter-to-allison.

294 **"I'd see Allison"** . . . **"hold on to"**: Quoted in Kisseloff, *Generation on Fire*, pp. 261–63.

295 **"People said"** . . . **"enjoying life"**: Quoted in Kisseloff, *Generation on Fire*, p. 264.

295 **"It [was] a healing"** . . . **"Allison with?"**: Quoted in Kisseloff, *Generation on Fire*, p. 261.

295 **"I said that"** . . . **"for Bill"**: Florence Schroeder to Gregory Payne, excerpted in J. Gregory Payne, *MAYDAY: Kent State* (Kendall/Hunt, 1981), pp. 75–76; and Florence Schroeder to Gregory Payne, March 16, 1977, Accession 1983-M-017, Box 1, KSC, SML, YU.

296 **"The individuals who"** . . . **"for Rhodes"**: Quoted in Ron Henderson, "18 Months Later: Families of Kent Dead Speak Out," *American Report*, November 12, 1971.

296 **"I think one bullet"**: Quoted in Jacqueline Marino, "Fragments of May 4" [radio broadcast], WKSU, May 1, 2020.

296 **"was supposed to"** . . . **"loaded rifles"**: Interview with Sandra Lee "Sandy" Scheuer's Father, 1970, Youtube.com.

296 **"She was the most"**: "Our Beloved Sandy Is Gone Forever," in *The Eloquence of Protest: Voices of the 70's*, ed. Harrison E. Salisbury (Houghton Mifflin, 1972), p. 199.

297 **"I could not stand"** . . . **"the backyard"**: Interview with Martin and Sarah Scheuer, June 1977, James Munves Papers, Box 1, KSC, SML, YU.

297 **"loved them so"** . . . **"my heart"**: Quoted in Payne, *MAYDAY*, p. 84.

297 **"What is that?"** . . . **"in heaven"**: Interview with Sandra Lee "Sandy" Scheuer's Father, 1970.

297 **"I'm not"** . . . **"wrong time"**: Quoted in Howard E. Royer, "Non-Violence Is the Only Way," *Messenger*, January 1, 1971.

297 **"his friendliness"**: Robert G. Hummerstone, "The Fifth Victim of Kent State," *Life*, October 16, 1970, p. 44.

297 **"He was"** . . . **"be depressed"**: Paul Keane, "They Took His Legs at Kent State 50 Years Ago, but Not His Heart," *Plain Dealer* (Cleveland, OH), January 17, 2020.

298 **"I tried to turn"**: Quoted in Mary Sue Rosenberger, "Healing the Wounds of Kent State," *Messenger*, July 1990, p. 12.

298 **"The sight of"**: Paul Keane Notes, Accession 1989-M-048, Box 34, KSC, SM, YU; and Paul Keane, "Remembering the Kent State Shooting Survivors," nhregister.com.

299 **"I had grown up"** . . . **"my legs"**: Quoted in *National Observer* (Washington, DC), May 3, 1975.

299 **"There are days"** . . . **"who shot me"**: Quoted in Rosenberger, "Healing the Wounds of Kent State," pp. 13–14.

299 **"It wouldn't be"** . . . **"it comes"**: Quoted in *National Observer* (Washington, DC), May 3, 1975.

299 **"I can't live"**: Quoted in Rosenberger, "Healing the Wounds of Kent State," p. 12.

299 **"The National Guard"** . . . **"this nightmare"**: Rosenberger, "Healing the Wounds of Kent State," p. 14.

300 **Dean still blamed**: "*CBS Morning*, May 4, 1990," Box 95A, Tape 61, May 4 Collection, Kent State University Library (hereafter cited as M4C, KSUL).

300 **"Our job"** . . . **"political system"**: Quoted in Rosenberger, "Healing the Wounds of Kent State," p. 14.

300 **"What happened"**: Quoted in Sarah Crump, "May 4 Journal," *Cleveland Magazine*, May 1995, p. 60.

300 **While on his daily**: Paul Keane, "Kent State Shooting Survivor Dean Kahler Perseveres, Despite Broken Bones," *Plain Dealer* (Cleveland, OH), August 6, 2021.

301 **"I was dealing with"**: Quoted in Lisa Abraham, "May 4: Where the Nine Wounded Are Now," *Kent State Magazine*, Spring/Summer 2020, p. 20.

301 **"The lessons I take"**: Quoted in Malcolm X Abram, "Kent State Shootings: Joe Lewis Reflects on Massacre 50 Years Later," *Akron Beacon Journal*, May 2, 2020.

301 **"For me"** . . . **"very complicated"**: Quoted in Abram, "Kent State Shootings."

302 **"I was a stupid fool"** . . . **"living today"**: Interview with John Cleary, James Munves Papers, Box 1, KSC, SML, YU.

302 **"very sympathetic"**: Interview with John Cleary, James Munves Papers, Box 1, KSC, SML, YU.

302 **"very cynical"** . . . **"Why try?"**: Interview with John Cleary, James Munves Papers, Box 1, KSC, SML, YU.

302 **"Some people"** . . . **"happen again"**: Quoted in *National Observer* (Washington, DC), May 3, 1975.

302 **"to not let"**: Quoted in Abraham, "May 4," p. 18.

302 **"made me look"**: Quoted in Erin Kosnac and Melissa Hostetler, "Then I Was Shot," *The Burr*, May 4, 2000, p. 19.

303 **"I'm glad just"**: Quoted in *Akron Beacon Journal*, May 3, 2020.

303 **"total bankruptcy"** . . . **"on violence"**: Quoted in *Plain Dealer* (Cleveland, OH), May 5, 1972, p. 10-A; and *Youngstown Vindicator*, May 5, 1972.

303 **"I would like to see"**: Interview with Tom Grace, James Munves Papers, Box 1, KSC, SML, YU.

303 **"I would have liked"** . . . **"are armed"**: Interview with Tom Grace, James Munves Papers, Box 1, KSC, SML, YU.

303 **"Once fate"**: Quoted in *Akron Beacon Journal*, May 3, 2020.

303 **"My intention"**: Quoted in Abraham, "May 4," p. 19.

303 **"Kent State has come"**: Quoted in Abraham, "May 4," p. 19.

304 **Some thought he suffered**: Interview with Albert Canfora, James Munves Papers, Box 1, KSC, SML, YU.

304 **"the system . . . the people"**: Interview with Alan Canfora, May 1977, James Munves Papers, Box 1, KSC, SML, YU.

304 **"we don't have"**: Quoted in *Washington Post*, May 5, 1995.

304 **"Pugnacious and partisan"**: www.s3-live.kent.edu/s3fs-root/s3fs-public/210209-spsu -05-10-21-p54-55.pdf.

304 **Alan's sharp elbows**: See, for example, the columns of Regina Brett in the *Akron Beacon Journal*, February 15 and 20, 1996.

304 **"His passion"** . . . **"was known"**: Derf Backderf quoted in *New York Times*, January 16, 2021.

305 "Unfortunately" . . . "considerably": Quoted in *AARP Bulletin*, May 4, 2010.

305 "I realized how": Interview with Doug Wrentmore, June 25, 1977, James Munves Papers, Box 1, KSC, SML, YU.

305 "could no longer" . . . "in my life": Quoted in James A. Michener, *Kent State: What Happened and Why* (Random House, Reader's Digest Books, 1971), pp. 476–78.

306 "karmatic link": Interview with Doug Wrentmore, June 25, 1977, James Munves Papers, Box 1, KSC, SML, YU.

306 "I have a great deal": Quoted in *National Observer* (Washington, DC), May 3, 1975.

306 "I don't blame" . . . "the same thing": Taped interview with Robby Stamps, October 9, 1970, James A. Michener Papers, Manuscript Division, Library of Congress, Washington, D.C.

306 "If I could find": Robert Stamps Testimony Before Special State Grand Jury, Accession 1989-M-048, Box 37, KSC, SML, YU.

306 "What I thought" . . . "highest bidder": Quoted in Kosnac and Hostetler, "Then I Was Shot," p. 20.

306 Robby's alienation: William Gardner interview with Robert Stamps, November 21, 1973, MS 1800, Box 75, KSC, SML, YU.

307 "Ohio's been blind": Quoted in *Akron Beacon Journal*, March 6, 1996.

307 "I want to forget": Interview with Robby Stamps, James Munves Papers, Box 1, KSC, SML, YU.

307 "We just don't": Quoted in Kosnac and Hostetler, "Then I Was Shot," p. 18.

307 "Of course": Quoted in Kosnac and Hostetler, "Then I Was Shot," p. 18.

307 "it is bad to hate": Interview with Scott MacKenzie, James Munves Papers, Box 1, KSC, SML, YU.

307 Jim Russell: "Medical Expenses—Jim Russell, Injured May 4, 1970," MS 1800, Box 73, KSC, SML, YU.

307 "was on" . . . "a student": Quoted in Steve Duin, "The Long Road Back from Kent State," *The Oregonian*, July 1, 2007.

308 "This Oregon country": Quoted in Steve Duin, "Kent State: Not Forgiven, Not Forgotten," *The Oregonian*, May 4, 1995.

308 "He didn't want" . . . "after him": Quoted in Duin, "The Long Road Back."

308 "never come" . . . "a sham.": Quoted in Duin, "Kent State."

308 "The campus can burn": Quoted in *The Burr*, May 4, 2000, p. 17.

308 "helped each other": Quoted in Duin, "Kent State."

308 "I had five great years": Quoted in *Akron Beacon Journal*, June 28, 2007.

308 "That picture" . . . "who you are": Quoted in Patricia McCormick, "The Girl in the Kent State Photo," *Washington Post*, April 20, 2021.

309 "It really destroyed": Quoted in *Orlando Sentinel*, 1990.

309 "I was too afraid" . . . "was treated": Quoted in McCormick, "The Girl in the Kent State Photo."

309 "It's been fifty years": Quoted in McCormick, "The Girl in the Kent State Photo."

309 "This is it" . . . "been affected": Quoted in Howard Means, *67 Shots: Kent State and the End of American Innocence* (Da Capo Press, 2016), p. 103.

310 "Certainly" . . . "just happened": Quoted in *Plain Dealer* (Cleveland, OH), May 1, 2000, p. 7-A; and *AARP Bulletin*, May 4, 2010.

310 "I think that" . . . "forgave themselves": Arthur Krummel telephone interview, April 1, 2020, Kent State Guardsmen Oral History Project, Ohio Northern University (hereafter cited as KSGOHP, ONU).

310 **"To have gone"** . . . **"you forever"**: Connie Sickels interview with Bruce Dzeda, May 2, 1995, KSSOHP.

310 **"Those men"** . . . **"all sorry it happened"**: Sandra Halem interview with anonymous guardsman, May 2, 2000, KSSOHP.

310 **"No one in the guard"**: Interview 5 of 5 with Laura Davis and Carol Barbato, April 1, 2007, Laura Davis Papers (hereafter cited as LDP), M4C, KSUL.

311 **"I don't think"** . . . **"the trial?"**: Quoted in *Cincinnati Enquirer*, May 1, 1995, p. A4.

311 **"took it really hard"**: Interview 4 of 5 with Laura Davis and Carol Barbato, April 1, 2007, LDP, M4C, KSUL.

311 **"nervous, depressed"**: William A. Powell, M.D., to Charles E. Brown, November 21, 1978, Heidloff-Reichard Papers, Box 72, Folder 12, M4C, KSUL.

311 **"I knew a couple"** . . . **"he did or not"**: Keith Crilow telephone interview, February 28, 2020, KSGOHP, ONU.

311 **"It was very painful"** . . . **"out to them"**: Jerry Damerow interview, March 11, 2020, KSGOHP, ONU.

311 **"It was something"**: Terry Lucas, quoted in Crump, "May 4 Journal," p. 61.

312 **"the ones who"**: Author's telephone interview with B. J. Long, May 5, 2022.

312 **"It affected"** . . . **"the clock"**: Author's interview with Ron Gammell, October 24, 2020.

312 **"I think about"** . . . **"your memory"** Author's telephone interview with B. J. Long, May 5, 2022.

312 **"simple"** . . . **"done differently?"**: Quoted in Edward Walsh, "At Kent State, Remembering 13 Seconds After 25 Years," *Washington Post*, May 5, 1995.

312 **"What kind"** . . . **"different outcome"**: Arthur Krummel telephone interview, April 1, 2020, KSGOHP, ONU.

313 **"We're deeply regretful"**: Quoted in National Geographic, *Kent State 2* [documentary].

313 **"Oh my God"**: *Cincinnati Enquirer*, May 1, 1995, p. A4.

313 **"I respected"**: Matt McManus to author, September 19, 2020.

313 **"Can you imagine"**: Author's interview with Matt McManus, October 24, 2020.

313 **"You have a murderer"**: *Cincinnati Enquirer*, May 1, 1995, p. A4.

313 **"It worked perfectly"** . . . **"rid of the pain"**: Author's interview with Matt McManus, October 24, 2020.

314 **"I made"** . . . **"to anything"**: Kathleen Siebert Medicus interview with Amy Shriver Dreussi, May 13, 2020, KSSOHP.

314 **"It put 'Paid'"** . . . **"in the afternoon"**: Connie Sickels interview with Bruce Dzeda, May 2, 1995, KSSOHP.

Select Bibliography of Published Sources

Abraham, Lisa. "May 4: Where the Nine Wounded Are Now." *Kent State Magazine*, Spring/ Summer 2020, pp. 18–20.

"Tragedy in Our Midst—A Special Report." *Akron Beacon Journal*, May 24, 1970.

Ayers, Bill. *Fugitive Days: A Memoir*. Beacon Press, 2001.

Barbato, Carole A., and Laura L. Davis. *Democratic Narrative, History, and Memory*. Kent State University Press, 2012.

Berger, Dan. *Outlaws of America: The Weather Underground and the Politics of Solidarity*. AK Press, 2006.

Bills, Scott L., ed. *Kent State/May 4: Echoes Through a Decade*. Kent State University Press, 1982.

———. "The Sixties, Kent State, and Historical Memory." *Vietnam Generation* 2, no. 2 (1995): pp. 173–80.

Burrough, Bryan. *Days of Rage: America's Radical Underground, the FBI, and the Forgotten Age of Revolutionary Violence*. Penguin Press, 2015.

Caputo, Phillip. *13 Seconds: A Look Back at the Kent State Shootings*. Penguin, 2005.

Casale, Ottavio M., and Louis Paskoff, eds. *The Kent Affair: Documents and Interpretations*. Houghton Mifflin, 1971.

Collier, Peter, and David Horowitz. "Doing It: The Inside Story of the Rise and Fall of the Weather Underground." *Rolling Stone*, September 30, 1982.

Crump, Sarah. "May 4 Journal." *Cleveland Magazine*, May 1995, pp. 58–63.

Davies, Peter. *The Truth About Kent State: A Challenge to the American Conscience*. Farrar, Straus and Giroux, 1973.

Eszterhas, Joe. "Ohio Honors Its Dead: One Nation, Under God, Indivisible, with Liberty and Justice for All." *Rolling Stone*, June 10, 1971, pp. 14–18.

Eszterhas, Joe, and Michael D. Roberts. "James Michener's Kent State: A Study in Distortion." *The Progressive*, September 1971, pp. 35–40.

———. *Thirteen Seconds: Confrontation at Kent State*. Dodd, Mead, 1970.

Federal Bureau of Investigation. *Weather Underground Organization (Weathermen): Declassified FBI Files*. JV Publications, n.d.

Fitt, Albert B. "The National Guard and Civil Disturbance." *City: Magazine of Urban Life and Environment*, August/September 1970, pp. 41–43.

Furlong, William Barry. "The Guardsmen's View of the Tragedy at Kent State." *New York Times Magazine*, June 21, 1970, pp. 12–13, 64, 68–70.

Gallagher, Thomas. "Tragedy at Kent State." *Good Housekeeping*, October 1970, pp. 82–83, 142, 144–48.

Gilbert, David. *Love and Struggle: My Life in SDS, the Weather Underground, and Beyond*. PM Press, 2012.

Gordon, William A. *The Fourth of May: Killings and Coverups at Kent State*. Prometheus Books, 1990.

Grace, Thomas M. *Kent State: Death and Dissent in the Long Sixties*. University of Massachusetts Press, 2016.

Grant, Ed, and Mike Hill. *I Was There: What Really Went on at Kent State*. C. S. S. Publishing, 1974.

Grathwohl, Larry as told to Frank Reagan. *Bringing Down America: An FBI Informer with the Weathermen*. Arlington House, 1976.

Heineman, Kenneth J. *Campus Wars: The Peace Movement at American State Universities in the Vietnam Era*. New York University Press, 1993.

Henderson, Ron. "18 Months Later: Families of Kent Dead Speak Out." *American Report*, November 12, 1971.

Hensley, Thomas R., and Jerry M. Lewis, eds. *Kent State and May 4th: A Social Science Perspective*, 3rd ed. Kent State University Press, 2010.

Hunt, Nigel, and Sue McHale. "Memory and Meaning: Individual and Social Aspects of Memory Narratives." *Journal of Loss and Trauma* 13 (2008): pp. 42–58.

Jacobs, Harold, ed. *Weatherman*. Ramparts Press, 1970.

Jones, Thai. *A Radical Line: From the Labor Movement to the Weather Underground, One Family's Century of Conscience*. Free Press, 2004.

Keller, Gordon W. "Kent State a Year Later." *Dissent*, April 1971, pp. 171–74.

Kelner, Joseph, and James Munves. *The Kent State Coverup*. Harper & Row, 1980.

Keniston, Kenneth. "The Agony of the Counterculture." In *The Eloquence of Protest: Voices of the 70's*, edited by Harrison E. Salisbury. Houghton Mifflin, 1972.

——. *Young Radicals: Notes on Committed Youth*. Harcourt, Brace & World, 1968.

——. *Youth and Dissent: The Rise of a New Opposition*. Harcourt Brace Jovanovich, 1971.

Kisseloff, Jeff. *Generation on Fire: Voices of Protest from the 1960s*. University Press of Kentucky, 2007.

Kosnac, Erin, and Melissa Hostetler. "Then I Was Shot." *The Burr*, May 4, 2000, pp. 15–21.

Kuhn, David Paul. *The Hardhat Riot: Nixon, New York City, and the Dawn of the White Working-Class Revolution*. Oxford University Press, 2020.

Lepore, Jill. "Kent State and the War That Never Ended." *New Yorker*, May 4, 2020.

Lerner, Jonathan. "I Was a Terrorist." *Washington Post*, February 24, 2002.

Lombardi, John. "Kent State Shootings: A Lot of People Were Crying, and the Guard Walked Away." *Rolling Stone*, June 11, 1970.

Means, Howard. *67 Shots: Kent State and the End of American Innocence*. Da Capo Press, 2016.

Methvin, Eugene H. "SDS: Engineers of Campus Chaos." *Reader's Digest*, October 1968, pp. 103–8.

Michener, James A. *Kent State: What Happened and Why*. Random House, Reader's Digest Books, 1971.

Morrison, Joan, and Robert K. Morrison. *From Camelot to Kent State: The Sixties Experience in the Words of Those Who Lived It.* Times Books, 1987.

O'Brien, Conor Cruise. "America First." *New York Review of Books*, January 29, 1970, pp. 8–14.

Oglesby, Carl. *Ravens in the Storm: A Personal History of the 1960s Antiwar Movement.* Scribner, 2008.

O'Hara, John Fitzgerald. "Kent State/May 4 and Postwar Memory." *American Quarterly* 58, no. 2 (June 2006): pp. 301–28.

O'Neill, William L. *Coming Apart: An Informal History of America in the 1960's.* Quadrangle Books, 1971.

Payne, J. Gregory. *MAYDAY: Kent State.* Kendall/Hunt, 1981.

Powers, Thomas. *Diana: The Making of a Terrorist.* Houghton Mifflin, 1971.

Rosenblatt, Stanley. *Justice Denied.* Nash Publishing, 1971.

Rudd, Mark. *Underground: My Life with SDS and the Weathermen.* William Morrow, 2009.

Sale, Kirkpatrick. *SDS.* Random House, 1973.

Salisbury, Harrison E., ed. *The Eloquence of Protest: Voices of the 70's.* Houghton Mifflin, 1972.

Sayre, Nora. "Kent State: Victims, Survivors, Heirs." *Ms*, September 11, 1975.

Scranton, William W. *Report of the President's Commission on Campus Unrest.* Avon Books, 1971.

Shriver, Phillip R. *The Years of Youth: Kent State University, 1910–1960.* Kent State University Press, 1960.

Simpson, Craig S., and Gregory S. Wilson. *Above the Shots: An Oral History of the Kent State Shootings.* Kent State University Press, 2016.

Stern, Susan. *With the Weathermen: The Personal Journey of a Revolutionary Woman.* Doubleday, 1975.

Stone, I. F. *The Killings at Kent State: How Murder Went Unpunished.* New York Review Books, 1971.

U.S. Senate, Committee on the Judiciary, 94th Congress, 1st Session. *The Weather Underground.* U.S. Government Printing Office, 1975.

Varon, Jeremy. *Bringing the War Home: The Weather Underground, the Red Army Faction, and Revolutionary Violence in the Sixties and Seventies.* University of California Press, 2004.

Viorst, Milton. *Fire in the Streets: America in the 1960s.* Simon & Schuster, 1979.

Wells, Tom. *The War Within: America's Battle over Vietnam.* University of California Press, 1994.

Wilkerson, Cathy. *Flying Too Close to the Sun: My Life and Times as a Weatherman.* Seven Stories Press, 2007.

Illustration Credits

Index

Page numbers in *italics* refer to photos.